The Films of JACK NICHOLSON

The Films of
JACK NICHOLSON

by Douglas Brode

A CITADEL PRESS BOOK
PUBLISHED BY CAROL PUBLISHING GROUP

ACKNOWLEDGMENTS: With appreciation to Scott Lecleau, Mike Greenstein, Lou Gaul, Joyce Persico, Paul Willistein, Annette Lopercio O'Toole, Gary Van Dusen, and to my friends at Allied Artists, Filmgroup, Dynasty Films, Universal, United Artists, 20th Century-Fox, American International Pictures, Grand National Pictures, Warner Brothers, Medallion Pictures, Lippert Pictures, Santa Clara Films, Proteus Films, Fanfare Films, Paragon Pictures, Raybert Productions, Columbia Pictures, Paramount Pictures, Avco Embassy, Miramax Films, and Metro-Goldwyn-Mayer.

Library of Congress Cataloging-in-Publication Data

Brode, Douglas, 1943–
    The films of Jack Nicholson / Douglas Brode. — Rev. & updated.
        p. m.
    "A Citadel Press book."
    ISBN 0–8065–1834–0 (pbk.)
    1. Nicholson, Jack—Criticism and interpretation. I. Title.
PN2287.N5B76 1996
791.43´028´092—dc20
                                                    96–36129
                                                      CIP

First Carol Publishing Group Edition 1990

A Citadel Press Book
Published by Carol Publishing Group

Editorial, sales and distribution, rights and permissions inquiries should be addressed to Carol Publishing Group
120 Enterprise Avenue
Secaucus, N.J. 07094

In Canada: Canadian Manda Group
One Atlantic Avenue, Suite 105
Toronto, Ontario M6K 3E7

designed by A. Christopher Simon

Carol Publishing Group books are available at special discounts for bulk purchases, for sales promotions, fund raising, or educational purposes. Special editions can be created to specifications. For details contact: Special Sales Department, Carol Publishing Group, 120 Enterprise Ave., Secaucus, NJ 07094

Manufactured in the United States of America
10 9 8 7 6 5 4 3 2 1

For My Son

SHEA THAXTER BRODE

who just loves watchin' that man
with the cobra eyes

Contents

Introduction

COBRA EYES, KILLER SMILE

"Everything I do in the movies," Jack Nicholson claimed not so long ago, "is autobiographical, no matter what the surface says." But that statement may confuse even his most dedicated fans. Autobiographical? How can that be, when he's played a redneck oil rigger, a world-famous writer, a mad-dog killer, a suave private eye and an insane asylum inmate, a macho sailor and an owl-eyed intellectual, a mindless idiot and an idealistic communist organizer? Each character is so different from the next! In fact, to understand the correctness of his point, one has to trace Nicholson's own life, then view the films in light of where he's been, what he's done, and who he is.

The young Jack Nicholson had a normal family and a definable if less than dependable father figure, or so he thought. His parents were John and Ethel May Nicholson; his oldest sister was named June. At least, that was the apparent reality during his boyhood years. Following his birth on April 22, 1937, Jack was raised by them (and another "sister," Lorraine, aged 14 when Jack was born) in Neptune City, a small New Jersey coastal town. His "father" may not have been around very often—running off when he so chose, showing up occasionally, finding work when he could as a sign painter or window dresser but more often getting lost in an alcoholic stupor. Yet by all accounts he liked his "son," sometimes dragging the boy along to the pubs; Jack would later recall John downing raw brandies while the boy stood by, sipping a sarsaparilla.

Later, Nicholson would express no bitterness toward John Nicholson: He was "a quiet, melancholy, tragic figure," he would claim, and "a very soft man." But no one, however forgiving, could claim John was a good provider. Fortunately Jack's "mother" came through by

A Rogue's Gallery: clockwise, from top left, George Hanson (*Easy Rider*), Bobby Eroica Dupea (*Five Easy Pieces*), J. J. Gittes (*Chinatown*), Billy "Bad Ass" Buddusky (*The Last Detail*), and (center) Randall Patrick McMurphy (*One Flew Over the Cuckoo's Nest*).

The Two Sides of Jack Nicholson: Dapper and elegant, and looking very Establishment, his Jekyll side . . .

. . . and wild and brazen, looking most bohemian, Jack's Hyde self.

turning her lower-middle-class household into a successful beauty parlor. At first, she couldn't afford to open a professional salon; even when her makeshift business showed a profit, she continued the work/home arrangement in a larger house to which they moved. Now, though, Ethel May was able to give Jack what he would later recall as a "comfortable, middle-class" upbringing.

Certainly, he was not the only boy raised by a houseful of strong women and a weak father. ("I was surrounded by women and hair dryers, and under such circumstances," he once intriguingly reflected, "it's a miracle I didn't turn out to be a fag.") But the worst was yet to come, for the father wasn't a father, and one sister was actually his mother, the other an aunt. How much of an inkling Jack had over the years is hard to say, but with his intelligence and insight he must, at regular intervals, have guessed all was not as he'd been asked to believe. For instance, it was at this point in his life that Jack developed a revealing habit. He refused to address these relatives by their actual names, using instead an alternative, colorful nickname for each, as if by renaming every person in his life he would remove them from the world at large and order them within a private universe of his own making. Ethel May became "Mud,"

Lorraine was "Rain," her husband George ("As good a [substitute] father as anybody's ever going to get or need," Jack once said of him), "Shorty." Tellingly, though, the "father"—John—was by all accounts spared such a rechristening.

In a classic case of identity crisis, Jack would eventually face what he'd had hints of all along: His parents were actually his grandparents, while the woman raised as his sister had born him out of wedlock. To give the boy an illusion of normalcy, she'd cajoled her parents into carrying on an elaborate charade ending only when June died in 1975. At that time, Lorraine at last admitted the truth, forcing Jack—who flew home for the funeral—to finally face the loss not only of a beloved person but also of the official history of his life up to that point. While he's always claimed he had no notion of the true state of affairs, he must have guessed; how else explain the fact that, years before receiving this news, Nicholson publicly claimed to harbor "a lot of antifamily feelings," insisting that "a lot of the things people are *bleeped* up about at this moment can be traced back to family structures." Jack may have been commenting on the larger social scene, but what's fascinating is how much the statement reveals about himself.

Ironically, our most contemporary actor can effectively assume classic roles: here, a throwback to the thirties, as Jack clowns on the set of *Chinatown*, but looks very classy . . .

. . . though always leading a double life, he can be the opposite; here, rangy and raunchy, while relaxing on the set of *The Missouri Breaks*.

In 1969, he told *After Dark* that he was excited about a play called *In Celebration* he'd caught in London: "All the characters are members of a family, who [think they] know each other very well and understand each other. . . . [In the] climactic scene, everything comes out, all of the revelations and the shouting." In 1984, when asked if he and live-in girlfriend Anjelica Huston would ever have children, a mature, mellowed Jack grew somber and said: "I'm very moved by [the idea of] family." Though he remains jovial on the surface, the betrayal has obviously taken its toll. "Jack's got a real hurt deep down inside," explains one old friend who chooses to remain anonymous, "and there's no way of resolving it, ever."

Several years before being forced to confront the truth, Jack admitted that during his first experiment with L.S.D. in the early sixties, "I became conscious of very early emotions about not being wanted—feeling that I was a problem to my family as an infant." When *The New York Times* asked him about social causes, Jack caustically replied: "I have my own favorite downtrodden minority. It's the bastard, the illegitimately born." This may also explain why, even though Jack takes a liberal political position on almost every issue, he's against

abortion: "As an illegitimate child born . . . to a broken lower-middle-class family, you're an automatic abortion with most people today. So it's very easy for me."

To this day, Nicholson does not know who his father really is, though he maintains a positive attitude: "I've got the blood of kings flowing in my veins, is my point of view," he once claimed. But the real-life confusion of identity adds a special dimension to the relentless pursuit of fathers and substitute father figures in the films, as well as the love-hate relationships with families who seem caring but turn out to harbor deep, dark secrets. Like father, like son? Jack, when asked by *People* to identify his one regret in life, replied, "I've always wanted more children." But Susan Anspach insists she and Jack conceived a son while they were filming *Five Easy Pieces*. "We had guarded the secret for years," she said, "but everyone knew, except the public." Jack replied: "She says that all the time, but because of the way she's been toward me, I've never been allowed a real avenue to find out about it." Yet when asked if he'd ever spoken with her about it or met with the boy, his reaction was uncharacteristically curt: "No."

Perhaps the young Jack's confused home situation helps explain why, at school (Roosevelt Elementary and

To begin at the beginning . . . the young Jack, with aspiring actress Judy Carne and Eddie Foy, Jr. in the early 1960s TV drama, "Fair Warning."

In the mid-sixties, Jack became a cinematic representative of the youth cult that preceded the hippies: the biker-badguy as hero of rebellious teens; the film is *Rebel Rousers*.

later Manasquan High), he led two lives, scholastically a straight A student, socially something of a troublemaker. Jack was a paradox to teachers and administrators: While his grades placed him in the top two percent of his class, Jack's antics got him suspended several times for smoking, swearing, and vandalism. Even his grandest antisocial act seems a perfect precursor to those of his best remembered movie characters: He destroyed sports equipment belonging to a visiting team Jack believed had cheated his pals of a victory. If it's true that the kind of a boy you are, the kind of a man you will be, then Jack retained a Jekyll/Hyde quality in his later life.

Freelance writer Robert Kerwin, interviewing superstar Nicholson a quarter-century later, was fascinated that the actor wore "a clean white cap, the old-time kind with a hard bill and a snap button. Pull the peak down on your eyes and you look like a 1930s poolroom bum; turn the cap around, and you're sweetness and innocence." Bill Davidson was intrigued to see that the superstar "still wears the rumpled blue jeans, but he also might show up unpredictably in an immaculate pinstriped suit and proper tie." In 1977, Jack explained that he hoped to someday do a film about Howard Hughes, in which the aged billionaire recluse manages to slip out of the penthouse where everyone thinks he's wasting away and thoroughly enjoys himself in another identity.

"I know a lot of people who've established double identities," Jack once whispered.

So when asked in a 1976 interview (while making *One Flew Over the Cuckoo's Nest*, a film about insanity) what actors have in common with schizophrenics, Jack flashed his killer smile and enthusiastically answered: "Multiple identities." Reflecting on his own early work, he immediately points out the double identities: "For years, I either played the clean-cut boy next door or the murderer of a family of five." In fact, a close literal examination of his early films reveals he never actually played either of those parts, though that hardly makes his perception any the less significant. Melvin Maddocks would, years later, touch on double identities as the key to Nicholson's onscreen appeal: "No actor since Marlon Brando has been so capable of terrorizing an audience by a show of temper," he wrote in the *Monitor*, "but his rages collapse as quickly as those extraordinarily charming smiles that on rare occasions spread across Nicholson's face."

Nicholson's post-stardom lifestyle provided evidence of a double identity, as in 1975 his garage housed both a beat-up 1967 VW and a brand new $23,000 Mercedes-Benz 600. Close friend Helena Kallianiotes notes the double identity can be seen in Jack's physique: a workman's body with an aristocrat's feet. "What I see,"inter-

In the late sixties, Jack emerged as a screen symbol of the counterculture, though he personally never felt comfortable with that (or any other) simplistic labelling. With Susan Strasberg on the set of *Psych-Out*.

A full-fledged star, at long last: Jack clearly relishes posing for a publicity still as, in the early seventies, he received leading roles in such important films as *Carnal Knowledge*.

viewer Ovid Demaris noted in 1984, "is a man who affects an impish façade but conveys the energy of a coiled spring." As early as 1969, interviewer Neal Weaver observed "a certain marvelous incongruity in the very idea of a bearded Underground type just being at the Regency [Hotel]."

As a high schooler, Jack developed in his writing assignments not one but two imaginary alter egos: a wise genie and an innocent boy. At graduation, his friends voted him both Class Optimist and Class Pessimist. His enduring fascination with double identities would eventually lead him to acting: "The actor is Camus's ideal existential hero," he said in 1986, "because if the idea is to live a more vital life, therefore the man who lives more lives is in a better position than the guy who lives just one." Surprisingly, he didn't emerge as a bright light of the drama club and made few cultural contributions to the school; his "theatrics" were limited to a performance of "Managua Nicaragua" at a talent show and an impromptu turning of himself into a clown with chalk dust when forced to sit on a dunce chair.

But show business ran in his blood: June left home when Jack was four to perform with the *Earl Carroll Vanities* in Florida. During her absence, Jack divided his time between the baseball team and girls, though friends recall there was little indication he'd ever become a

13

Refusing to be typecast, Jack played the dapper detective in *Chinatown* . . .

. . . and the rough-and-tumble career sailor in *The Last Detail*.

Ultimately, though, he seemed most comfortable when playing loners in search of their place in the universe: Here, Jack's existentialist character from *The Passenger* appears eager to believe in the old values symbolized by the cross, though his deep doubts about whether he inhabits a meaningful universe make that difficult.

By the mid-seventies, Jack appeared mellow and mature; still, there's a trace of the devil in those eyes.

14

A striking pose: Jack's uniquely appealing combination of
intellectuality and masculinity shine through in this mood-
drenched portrait.

world-class sex symbol. Jack's body was short, his face mostly babyfat. Everybody liked him (he was a candidate for Most Popular in the senior elections) but, as old friend George Anderson recalled in 1974, "he wasn't one of the heroes, though he made them his friends." Another classmate recalls the same information somewhat less flatteringly: "A fat Irish kid who wasn't good enough to play basketball so he managed the team."

Jack graduated from high school in 1954. Teachers believed his future lay in engineering, for he was offered an attractive scholarship at the University of Delaware. "Sister" June had meanwhile moved to Los Angeles with her two children, having married and divorced a glamorous test pilot (and son of a wealthy Eastern brain surgeon) she met in Miami. June's life had been a fascinating one: working her way up from gypsy dancer to Pinky Lee's "straight" lady, she had also labored in the control tower at Willow Run, the central domestic-sending center for the military in World War II. Following her upscale marriage, June had lived a country club existence in Stony Brook, and Jack spent his summers there, adding to his sense of double identities as the boy from working class New Jersey tried to adjust to a ritzy Long Island lifestyle. But that was ancient history now: June was once again on her own, in Los Angeles, and indicated a desire to get to know her "kid brother" better.

Jack accepted her invitation to spend his post-graduation summer with her. He wasn't altogether sure if he wanted to go to school, at least right away. He had been intellectually precocious enough to skip a grade and was tired of being a year younger than everyone around him. Besides, he feared he was too lazy to be a good student. No sooner had he arrived in L.A. than he found the detour in life that would in time lead him down a long, convoluted path to international celebrity: the movie business.

Jack quickly decided he might like to write for films. That wasn't surprising, since the caption under his graduation photo in the yearbook stated: "Enthusiastic writer of those English compositions," and old friends still recall him as the boy nicknamed "The Weaver," owing to his talent for weaving intricate, richly textured sentences. Even his hard times had pushed Jack toward writing: when during his Sophomore year he had to stay after school every day and write a 1,000 word essay as punishment, he'd turned it into a pleasure by applying his imagination to the compositons.

Without a clue as to how he might start writing for profit, Jack found menial work as a part-time sales clerk at a toystore and hung out in pool halls where he proved an adept hustler. That, and some success at the race track, allowed him to buy his first car, a '49 Studebaker. Several times, he'd have four winners in one afternoon

and head home with $300 or $400. One day, though, he lost on the last race, then couldn't find his car in the parking lot. From then on, he stayed clear of the track.

But any thought of following up on that scholarship dissipated when he landed his first job with a major movie studio—as mail sorter at MGM, where he was paid $30 a week to arrange and classify fan letters kids had sent to those animated stars, Tom and Jerry. Jack took the job mainly so he could gawk at the big stars working there. "Everybody's interested in seeing movie stars," he'd admit after becoming one himself.

The pay at MGM wasn't great so he began a betting pool. Jack caught the attention of studio bigwigs by aggressively addressing the top executives on a first-name basis. Where, the moguls wondered, did this Irish kid acquire such chutzpah? In his spare time, though, Jack furthered his interest in writing by reading. He waded through books that had not been on the recommended list in high school, but were certainly required for anyone discovering he was one of the "angry young men" of the fifties. This group found their literary inspiration in the works of Jack Kerouac and their cultural icon in the screen presence of James Dean. Hollywood was suddenly full of rebels without causes, and Jack learned that to communicate intelligently with others of this ilk, he had to begin his informal education with J.D. Salinger's *Catcher in the Rye*, then move on to Existential and Zen Buddhist works.

Despite his interest in writing, Nicholson noticed that most of the young men trying to break into movies were taking acting lessons, forming little theatre groups to ply their craft while waiting for the hoped-for auditions and dreamed-of "big break." It was reassuring to be with other people of the same age, to know one wasn't alone in attempting to break down the doors of the monolithic studio system. Jack joined a group called The Players' Ring. They survived on the very edge of respectability; membership in the repertory group meant not only involvement in all aspects of production but, after hours, swiping wood from a local timber yard to use for floorboards, or snitching lighting equipment from an all-night supermarket. The most money he ever made for one week's work was $14. There was always hope, though: Michael Landon, Edd Byrnes, and Robert Fuller co-starred with Jack in a production of *Tea and Sympathy*; all three were spotted by talent agents and soon worked on TV's *Bonanza*, *77 Sunset Strip*, and *Laramie*. "I just lay around," Jack would bitterly remember, "still 'preparing.' " His stardom would eventually far outstrip theirs, but for years he seethed with barely repressed jealousy.

Another Hollywood-fringe staple was taking acting lessons from some established performer. Jack's first

Meeting with the press: Jack speaks with reporters (the author is on the left) during the press conference preceding the national release of *One Flew Over the Cuckoo's Nest.* (Photo by Paul Schumach)

With co-stars Anjelica Huston and William Hickey, Jack faced a considerably less enthusiastic (some would say "hostile") group of reporters following the premiere of *Prizzi's Honor.*

A family portrait: Jack (looking less than amused), Kathleen Turner, director John Huston, and Anjelica all pose for a publicity shot during their *Prizzi's Honor* experience.

classes were with experienced but out-of-work actors Joe Flynn and Martin Landau. Landau told the impressionable young Nicholson that "all art is one thing—a stimulating point of departure." That idea would prove basic to all his work, explaining why, as a superstar, he avoids escapist fluff as consistently as he does didactic tracts. "What you're supposed to do," he says, "is keep people vitally interested in the world they live in." It was in such a class that he met two other hopefuls, Robert Towne and Roger Corman; the three became close friends, swearing someday they would make movies together. That proved to be no mere pipe dream.

But even before the first sweet smell of success, this was an exciting time; in an era following the Beats and predating the Hippies, Jack and his friends emerged as a transitional group of West Coast Bohemians, a bridge between Lawrence Ferlinghetti and Bob Dylan. There was the thrill of meeting other young talents, trying to guess who would leave a mark on American culture and who would pass unnoticed; hanging out in the since-defunct coffeehouses like The Unicorn, eating at Barney's Beanery, playing darts in the Rain Check bar; freaky experiences at the salons held by Samson DeVreer, a male witch; parties with the attractive and liberated young women who were always around, always available.

For a while, Jack shared a place at the corner of Fountain and Gardner with pals Don Devlin and Harry Gittes, which by Jack's own admission "was the wildest house in Hollywood." By some accounts, though, Jack was still more likely to inspire trusting friendship than true infatuation. Actress Sally Kellerman, recalling that era, cited being unhappily in love with someone else and sitting on Jack's lap, pouring her heart out to him. Far from the menacing macho character he's so effectively played, Jack struck her as "the funniest man in the world, and always available when I needed him—a true friend."

Hard liquor didn't appeal to Nicholson; perhaps he was haunted by too many dark memories of the man he believed to be his father. Still, character actor Harry Dean Stanton (*Repo Man*) recalls: "Whenever I think of Jack from that period, I always see him with a cheap red wine on his lips." Occasionally, reality would intrude: Jack had to fulfill his military responsibility, and did so working with an airfield crash crew in the capacity of fireman.

Meanwhile, there were brief brushes with the big-time: Producer Joe Pasternak, who took a liking to Jack, arranged for him to have a bona-fide Big Studio screen test, and, as self-defeating as some of the characters he has played, Jack didn't bother to memorize his dialogue and bombed badly. Even acting class presented prob-

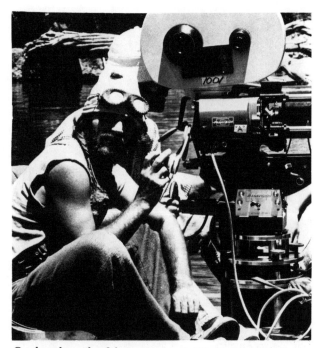

On the other side of the camera: Jack directs *Goin' South*.

lems. Teacher Jeff Corey complained that, in his acting, Nicholson didn't show him any "poetry." "Maybe, Jeff," Jack answered, "you don't see the poetry I'm showing you."

Then the dream came true. Jack's twentieth birthday present was from his friend Roger Corman, who had quit trying to break into the Hollywood mainstream and instead gone into business for himself. Now an independent producer, Corman turned out lurid low-budget films for the youth market. Nicholson was given the leading role in *Cry Baby Killer*, one of the countless misunderstood-teen flicks. Better still, Jack—who had initially been drawn to movies in hopes of becoming a screenwriter—was allowed to work on the script of this and many of the other Corman quickies. Indeed, "allowed to" may be understating it. The Corman company made films the way improvisational companies create comedy, with everyone throwing in any idea they come up with in hopes something might click. Always working in those early days as writer-director-producer-actor (however unofficially), Jack would later reflect: "I was the first person of my own generation to be one of these hyphenated people." He also learned that he most enjoyed working when he was a full collaborator on a project, rather than merely a chesspiece in the hands of a director.

But movie stardom, even on such a less than prestigious level, was for the time being short-lived. Nicholson proved difficult to cast, neither good-looking enough for leads nor offbeat enough for character roles.

Always the improvisor and collaborator, Jack adds a detail during the shooting of *The Postman Always Rings Twice*, suggesting the use of a gun as prop as director Bob Rafelson *(left)* instructs the other actors.

Later that same day, Rafelson, Jessica Lange, Jack, cinematographer Sven Nykvist and the rest of their crew gather around a video recorder to watch the results of their work.

Relaxing on the set of *The Missouri Breaks* with longtime idol and then-recent neighbor, Marlon Brando; Jack can't take his eyes off his co-star, who apparently can't take his own eyes off the camera.

He still fondly remembers the comment of one producer who sensed there was something special if undefinable in this young man: "Gee, Jack," the guy told him, "I don't really know what we could use you for, but if and when we do need you, we'll need you very badly!" He found some employment on TV shows like "Divorce Court" and "Matinee Theater," then returned to acting classes. Several times, he thought his shot was in front of him, only to find himself starting all over again. No wonder he and another frustrated writer-director-actor, Monte Hellman, penned a screenplay based on The Myth of

19

Nicholson, director and actor: pensive and
enigmatic, accessible and easy-going

Sisyphus—embodying man's eternal uphill struggle, the
goal of which can never be fully achieved—which has to
this day gone unproduced. "Man's dignity," Jack later
reflected, "is the trip down the mountain."

Those hungry years both scared and scarred him.
"When you're not accepted, you cease to think of yourself as special," he would recall from the vantage point of
superstardom. "I had doubts, which is a horrible quality
for a human being to live with." Still, one old friend
insists that even during this lean period Jack "always
thought of himself as a movie star." Years later, Jack
would admit he was lucky to take so long arriving.
"Better this way, than making it at 22 and then going
downhill. Look at other guys my age—I mean, where is
Troy Donahue at? I think being a late success was one of
my greatest pieces of luck."

In hindsight, perhaps. Back then, he hungered for a
touch of success. In time it came, however modestly. In
1960, Corman finally awarded Jack roles in several more
quickies. He may not have been famous, but he was
certainly becoming experienced. And while mainstream
moviegoers may not yet have seen him onscreen, the
teens who would shortly emerge as the most important
"target audience" had, at drive-ins and double bills,
enjoyed their first glimpse of that incredible smile Molly
Haskell would one day claim extends "beyond the moment or the person to whom it is directed." But for more
than a decade, an inwardly troubled Jack wondered if

he'd ever crack the big time. "I couldn't even get inter-
viewed for *The Graduate*," he later recalled. "They saw
every actor I had lunch with."

By 1962, Jack was married to actress Sandra Knight,
who likewise earned a living working for Corman. A year
later their daughter, Jennifer, was born, and friends
immediately noted Jack's sincere attempt to slip into a
more sedate lifestyle. For a while, irresponsible pleasure-
seeking was replaced by a proper home-life, as Jack made
a stab at being the kind of husband-father he'd never
himself known. But Corman didn't pay much, and to
make ends meet, Jack eventually balanced acting by day
with a moonlighting stint which returned him to his first
love, writing scripts. His double existence as writer and
actor didn't leave much time for his other double-
existence, Hollywood filmmaker and husband/father:
"I've blown a lot of significant relationships in my life,"
he eventually told *Playboy*, "because I was working and
didn't have time to deal with a major crisis."

Even at this early point, Nicholson showed signs of
artistic ambition; like other young talents in his clique,
he longed to move beyond exploitation and into the
realm of art. Jack and Monte Hellman formed Proteus
Films, and Nicholson literally carried the offbeat westerns they filmed to the Cannes festival in cartons.

That trip changed his life, his career, his sensibility. In
Hollywood, Jack had been dealing with the slick style of
producers, men who think of movies as material to be

20

marketed. At Cannes, he spoke with such revolutionary artists as Jean-Luc Godard. Ideas came to Jack like epiphanies: films, he suddenly realized, could alter the public's perceptions of the world, could exert complex political impact, could be made not to turn a quick profit but to turn people around in their points-of-view. For years, Nicholson had been living in the heart of what was supposedly the world's moviemaking capital. Now, he realized, there was an alternative way of approaching movies. For the European director, film as art was not a notion hauled out once a year on Oscar night, but a code to live and work by. Nicholson returned to Hollywood, but carried the continental vision home with him.

Then, as Nicholson's marriage crumbled (lamentably, he would later admit his "secret inner pressure about monogamy," while insisting, "I have a good relationship with my ex-wife—our marriage was lived out rather than failed"), his career took off.

The youth rebellion of the late sixties was about to happen. As an actor and writer, Jack was clearly the proper talent to bring the emerging pop scene to life onscreen. He and his friends had, after all, practically invented it.

So Jack wrote scripts about acid after experimenting with L.S.D. to make his screenplay more valid. He hung out on Sunset Strip with the young people who sensed something exciting was in the air, politically and culturally. Presenting (some would say selling) this idealized image of the counterculture to the confused youth of America, Jack and collaborator/chums like Bob Rafelson were in the forefront of what was happening. All that was needed now was a film which, by conscious intention or happy accident, would wrap all the varied elements of the expanding hippie culture into a single vision. The *Rebel Without a Cause* of 1969 was waiting to be made.

Easy Rider proved to be that film. When full-scale success finally came, Jack—knowing he'd paid his dues many times over—had no problem dealing with it: "There are two ways up the ladder, hand over hand or scratching and clawing," he would later say, adding with a grin: "It's sure been tough on my nails." Shortly, Nicholson fulfilled the promise reviewers had noted with a series of remarkably varied and in-depth characterizations. No passing symbol of hippie youth, Jack was clearly an actor of almost unlimited potential: "They wanted me to line up with the longhairs," Jack would later recall of that turbulent period. "I'm comfortable in that environment and have a lot of friends in it, but it never was what I really wanted to be."

Instead, Jack drew on two different but equally admirable traditions. On the one hand, he appeared a throwback to the great stars of the thirties and forties, with a presence that reminded viewers and critics of Bogart and Garfield; on the other, he was clearly the spiritual descendant of such alienated loners of the fifties and sixties as Brando and Clift. In Nicholson, the old Hollywood and the new merged in a magical way, the "double identity" of the man extending even to his unique brand of stardom. The *Village Voice* acknowledged that quality when it hailed Jack as "Bogart in the age of rock 'n' roll," and Rex Reed similarly tagged Jack as "a man with both feet planted firmly on the opposite banks of The Generation Gap."

As it turned out, the hippies did not take over Hollywood; *Easy Rider* may have been the surprise hit of 1969, but, more surprising still, *Airport*—a blockbuster return to the studio formula film, complete with an old-fashioned all-star cast and a conventional style—emerged as the box-office success of 1970, not only with older audiences but (significantly) with youthful moviegoers as well. Jack survived the swing back because audiences responded to a happy marriage of past and present in his performances. Journalists had a field day proclaiming him the (onscreen) man of the hour: "As James Stewart epitomized the New Deal Average Joe," Tad Gallagher wrote, "Jack Nicholson represents a generation split by the urge to change things and the need to survive" with certain traditions intact. But when one publication hailed him as the screen incarnation of "The Man of the Seventies," Jack responded with mixed emotions: "The press will grasp for anything simplistic, so they tag me a man of the seventies, or *the* man. Sure, I am, but it's because I'm not simplistic. It's because I'm open. What I represent is change."

Certainly, there was nothing "simplistic" about his performances or career choices. Jack refused to coast on his popularity, instead taking serious risks, career-wise. Agents and producers shook their heads and shuddered, certain Nicholson would destroy his delicate stardom by passing up prestige productions—*The Godfather* and *The Sting* among them—to work on less glossy, less financially certain, more artistically stimulating films. Which is not to suggest he ever turned anti-capitalist. "Don't get the idea I'm against money," he once reflected. "I'm not. I'm very cautious about what I do . . . because one day a couple of years ago I heard something that surprised me. John Wayne was broke. *John Wayne!* That's something to think about when planning a career, how ephemeral movie money is." In another context, he told interviewer Helen Dudar he owns a piece of every movie he now makes, flatly admitting: "I didn't get into the film business to be poor."

In fact, there are polar reactions concerning Jack and money. Mike Nichols insists Jack always has "several thousand bucks out" in the hands of old friends who have run into hard times; Roman Polanski describes Jack

Part beatnik and part Establishment, a bemused, drowsy-eyed Jack Nicholson, sporting a bohemian beret to offset his elegant tux, nonnchalantly parties with Hollywood notables at the big bash following the 47th annual Academy Awards.

Jack, overlooked once again, manages a charitable smile as Jack Rollins (rear) and Charles Joffe accept yet another Oscar for Woody Allen's *Annie Hall* at the 50th annual Academy Awards.

as "stingier than W. C. Fields." Jack's paradoxical attitude toward money became evident once when, at the upscale restaurant Maxim's, Jack magnanimously picked up a $600 check. Upon learning that a dinner companion, who tried to treat but had been out-maneuvered by Jack, could have written it off as a business expense, Nicholson fell into a deep depression. People lucky enough to visit his Hollywood Hills home see evidence of Jack's mixed attitude toward money. Proudly displayed among the great works of art is a platter of shredded dollars.

Yet money has always taken a backseat to more intriguing matters, such as the fairer sex. During the early seventies, Nicholson was (along with his pal Warren Beatty) associated with numerous beautiful women, model-turned-actress Mimi Machu and singer-turned-actress Michelle Phillips most prominent among them. A decade later, Margaret Trudeau, estranged wife of then Canadian Prime Minister Pierre, would brag in her autobiography, *Beyond Reason*, of a wild affair with Jack, insisting on torrid lovemaking in his car: "I discovered just how much room there is in the back seat of a Daimler." Clearly, Jack was no longer only a pal to some of the lovely ladies.

Attempting to define his sex appeal, friend Candice Bergen muses about Jack's "cobra eyes." Another friend,

former *Vogue* editor Diana Vreeland, admitted, "That smile of his is simply a killer; Jack must know it's devastating, because he uses it very rarely." And a well-known Hollywood beauty once slyly noted that, "If all the women Nicholson's had affairs with voted for him, he'd be a shoo-in at the Academy Awards." Jack himself confessed (apparently straightfaced) that, "I've never been in an orgy of more than three people."

In time, though, he settled into a long-term relationship with Anjelica Huston, renamed "Toots." They lived together in a house in the mountains overlooking Beverly Hills, appropriately flanked by neighbors representing the opposite poles of the Old Hollywood, philosophically as well as physically: Charlton Heston on the right, Marlon Brando on the left.

In 1982, Anjelica did move into her own home with four cats and a dog, though the seemingly strained, obviously special relationship survived tabloid stories of Jack's supposed Trudeau affair and Anjelica's own involvement with Ryan O'Neal. "I keep asking her to marry me," Jack has said, "and she keeps turning me down." As to why they survive as a couple, with dignity if with difficulty, Anjelica simply states, "He makes my blood boil." Part of the strain on their relationship in the late eighties arose from the fact that countless other women felt the same way. Recently, one actress posed for

Playboy while discussing her alleged affair with Nicholson in the most intimate terms, while another lady announced she was carrying his child. Considering Jack's own background, the latter claim (if indeed true) leaves one with the impression that in time, Jack became a virtual clone of the father he never knew.

Still, as long as Jack and **Anjelica** remained a couple, they were perceived and portrayed as the spiritual center of the hip young Hollywood; but in search of privacy and removal from such unsought status, they often slipped away to Aspen, returning to L.A. when work beckoned.

Throughout the early seventies, the excellence of that work earned Jack a nearly annual Oscar nomination but no statuette. And despite his image as something of an anti-Establishment outlaw/star, Jack (in stark contrast to the condescending attitudes of Dustin Hoffman and George C. Scott) showed up dutifully every year at the movie Establishment's big ceremony. But he kept losing out to beloved old-timers like Gig Young, Jack Lemmon, and Art Carney. At last, running out of patience, he growled that, "Maybe by 1976, I'll [be old enough to] get a little of that sentimentality vote myself." Friend Quincy Jones insisted, "Next year, they'll run out of old dudes to vote for." He was right; Jack at last won an Oscar for his shattering performance in the screen adaptation of *One Flew Over the Cuckoo's Nest*.

Still, there have been disappointments and setbacks. *Napoleon*, the epic he and Stanley Kubrick have always hoped to do together, will most likely not get made. *Moontrap*, a novel he's always wanted to adapt to the screen and direct (but not star in) may never happen. He has another unrealized project: "I'm going to come out with the real Howard Hughes. Which is going to be nothing but my fantasy about what it's like." A remarkable statement, considering the blurring of objective and subjective reality, the insistence that the "real" Howard Hughes would be Jack Nicholson's "fantasy" of him.

The eighties was certainly an awkward time for him, both socially and artistically. With his liberal political bent, he's less than comfortable with the country's shift to the right, less than happy with the fact Hollywood has returned to the old-fashioned formula films, but without duplicating the charm or craftsmanship evident in the pictures produced during the studio era. No one in Hollywood wants to make a modest success, only a mammoth blockbuster that will outdraw *E.T.*: "That's not good for me," Jack says, "because I tend to shy away from those kind of movies." Today's megahit mentality only "narrows the avenues that are open for people to explore." He survives by seeking out the most interesting film projects that come his way, never even considering what most actors look at first (the size of his role, the number of lines, how sympathetic the character is) but deciding on whether he believes in the film itself, whether participation will be both fun and a challenge. "My thought," he's been quoted as saying, "is that I should try and do what other people can't do. I should be very esoteric and hope it will communicate." That helps explain why, for every box-office record breaking blockbuster like *Batman*, there's also a more personal little picture like *Ironweed*; *Broadcast News* and *Two Jakes* are attempts to blend the best qualities of audience pleasing blockbuster entertainment with serious films that communicate.

Often, his choices have less to do with the merits of the script than who the director will be; Jack passed on *Witness* before Peter Weir was signed to helm that

A winner at last: Jack Nicholson grips his own statuette, sharing the moment of glory with co-producer Saul Zaentz, co-star Louise Fletcher, and co-producer Michael Douglas as *Cuckoo's Nest* sweeps the 1975 awards.

project, and insists he would have done the film if he had only known. "Once I'm in," he explains, "all I want to know is what the director wants. I don't want to be the one who robs this guy of his chance to express his vision, whether or not it's mine. My whole craft is developed to be able to do what that guy wants." Which is why there's no such thing as a Jack Nicholson movie or a Jack Nicholson role; unlike a Clint Eastwood or a Sylvester Stallone, he's not concerned with image, prefering to direct only if he won't be in the film. Jack relishes having the director elicit his creative, collaborative input, but never uses his superstar status to wrest control of the film away from him.

Politically, he bides his time, waiting for "another McGovern to come along" so he can get the juices going once more, even if the outcome is as disappointing for him as it was last time around. Because it's the Sisyphian effort that counts: "You are what you do," he said in 1977. In that same *Arts Journal* interview, he also made clear his attitude on making movies and campaigning for candidates is one and the same: "I have an artistic-political philosophy; it's Zen Buddhist; skirt the authorities."

He's a dedicated Los Angeles Lakers fan who will fly cross country to catch one of their games, likes to ski, roller skate, and play tennis. He collects effigies of pigs (stuffed toy swine, carved wooden hogs), claiming that, "When pigs became the symbol of evil, I adopted them." He enjoys continuing to cultivate what *Time* once described as his "deliberately scuffed, slightly sinister popular image," gleefully noting it's impossible to type him, in part owing to the varying reactions he elicits: "Someone 50 thinks I'm a dope fiend," he said in 1975, "while someone 15 thinks I'm too mild a guy." Uninterested in poppers or chic cocaine, he admitted: "I know it's not fashionable to be an old pothead, but what can I do? That's pretty much my level."

And he reads. Dostoyevsky and Proust are his favorites, but more often he's too burdened with scripts. "That's all I do, read scripts," he once wailed. "I have this dream that my poor deceased mother is going to come up out of her grave someday and beckon me over: 'Psssst, come here, son, I want you to have a look at this script I've got for you.'

"I think the most impressive thing about me," Jack told interviewers Robert David Crane and Christopher Fryer in 1975, "is that I've done 20 to 25 films, and none of the characters are alike." Since that time, the number has doubled but the statement remains true. Jack has—more than any other contemporary actor—resisted the temptation to slip into an all-purpose star persona. Instead, he has consistently stretched himself as an actor, playing the widest range of characters in movies that

seemingly have nothing in common except his presence. "Unpredictability," he has said, "is the most arresting quality an actor can have."

"Despite his trademarks," Mel Gussow once wrote, "the cocky smile and the casual insouciance with which his characters confront authority, he seems more than most actors to be transformed with each role." Jack's not so much a latter day man of a thousand faces, hiding a single characterization behind endless masks, as he is a man able to make a single face express a thousand personalities. "What is stardom for," Jack scoffs, "if you don't take chances?" Easy enough to say, but the impressive part is that Jack's actually lived up to that code: Each Nicholson character (the overall success or failure of any individual film notwithstanding) emerges as a clearly defined human being, a uniquely realized man rather than an excuse for a "star turn."

Jack begrudgingly admits that, "People expect me to do rips I do in films: bawling out waitresses and that," though he's concerned when they don't likewise recall his other, understated performances. "It's a compliment, I guess, to be identified so closely with [some of] my roles. I suppose I did them well enough that people confuse me with the characters. But I'm an actor."

Critics as well as audiences have continually tried to saddle him with a set persona, based on particular, popular parts. In 1975, Bill Davidson wrote in *The New York Times* that *Cuckoo's Nest* "continues the long string of anti-hero roles which have brought Nicholson both fame and fortune"; eleven years later, Ron Rosenbaum wrote in the same publication that the "Nicholson film persona tends toward world-weary disillusion and cool cynicism." But their comments are as untrue of the characters in *King of Marvin Gardens*, *Tommy*, and *The Fortune* as they are accurate for *Carnal Knowledge*, *Chinatown*, and *The Last Detail*. *Parade* magazine can report that "in almost all his films, Nicholson has played the perennial loser, the loony, the misfit destroyed by forces beyond his control or comprehension, the quintessential anti-hero," but such a conclusion can be reached only by ignoring more characterizations than one observes. Jack only scoffs at critical attempts to draw parallels between the dissimilar men he's brought to vivid life: "They try to make all the roles I've played into one unified archetypal character that I represent," he says, "but the difference between *Easy Rider* and Mc-Murphy is as big as that between *Henry V* and *Hamlet*."

On closer examination, though, Nicholson does reveal something of himself, however subtly. Jack resembles an artist who sketches other people's faces but, perhaps unknowingly, is drawn to subjects that allow him to come to grips with forces within himself; a painter who has never done a self-portrait but unconsciously paints other people so their divergent faces all, in some way, come to resemble his own. While the spectrum of his work belies any simple notion of "a Jack Nicholson role," these vividly realized men—so strikingly different from one another in terms of social status, level of intelligence and education, values and virtues, manners and morals—can indeed be seen as a body of portraits organized around recurring concepts. Consciously, Nicholson may have chosen the parts because the clear-cut differences forced him to perform a dramatic stretch each time out. But his choices reveal much about the man who chose to play them all.

Notice how many of the characters are writers. The lowlife hoodlum he played in the junk-movie *Rebel Rousers* was named Poet; a decade and a half later, Jack turned up as the real-life Eugene O'Neill in *Reds*. And in *The Shining*, he "captures, for all time [and] with horrifying verisimilitude, the impotent fury of the blocked writer," according to Ron Rosenbaum. More basic still, each of his characters has been involved, either openly or on some implicit level, on a two-part life-journey: a search for his own true identity, accompanied by an attempt to resolve ambiguous attitudes toward either an actual family or a substitute one, very often with a focus on a turbulent relationship with a father or foster-father figure.

First, the search, a motif Nicholson is himself fully aware of, both in his life and in his work. "The search for me and for the character is compulsive," he would eventually reflect. "There's never been a time in my life when that wasn't going on." So George Hanson in *Easy Rider* impulsively leaves his respectable, dull smalltown existence when a pair of exotic passersby promise to be his alternative family, while Bobby Dupea in *Five Easy Pieces* conversely leaves the freedom of the open road to try and rejoin the sort of Establishment family Hanson walked out on. Notice too the remarkable number of Nicholson characters whose search for their selves rules out any lasting commitment to a single woman or an extended family situation. Many others, having made such a commitment, find the search-for-self threatened by a man-woman relationship that can kill a man's sense of individual identity. In *Prizzi's Honor* the "killing" finally becomes literal.

The Nicholson character in *The Shining* attempts to murder not only his wife but also his small son when he begins to believe his family encroaches on his individual freedom as a writer. Other Nicholson characters actively seek out alternate families: the hippie cults in *Easy Rider*, the Navy in *The Last Detail*, the fellow inmates in *Cuckoo's Nest*, the outlaw gang in *The Missouri Breaks*, the union in *The Last Tycoon*.

Likewise, in real life, Jack has done the same

thing: "Bob (Rafelson) and Carol (Eastman) are among a number of actors, writers and directors I've hung around with for years whom I consider my surrogate family," he told *Playboy* in the early seventies. "I have very familial feelings about them." The very idea of family haunts the films of Jack Nicholson, reaching a logical conclusion in that corrupted caricature of the family, the Mafia, in *Prizzi*. There, Nicholson's character must deal with an outrageous notion of the traditional father figure, his godfather.

But dealing with fathers, or substitute father figures, is nothing new for Nicholson characters. The beachside confrontation between Bobby Dupea and his wheel-

A winner once again! Jack joins Shirley MacLaine and writer-director James L. Brooks as they likewise sweep the awards with 1983's *Terms of Endearment*.

chair-bound father in *Five Easy Pieces* remains one of the most moving and memorable moments in film history. Relationships with father figures are basic to *King of Marvin Gardens*, *Chinatown*, *The Shining*, and Nicholson's directorial debut, *Drive, He Said*.

Even his interest in the unrealized *Napoleon* project has more to do with personal expression than historical consideration. "When I was thinking about him," Jack told the *Times* in 1986, "I got a feeling of autobiography about it—in the sense that he was a man who conquered the world twice. And became a symbol for the Devil. That's the way they described him in England. But he was ultimately the man who overthrew feudalism, after all. . . . Up until that time, it was all about family. And now, after him, you could just be who you are. . . ." Likewise, Jack conquered the world twice as an actor, considering his comeback with *Terms of Endearment*; he

might have seemed Satanic to those who feared the youth culture, but he exerted a positive force, displaying a double identity not unlike Bonaparte's. The temporary success of the counterculture and the social change Jack wrought with *Easy Rider* overthrew the "feudalism" of mainstream America in the mid-sixties; Jack needed to go beyond the restrictions that family places on one's identity and be just who he is. . . .

There are in Nicholson's work consistent elements that bind up what at first appears an eclectic, haphazard series of career choices. In an understated manner, Nicholson has been using the film medium and his acting career as a form of self-expression: clearly, he's drawn to roles that relate to him on a deeply personal level. After all, summarize the life of Jack Nicholson and you have what sounds like the scenario for a Jack Nicholson film.

A winner for all seasons: Jack Nicholson, enjoying every moment of his success, and rightly so.

THE FILMS

The local teenage toughs (looking non-coincidentally like the kids who hassled James Dean in *Rebel Without a Cause*), plot to give Jimmy a tough time, as Joey (Ralph Reed) reveals his pistol to Manny (Brett Halsey, center) and friends.

Between two worlds: teen-outsider Jimmy holds a middle-class lady (Barbara Knudson) hostage, as a poor black worker (Jordan Whitefield) looks on helplessly.

Jimmy (Jack) has been badly beaten, and cannot know that he is being set up; the unknown little actor speaking with Brett Halsey appears to be a road company stand-in for Nick Adams, king of the teen weasels in *Rebel Without a Cause*.

AN ACTOR IN EMBRYO:

Cry Baby Killer

(1958)
AN ALLIED ARTISTS RELEASE

CAST:

Harry Lauter (*Porter*); Jack Nicholson (*Jimmy Walker*); Carolyn Mitchell (*Carole*); Brett Halsey (*Manny*); Lynn Cartwright (*Julie*); Ralph Reed (*Joey*); John Shay (*Gannon*); also, Leo Gordon and Roger Corman (*Extras*).

CREDITS:

Director, Jus Addis; producers, David Kramarsky and David March; screenplay, Leo Gordon and Melvin Levy, from a story by Leo Gordon; cinematography, Floyd Crosby; editor, Irene Morra; music, Gerald Fried with a song by Dick Kallman; running time: 62 mins.

Jack is one of the rare Hollywood stars who played the lead in his very first film. But considering the questionable quality of the movie, that's less impressive than it might at first seem. For *Cry Baby Killer* is one of the dozens of cheaply produced flicks released in the wake of *Rebel Without a Cause* in 1955, attempting to cash-in on its phenomenal impact on America's youth.

Though Roger Corman is not officially listed on the film's credits as producer, this was in fact the first collaborative effort between Jack and that schlockmeister of B-budget exploitation flicks. *Cry Baby* was, in all respects, a "quickie," made in a scant week and a half, at an estimated budget of under $7,000. Most of it was shot on a single set, but the effectively moody lighting and angular photography (the result either of an expressionistic approach or utter inexperience) lent it an awkward visual sensibility its limited but enthusiastic youthful audience could happily forgive; it was the angst of the

Jimmy grows more violent, threatening to turn into the very kind of delinquent the police mistakenly believe him to be.

title character they directly related to.

The distribution was limited, at best. *Cry Baby* was lucky to get the bottom half of a double bill at the drive-in; some other teens discovered it at rainy matinees in second-string theaters, where the kids could neck whenever the action onscreen slowed down. In fact, that wasn't often. Corman and his cohorts created films with a breakneck pace that played perfectly to the adolescents of the 1950s. His B-budget movies were a kind of unofficial alternative cinema, damned by the same teachers and civic leaders who likewise looked down on rock 'n' roll, eagerly awaited by kids who defied their elders. In time, that music would come to be accepted as a legitimate part of American popular culture. Similarly, the Corman films, dismissed at the time by serious critics as unreviewable junk, would—with their raw energy and alarming visual effects—stand the test of time better than many of their more prestigious movie competitors.

Nicholson was an essential part of the Corman company and an important influence on that entire subculture of the movie business. While *Cry Baby* is far from being a classic of its kind, it's certainly the consummate example of the fifties youth genre. Years later, recalling this and similar films, Jack would gleefully claim: "I always played psychos . . . there were a lot of juvenile-delinquent [pictures] in those days. I was usually (cast as) some crummy, cruddy person." It's hard to believe he could have been thinking of any film but *Cry Baby*, for in it, he's Jimmy, a misunderstood youth; it seems

obvious Corman and writer Leo Gordon (best known as a character actor specializing in cruel tough guys) wanted to stress the connection between him and the late Jimmy Dean.

The advertising for the picture proudly announced: "from Teen Rebel to Mad-Dog Killer!" In fact, that line was more sensational than anything in the film. Jimmy is a vulnerable high schooler (and an identification figure for the kids watching) first encountered, logically enough, at a drive-in theater—the very place where the film was likely to be seen. Jimmy is there trying to rekindle his relationship with a former girlfriend, Carole, an awkward emotional situation teens in the audience could easily empathize with. When several tough characters from Jimmy's high school flirt with Carole, then hassle Jimmy when he warns them away, it wasn't difficult for the film's audience to relate to his anger.

That quality of audience identification makes clear how strong a grasp the Corman company had on the mindset of their audience. After setting up (without

After seeing his life turned into a media event, Jimmy is persuaded to surrender by a sincere, sensitive adult (Harry Lauter, far right); the scene is an upbeat restaging of the considerably more pessimistic finale from Nicholas Ray's *Rebel Without a Cause*.

subtlety, but with considerable impact) an incident that could happen to any viewer if the fickle finger of fate should point in his direction, the filmmakers then carried through a nightmare scenario of the possible outcome. Jimmy is roughed up by the trio, and slugs one of the guys. Hoodlums all, they pull a gun and threaten him. But when in the ensuing confusion the gun is dropped, Jimmy grabs it. As the tough boys approach him, he fires and shoots two of them, and mistakenly believes he's killed them both. Terrified, Jimmy flees and, in his desperation, takes a mother and her child as hostages. He then holds them, along with a black working man, in the supply room of a store. The situation, which began as a mere youth scuffle, quickly mushrooms into a serious issue that cuts across the age barrier and affects the entire town.

There is clearly the possibility here for strong social statement. But didacticism was not in Corman's vocabulary, so for better or worse, his film raises intriguing issues only to skirt their implications. This might have been powerful stuff indeed if the relatively innocent Jimmy were (like Sal Mineo's character in *Rebel*) shot down for a crime he didn't commit. Instead, Carole shows up, claiming she loves Jimmy, also convincing him no irreparable harm has been done. Jimmy then allows the hostages to be rescued and happily surrenders when assured he can submit a self-defense plea.

Critic Derek Sylvester would complain the film featured "vapid, clumsily handled attempts at satire, directed against just those excesses of mob voyeurism to which the movie pandered." Likewise, Nicholson biographer David Downing insisted it was "not the sort of film to provide anyone with instant stardom." In fact, on its initial release, *Cry Baby* was considered too lowbrow to be reviewed by most major newspapers. But in En-

gland, it did receive attention: The highbrow journal *Films and Filming* complimented "the strongly humane attitude," while the *Monthly Film Bulletin* noted "a direct honesty of approach" that set this apart from the run-of-the-mill teen exploitation flicks.

Jack's performance was both energetic and amateurish. Even his most fervent admirers admit they enjoy this for nostalgia and cult value, rather than any hard evidence of the world-class actor who would in time emerge. In retrospect, though, Richard Goldstein noted that, "To this shadow of *The Desperate Hours*, Nicholson adds a confounding aloofness, completely at odds with the vulnerability which audiences demanded from juvenile delinquents in those days." Years later, *People* would claim: "Like Dean, Nicholson speaks for the single soul in its uphill struggles with mass civilization." However tentatively, that "voice" began with *Cry Baby Killer*. And the film does demonstrate at least a peripheral relationship to Jack's personal element in his work, with its hero who lives a double existence—at once a wimp who can't get his girlfriend back and a tough guy who inadvertently terrorizes an entire town.

Jack does have his moments—spontaneous bits of business, a fascinating look of bewilderment that occasionally crosses his eyes—which allow us a glimpse of his eventual approach toward acting. There's no doubt he enjoyed the experience of seeing his name above the title, if in a relatively perfunctory picture, and has expressed no regrets: "I'm very grateful for the rhythm of my career. It's true that some of my early pictures were really horrible, and I'm happy that most people haven't seen them. But I wouldn't have wanted to be successful as a young actor, because then you're placed in the position where you have to mature offstage."

Little Shop of Horrors

(1960)
A FILMGROUP RELEASE

CAST:

Jonathan Haze (*Seymour Krelboind*); Jackie Joseph (*Audrey*); Mel Welles (*Gravis Mushnick*); Dick Miller (*Fouch*); Myrtle Vail (*Winifred*); Leola Wendorff (*Mrs. Shiva*); Jack Nicholson (*Wilbur Force*).

CREDITS:

Director, Roger Corman; producer, Roger Corman; screenplay, Charles B. Griffith; cinematography, Arch Dalzell; editor, Marshall Neilan, Jr.; music, Fred Katz; art director, Daniel Haller; running time: 70 mins.

The cult following for *Little Shop* began in the mid-sixties, when college students at campuses large and small, prestigious and unknown, would notice in their local TV listings that the weird little film they'd seen several years earlier while in junior high school was going to play on television. Guiltily, a student would slip down to the dormitory or frat house recreation room with plans of catching it again after Johnny Carson was over and everyone else had gone to bed. To his amazement, the student would discover that everybody else was already assembled, waiting for *Little Shop* to start, eagerly anticipating the monster movie from their youth that had been so unbelievably bad it rated, in its own special way, as quite good. Whenever another student showed up, everyone already gathered to watch would look up at the late comer and gleefully shout: "Feed me!" Then everybody would break into the laughter of recognition. Only later, when such students had gone their separate ways and entered the work force, did they

realize precisely the same experience had happened on most other campuses: a true cult movie had spontaneously, unconsciously come into being.

Basically, Corman and company had set out to make a monster movie about a man-eating plant. But several hours into filming they realized their special effects were so decidedly non-special, their script so silly, their production values so completely non-existent that, if they shot the work as a "serious" scary film, it would be hooted off the screen. There was only one way to salvage things: Make the viewer aware of the fact that they, the filmmakers, knew what a dreadful film they were making by constantly kidding themselves and winking at the audience. If what Susan Sontag would identify as high camp didn't exist before *Little Shop*, then perhaps the concept began here. Roger and Jack may themselves have been unaware, on a conscious level, of trying to do anything but turn out an exploitation flick as quickly as possible. However unwittingly, though, the result was a film that would eventually be shown in museum retrospectives and discussed in lofty journals as a key work of American culture. In time, of course, it would also be the subject of a Broadway musical. Adults who, some twenty years earlier, thoroughly enjoyed a tacky little film would pay thirty dollars or more per ticket to see an upscale restaging of the story.

The focal character is Seymour (Jonathan Haze), a wimp who works in a floral shop. When not involved in what amounts to slave labor for his demanding boss, Seymour spends his time trying to develop a unique hybrid plant that will re-establish the importance of their shop, which has fallen on hard times ever since the

Seymour (Jonathan Haze), Audrey (Jackie Joseph), and the shop owner (Mel Welles) inspect "Audrey II."

Wilbur Force (Jack), repressed masochist, shows up at the dentist's office for his weekly allotment of pain.

"No novocaine—it dulls the senses!"

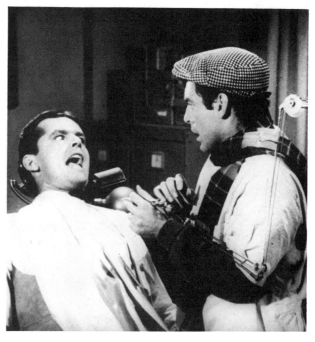

neighborhood around them began deteriorating. Seymour does indeed come up with such a plant, and people eagerly line up to see it. The problem is, Audrey (named after Seymour's girlfriend) thrives on blood and commands Seymour in no uncertain terms: "Feed me!" Seymour, so often the victim of beatings and beratings by

The film's cult status led to a Broadway musical and, coming full circle, Universal's big-budget 1986 remake with Rick Moranis and Ellen Greene as Seymour and Audrey.

hoodlums, finds himself transformed into a victimizer; for him, though, there will be no happy ending.

Seymour's first foray for food involves the accidental killing of a man he knocks under a speeding train. Later, Seymour does in a vicious dentist and his boss kills a would-be thief who breaks into the floral shop; both provide the hungry plant with meals. A pair of cops, Frank Stoolie and Joe Fink, eventually figure out what's happening, and Seymour, rather than face jail, allows himself to be devoured by the plant, taking with him a knife he uses to end his creation's reign of terror: essentially, he's Dr. Frankenstein transformed into a late-fifties teen fink. As the faces of the victims gaze on (they all show up on Audrey's petals), it is the monster Audrey rather than the woman of the same name who claims Seymour for her own.

"One of the most memorable for me," is the way Jack, entrenched as a Hollywood star, would look back on *Little Shop* among the cheapies and quickies he did for Corman. "Spoof" is the best term to describe the film, and, in the words of Derek Sylvester, an "amiable, knowing" one at that, with an "endearingly tatty" monster and a charming, clever tendency to "shamelessly flaunt its Poverty Row sets." Likewise, David Downing claimed the creature was "classically unconvincing," while one wag of a critic labelled it "the best full-length horror comedy ever made in two days."

Most serious critics of the time either dismissed the film with a smug review or considered it beneath both contempt and criticism. Only *Variety* (in the person of

"Tube") offered a remarkably perceptive commentary of the sort most critics would be incapable of until the film had, with the passing of years, established its own strange but lofty reputation. Noting the brief shooting schedule and bargain basement budget, the April 20, 1961, review went on to claim that "limited fiscal resources haven't deterred Roger Corman and his game, resourceful little Filmgroup from whipping up a serviceable parody of a typical screen horror number. It makes a handy supporting attraction for shock features, supplying both comedy relief and offbeat diversion."

Tube went on to claim that the film was "one big 'sick' joke, but essentially harmless and good natured," noting that this was "low comedy, to be sure, and the per cent of parody is considerably less than 50-50, but the film comes up with several good laughs via its wild disregard for reality and its wacky characterizations." None was wackier than the bit supplied by Nicholson: Wilbur Force, the wild-eyed masochist who shows up at a sadistic dentist's office happily prepared for the pain. "This is going to hurt you more than it does me," the sadistic dentist tells Wilbur, but that only draws a masochistically pleased response: "No novocaine! It dulls the senses." Wilbur feels the need to justify his pleasure in pain: "There's a real feeling of growth, of progress," he muses, "when the drill goes in." But we grasp his real reason for being there when the dentist pauses a moment in his drilling and Wilbur, thoroughly disarmed, screeches: "Oh, my God, don't stop now." When the drilling is completed, Wilbur seems a tad disappointed:

"Aren't you going to pull any?" he whines. At last leaving (and now with a lisp as the result of the dental work), he sighs: "I can truly say I've never enjoyed myself so much."

When *Variety* commented that the acting is "pleasantly preposterous," it seems safe to assume the unnamed Nicholson was primary in Tube's mind. Most actors, stuck in such parts early in their careers, resent the brevity of their roles and dream of a day when they can assume center stage; but even after achieving superstardom, Jack would enjoy taking wild risks by playing similar off-center cameo characters, and his taste for such intriguing roles dates from his work in this film.

"Comic support is broad, sick, and low," one critic claimed, "but it plays." Indeed, it did; it does more than a quarter century later.

It would be a while yet before Jack was given official collaborative input into the films he and Corman concocted. But he contributed far more to this cult-classic than the credits allow. Seymour is, after all, the first of a breed of characters Jack would throughout his career write and/or portray: a man who leads a double existence, a mild, victimized middleclass storekeeper by day, and a grim, victimizing killer working outside the law at night.

Audrey Lives! Rick Moranis and friend, circa 1986.

35

Too Soon to Love

(1960)
A UNIVERSAL RELEASE OF A DYNASTY FILM

CAST:

Jennifer West *(Cathy Taylor)*; Richard Evans *(Jim Mills)*; Warren Parker *(Mr. Taylor)*; Ralph Manza *(Hughie Winemann)*; Jack Nicholson *(Buddy)*; Jacqueline Schwab *(Irene)*; Billie Bird *(Mrs. Jefferson)*; William Keen *(The Doctor)*.

CREDITS:

Director, Richard Rush; producer, Mark Lipsky; screenplay, Lazlo Gorog and Richard Rush; cinematography, William Thompson; editor, Stephen Arnsten; music, Ronald Stein; running time: 85 mins.

For his third film, Jack returned to the genre of his first, yet another quickie in the *Rebel Without a Cause* mold about misunderstood teenagers and their problems dealing with insensitive adults. This time, though, Jack did not play the lead but the hero's sidekick, and the amount of thought that went into the creation of his character can be seen in the name: "Buddy" is the good guy's buddy. The hastiness in every aspect of production is evident, for this film lacks the modest impact of *Cry Baby Killer*, which may be rated as sensationalism but has an undeniable crackling sense of excitement to it. *Too Soon* is mostly slow and dreary.

In fact, the film's only real claim to fame is the theme, which is gutsier than the filmmaking itself: Abortion is here treated openly as an existing alternative to early marriage for teenage couples with (as people once euphemistically put it) a "problem." If in an age of made-for-TV movies that treat abortion as one more "problem

of the week" issue that sounds less than scintillating, it's important to remember this was made at the tail-end of the repressed fifties.

But if the shooting schedule for *Too Soon* was completed during the last year of that decade, the film was released during the first year of the sixties, an era that would explode in psychedelic images onscreen. So *Too Soon* may deserve a minor niche in the history of youth films as the bridge between the two periods and the very different styles and attitudes they embodied.

The heavies of the piece are virtual retreads of the constantly bickering Mom and Dad from *Rebel*, who following that film's success had emerged as stock characters in films calculated for teen audiences. Once more, it's the parents' lack of sympathy for or interest in their offspring that causes the bewildered but fundamentally decent kids to become rebels.

Substituted for Dean and Natalie Wood are Richard Evans as yet another troubled teen named Jim and his girlfriend Cathy (Jennifer West). Her overbearing father insists on keeping the romantically inclined kids from seeing each other, which only causes them to meet on the sly. Seen kissing in public by the local police, they are dragged down to the station house. Realizing they must continue their relationship in absolute secrecy, Jim and Cathy find just such a place to meet, and shortly thereafter Cathy is pregnant. Deciding abortion is the only way out, Jim gets involved in a robbery to pay for it, while Cathy attempts suicide. At the end, they decide to marry, hoping they will not turn out like their parents.

The movie's message, of course, was that the parents and police (insensitive adults and authority figures in

As Buddy (center right), Jack tangles with yet another of the Nick Adams lookalikes who played the weasely bad teenagers in so many post-*Rebel Without a Cause* youth exploitation flicks.

Troubled teenagers: Richard Evans and Jennifer West as Jim and Cathy, the latest couple to stand in for James Dean and Natalie Wood.

general) created the problem by forcing the kids to love in private. If society had taken a more understanding attitude to their initial kissing, we are led to believe, Jim and Cathy would have gone on harmlessly petting in public, and the relationship would have gone no further. The problem with message movies like this is that they played almost exclusively to a teen audience, where they preached to the converted; the up-tight parents who needed to be persuaded that a certain amount of teen affection was nice and normal never went to see these films, so any positive effect was blunted.

As Jim's "buddy," Jack Nicholson was largely over-looked by those few critics who deigned to review the picture, though in *Variety*, "Powe" singled him out as someone who did "contribute" to the overall effect. Of the movie itself Powe argued: "The wages of sin . . . are both grim and dreary. This is the strongest recommenda-tion that can be made for the film, which is otherwise an inept retelling of a familiar story." A far tougher view was offered in the *New York Daily News*, which used this minor enterprise as an excuse to complain moralistically that, "Irresponsible fringes of the industry, sans money or talent, are flooding the market with pictures constructed solely on the appeal of amoral youth . . . like too many others, *Too Soon to Love* is an obviously expendable venture, although it is far less salacious than some. . . ." Generally, the film was treated more sympathetically in England, where *Film Daily* heralded it as "an earnest probing drama of teenagers" who were here "treated with candor and dramatic effectiveness." If the outrage of the *Daily News* seems a bit overblown for such a relatively low-key effort, then the attitude of *Film Daily* appears somewhat over-generous.

This genial, contrived, harmless item would be barely worth mentioning were it not for the fact that it marked Nicholson's first contact with a director who would play a significant role in Jack's development as a screen actor. Richard Rush would guide him through four future films (to date), and while none were masterpieces (Rush's only significant film, *The Stunt Man*, would star Peter O'Toole), they would all prove more visually arresting than *Too Soon to Love*. Like those others, this was an independent project Rush talked Universal into taking on. As the sixties wore on, more and more independently minded moviemakers would follow that route, and Jack—in on such projects early—was at the forefront of that movement.

Variety had commented that Jack did clearly "contribute" to the movie. Is it possible their comment is an understatement? Their reviewer was referring to his acting, though Jack was already intrigued with the idea of writing movies and, having worked twice for Corman, was used to collaborating beyond performance. He would say, years later, "I have my favorite minority—the unborn," facing the fact which he must have implicitly understood all along—he was illegitimate. On the abortion issue, he's aware of going against the grain of his usual political allies: "I'm very contra my constituency in terms of abortion because I'm positively against it. I don't have the right to any other view. My only emotion is gratitude, literally, for my life. If [his mother and grandmother had been] of less character, I would never have gotten to live." Though he knew none of the particulars in 1960, Jack would learn that his own mother had gone through a drama—deciding whether or not to abort—almost identical to the one that Cathy here endures. In the film, Cathy makes precisely the same decision Jack would later learn that June had arrived at. The parallel to his life is uncanny, cinching the connection between the film and his own ongoing inner psychological drama.

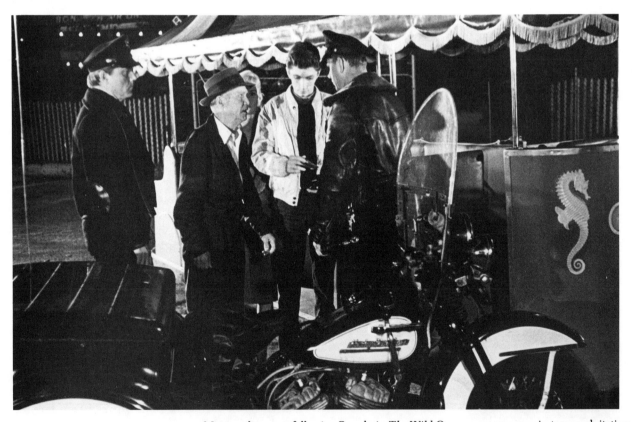

Motorcycles were, following Brando in *The Wild One*, necessary props in teen exploitation films (even if they belonged to cops) and were hauled out once again in *Too Soon to Love*. Press material from Universal-International optimistically hailed this as "a deftly-etched story of restless youth."

THE BIG LEAGUES:

Studs Lonigan

(1960)
A UNITED ARTISTS RELEASE

Weary Reilly (Jack Nicholson) is dragged down
to the station house by some tough Irish cops.

CAST:

Christopher Knight *(Studs Lonigan)*; Frank Gorshin
(Kenny Killarney); Venetia Stevenson *(Lucy Scanlon)*;
Carolyn Craig *(Catherine Banahan)*; Jack Nicholson
(Weary Reilly); Robert Casper *(Paulie Haggerty)*; Dick
Foran *(Patrick Lonigan)*; Jay C. Flippen *(Father
Gilhooey)*; Kathy Johnson *(Frances Lonigan)*; Jack Krus-
chen *(Charlie)*; Mme. Spivy *(Mother Josephine)*.

CREDITS:

Director, Irving Lerner; producer, Philip Yordan; screenplay, Philip Yordan from the trilogy of novels by James
T. Farrell; cinematography, Arthur Feindel; editor,
Verna Fields; music, Gerrald Goldsmith; running time:
95 mins.

At last, Jack was cast in a major Hollywood motion
picture, the long-awaited film version of James T. Farrell's once-scandalous but critically acclaimed study of
lowlife teenagers. A classic of gritty, uncompromising
realism, the trilogy had often been taken to task for its
unsparing use of gutter language, but no one could deny
its raw power of brutal conviction. In fact, Farrell's three
books were considered so tough in theme (as well as
intimidatingly enormous in scope) that no studio had
dared approach them during the thirties, when they were
written. But in time, the edge of controversy had passed.
What survived was the literary reputation; a masterwork
awaited screen interpretation, and Jack was involved in
this ambitious undertaking.

Remarkably, *Studs Lonigan* rates as one of the least
interesting of Nicholson's early vehicles, for almost
everything about the movie appears absolutely wrong-
headed. The novels offered an emotional rather than
physical picaresque, carrying its central character—a
tough Irish Catholic hoodlum raised in a Chicago
slum—through journeys of the heart, as he finds his life
turning topsy turvy when the boom of the twenties
breaks down into the bust of the thirties. Such internal,
episodic material works well in prose, but is less successful in a motion picture, where viewers expect a strong
storyline. Farrell had layered incident upon incident; no
one of the myriad anecdotes was significant in and of
itself, though by book's end a tremendous power had
been amassed through deliberate accumulation of anecdotes. For the film, it was necessary to select (at most)
one in every ten episodes, which put undue stress on
those chosen; they were forced to carry more weight in
the depiction of the deterioration of Studs' personality
than they could support.

Studs Lonigan was one of those novels (like J. D.
Salinger's *Catcher in the Rye* or Jack Kerouac's *On the
Road*) which sensitive young men looked upon as a
Bible: a novel interpreted not as a mere story, but as a

level at all: It is neither comprehensible as casual entertainment nor intriguing as an adaptation of a classic. Worst of all, it is pretentious: A B-budget quickie like *Cry Baby Killer* made fewer claims for itself but in fact captured more of the anger, confusion, and frustration of male youth than this "literary" project did.

Despite his character's nickname, Jack is energetic enough as Weary Reilly to make one wish he'd been given the lead. Certainly, the theme of both book and film—the young man who is accepted by his peer group but senses he is essentially different from them, fighting to keep from slipping into the more mundane life-styles they succumb to, continuing on an inarticulate but endless search for himself—was material that would have lent itself well to Nicholson the person as well as Nicholson the actor. Like Jack, and like certain of his key characters, Studs's drama grows out of his bridging of two worlds: He is in the streets but emotionally and

Weary (Jack) demonstrates how he got his nickname. Another gang member, Kenny Killarney (Frank Gorshin, far right) looks a bit more animated.

kind of blueprint for life, dealing as it did with a young man's cocky, arrogant attitudes and accompanying belief that the world is his oyster, and following him through to eventual disillusionment as he in time realizes his life will not be special, that he will die and be forgotten.

The role called for an actor as intense as James Dean. Christopher Knight, however, looked like a second-string Dean imitator, appearing weak rather than sensitive. He's especially ineffective in the scenes with fellow gang members, for Jack and the others look and act convincingly menacing. Jack would later claim he was awarded the role of "Weary" Reilly because he was the only actor in Hollywood willing to read the entire trilogy, a requirement the well-intentioned and high-minded but only modestly talented filmmaker Irving Lerner made of his cast members.

The film veers between the overly arty (as the gang members hang out near a carousel, we are treated to strange angle shots on the wooden horses) and the absolutely sordid (a brutal and, in the abbreviated film version, unmotivated attack on an innocent woman). Sometimes, the two approaches cross in bizarre ways, as when Studs visits his attractive high school teacher (Helen Westcott); as she walks around the apartment, we see his mental fantasies of her performing a striptease. This is handled so ineptly that it looks silly.

The movie is lethargic, and satisfies on absolutely no

intellectually not of them, yet his attempts to move into the life-style his attractive teacher symbolizes (with its emphasis on mental and moral values) are hindered by his street experiences. In this sense, Studs is a prototype of roles Jack would often be drawn to.

Certainly, Jack and actor/impressionist Frank Gorshin steal every scene they're in with their apparently improvised bits of business which cut through the film's crushing rigidity. But critics of the time failed to single out Nicholson's contribution; instead they analyzed the film's many failings. In the *New York Post*, Irene Thirer called it "a curiously concocted, hodge-podge affair," claiming it was done "imaginatively, though odd and static . . . it is a taxing picture, a *think* film but it lacks real passion, fire and flowing continuity." Paul V. Beckley, writing in the *Herald Tribune*, claimed it was "no more than a pale flicker of Farrell's massive trilogy . . . nor does it quite make its point as a film," adding that the

novel's powerful sense of "spiritless despondency" was only "limpingly" recreated.

Alone among critics, Howard Thompson of *The New York Times* defended the film, claiming it was "a pretty good movie, in some ways a very fine one," insisting that the effect was "haunting." Most audiences, though, saw the film as a failure. Farrell's books had been heatedly debated as raw social realism or vulgar sensationalism. No one debated the film, for it did not appear particularly powerful or appealing as either possibility.

Weary *(second from right)* smokes and gambles with the gang members; only Studs (Christopher Knight, far right) will come to see the emptiness of their lives.

Christopher Knight (second from right) lacked the talent and charisma to bring James T. Farrell's character to life; Jack *(far right)* was sadly wasted in a supporting role, though he might have done well by the title character.

LOVE ME AND THERE IS NO
FEAR:

The Wild Ride

(1960)
A FILMGROUP PRESENTATION

CAST:

Jack Nicholson *(Johnny Varron)*; Georgianna Carter *(Nancy)*; Robert Bean *(Dave)*.

CREDITS:

Director, Harvey Berman; producer, Harvey Berman; screenplay, Ann Porter and Marion Rothman; cinematography, Taylor Sloan; editor, William Mayer; running time: 63 mins.

Jack returned to the folds of Roger Corman and his independently-minded features for *The Wild Ride*, perhaps the least impressive of his early exploitation flicks. If only it had lived up to its title, the film might have offered some fun, but judged even as sensationalism, this is unexceptional stuff, lame rather than lurid.

Jack plays Johnny Varron, a vicious psychotic killer who terrorizes innocent people. If *Cry Baby Killer* had been an attempt to capitalize on *Rebel Without a Cause*, then this film was likewise a rip-off of another archetypal image of youthful rebellion from the fifties, *The Wild One*, for Nicholson played a biker—his first. If the film had the energy of, say, *Hell's Angels on Wheels*, it might have offered kinetic if overblown excitement. But of all Jack's early films, this one has the least "cult" interest.

Jack has no illusions about the quality of films like *Wild Ride* or the monster movies that followed: "I never dug them. I'm not a nostalgic person. They were just bad. The people who never saw my [early] movies are better off in life than I am, but like all other actors, I needed the work. I did all those [teen angst and horror

Back in the James Dean mold, Jack plays Johnny Varron—one more variation on the 1950s-style troubled teenager, this time in the tradition of Marlon Brando's "Johnny" from *The Wild One*. By 1960 the genre was quickly wearing out, waiting for the biker films to replace them. Georgianna Carter is the girl.

A pensive moment at the schoolyard, as Johnny Varron (Jack) and Nancy squarely face the severity of their problems.

One critic called Johnny "a *Cry Baby Killer* on a motorbike"; here, we see him messing up the girl who defies him.

flicks] because they were the only jobs I could get. Nobody wanted me." But Jack has never been contemptuous of the Corman quickies or of the man who turned them out. Noting the array of talent given their first shots by Corman during the sixties, Jack recently reminded interviewers of how few new directors were allowed such a chance to work by the major studios. "He's the best producer I've met in the business," Jack insisted. "The man carried me for seven years. I feel tremendously indebted to him." He has also noted that the paltriness of the material may have actually helped him develop an ability to create in-depth characters beyond what was to be found in a rather elementary script: "With lines like 'Love me and there is no fear,' I had to learn how to act—to keep myself and the audience from breaking up!"

43

Cast in his earlier films as a misunderstood teenager molested by hoodlums, Jack this time out demonstrated the Jekyll-Hyde quality that would mark his career. Here he plays one of the tough guys who beats up on unsuspecting kids.

More of the same: Jack and friend (Robert Bean) in action.

SON OF A GUN:

The Broken Land

(1962)
A 20TH CENTURY-FOX RELEASE

CAST:

Kent Taylor *(Jim Kogan)*; Dianna Darrin *(Mavra Aikens)*; Jody McCrea *(Ed Flynn)*; Robert Sampson *(Gabe Dunson)*; Jack Nicholson *(Will Broicous)*; Gary Snead *(Billy Bell)*.

CREDITS:

Director, John Bushelman; producer, Leonard Schwartz; screenplay, Edward Lakso; cinematography, Floyd Crosby; editor, Carl Pierson; music, Richard LaSalle; running time: 60 mins.

Some of Jack's most interesting projects have been westerns, but his first would hardly qualify for such praise. Like *The Wild Ride, The Broken Land* is one of the rare Corman quickies lacking the zest and excitement usually associated with that director's work. The press releases for the film described it, in glowing terms, as an "off-beat adventure drama, depicting the hardships and terrors encountered by the inhabitants of a small western town, dominated by a sadistic marshal." Corman and company managed to talk a major releasing company, 20th Century-Fox, into handling the movie's distribution, perhaps because the film at least had some minimal production values—it was shot in DeLuxe Color and CinemaScope process, which marginally distinguished it from the usual Corman fodder. Yet, considering the film's minimal hour-long running time, such "A" film qualities seem incongruous embellishments. Thematically, the movie bore more resemblance to a youth exploitation film than it did to *High Noon, The*

As Broicous, Jack appears to have less in common with the real-life westerner nicknamed "Curly Bill" by Wyatt Earp than with the sensitive, alienated, deeply troubled teen heroes he and most other young actors had been playing ever since the advent of James Dean. Here, Dianna Darrin attempts to comfort him.

Broicous (Jack Nicholson) and friends inadvertantly find themselves "kidnappers" when they stop the stage. Dianna Darrin plays Mavra Aikens.

Many of Jack's later films would deal with a corrupt, all-powerful member of the Establishment preying on young people; the precursor of such characters is the sheriff, Jim Kogan, played by Kent Taylor, no stranger to westerns following his *Rough Riders* TV series.

Gunfighter, or any of the other "big" westerns of the previous decade, focusing on a group of teenagers driven into a life of crime by an insensitive adult. The film, its pre-release hype insisted, "combines the talents of some promising newcomers with popular favorites." Just who the popular favorites were remains to be seen (top-billed Kent Taylor is best known for his syndicated TV series *Boston Blackie*), but for once, the hype proved more correct than the writer could have possibly guessed: Jack was certainly promising, if not precisely a newcomer.

A sadistic officer of the law who obeys the letter if not the spirit of democratic principles, Marshal Jim Kogan (Taylor) completely dominates the everyday life of his small, isolated town. Out of sheer cussedness, he jails Will Broicous (Nicholson), the well-meaning son of a well-known shootist. Shortly thereafter, Kogan also imprisons Billy Bell (Gary Snead) and Gabe Dunson (Robert Sampson) after catching them attempting to help Will escape. Suspicious about the intentions of a pretty young waitress, Kogan tells Mavra (Dianna Darrin) to get out of town. Before she leaves, though, Mavra visits the trio of young men and slips them a key to their cell. As she departs, the Marshal's deputy and mayor's son, Ed Flynn (Jody McCrea), spot her.

Will, Billy, and Gabe disappear into the nearby mountains and hide. When a stagecoach passes by with Mavra on it, they try and stop it to thank her for the help. Mistakenly, the stage driver assumes they are hold-up men and throws down the money box. The three take both the money and Mavra; as they try and leave the territory, Mavra finds herself falling in love with Gabe. When the four hide out in the hills, they are surrounded

46

The young deputy Ed Flynn (Jody Mc-Crea) finds himself torn between his duty to the marshal (Kent Taylor) and his instinctive feel for the young people who have been forced into the outlaw existence by an unfeeling, uncomprehending system.

by Kogan, Flynn, and members of a posse. Will and Gabe manage to get the drop on the lawman and force them to leave, allowing them to take the money; when Kogan decides to go back on his word, he's resisted by Ed, who is killed. Kogan then kills Billy and arrests the others, bringing them back to town.

Upon reaching their tenuous outpost of civilization, the group faces some angry townspersons. Mavra reveals that Kogan violated many of the local women (herself included) when he ruled the area as an army officer during the Civil War. Upon learning this, Gabe fights Kogan with his fists and beats him. Kogan crawls away, powerless, leaving Gabe and Mavra in an embrace.

Dianna Darrin was the beautiful blonde making her debut in this outdoors programmer; she would not be heard from again. Jody McCrea ended up playing the supporting role of "Meathead" in the *Beach Party* movies, never achieving the full stardom of his famous father, Joel. And Kent Taylor pretty much faded away following the limp box-office for this B feature. Jack alone would move on. The name of his character is intriguing, for it's the only one in the film that appears historical. There really was a "Curly Bill" Brocious, a friend to the Clantons during the bloody days in Tombstone, Arizona. Whether Jack's character is supposed to be the son of that Brocious (and somebody connected with the screenplay misspelled it) is unclear.

It's worth mentioning, though, that this was the first film in which Jack visibly metamorphosed into what would later be called "the man with the killer eyes." There is a dangerous quality about Will that comes from Jack's emerging presence rather than anything in the

The film's attractive (but afterwards little-seen) top-billed stars, Jody McCrea and Dianna Darrin.

mundane script. Likewise, there is a plot element in the film that at least tangentially links it to Jack's later, more impressive works: The reason Will is arrested by the marshal is the lawman's belief that, as critic Derek Sylvester put it, "the sins of the father should be atoned for by punishment of the son." Of course, we never see the father in the film, but his boy suffers great humiliation and pain owing to his kinship with a man he apparently doesn't know. There is a bizarre and intriguing link in that to Jack's own life as well as to other pictures in which Nicholson protagonists have been haunted by the presence of a father figure they never knew. There is also a link to Jack's eventual attitude that youth cults do not (as compared to the corrupted adults)

have all the answers, for the gang members are not a trusting bunch of buddies. As Broicous says at one point: "It's not love that holds us together . . . it's hate. Hate for Kogan and the others like him in all the towns we've ever been in." That line is not bad and is neatly delivered in the film by Jack. It captures something of the complexity of his own view of outlaw youth, at odds with the Establishment but never at peace with themselves.

There was little critical reaction at the time. Hindsight comments have correctly tagged it an acceptable, undistinguished film: *The Broken Land* has been called "routine" (Leonard Maltin), "typical" (David Downing), "fiasco" (Derek Sylvester). That last epithet seems a bit harsh: The film is not so much awful as it is ordinary.

Class-consciousness in the old west: Good badmen and bad goodmen eye the women and convey their power struggle through body language. Like so many later Nicholson films, *Broken Land* features, in Ed Flynn, a youth attempting to join the Establishment, a hero who has one foot firmly planted on each side of the Generation Gap.

"NEVERMORE!":

The Raven

(1963)
AN AMERICAN INTERNATIONAL RELEASE

Halfway between a romantic lead and scene-stealing buffoon, Roxford Bedlo (Jack Nicholson) kisses the hand of Craven's pretty daughter Estelle (Olive Sturgess) while Craven (Vincent Price) and Bedlo's own father (Peter Lorre) gaze on. This was a comic-horror variation on the serious theme of Generation Gap misunderstandings which would (no pun intended) haunt Jack's later work.

CAST:

Vincent Price (*Dr. Erasmus Craven*); Peter Lorre (*Dr. Bedlo*); Boris Karloff (*Dr. Scarabus*); Hazel Court (*Lenore Craven*); Olive Sturgess (*Estelle Craven*); Jack Nicholson (*Roxford Bedlo*); Connie Wallace (*Maid Servant*); William Baskin (*Grimes*); Aaron Saxon (*Gort*).

CREDITS:

Director, Roger Corman; producer, Roger Corman; screenplay, Richard Matheson, inspired by the poem by Edgar Allan Poe; cinematography, Floyd Crosby; editor, Ronald Sinclair; music, Les Baxter; production designer, Daniel Haller; sound, John Bury; running time: 85 mins.

Though Jack had been working with Roger Corman on and off for five years, *The Raven* marked their first official director-actor effort. *The Raven* also represents the end of a tradition at American International. Several years earlier, Corman had turned out *House of Usher*, which expanded on an Edgar Allan Poe story, starring Vincent Price as the haunted hero, featuring marvelously atmospheric sets which, in the heightened atmosphere of color photography, lent a formidable sense of gothic eeriness. The arty film proved a hit, so Corman mounted a succession of Poe adaptations: *The Pit and the Pendulum, The Premature Burial, The Masque of Red Death*. But after several movies, the effect was less terrifying than simply fun: like taking a ride through a fun house for the third time, laughing where you once jumped with fear. Corman, sensing this, smartly chose

to add humor. The result was surprisingly appealing; along with *Abbott and Costello meet Frankenstein* and Bob Hope's version of *The Cat and the Canary*, this is one of the most successful comedy-thrillers Hollywood has given us.

The film begins as though, like previous Poe adaptations, it will be played "straight": In the mid-fifteen hundreds, the mad magician Dr. Craven (Price) stands amid a dazzlingly designed set, reciting Poe's famous poem in the kind of elevated, hammy, archly theatrical voice Price is famous (some would say infamous) for. Then the blackbird enters, and the subsequent lines are addressed directly to him. Will I ever see Lenore? Price muses. Every schoolchild thinks he knows the answer: "Nevermore . . ." Instead, in Peter Lorre's voice, the Raven replies, "How the hell should I know?"

From that point on, there is little if any relationship to the poem from which the film derives its title. "The Raven" is in fact another magician, Dr. Bedlo, who has taken bird form after being put under a diabolical spell by his archenemy, Dr. Scarabus (Boris Karloff) for the affront of challenging his dominance as greatest practitioner of dark arts. Craven is kind enough to restore

"Take that, you . . .!" Roxford tackles one of the palace guards.

Wholesome if dimwitted, Roxford (Jack) stands dutifully behind his ladylove while she listens attentively to her father.

The evil Lenore (Hazel Court, in dark cape) defies her husband Craven (Vincent Price) and entraps Roxford and Estelle.

Bedlo to human form, and admits to him that he's obsessed with finding his beautiful wife Lenore, who disappeared from the castle some time earlier. Bedlo informs Craven that a woman who fits Lenore's description has been seen in the haunted palace of Scarabus. Hoping together they may be able to defeat this monstrous man, Craven and Bedlo head toward his home.

Making the journey with them is Craven's lovely daughter (Olive Sturgess) and Bedlo's strange son (Nicholson). The terrible truth they learn upon arriving is that Lenore (Hazel Court) has not been kidnapped but is the willing mistress of Scarabus. This figure of evil has indeed been hoping his two enemies would foolishly travel here and fall into his hands. Shortly, our intrepid band of heroes is imprisoned, as Scarabus insists he'll torture poor Estelle if Craven does not reveal all his great magical secrets. But the over-proud Scarabus makes the fatal mistake of once more turning Bedlo into a raven; the bird bites the bonds that hold the others, and they confront the villain.

What follows is the film's *pièce-de-résistance*: Amid the remarkably moody shadows of the great castle, Price and Karloff face off in a lengthy, elaborate duel, each summoning up his wildest bits of sorcery to outdo the other. There are plenty of visual effects that look impressively expensive for a film from the ordinarily cut-rate Corman. Much of the movie's appeal derives from the clever script by Richard Matheson, a novelist (*I Am Legend*, *The Shrinking Man*) turned screenwriter who was responsible for the best films created by the Corman company.

Nicholson's goofy comic turn as the male romantic lead did not win him much attention during the initial release. Writing for *Variety*, "Whit" merely said that Nicholson, like Miss Sturgess, was able to "lend effective support." David Downing claimed that Jack "played the Zeppo character to this bunch of weirdos," surmising that he "must have enjoyed watching them ham it up." In a considerably less charitable tone, Derek Sylvester noted that "Nicholson was clearly ill-at-ease with such Grand Guignol high jinks." However silly the project, Jack was again playing the son of a man for whose crimes he must suffer.

That could hardly have been a conscious choice this early in his career. Jack was doubtless glad to be trying his hand at comedy and doing so in the role of a nice, normal (if dumb) fellow, however abnormal the situations he found himself embroiled in. It was the first of his films to receive generally favorable reviews. As *Variety* put it: "Edgar Allan Poe might turn over in his crypt at this nonsensical adaptation of his immortal poem, but audiences will find the spooky goings on . . . a cornpop of considerable comedic dimensions." It called the screenplay "skillful, imaginative" and noted that Corman "takes this premise and develops it expertly."

The Terror

(1963)
GRAND NATIONAL PICTURES

CAST:

Boris Karloff *(Baron von Leppe)*; Jack Nicholson *(Andre Duvalier)*; Sandra Knight *(Helene)*; Richard Miller *(Stefan)*; Dorothy Neumann *(Old Woman)*; Jonathan Haze *(Gustaff)*.

CREDITS:

Director, Roger Corman; producer, Roger Corman; writers, Leo Gordon and Jack Hill; cinematography, John Nickolaus; editor, Stuart O'Brien; music, Ronald Stein; running time: 81 mins.

When Corman realized that shooting for *The Raven* had been completed two days ahead of schedule, but that the sets he'd rented (payment in advance) would remain unused for that upcoming 48-hour-period, he decided to knock off a second film in the remaining time. *The Raven* had been carefully scripted and shot, about as close to an "A" feature as the Corman company came. *The Terror*, however, was a hastily tacked together exploitation vehicle, though it looked considerably more impressive owing to the presence of those various leftover sets and costumes it had been rapidly assembled to capitalize on.

Comparing the two films is a little like comparing a turkey dinner on Thanksgiving Day with a serving of the leftovers later in the week—the ingredients are essentially the same, but there's a lack of elaborateness to the way they're presented.

Whereas *The Raven* appears polished, *The Terror* looks exactly like what it is: a makeshift affair. Critic Leonard Maltin would label it "engaging chiller nonsense."

Jack Nicholson as Andre Duvalier.

Sandra Knight, in real-life Mrs. Jack Nicholson at the time, portrays the enigmatic,
beautiful female spirit who enraptures Andre.

Much later, Corman gleefully recalled for critics that he had the cameras rolling before even the barest blueprint of a script was ready. Karloff claimed he saw impending disaster, because not only was there no finished script, there was not even the barest outline of a story! In Karloff's words: "As [the magnificent sets from *The Raven*] were being pulled down around [us], Roger was dashing around with me and a camera two steps ahead of the wreckers."

In fact, some crew members who witnessed the creation of the movie insist Corman exaggerates, playing up to his own legend: shooting went on for a full three days, and there was even another weekend given over to filming additional material. Corman has always delighted in his prowess at working under financial and time pressures, and like many moviemakers enjoys sustaining and augmenting his popular image. Still, as one film historian put it, *The Terror* was "economical even by Corman standards." The film boasts the same visual sense of stylish eeriness that marks its predecessor, *The Raven*, though the narrative here lacks the sharp structure, sense of character, and undercurrent of self-satire that were so appealing in that previous Poe adaptation.

The ostensible lead is Nicholson as Andre Duvalier, a veteran of the Napoleonic wars who mysteriously finds himself on the shore of a strange land, apparently Prussia. As dry-ice fog whirls around him, he follows a strange, beautiful young woman (Sandra Knight) who appears to him in a vision just in time to save him from an apparent drowning beneath the ice, then vanishes like a will-o-the-wisp. An elderly woman nurses him during his infirmity, then hints at where he might find the lovely lady he's become obsessed with. The journey after her takes him to the ancient palace of Baron von Leppe (Karloff), where he spots a portrait of the Baron's deceased wife and notices she looks remarkably like his inamorata. In fact, the attractive woman he met is a creation of the old crone, who is actually a witch trying to drive the Baron insane for a crime she believes (whether rightly or wrongly is never established) he committed against her dead son. The Baron is driven to madness, and as the castle comes down around him, Andre attempts to escape with the girl. But being a mere vision, she dissolves in his arms.

Though Corman worked quite independently, he was in fact a member of the directors' union. And since he

At first, the old crone (Dorothy Neumann) resists Andre's entreaties . . .

. . . though he finds a means to convince her he's serious about finding the pretty young witch-woman.

The gothic sets, held over from *The Raven*, give the film a far more expensive look than would have otherwise been possible for such a quickie-flick.

was shooting the film rapidly because of the nearly nonexistent budget, he had to cease work after two days of filming interiors because he couldn't afford to continue while remaining loyal to union procedures. So he necessarily turned the picture over to a number of those bright young people who cut their teeth working on his quickie projects and, being unaffiliated with the union at this point, could work without causing infractions. Francis Ford Coppola insists he worked on exteriors, as did Monte Hellman. Corman himself claims Jack was allowed to direct a couple of scenes, and Jack has mentioned in interviews that he contributed to the script.

Perhaps that explains why a key theme, developed in far more sophisticated ways in future collaborations, is at least introduced here. Jack's characters will often attempt to hold women but lose them, owing to the fact that the men are in love with their own mental images of the women rather than the flesh-and-blood women themselves. Jack has always believed he ought to have played *The Great Gatsby*, which is the classic variation on this theme. Characters as diverse as the hedonist Jonathan in *Carnal Knowledge* and the idealistic Charlie in *The Border* suffer from similar problems. Notably, Jack's early (and admittedly) junk movie experiences allowed him to introduce, in successive films, the key themes of his career.

Importantly, then, this otherwise forgettable film marked Jack's total involvement in the collaborative business of making movies; his eventual projects as writer and director would stem from the fact that his appetite for moviemaking endeavors other than acting were whetted here. The film is also a curio in that it marks the only time Jack and the then Mrs. Nicholson appeared onscreen together.

As far as Jack's acting goes, the film did considerably less for him. One critic complained that he looked "lost," another that he appeared "stilted and wooden." Considering the process by which the film was made, it's not hard to understand why! Still, the pieces of his career were beginning to fit into place, for Jack was on his way to becoming the first of a new breed of movie actors who would immerse themselves in all aspects of production.

JACK NICHOLSON, SCREENWRITER:

Thunder Island

(1963)
A 20TH CENTURY-FOX RELEASE

CAST:

Gene Nelson *(Billy Poole)*; Fay Spain *(Helen Dodge)*; Brian Kelly *(Vincent Dodge)*; Miriam Colon *(Anita Chavez)*; Art Bedard *(Ramon Alou)*; Antonio Torres Martino *(Col. Cepeda)*; Esther Sandoval *(Rena)*; Jose De San Anton *(Antonio Perez)*; Evelyn Kaufman *(Jo)*; Stephanie Rifkinson *(Linda Perez)*.

CREDITS:

Director, Jack Leewood; producer, Jack Leewood; screenplay, Jack Nicholson and Don Devlin; cinematography, John Nickolaus; editor, Jodie Copelan; music, Paul Sawtell and Bert Shefter; running time: 65 mins.

With *The Terror*, Jack's interest in writing had been reawakened. His next project did not involve him as an actor but only as scripter of a B-budget action film.

In the early sixties, 20th Century-Fox—one of the "majors"—had developed a system whereby it continued its own studio assembly line approach toward the making of "A" features while also encouraging the new independents. The "Associated Producers" constituted a wing within the Fox organization that allowed Corman-like companies to create their own items with the assurance their work would find an audience through the efforts of this well-known distributor. This made for some pretty strange items. *Thunder Island*, for instance, runs barely over an hour, yet it was shot in the CinemaScope process usually reserved for upscale product. According to the persevering Hollywood legend, Corman was impressed enough by Jack's work as a volunteer writer on *The Terror*

The villains: Hit man (Gene Nelson) and Dragon Lady (Miriam Colon) plan the assassination.

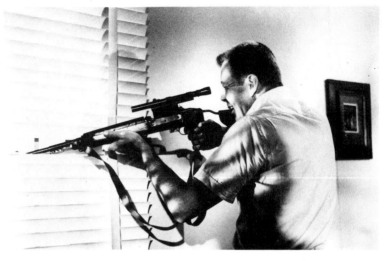

Together with writing partner Don Devlin, Jack developed a scenario that featured a surprisingly complex view of international politics . . .

. . . and even predicted the assassination conspiracy theories which were shortly to obsess all Americans.

to suggest he ought to concentrate on that aspect of moviemaking. Given such a vote of confidence, Jack and friend Don Devlin followed the only advice they'd been given—"Make it a thriller!"—and in less than three weeks' time turned out the first draft for *Thunder Island*.

The movie was set in the Caribbean and shot off the coast of Puerto Rico, where it was then possible to film on a minuscule budget. And for a "first script," *Thunder Island* is, if not entirely successful, then at least consistently interesting, with a fascinating double focus developed during its abbreviated running time. Nicholson and Devlin set up a tumultuous political situation in which a small band of "idealistic" Latin American political leaders, fearing that the exiled corrupt dictator who once ran their small country is about to stage a return coup, decide they must hire a hit man to eliminate this verminlike warlord once and for all. Billy Poole (Gene Nelson), a truly despicable mercenary, is the man they recruit, and he, working with a beautiful, treacherous female, Anita (Miriam Colon), who serves as the messenger between the "idealists" and the cold-blooded killer, begins his plan for an assassination.

But this plot constantly makes way for one involving the likable Vincent (Brian Kelly), a refugee from Madison Avenue who now runs a charter fishing boat, and his pretty but frustrated wife, Helen (Fay Spain), who misses big city life. They are always at each other over the tenuous nature of their current gypsy-like life-style. Then Vincent finally makes a big score that will let them live comfortably for a while, as he takes on a new client willing to pay him plenty for a private cruise. What

Vincent and Helen gradually realize, however, is that their gruff, uncommunicative "guest" is a hired killer, while they are unwitting and unwilling accomplices. A fundamentally decent man, Vincent refuses to have anything to do with a political murder once he grasps what is going on, until the hit man kidnaps his wife in order to blackmail Vincent into cooperating with the plan. Vincent finds himself in the same moral position as Jack's eventual character in *The Border*, initially trying to resolve his wife's desire for a pat mainstream life-style with his own need to find an alternative to that, and his eventual trauma as his public and private loyalties clash.

In time, Vincent and Helen will defeat the killer, who is a bizarre combination of health food nut (constantly eating raisins) and sadist—yet another Nicholson creation who displays a double existence. And following a whirlwind chase around El Morro castle, the heroes will find their own personal relationship revitalized by their shared adventure. If much of the plotting is perfunctory and, at times, predictable, there is much that is impressive in Jack's first, fast stab at screenwriting. After all, in a mere matter of days he turned out a script filled with fascinating dark edges and surprising powers of prediction.

The film was released in September, 1963, just two months before the assassination of John F. Kennedy. It deals economically and effectively with the modern world envisioned as a place where political leaders are sitting targets for complicated conspiracies. In this, Jack was, like all good artists, able to plug in to an emerging sensibility and articulate the situation before it surfaced.

As political values, money motivation, and sexual tensions clash, the villains find themselves ever more anxious.

minutive size." He also pointed out the qualities of the "workmanlike original" script Jack had helped fashion.

Tube went on to complain that, if the film had a fault, the dictator in question is "too nebulous" a figure. In retrospect, that appears basic to the film's impact. If we knew more about him—i.e., clearly understood whether he was basically good or bad—it would make the movie conventional. The ambiguity of the target of all the

Similarly, he projected into this script the kind of cynical wisdom which, some ten years later, would be accepted as common knowledge: His vision of idealists unknowingly corrupting themselves in order to eliminate a man of evil, though through their questionable methods doing something far more evil than even their prey was capable of, is the kind of plot device we expect from a post-Watergate film. Even having the dictator get away with his life is a fascinating plot device, for it suggests that the hero and heroine, in stopping a murderous act, have actually set up a situation whereby intolerance and viciousness may continue. It's hard for a character to commit a courageous act without it creating unpleasant resonances.

No wonder, then, that most critics were kind. In the *New York Herald Tribune*, John Gruen dismissed the film by saying that "Brevity is *Thunder Island*'s greatest asset," adding little in the way of commentary other than that the actors were all "adequate in their roles." But one British reviewer claimed the movie was "decidedly above average," while *Variety* went further still with its praise. In the presence of "Tube," the paper gushed: "Skillfully designed and executed within the limited possibilities of an extremely modest expenditure, *Thunder Island* is a commendable example of frankly 'B' picture craftsmanship—unpretentiously tailored . . . but pound for pound, dollar-for-dollar a cut above average for its di-

running around makes the movie intriguing, and a predecessor of the kind of work which depicts our ever more confused and complex world. No wonder Jack emerged as the perfect film presence to project that world. A full five years before anyone else in Hollywood acknowledged such a situation existed, Nicholson was busily dramatizing it.

The Caribbean settings lend *Thunder Island* its raw sense of conviction and authenticity.

As an earnest seaman, Jack grimaces while Pulver (Robert Walker) and Doc (Walter Matthau) attend to the Captain (Burl Ives). Judging from the look, could Jack possibly be considering the quality of the movie he's in?

WATERLOGGED:

Ensign Pulver

(1964)
A WARNER BROTHERS RELEASE

CAST:

Robert Walker, Jr. *(Ensign Pulver)*; Burl Ives *(The Captain)*; Walter Matthau *(Doc)*; Millie Perkins *(Scotty)*; Tommy Sands *(Bruno)*; Kay Medford *(Head Nurse)*; Larry Hagman *(Billings)*; Gerald O'Laughlin *(LaSueur)*; Sal Papa *(Gabrowski)*; Al Freeman, Jr. *(Taru)*; James Farentino *(Insigna)*; James Coco *(Skouras)*; Diana Sands *(Mila)*; Jack Nicholson *(Seaman)*.

CREDITS:

Director, Joshua Logan; producer, Joshua Logan; screenplay, Joshua Logan and Peter S. Feibleman, from a play by Joshua Logan and Thomas Heggen, based on characters created by Thomas Heggen in his novel *Mister Roberts*; editor, William Reynolds; cinematography (Technicolor), Charles Lawton; music, George Duning; assistant director, Daniel McCauley; running time: 104 mins.

Ensign Pulver proved a disaster of the first order, and a career killer for many of the people involved—both in front of and behind the camera. Reputations were at stake. This was the long-awaited sequel to *Mister Roberts*, which had won an Oscar for Jack Lemmon in the scene-stealing role of the lovable coward who rises to heroic proportions when his mentor (Henry Fonda) is killed in a plane crash. Warner Brothers and filmmaker Joshua Logan had long attempted to persuade Lemmon to return to the role for a sequel, but he steadfastly refused. And rightly so: Lemmon was savvy enough to realize he had carried his character on an arc from

shallow hustler to a commited, worthwhile human being. It was the growth he'd shown in the role which so impressed people, and the scripts he read for the possible sequel were not able to match that. In them, Pulver was either another Mister Roberts at this point in his life, or had reverted to being his old self.

But even without Lemmon, Warners and Logan were bound and determined to move ahead on the project, at last settling on Robert Walker, son of the star of such 1940s films as *Since You Went Away, Strangers on a Train*, and *See Here, Private Hargrove*. In the last film, Walker had demonstrated a cocky charm not unlike that of Lemmon's later characterization of Pulver; and if the young Walker could only duplicate Dad's appeal, he might pull off the role of the maturing Ensign.

Like another son of a famous star who began working in films at about the same time, Peter Fonda, Walker managed to project something of his father's charm while also seeming very much a symbol of the early 1960s' sensitive young man. In fact, if anyone were to suggest at the time that this quietly handsome fellow would never again play the lead in a major movie while the silly-looking chap seen in the background talking into a phone would emerge as one of the all-time great screen legends, that comment would probably have been met with howls. But fate plays funny tricks, and such turnabouts do occur. In Jack's first great vehicle, 1969's *Easy Rider*, it would ironically be Walker who played a bit part, just as Jack stepped forward toward superstardom.

Filming took place aboard an AKL (a form of Navy cargo ship) out of Puerto Marques, just eight miles from Acapulco, so at least Jack and the others involved had the chance to see some remarkable scenery while shooting. "It has everything the South Seas offers in beauty, light, and blue water, and is only three hours from Hollywood," Logan said. But fate did not intend this to be a successful follow-up to a film which in fact needed no sequel. This became apparent early on when the only member of the original *Mister Roberts* cast to repeat his characterization in the sequel (Joseph Marr as "Dowdy") lost his footing and fell 12 feet to the ship's deck, fracturing several ribs in the process. In late September, 1963, Logan's cast and crew finished their location shooting and returned to Hollywood, where interior filming was completed at Warners' Burbank studio.

Five months later, the film opened to reviews more damning than a director could summon up in his worst nightmares. "I think I first began to feel sick during the showing of *Ensign Pulver*," critic Leo Mishkin wrote in *The Morning Telegraph*, "when young Walker insisted on referring to the derriere of the human anatomy as the 'bewtocks.' This was a joke, son, and you were supposed to laugh your head off. . . . Sequels are notoriously second rate to the originals from which they are derived, but this goes beyond all bounds of taste, discretion and sensitivity." Mishkin summed the film up as "a grotesque, preposterous and utterly dismaying catastrophe."

Few would argue with him. The story was an embarrassing one in which seaman Bruno (played by a young but already over-the-hill pop singer, Tommy Sands) was refused permission to go home and comfort his wife after their baby girl had died. Dead babies have never been a particularly effective basis for lighthearted comedy-dramas, and while Logan may have felt he was taking a risky, courageous route by including this, it backfired on him. No better was the scene in which the Captain (huffily-puffily played by Burl Ives), adrift at sea with Pulver, drones on and on about the horrible childhood that made him the nasty man he is. The scene might have been employed to lend the Captain a certain sympathy heretofore denied him, but instead it is only the source of an ugly plot twist when Pulver jots down all the near-incoherent man's memories in order to blackmail him at some later date.

Archer Winsten of the *New York Post* rightly complained that, "The incidents dreamed up to make another story are a terribly phony and not especially funny lot." In *Variety*, "Tube" stated that, "*Ensign Pulver* does not have much going for it." One of the few fascinating elements about this deliriously dull movie is the oddball

Robert Walker, Jr., as Ensign Pulver. This was his one and only film lead.

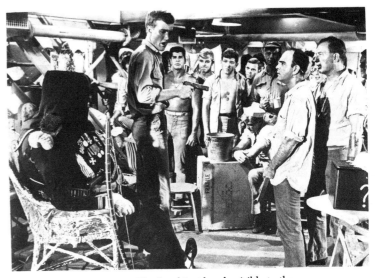

Pulver confronts the crew. The head just barely visible to the left of Pulver's back belongs to Jack.

cast, which included actors on the way up and others on the way down who briefly met in this no-man's-land. Nicholson and Matthau would soon achieve superstardom; Tommy Sands and Millie Perkins had had their moment in the sun. Nicholson's latest brief flirtation with big-budget filmmaking proved as unrewarding as his first; it's not difficult to understand why he quickly retreated to the more energetic shoestring productions of Corman and company.

FIGHTING THE GOOD FIGHT:

Back Door to Hell

(1964)
A MEDALLION PICTURES RELEASE

CAST:

Jimmie Rodgers (*Lt. Craig*); Jack Nicholson (*Burnett*); John Hackett (*Jersey*); Annabelle Huggins (*Maria*); Conrad Maga (*Paco*); Johnny Monteiro (*Ramundo*); Joe Sison (*The Japanese Captain*).

CREDITS:

Director, Monte Hellman; producer, Fred Roos; screenwriters, Richard Guttman and John Hackett; photography, Mars Rasca; editor, Fely Cristomo; music, Mike Velarde; running time: 68 mins.

Jack's next quickie, *Back Door to Hell*, is rarely if ever revived; it is so unavailable that until recently Leonard Maltin didn't consider it worthy of a line or two in his encyclopedic *TV Movies*. But this mildly engaging junk movie deserves at least passing attention, if only for Nicholson's first actor-director collaboration with a filmmaker who would shortly guide him through several fascinating vehicles.

That filmmaker is Monte Hellman, another graduate of the Corman school of filmmaking, in which scripts were often so "thumbnail" in their approach that directors were literally forced to visually invent. Like Francis Ford Coppola, Martin Scorsese, and Peter Bogdanovich, Monte Hellman graduated from that unofficial university, and while Hellman never did have a big hit on the order of *The Godfather*, *Raging Bull*, or *The Last Picture Show*, he remains a gifted moviemaker whose unique abilities have never been properly tapped.

Hellman was 32 when he and Nicholson completed

As Burnett, Jack (*far left*) confers with his fellow adventurers on the best way to complete their mission.

their first picture, though they previously became friends while working in various capacities for Corman. Jack, with his native intelligence but lack of higher education ("One of my biggest regrets is that I'm not academically trained," he has said), was immediately struck by Hellman's familiarity with philosophic, intellectual, and artistic concepts owing to his background as a Drama major at Stanford and his advanced work in film studies at UCLA. Hellman was a fascinating case of an intellectual who was not in any way pretentious, which is why, among his early credits, he could list himself as director of both a live theatre production of Samuel Beckett's *Waiting for Godot* and the exploitation flick *Beast from the Haunted Cave*. Nicholson was taken with the casual, good-humored manner with which Hellman could drift

Burnett, concerned, awaits the decision of Paco (Conrad Maga, left) and Jersey (John Hackett) on how to proceed with their mission.

from the lofty demands of the former to the lighter responsibilities of the latter.

It's not surprising, then, that after they worked together in various capacities on *The Terror*, Jack and Monte collaborated on a screenplay. Called *Epitaph*, the never-produced work drew on their actual experiences as occasionally employed actors; it also could have broken new ground by being among the first Hollywood films to deal with the issue of abortion on an uncompromising level. Once again, Jack put his deeply felt personal interests into his work. But before they could get that project off the ground, the two were given the chance to collaborate on several less demanding projects, so *Epitaph* never did get made.

If nothing else, *Back Door to Hell* gave Jack the chance to see a little more of the world. Filmed in the Philippines, it brought Nicholson to Manila; that is, when he was not running around in the jungle playing one of a trio of American soldiers during World War II who shoot it out with the Japanese.

The mission of these men (screenwriter John Hackett and singer-turned-actor Jimmie Rodgers played the others) is to scout the island, learn the number and positioning of the Japanese troops, and report this information to their superiors before the main force of Americans make their attack. This information is easily picked up from

As Jersey, John Hackett looks like a precursor of *Miami Vice's* oft-unshaven Don Johnson as he confers with a pretty guerrilla warrior, Maria (Annabell Huggins).

As Lt. Craig, pop balladeer Jimmie ("Kisses Sweeter than Wine . . .") Rodgers *(right)* received a few movie roles as a spin-off of his singing stardom. His only major lead was in the Civil War adventure *The Little Shepherd of Kingdom Come*.

In a rare on-location shot, Monte leads his cast and crew through the underbrush to make ready for another day's shooting.

various natives, who are fervently anti-Japanese. But when the Japanese officers realize the natives have been supplying the American scouts with information, they plan to teach them a lesson by killing all the children in the village. To thwart this, the three Americans slip into the Japanese camp and shoot it out with them. At the same time, the Americans relay the important data to their commanders back at the base.

Most critics (among those who even deigned to write about the picture) had little to say in its favor. Derek Sylvester dismisses it as "an undistinguished World War II programmer" (which in many respects is accurate enough) burdened by a "labored, derivative script" (again, quite fair), nonetheless admiring Hellman's "sharp eye for location" but complaining "the movie spent too much of its relatively brief running time striving to counterpoint its facile gung-ho heroics with a modicum of anti-war sentiments." In a similar vein, David Downing insisted the mistake Nicholson and Hellman made was to "imagine the flimsy 'B' movie structure they were working in could bear the weight of any serious intent. The film ended up dissipated by its own contradictions; the script was so bad the direction seemed overblown."

Well, yes and no. . . . Certainly, this film was far from successful. But anyone who sees it today will note the contrast between the ordinary, stereotypical heroics of the script and the sharp, savage eye of Hellman (abetted,

no doubt, by the natural wit of Nicholson) which lends the movie a madcap, antic, iconoclastic element. It's as if a cliché action flick were endowed with a Marx Brothers quality. It would not be wise to venture any overblown claims for this. *Back Door to Hell* is hardly an auteurist masterpiece, waiting to be rediscovered by film societies and enshrined as a forgotten cult classic. But there is a fascinating discrepancy between the blandness of the writing and the boldness of the moviemaking that creates what serious fans of cinema like to label a "tension" in the work. Watching it, one senses the distinction between the routine events (the kind of *Gung Ho!* stuff that usually characterizes a mindless pro-war film) and the presence of an intelligent sensibility that sees beyond them and offers an anti-war statement. Even the basic plot premise—that the trio, trying to do good, almost cause a more terrible situation than previously existed—bears a certain similarity to the cynicism expressed in Jack's script for *Thunder Island*.

It is this adventurous quality, the chutzpah to try and turn a sow's ear of a script into a silk purse of a picture by filming an unremarkable genre piece in an ingenious way, that always characterized Corman's most clever protegés, Hellman and Nicholson among them. And if here the results are as interesting as they are unsuccessful, then *Back Door to Hell* at least paves the way for some of the more impressive pictures Jack and Monte would shortly create.

Burnett and Jersey enjoy a native repast when getting the word that the enemy's in the vicinity.

A TREMENDOUS PSYCHOPATH:

Flight to Fury

(1966)
A LIPPERT PICTURE

CAST:

Dewey Martin *(Joe Gaines)*; Fay Spain *(Destiny Cooper)*; Jack Nicholson *(Jay Wickam)*; Jacqueline Hellman *(Gloria Walsh)*; Vic Diaz *(Lorgren)*; Joseph Estrada *(Garuda)*; John Hackett *(Al Ross)*; Juliet Prado *(Lei Ling)*.

CREDITS:

Director, Monte Hellman; producer, Fred Ross; screenwriter, Jack Nicholson, from an original story by Monte Hellman and Fred Roos; photography, Mike Accion; running time: 62 mins. (original theatrical release print), 80 mins.

Flight to Fury—Jack's only made-for-TV movie, though in fact briefly released to theaters—marked another collaboration for Nicholson and director Monte Hellman, along with the producer of their previous picture, Fred Roos. The idea had been to go to the Philippines and make two pictures, one for theaters and one for television, back to back, using the same casts and crews, increasing their chances of showing a profit by coming up with a pair of films for little more than the price of one. This time, Jack had more to do: Instead of merely acting, as he had (officially, at least) in *Back Door to Hell*, he was allowed to create the screenplay, based on a story Hellman and Roos outlined. But being a television piece, *Flight to Fury* is understandably undernourished in terms of the excitement and manic unpredictability that marks *Back Door to Hell*. The script for that film may have been both stereotypical and predicta-

Rumpled diamond smuggler Jay Wickam (Nicholson) watches as Joe Gaines (Dewey Martin, center) and his Japanese cohort (Vic Uematsu) tend to a dying passenger when their small plane crashes.

ble, but that could hardly be said of the filmmaking, which rippled with offbeat bits and unexpected emotional edges. *Flight to Fury* is mostly matter-of-fact in a way that seems uncharacteristic for both Jack and Monte.

Less a programmer than potboiler, the film features Jack as diamond smuggler Jay Wickam, who nihilistically marches around Manila, searching for some stolen stones. Another of Jack's psychopathic types from that time, Wickam hops a plane with his motley crew of co-conspirators, hoping to slip away with the loot. But they crash in the jungle and, instead of working together to survive, turn on one another. Each is so interested in his own personal survival that, ironically, he ensures his own eventual demise by refusing to see that they can come through this only if they band together. This theme, so characteristic of Nicholson, would be developed in various later pictures. The idea of communal survival that will be seen in *Missouri Breaks* and *One Flew Over the Cuckoo's Nest* begins here.

If there is one truly surprising element to the picture, it is the ending and the way Nicholson's character meets his demise. "It's the one where I kill myself," Nicholson fondly recalled of the film almost two decades later, and that curt summation of the movie makes clear Nicholson's most vivid memory of a less than memorable movie. Jack was devouring masterworks by Camus and Nietzsche at the time when he drafted the screenplay for *Flight to Fury*, and those elements influenced the powerful attitude, if not the paltry artistry, of the picture. Realizing that the end is unavoidable, Wickam flashes one of those insane killer smiles Nicholson has become known for, turns to Joe Gaines (Dewey Martin), and laughingly claims, "Nobody can kill me." Then he takes his own life.

Because it was a television film, *Flight* has never been widely reviewed. In interviews, however, Nicholson has consistently cited this as the only entry among his exploitation pictures that he remembers with much fondness, because he got to play "a tremendous psychopath . . . that's one of my early movies I do like." It also continued a key pattern in his work—making two films in a row, with similar themes worked and reworked, but with Jack tackling a very different kind of character (the two polar possibilities, exhibiting his "double-existence" theme) in each. There would be two westerns, two biker films, and two psychedelic movies; there had already been two *Rebel Without a Cause* ripoffs and two horror films. Naturally, then, there were two Manila-made adventures, with Jack an idealist in one and a nihilist in the other.

White-suited Wickam contemplates a diamond heist at the gambling table while noticing something familiar about the Oriental lady at the right, Lei Ling Forsythe (Juliet Pardo)

Lei Ling opens her closet to find Wickam poised to strangle her.

A McLUHAN MYSTERY:

The Shooting

(1966)
A SANTA CLARA FILM

Jack Nicholson as Billy Spear.

CAST:

Warren Oates *(Willet Gashade)*; Will Hutchins *(Coley)*; Millie Perkins *(The Woman)*; Jack Nicholson *(Billy Spear)*; B. J. Merholz *(Leland Drum)*; Cuy el Tsosie *(Indian)*.

CREDITS:

Director, Monte Hellman; producers, Monte Hellman and Jack Nicholson; screenwriter, Adrien Joyce (a.k.a. Carol Eastman); photography, Gregory Sandor; editor, Monte Hellman; music, Richard Markovitz; running time: 82 mins.

The Shooting must be accorded a special place not only in any cataloguing of Nicholson's career but also in the iconography of the western film, for this—and its companion piece, *Ride the Whirlwind*—represents the ability of the western to survive as a genre by adjusting to our ever changing psychological landscape. Simply, the old west has become, for Americans, what the Arthurian romance is to the British: a dimly remembered era of history in which facts have become exaggerated into legends.

We palm off our preoccupations of the present on the western, allowing us to unconsciously address our current fears by imposing them on a historical context. And the westerns of the late 1960s would turn ever more bitter and existential: Westerns violent *(The Wild Bunch)*, sweet-spirited *(Butch Cassidy and the Sundance Kid)*, and sometimes alternately violent and sweet-spirited *(Little Big Man)* would effectively capture the revo-

lutionary sensibility of the sixties. In many respects, the predecessor of these representative 1960s westerns was *The Shooting*.

Nicholson and Hellman helped pioneer (no pun intended) the avenues open to this form with the pair of moody, melancholic, mythical pictures they shot, back to back (an economical rather than aesthetic decision), in 1966 in the Utah Desert. Roger Corman okayed an oater for the next Nicholson/Hellman collaboration, then suggested they employ a single crew and cast but shoot two pictures in rapid succession, an approach that had proven lucrative with their twin horror flicks and Manila-made action movies. So while Jack knocked off the screenplay for *Ride the Whirlwind*, writer Carol Eastman (who had met Jack and Monte during their acting workshop days, and here worked under the nom de plume Adrien Joyce) developed the plot for its companion piece, *The Shooting*. Each of the films is of great interest, but they are best appreciated in comparison, offering a double-barreled shotgun blast of sixties-style existential ambiguity outfitted in the garb of nineteenth-century romantic fiction. Neither fish nor fowl—too strange and subtle for the drive-in audience, too obviously shot on a shoestring budget to allow much mainstream attention—the films failed in America but stirred considerable interest and controversy on the continent, especially in France, where the western hero was already perceived by highbrow fans of lowbrow films as America's pop-culture prototype of a Camus-like alienated man.

Watching *The Shooting* is a little like seeing a traditional western hero such as *The Virginian* after he's somehow been slipped some L.S.D. "Ambiguous and allusive" is the way one critic described the impact of this enigmatic, arresting picture. The film is framed by a dark, gloomy recurring vision; it begins and ends with the parallel deaths of two men—or, according to one interpretation, the bizarre double death of the man presumably killed in the opening. A fellow named Coigne is never actually glimpsed, but his presence hovers over this story like an ominous cloud. During the early moments of the drama, we learn that Coigne has disappeared, though just why is never made clear. What we do know is that an isolated mine is the scene of some brutal action the main character, Willet Gashade (Warren Oates), has just missed.

He arrives at the mine to discover that his brother Coigne is gone. The former bounty hunter then attempts to learn from one of his two partners why that is so. Hysterically, the semi-retarded Coley (Will Hutchins), a perennial boy-man, tries to explain what happened to their buddy, Leland Drum, who apparently now inhabits a freshly dug grave near the mine. Coley's rantings and ravings are too confusing to allow Willet any understanding of just why Drum is dead, but it is apparent that Willet's brother Coigne was involved in a violent incident in the nearest town, during which a man was ridden down and a child also killed. But whether Coigne actually did the double murder, or whether the death of Drum is related to any of this, Willet (and we, the audience) cannot grasp. All we know is that someone (presumably Drum) is in that grave, and Coigne (presumably still alive) has run away.

Adding to the complexity is the fact that on his way back to the mine, Willet was seen creating clear trails he hoped would be spotted by a mysterious man we sense was following him; but just who that pursuer was, and what he wanted, we do not know. At any rate, Willet attempts to put his life in order while caring for Coley. Shortly thereafter, though, a strange, attractive woman (Millie Perkins) walks into their camp, offers to buy a house from Gashade, then offers him even more money if he will accompany her across the desert on a mission, though she will not reveal to him the nature of her trek.

An existential trek into the wasteland. For the first time in an American film, the riders of the purple sage appeared to have been created by Ingmar Bergman rather than Zane Grey.

69

The enigmatic woman (Millie Perkins) and the existential man (Jack); the period would be more directly contemporary, but the relationship essentially unchanged, in such later films as *The Passenger*.

Jack, usually seen throwing punches, here takes one: the mythic American western is given a hypnotic ambience and a contemporary ring.

Willet has few other options open to him, so he and Coley begin the journey toward an unknown destination and an equally unknown purpose. Coley begins to seem as though under some spell cast on him by the beautiful witch-like lady. As they travel, another figure on horseback begins to parallel their every move; whether or not he is the mysterious man Willet originally tried to throw off his trail, we do not know. Even more enigmatic than the woman herself, he is eventually identified as Billy Spear (Nicholson), a cold-blooded killer who may or may not be the man earlier spotted trailing Willet. Or, possibly, the man involved in the killing of Drum—if Drum is indeed dead!

In time, the woman's horse dies, and the steely-eyed Spears forces Coley to give his mount up to her, then allows the delirious Coley to wander out onto the desert to his certain death. In fact, Coley survives by taking the horse of an unidentifiable dead man (Coigne? Drum? the mysterious pursuer from the first scene?) and rejoins the group. But in a sequence that perfectly captures the film's remarkable sense of the absurd, Billy Spear then shoots Coley down. In the struggle that follows, Willet breaks the killer's gunhand, leaving him defenseless. But when Willet looks around, he realizes that the woman has disappeared. Did she in fact ever exist, or was she some figment of his imagination? Is any of this happening, or is it all Willet's dark daydream on the ride back to camp with which the film began?

In the much-discussed final sequence, Willet enters a canyon and sees the woman taking aim at a man. Willet rushes in, trying to stop the shooting, as he appears to recognize the woman's target. Shots are fired, but we can't be sure who has fired at whom. The woman drops, as does her adversary, but whether both or neither is dead, we don't know. In fact, Willet may also have been mortally wounded in the exchange of shots. But if he is indeed dying, he at least manages to cry out a single word before he goes under: "Coigne!" Is he joining his brother, who he now realizes is in fact dead, as he, too, soon will be? Or is Willet going to survive, but realizes that his brother is the man the woman has been following, suggesting she may have been the wife and mother of the man and child killed (perhaps by Coigne) back in the town?

The Shooting presents us with these possibilities, but does not insist on any: It is every bit as obscure as a European art film of the sort Michelangelo Antonioni was even then making. In fact, the movie's enigmatic mood and nearly incomprehensible narrative of a journey with an ambiguous (at best) destination has more than a little in common with *L'Avventura* (1960), and at odd moments Millie Perkins actually resembles Antonioni's famed star, Monica Vitti, with her impenetrable face.

By movie's end, we are uncertain if Coigne ever existed, or if he is merely a projection by Willet of some other side of himself—Nicholson's own double-existence theme neatly expressed. More than one critic noted that the final shooting, in which it's impossible to decipher how many bullets are fired by whom or for what reasons, looked remarkably like news footage of the assassination of President Kennedy. Then again, the entire story moves with a wary pace suggesting this is more allegory than adventure film.

Jack's remarkable career would be based on his ability to fuse art with entertainment, to seek out projects allowing him to remain popular with the mass audience while never playing down to that public, instead insisting on more demanding pictures than other stars settled for. Jack plays the Mr. Hyde of the piece, a strange, psychotic mystery man. It made sense, then, that he would jump at the chance to do the Dr. Jekyll role in this film's companion-piece. From watching the two films, what we learn about Jack as an actor is his early insistence on avoiding typecasting. What we learn about him as a writer is his absorption in Camus as well as cowboys; his attempt to blend the two makes for a film that is enigmatic, elliptical, and ambiguous, or ponderous, preposterous, and pretentious, depending on how you look at it. As Jack told *Ramparts* in the early 1970s, the two films are "the last step forward that the western form has taken. They touch a deeper level of reality in historical context . . . because the philosophical roots of the films are based in existential" thinking.

Jack has also referred to the film as "a McLuhan Mystery," emphasizing the degree to which the late Marshall McLuhan's theories on media influenced him at an early age. The mystery here is based on the very properties of the film medium; it grows out of the way in which the camera, seemingly the world's greatest recording device, in fact shows us only a single angle on reality, withholding all other viewpoints and thereby revealing less than it conceals. The identity of the killers and the killed, like the earlier identity of the mystery man, are fascinating largely because they are captured by the camera but not penetrated by it. The medium, McLuhan wrote, is the message; in the hands of capable practitioners, the most significant element we experience is an experimentation with the limits and ranges of the medium itself. In *The Shooting*, Jack and Monte Hellman took the western one step beyond anything it had previously achieved.

AN EXISTENTIAL WESTERN:

Ride in the Whirlwind

(1966)
A PROTEUS FILM

CAST:

Cameron Mitchell *(Vern)*; Jack Nicholson *(Wes)*; Millie
Perkins *(Abby)*; Tom Fuler *(Otis)*; Katherine Squire
(Catherine); George Mitchell *(Evan)*; Brandon Caroll
(The Sheriff).

CREDITS:

Director, Monte Hellman; producers, Monte Hellman
and Jack Nicholson; screenwriter, Jack Nicholson; cinematography, Gregory Sandor; editor, Monte Hellman;
music, Robert Drasnin; running time: 82 mins.

In addition to the co-starring team of Jack and Millie
Perkins, the second of the Monte Hellman/Jack
Nicholson westerns has another key element in common
with the first: the concept of characters pursued by a
mysterious, menacing person we never see. Just as *The
Shooting* opened with the vision of a one-time shady
character attempting to go straight but relentlessly
hounded (in a *Les Miserables* sense) by a powerful
presence the viewer never clearly comprehends, so too
does this film. If anything, it's even more ambiguous
than the first; no one can even say for sure what the title
is: alternately listed as *Ride in the Whirlwind* and *Ride
the Whirlwind*.

Here, a couple of genial cowboys are forced to leave
the homestead they've established when a character
similar to the one from the other film (perhaps the same
character) is rumored closing in on them. This time, at
least, the terrifying presence at least has a name; crypti-
cally enough, he's referred to throughout as 'Cain.'

Two lone cowboys (Jack and Cameron Mitchell) are mistaken
for outlaws and relentlessly tracked across a stark terrain that
looks more like T. S. Eliot's Wasteland than the traditional
Painted Desert.

Fascinatingly, we do not know if Cain is a lawman,
dogging them for previous outlaw deeds, or some man
they once wronged or believes he was once wronged by
them. Whereas most previous American movies (especially westerns) were constructed on the basis that the
more information we know about the characters, the
more satisfying the film will be, *Ride in the Whirlwind* is
closer in nature to the enigmatic European films that
often withhold information from the viewer. It was
ahead of its time. A year later, *Bonnie and Clyde* would
become a runaway hit by taking such artfilm approaches
and layering them onto what seemed an exploitation
script.

But if *Bonnie and Clyde* proved the breakthrough
film, *Ride in the Whirlwind* ought to rightly be consid-

The cowboy and the lady: Jack and, once again, Millie Perkins, here cast as Abby.

ered its predecessor, the true pioneer of the sort of picture that would emerge as the representative moviemaking style of the late 1960s.

As in *The Shooting*, the characters embark on a journey that is without a destination or, if an objective is perceived at all, is but dimly understood. The notion that Americans (represented by the two anti-heroes) are lost and lonely is perfectly captured by the Yin/Yang relationship of Vern (Cameron Mitchell) and Wes (Nicholson), for they are the opposites that not only attract but in fact form a complete whole through their diametrically opposed attitudes. Vern spends his time longing for the bygone paradise of their homestead, which in his mind he elevates to the level of a lost Eden. We have an ironic angle on his attitude, having seen how humble (at best) this abode was. The longer Vern is away from the place, the more perfect it becomes in his mind. He is the

Jack (far right) and the other cowboys (Cameron Mitchell and Tom Fuler) discover that far from the pioneer spirit they've heard about, the real west is a land of bitter men, dashed dreams, and random violence.

In strong contrast to the charming homestead in George Stevens' 1950s classic *Shane*, the anti-heroes of a 1960s western find only a harsh, crude cabin.

prisoner of his own romanticism, idealizing the ranch out of all proportion, trapped by his all-encompassing nostalgia. In contrast, there is Wes, who seems almost freed by their need to run from the homestead, which had become a kind of trap. It makes sense that Nicholson, a victim of wanderlust, would as a writer create such a character for himself to play. Wes implicitly understands that only by embarking on a physical odyssey can he ever complete his inward journey toward understanding. His only motivation is the hope he will come to this knowledge, however difficult it proves to be when faced.

He is like so many future Nicholson characters, as summed up by Melvin Maddocks: "Hope for a Nicholson character is practically subliminal, the shadow of a shadow. . . . But without the element of hope, Nicholson's characters make no sense. For they are closet romantics. Wearing cynical masks, savagely mocking their audiences and themselves, they are nevertheless pilgrims on quests." Maddocks was in fact talking primarily about *The Passenger*, but this seems a fitting description of Wes. And a fitting description of Jack himself, for Nicholson's own life journey resembles the kind of script he had been fashioning as a writer; it's as though his stories were projections of the coming to terms with the truth about his own identity that would in time become the central reality of his life.

Jack's work, then, is inseparable from his life. It makes sense to believe that in these two films, which fully reveal Nicholson only when seen back to back, he dramatized the two sides of himself, the Jekyll and Hyde extremes. Billy Spear in *The Shooting* is the dark side of Jack Nicholson, the aspect of him people perceive as menacing in a darkly appealing way, the side of Jack they are commenting on when they speak of The Man with the Killer Smile. But there is the other side, the Jack

Nicholson who even today strikes people as boyish, gentle, trustworthy, steadfast, dependable. This is characterized in *Ride the Whirlwind*, where Wes is softspoken but strong, likeable if occasionally laconic, forever youthful and paradoxically old-fashioned in manner and value. Watching the two films on a double bill, it's amazing to conceive that Billy Spear and Wes are played by the same actor, so dazzlingly convincing is Jack as the cold-blooded killer and the charming boy-man.

One critic called *Ride in the Whirlwind* "an Existential western," a phrase that nicely captures the film's puzzling quality, and also its hipness. Jack and Monte developed a scenario based on the notion of people being at the mercy of a fickle, godless fate working in an absurd and cruel universe. The cowboys who are at the film's focus initially number three, but one does not survive the hand they are dealt early on. When these drifters

74

encounter a group of strangers camped on a prairie that can only be described as visually existential in its abiding starkness, they have no way of knowing these men are outlaws. It is their bad luck to have accepted the food and water of the camp at the moment when a group of lawmen arrive and assume everyone present must be a member of the gang they're after. The Nicholson character here, then, presages the role he would play in *The Passenger*, a man whose internal identity is at odds with the way in which the surrounding society chooses to see him. In time, he himself cannot quite understand who he is: If so many people choose to insist he is an outlaw, then perhaps they are right and it is he who is wrong.

The effect of both *The Shooting* and *Ride in the Whirlwind* has often been described as "mythic," and Jack himself has identified the single myth that most intrigued him at the time he and Monte were working on the scripts: Albert Camus's famed essay in which he translated the Myth of Sisyphus for twentieth-century readers, finding in it a bleak vision of people attempting to maintain a sense of self-worth in a clouded, meaningless universe. Or as Jack himself would later paraphrase it, "Man's only dignity is in his return down the mountain after pushing up the stone . . . that's what our film was about."

There is no clear beginning or ending to either picture, for they do not proceed from the notion that life is neatly ordered, but rather is a dimly understood fragment in which people are pawns in some chess game they cannot hope to comprehend. Within the absurdity of that situation, they must continue to strive, to hope their struggles (however useless they prove to be) will at least have lent their lives a sense of worth; the struggle will have defined those who struggle even if, in any worldly sense, it accomplishes nothing.

In order to illustrate this, screenwriter Nicholson played off a pre-existing situation from the classic western *Shane* (1952), a product of a more ordered and positive period when, during the Eisenhower years, most people trusted that life was simple, accomplishment was possible, and achievements could be measured. In that film, the wandering western hero comes across an ideal-looking farm, and helps the father cut away one last vestige of raw nature, a tree stump, conveying to the audience the idea that life can be ordered, progress can be made, imperfection can be cut away. In Jack's film, there is once again a homestead, only it is bleak. There is once more a father figure and a tree stump. But the stump will not be cut away, despite the continued efforts of the western hero and the father figure to do so. In *Shane*, the characters' sense of self-worth and their belief in meaningful action could be attained by looking at their accomplishment. In *Ride in the Whirlwind*, there is no such consummation, and characters must achieve any such sense through their efforts, not the accomplishments of those efforts. Jack was not, as a screenwriter, simply swiping the situation from *Shane* to pad out his picture; he was summoning up the popular memory of that movie in order to reverse the outcome and challenge everything *Shane*, as a work, "says" to an audience.

If *Shane* stood as a characteristic western of the early fifties, *Ride in the Whirlwind* neatly forces a comparison with that picture while insisting on a different outcome of events as a result of the changing value scheme. Jack has noted his refusal to do any neat dramaturgy; next to *Whirlwind*, "*High Noon* is pure Ibsen—the forces neatly aligned, the moral issues clear as the hands on a clock." In comparison, watching *Whirlwind* is like the famous scene from a Bergman movie in which a character looks at a clock with no hands: nothing is neat, and the moral issues are kept purposefully clouded.

The cowboys attempt to surrender, but are soon forced to run once more as they are mistaken for outlaws.

VARIATIONS ON A GRIN:

Hell's Angels on Wheels

(1967)
FANFARE FILMS

CAST:

Jack Nicholson (*Poet*); Adam Rourke (*Buddy*); Sabrina
Scharf (*Shill*); Jana Taylor (*Abigale*); John Garwood
(*Jock*); Richard Anders (*Bull*); Mimi Machu (*Pearl*);
James Oliver (*Gypsy*); Jack Starrett (*Bingham*); Gary
Littlejohn (*Moley*); Bruno Vesota (*Justice of the Peace*);
Robert Kelljan (*Artist*); Kathryn Harrow (*Lori*); Sonny
Barger (*Himself/Angels Leader*).

CREDITS:

Director, Richard Rush; producer, Joe Solomon; screenplay, R. Wright Campbell; cinematography, Lazlo
Kovacs; editor, William Martin; assistant directors, Wil-
lard Kirkham and Bruce Satterlee; music, composed by
Stu Phillips and performed by The Poor; running time:
85 mins.; rating: R.

Hells Angels on Wheels (like its follow-up, *Rebel
Rousers*) represents an exercise in a less lofty form of
storytelling. The biker film had been born in 1954,
when producer Stanley Kramer concocted a social message movie based on an actual incident involving a
motorcycle gang taking over a small town. But instead of
a serious statement about rugged individualism as opposed to community ethics, what emerged was a cult
film for youthful audiences, with Marlon Brando's
"Johnny" turning into something neither Kramer nor
Brando had counted on: a leather-clad hero and role
model for impressionable teens. Surprisingly enough,
there was no immediate attempt by exploitation filmmakers to imitate that financially successful picture, per-

Poet (Jack Nicholson), an artististic soul inside a redneck's body,
is brutally beaten by several sailors owing to his nonconformist
attitudes, though he manages a cynical smile even as the
punches hit him; all the Nicholson themes are beginning to fall
into place.

haps because *The Wild One* had been so definitive in its
portrayal of the 1950s biker life-style that any further
presentation would seem limp and lukewarm by comparison.

76

Poet (Nicholson) finds himself being seduced by Shill (Sabrina Scharf).

Whether or not Poet is forcing himself on Shill, he appears to be meeting with no resistance.

It was not until twelve years later that the biker genre exploded in popularity following the release of Roger Corman's *The Wild Angels* (1966), as dazzlingly photographed and edited as it was filled with disastrous dialogue and dumb plotting. That combination of idiotic storyline and impressive visuals shaped the film's fate, critically speaking: In America, where the drama and dialogue were most closely scrutinized, the film was relegated to the déclassé drive-in circuit, assessed as flamboyant junk; in Europe (especially France), where the necessity for subtitles rendered language a negligible part of a film's artistry, *Angels* was hailed as a masterpiece. A picture relegated to the B-movie junkpile in the States (though extremely lucrative all the same) was chosen as the only American entry in the Cannes Film Festival's grand prize competitions.

The success of *The Wild Angels* led to a long line of biker flicks, most of them quickly thrown together, that cannot stand up under the close scrutiny that Jack's pair of thoughtful westerns deserve. *Hells Angels on Wheels* had one of those negligible scripts which might have been hurriedly scribbled on a matchbook cover, but provided a treat for the eyes and the ears thanks to flamboyant cinematography, crackerjack editing, and clever musical scoring. Indeed, "Robe," writing for *Vari-*

A race quickly degenerates into a violent spree of mindless destruction; that's Adam Roarke, second from right, as Buddy—which had been Jack's name back in *Too Soon to Love*.

Poet and Hell's Angels pals Bingham (Jack Starrett, left), Jock (John Garwood, right), and Buddy (Adam Roarke) prepare to take on all comers.

ety, complained that "the most depressing thing about this latest adventure of the Rover Boys is that such first-rate color camerawork was thrown away on such trivia. Either cameraman Kovacs is a still undiscovered talent or he's careless about where he points his lens. Beyond the cinematography, which manages to give over-photographed California highways a new and interesting look, there's little to recommend in this tedious treatment of what makes motorcycles tick."

Howard Thompson, in *The New York Times*, voiced a similar reaction: "Some very fine color photography is the sole distinction," he wrote. "Indeed, if the movie had matched the striking introduction of the credits, this obvious, raucous little exercise . . . would have been considerably more than a glorified cash-in on the notorious California motorcycle gang. . . . The rather dazed performances of the three principles, Rourke, Nicholson, and Sabrina Scharf, plus adroit use of a hand-held camera and the insular lingo, render the picture curiously convincing."

Variety has the distinction of being the first publication to see in Nicholson a quality that would take him beyond exploitation flicks and into mainstream superstardom, even though Robe chose to make his point in a less than flattering manner: "Acting by the entire cast is only average with Jack Nicholson's contribution as the non-conformist made up mostly of variations on a grin." Before very long,, Jack would in fact demonstrate how many variations were possible, and how basic it would be to his screen stardom.

AN AMUSING TIME CAPSULE:

Rebel Rousers

(1967)
A PARAGON PICTURE

CAST:

Cameron Mitchell *(Mr. Collier)*; Jack Nicholson *(Bunny)*; Bruce Dern *(J.J.)*; Diane Ladd *(Karen)*; [Harry] Dean Stanton, Neil Burstyn, Lou Procopio, Earl Finn, Phil Carey *(The Rebels)*; Robert Dix *(Miguel)*; and Sid Lawrence, Jim Logan, Bud Cardos, Helena Clayton, and "The Citizens of Chloride, Arizona."

CREDITS:

Director, Martin B. Cohen; producer, Martin B. Cohen; screenplay, Abe Polsky, Michael Kars, and Martin B. Cohen; cinematography, Leslie Kouvacs (a.k.a. Lazlo Kovacs); editor, Thor Brooks; music, William Loose; running time: 78 mins.; rating: R.

Again balancing sympathetically boyish roles with images of seductively dangerous characters, Jack followed his wholesome "Poet" in *Hells Angels on Wheels* with a chilling incarnation of the very kind of amoral biker he opposed in that picture. *Rebel Rousers* hardly deserves close critical scrutiny, for it is an imitation of an imitation, a lower budget variation on a genre that was shoestring to begin with. But for Nicholson buffs, it does provide not only an arresting characterization but several precursors of elements that would shortly pop up in more important pictures.

The storyline opens as a middle-class, Establishment-type architect named Collier (Cameron Mitchell) drives his car into a sleepy little southwestern town. He bumps into a biker, J.J. (Bruce Dern) and they recognize each other as good friends from high school. This unexpected

Jack Nicholson as Bunny.

79

The vicious Bunny (Jack) is kept from assaulting the pregnant Karen (Diane Ladd) by a more rational member of the gang, J. J. (Bruce Dern). This was the first of several collaborations for the two actors, who quickly became close friends.

The middle-class hero Collier (Cameron Mitchell) standing between the dark and bright sides of counterculture lifestyle.

reunion is brief but intense: Each man sees in the other an extreme possibility of the road not taken, for they were wild when kids, though one has straightened out and the other has not. They part, each man having enjoyed the stirring of old memories this brief encounter has caused.

The first half of the film alternates between the subsequent experiences of each man. J.J. joins his fellow bikers, including "Bunny" (Jack), the wildest among them, and, running afoul of the law, they are forced out of town. Collier, meanwhile, visits an isolated house, where he encounters Karen (Diane Ladd), the girlfriend he had made pregnant but did not want to marry; he had suggested an abortion instead. Insisting she would have her baby whether Collier chose to marry her or not, Karen ran away. Collier, truly in love, has spent considerable time and money locating her. But she doesn't believe in his sincerity, because Collier still speaks of an abortion as the solution. Karen refuses to return (presumably, to L.A.) with him, though she does agree to go for a drive and talk about it.

The two men cross paths once again. The Rebels, angry at their rude treatment, are hiding in the very seaside hills where Collier and Karen innocently drive. The gang members, drunk now, smash into the car, making the two "straights" their prisoners. When J.J. realizes it's his old buddy who has been taken prisoner,

he makes every effort to free him and his woman. But the gang members are in an ornery mood, and no longer respect his assumed leadership. In order to stall for time, J.J. suggests they have a drag race with the woman as the prize. He hopes to win Karen, then turn her back to Collier. But Bunny is too much of an opponent and wins the race. Only when the badly beaten Collier escapes and recruits help among the Mexican element of the community is Karen saved from the maniacs, meanwhile realizing the extent of Collier's love for her.

Perhaps some future film historian will yet make a case for Martin B. Cohen as an undiscovered auteur, able to slip his own values and themes into the structure of this seemingly insignificant genre picture. In the meantime, though, if *Rebel Rousers* has any interest at all, it is for Nicholson freaks, who will immediately notice that this budding writer/director/actor had input into what we see. Because even though his character is a supporting one (and the ostensible villain to boot), Jack's interests suffuse the film.

There is the initial meeting between the two protagonists—one straight, one counterculture—and the theme of double existences they embody. (In fact, the film's

Would anyone have guessed that the grungy, menacing character here seen assaulting Karen might emerge as one of the great figures of the screen?

Bunny and his companions take off with their bikes and their women.

impact is badly muted by the casting of Cameron Mitchell. A reject of the studio system, Mitchell clearly is at least ten years older than Dern. The casting makes the notion that the two graduated from high school together ridiculous.) We see an image of two men staring into a distorted mirror, revealing what each might have been rather than what he is, with the interesting angle that each man is secretly jealous: the hipster feels he missed out on the benefits of the straight life, the straight senses he's been too rigid to have had much fun.

There is the wool mariner's cap, pulled low over Jack's eyes, which may appear only a bizarre bit here, but would be recycled for a similar charmingly-dangerous character in *One Flew Over the Cuckoo's Nest*. Most significant, though, is the theme of a possible abortion, a father who may go through life without ever seeing his son, and a mother who, despite everything standing in her way, chooses to have her child rather than take a momentarily painful but in the long run easier way out. Jack's own situation in life comes remarkably close to the script of this film, which he (according to the credits) only acted in.

On a lighter note, *Rebel Rousers* provides the first co-starring role for Jack and close friend Dern ("Dernsie," Jack has warmly nicknamed him). The sixties biker films often served as unintentional "halfway houses" for Hollywood, where Establishment stars on the skids (like Mitchell) momentarily met stars of the future on the way up. At the time, it's doubtful anyone would have predicted serious stardom for either Dern or Nicholson, though they would in a short time achieve just that. In the meantime, this negligible little drive-in film allowed everyone to at least pay some bills.

A nifty *Time* simile neatly describes the way Jack comes off here: "He looks like an all-night coach passenger who is just beginning to realize he has slept through his stop." Or as critic Leonard Maltin, writing much later, put it, "Nicholson, decked out in outrageous striped pants, steals the show in this amusing time capsule." Just how amusing the film is may be a debatable point, but certainly the outrageousness of Jack's striped pants—the most flamboyant garb worn by anyone in any biker flick—is there for everyone to see when *Rebel Rousers* shows up on late night cable.

When questioned about *Rebel Rousers*, Jack allows the film a unique if less than elevated position in his canon of films: "I think it's the only movie of mine I've never seen."

BLOOD POISONING:

The *St.* Valentine's Day Massacre

(1967)
A 20TH CENTURY-FOX RELEASE

Jack *(third from right)* appeared in his first 1930s period piece, as the kind of greasy hit man J. J. Gittes would have made short work of.

CAST:

Jason Robards, Jr. *(Al Capone)*; George Segal *(Peter Gusenberg)*; Ralph Meeker *(Bugs Moran)*; Jean Hale *(Myrtle)*; Clint Ritchie *(Jack McGurn)*; Frank Silvera *(Sorello)*; Joseph Campanella *(Wienshank)*; Richard Bakalyan *(Scalisi)*; David Canary *(Frank Gusenberg)*; Bruce Dern *(May)*; Harold J. Stone *(Frank Nitti)*; Kurt Krueger *(James Clark)*; Paul Richards *(Charles Fischetti)*; Joseph Turkel *(Jake Guzik)*; John Agar *(Dion O'Banion)*; Tom Reese *(Newberry)*; Jan Merlin *(Willie Marks)*; Alex D'Arcy *(Aiello)*; Reed Hadley *(Hymie Weiss)*; Jack Nicholson *(Driver)*.

CREDITS:

Director, Roger Corman; producer, Roger Corman; screenplay, Howard Browne; cinematography, Milton Krasner; editor, William B. Murphy; music, Lionel Newman and Fred Steiner; running time: 100 mins.

In a famous 1972 *Esquire* magazine article, Peter Bogdanovich—who himself rose from the ranks of Roger Corman's unofficial academy for aspiring auteurs to make some big pictures—complained: "One of the most absurd questions I've heard: 'But do you think he can handle a big budget?' I never could figure out why time and money should be considered more difficult to deal with than speed and poverty."

But there seems little question that Roger Corman's worst films are his most expensive: *Von Richtofen and Brown*, a 1970 study of the Red Baron and his nemesis, and *The St. Valentine's Day Massacre*, an overblown gangster saga which seems little more than a retread of TV's *The Untouchables*. In the latter, instead of scraping together some vestiges to thinly suggest the historical period, Corman—who had at last won a contract with a "major" studio, 20th Century-Fox—now had the luxury of affording more than 50 vintage autos and all sorts of costuming, even tapping an esteemed name star—Jason Robards—for the lead. In fact, he at one point hoped to

Al Capone (Jason Robards) summons his men for a conference.

feature Orson Welles as Capone and Marlon Brando as Bugs Moran, though that didn't work out. George Segal, who had already appeared in such prestigious items as *Who's Afraid of Virginia Woolf?* and *Ship of Fools*, was persuaded to play a campy variation on James Cagney's classic characterization from *The Public Enemy*.

But the results, while never as lurid as previous Corman concoctions *(The Viking Women vs. The Sea Serpent, Mermaids of the Tiburon)* is lame and lackluster in a way those appealingly idiotic junk movies never were. *Massacre* is not an art film about gangsters (like *The Godfather*), nor is it engaging trash, such as 1965's *Young Dillinger* with Nick Adams. It's bland and boring, but never so outrageously bad that on a certain level it provides fun. Corman appeared to be taking seriously all those European claims that he might be a great filmmaker. By trying to live up to his lofty reputation he turned out a film devoid of all the daring visual imagery which appealed to French auteurist critics in the first place. As Archer Winsten wrote in the *New York Post*, "The picture makes you think of some beautiful, full-color reproduction in which research has supplied a plethora of detail, but no breath of life." Kathleen Carroll of the *New York Daily News* noted that the actors "behave like adults caught playing a kid's game. Corman does his film in a desultory, documentary style." The performers were never convincing in their parts, but seemed to be play-acting, doing charades in which they

impersonated not the real gangsters but doing spoofy send-ups of clichés from previous gangster pictures.

If there was any interesting element, it was the continuation of a trend in violent entertainment which had germinated with *Psycho*, blossomed with *The Wild Angels*, would be developed in *Bonnie and Clyde*, and which would later see such screen incarnations as *The Wild Bunch* and *Straw Dogs*. Many highbrow critics defended the violence as being socially relevant, deriving as it did from the atmosphere of political assassinations, civil rights protests, and the escalation of the Vietnam war. Understandably, Whitney Bolton of the *New York Morning Telegraph* considered this the most characteristic element of *Massacre*: "For my part, I never have seen a film in which outright, brutal, remorseless violence is so constant and unrelenting."

Bolton, who remembered 1929 Chicago firsthand, defended the film by claiming it was "vivid, unpredictable, insecure and terribly wild." Few agreed; most found the film static and (for Corman) uncharacteristically staid, devoid of the iconoclastic energy which suffused the year's other period-piece gangster film, *Bonnie and Clyde*. This, of course, eclipsed *Massacre* at the box-office thanks to a sensation of timeliness: It managed, as *Massacre* did not, to make the violence of our American past seem a fit correlation to the equally violent period of the late sixties. But Corman's *Massacre* appears to be tottering on the brink of being a *Blazing Saddles* type

Seven Against the Wall: disguised as police, Capone's hit men shoot down members of the Bugs Moran gang.

parody, without any of the wit that would make it an entertaining film.

In *The New York Times*, Bosley Crowther pointed out that the failure of the film extended even to the acting of the usually impressive Mr. Robards, claiming he did not "add any dimension to or even give a fair approximation of the appearance and nature of Capone. With a pair of scars pasted boldly on his angular Irish face and a fat cigar jutting pugnaciously out of his grimly clenched teeth, he does little more than manage to display a couple of the familiar façade features of the round-faced Italian gangland boss." Whereas several years earlier, Rod Steiger had attempted to remove the aura of cliché from Capone and portray him as a psychologically complex being, Robards—who like Steiger usually attempts to do something out of the ordinary with a stereotyped part—here settled for an exaggerated imitation of the cartoon-villain that Neville Brand had offered on TV.

Jack was in line for the part Bruce Dern eventually played, but turned it down. Perhaps, after the fun of doing unpretentious junk movies with Roger, Jack's instincts were strong enough to let him smell disaster in the air. As he later put it: "I said, 'Roger, I'll be perfectly honest with you, I don't want to do the lead. Do me a favor: Give me the smallest part with the longest run you can in the picture.' " Which he did. As the driver for the murderers, Jack worked three weeks (a full week longer than any of the Corman horror films in which he'd played leads) and earned more money in a Corman movie than ever before.

Jack has only one line of dialogue, but it is so cryptic, and delivered so uniquely by Nicholson, that no one can fail to recognize him. A gangster notices another criminal carefully greasing his bullets and inquires why. "It's garlic," Nicholson caustically observes. "The bullets don't kill ya. Ya die of blood poisoning."

George Segal and Jean Hale sit in for James Cagney and Jean Harlow in a scene that seems uncertain whether it's supposed to lovingly spoof or seriously revive *The Public Enemy*.

IS THIS TRIP NECESSARY?:

The Trip

(1967)
AN AMERICAN INTERNATIONAL PICTURE

The experiences of Paul (Peter Fonda) and Sally (Susan Strasberg) in the film closely parallel those of Jack and Sandra in real life: a bright young media man whose marriage is crumbling tries L.S.D., though that causes the final break in his relationship with his wife.

CAST:

Peter Fonda *(Paul Groves)*; Susan Strasberg *(Sally)*; Bruce Dern *(John)*; Dennis Hopper *(Max)*; Salli Sachse *(Glenn)*; Katherine Walsh *(Lulu)*; Barboura Morris *(Flo)*; Caren Bernsen, Dick Miller, Luana Anders, Tommy Signorelli, Mitzi Hoag, Judy Lang, Barbara Renson, Susan Walters, Frankie Smith *(Hippies)*.

CREDITS:

Director, Roger Corman; producer, Roger Corman; screenplay, Jack Nicholson; cinematography, Arch Dalzell; editor, Ronald Sinclair; music, The Electric Flag; running time: 85 mins.; rating: R.

Movie acting for Nicholson, at least in the kind of B pictures he'd been consigned to, seemed at this point little more than a way to earn one's bread and butter. "When I was paying my dues in this business," Jack would reflect from his later vantage point, "I constantly maintained that I was as good as anybody around. But unless somebody else says that about you, there's no way to believe it totally." And at some point, his belief suffered a crack. Then again, he had initially intended to write for the movies; if the acting was clearly not panning out, perhaps he had allowed himself to get sidetracked, needed to get back to his original ambition. *The Trip*—which he wrote but did not appear in—was the result of such feelings.

And, in fact, must have added to them as well, for as Jack once recalled to Rex Reed: "I had written a part for myself to play and didn't get to because Bruce Dern—

During his "trip," the hero—halfway between a successful Establishment businessman and a counter-culture hippie— finds solace with a beautiful flower child (Salli Sachse).

Dernsie—played it. Dernsie is Roger Corman's favorite actor . . . so I wasn't in it, but I met them all then." Jack couldn't even get to play a role he'd tailored expressly for himself! These were dark days indeed, as any final hope for eventual stardom came to seem more and more a pathetic pipe dream. But on the bright side, once again Jack was back in the folds of A.I.P. and its titular head, Roger Corman.

With their sharp perceptions of social trends, Corman and Nicholson could hardly help noticing that the harmless, worthless *Beach Party* pictures of the early sixties had at last worn out their welcome. Their innocent, innocuous view of teenagers suddenly seemed ridiculous, since kids were hearing radio news reports about civil rights violence, political assassinations, and a faraway place called Vietnam. Even the music on the radio was changing; that good ol' rock 'n' roll had given way to something called folk-rock, which in turn had been replaced by acid rock. A college professor, Dr. Timothy Leary, was urging his students to "tune in, turn on, drop-out."

Before long, serious filmmakers would be analyzing the phenomenon, as in Arthur Penn's ambitious *Alice's Restaurant*. In the meantime, the youth phenomenon and corresponding drug culture was the providence of those filmmakers whose quick methods and low budgets suggested more an exploitation than exploration of issues. Pictures made to quickly cash in on what might have been a passing phase could not be written or directed with the carefulness and consideration we expect from a "major" movie. But those cheaply made exploitation flicks very often did capture, in however crude a manner, something of the surface of events, simplified or romanticized as the vision may have been.

It made sense, then, that the first picture about L.S.D. (other than some "underground" movies) came from A.I.P., for the big studios—while desirous of young people's ticket money—were nervous about going too far, too fast. Neither Corman nor Nicholson feared to tread.

Jack's was the film in which "psychedelia" reached the big screen; it is experienced by the Peter Fonda character as he hallucinates under the influence of L.S.D. Jack was able to write it because he'd already lived it. "I was one of the first people in the country to take acid," he told *Playboy*. "It was in laboratory experiments on the West Coast. . . . At that time, I was a totally adventurous actor looking for experience to put in his mental filing cabinet for later contributions to art."

The Trip was that contribution. Fonda plays Paul, a creator of TV commercials who cannot stand the pressure of his job and the personal difficulties of breaking up with his wife Sally (Susan Strasberg). Jack and Sandra broke up at about the time he wrote this picture, when he admittedly experimented with L.S.D. under medical supervision to get an authentic sense of what he was

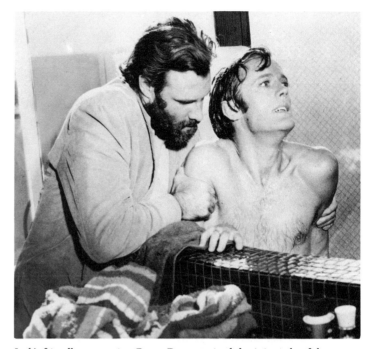

Jack's friendly-competitor Bruce Dern received the juicy role of the hero's best buddy, who has to help Fonda through a bad trip.

writing about. Sandra, who had once experienced a bad acid trip, ended their relationship because of it, and Jack incorporated that result of his research into the film along with the drug itself, thereby using this seemingly fictional film as a form of disguised autobiography. Paul is, after all, also searching for self-revelation, willing to turn on to the substances he's soon offered. Years later, Jack would admit: "Most of my divorce is written into *The Trip*."

Distraught, Paul allows his buddy John (Bruce Dern) to turn him on to L.S.D. at The Freakout, a drug club run by Max (Dennis Hopper). Shortly, Paul is flying high, picturing himself engaged in a Felliniesque fantasy, running along a beach, then through a forest where he's pursued by a pair of black-robed horseman who look like fugitives from a Bergman or Fellini film.

Bosley Crowther of *The New York Times* was one of the first to note the similarity between the imagery in this drive-in/grind house circuit item and what sophisticated viewers had already experienced in European art films: "If *The Trip* is a fair indication of what one sees when high on psychedelic drugs, take it from me the experience is not very different from looking at some of the phantasmagoric effects in movies like *Juliet of the Spirits*. . . ."

Indeed, both Roger and Jack were already hooked on the experimental quality of European movies. A relatively early effort like *The Trip* may seem naïve at best, blatantly imitative at worst, from today's perspective.

In images borrowed from Bergman, Fellini, and even earlier Corman horror flicks, Paul (Fonda) is brutalized on a medieval torture rack during one of his hallucinations.

But not all the hallucinations are bad: Salli Sachse shows how traditional Hollywood cheesecake could easily be updated for the hippie era.

Still, it's important to keep in mind that they were working on the quick, with none of the luxury of time for careful consideration. They saw the B-budget feature as a wide-open form, viewed largely by the young who were (at least for a brief while in the late sixties) more open to such experimentation than their parents. So the first major infusion of European styles took place not in the prestigious American films but in those sensational little items that entertained teens on a Saturday night at the drive-in.

Ann Guarino of the *New York Daily News* wrote: "Roger Corman holds attention with imaginative special effects that eventually knock your eyes out. He overdoes quick-cutting action sequences, especially in the last third of the film. A psychedelic nightclub scene with pulsating lights also unnecessarily strains the eyes. The result is more a camera happening in an unreal world than the commentary it supposedly sets out to be. Motives for theme and treatment are open to debate. . . . Its inconclusive ending is likely to leave viewers asking: 'Was this trip necessary?' "

Still, there are some interesting themes, including a similarity to Jean Cocteau's classic 1949 French film *Orpheus*, which likewise studied a frustrated, despairing would-be artist who fears he is a charlatan, his successful career merely satisfying the masses without saying anything of lasting significance. As obsessed with death as Paul, Orpheus likewise takes off on a trip (though there are no direct references to drugs in Cocteau's film, the imagery certainly appears drug-inspired) in which he is torn between two women and the mutually exclusive things they mean to him. On the one hand, he is a man, and wants a normal home life with his wife and eventual children; on the other, he is an artist, and to create, he senses he must experiment with the offbeat. His wife symbolizes life, which a side of him wants to continue living on the most everyday level. But a mysterious woman, a kind of dark and dangerous princess, symbolizes the other side of existence, the excitement which leads to great poetry but may also lead to one's destruction. The eternal artist's tragedy is that he wants it both ways, wants to possess both the straight life and the dark side. Wants, essentially, a double existence, as do so many Nicholson characters.

Like Orpheus, Paul is torn by this conflict: if his wife Sally is the straight life he seriously considers returning to, then the fascinating Glenn (Salli Sachse), who appears and reappears with the irregular fascination of The Princess in *Orpheus*, represents the strange stuff he wants to rub up against before going home. If Nicholson and Corman did not express their vision with the subtlety or sophistication of Cocteau, it's worth noting that Cocteau could carefully construct a film for an elite viewing audience, while the pressures of the marketplace forced Jack and Roger to work at a more hurried pace, and for a considerably less sophisticated target audience.

But there's a difference in attitude as well: At the end of *Orpheus*, the poet—having flirted with the dark side and survived—clearly settles into a middle-class existence. Archer Winsten of the *New York Post* asked: "Is Peter wiser than he was before he took the L.S.D.? One does not know. He has not returned to his original wife. It looks as if the new girl will be the new friend. The future seems less certain than ever." It's understandable Jack could, at this point, not end the film as Cocteau ended his, for Cocteau had made *Orpheus* as a mature, middle-aged filmmaker, while the still youthful Nicholson had not reached the same vantage point. *The Trip* ends on a note that must have perfectly reflected Jack's own point of view about his achievements and his ambitions at that time: total ambiguity.

THE OTHER SIDE OF ACID:

Psych-Out

(1968)
AN AMERICAN INTERNATIONAL PICTURE

The hippies manage to combine a funeral with an orgy.

CAST:

Susan Strasberg *(Jennie)*; Dean Stockwell *(Dave)*; Jack Nicholson *(Stoney)*; Bruce Dern *(Steve)*; Adam Rourke *(Ben)*; Max Julien *(Elwood)*; Henry Jaglom *(Warren)*.

CREDITS:

Director, Richard Rush; producer, Dick Clark; screenplay, E. Hunter Willett, Betty Ulius, from a story by E. Hunter Willett; cinematography, Lazlo Kovacs; editor, Ken Reynolds; music, Kronald Stein; running time: 101 mins.

There had been complementary teen angst flicks, horror films, Manila-based action tales, existential westerns, and biker epics. Naturally, there were two L.S.D. films as well. Jack wrote *The Trip* but did not appear in it; he appeared in *Psych-Out* but didn't (officially) contribute to the screenplay.

The central character here is a young woman, and whereas *The Trip* approached acid from a man's perspective, this film drew its point of view from Jenny (Susan Strasberg), a 17-year-old runaway. In that, she seems not so different from the real life little girls who were infected by the wanderlust spirit of the times and took off for the hippie haunts of New York's East Village or California's Haight-Ashbury; to a degree, Jennie is an exploitation of such troubled teens or a fair representative of them, depending on how successfully one feels this film transcends its quickie-flick origins.

Jennie shows up in San Francisco where she hopes to locate her artist brother, Steve (Dern), who is rumored to

be living there. She shows up at a hippie-haunt club and innocently asks questions, but when police raid the place, she's in danger of being whisked away to jail along with the hardened drug users. Three acid-rock performers playing a gig at the time of the raid decide to hide this sweet young thing, so Jennie is saved by Elwood (Max Julien), Ben (Adam Rourke), and Stoney (Nicholson).

Though she's grateful, Jennie's preoccupation continues to be the location of her brother. Because she knows of his love for painting, she stops by a local gallery in hopes maybe he'll show up there. Though Steve is not there, she does notice one of his paintings on display. He's definitely in the area, then, and Stoney believes another member of his rock group, Dave (Dean Stockwell), may be able to help locate Steve. Dave does indeed know Steve, and is able to tell them where Steve lives, but when Stoney and Jennie approach the place, there's no sign of him. The search continues, and Dave continues to help Jennie and Stoney, not because he's sincerely interested but because he hopes to seduce the pretty, vulnerable young woman. In time, he does: Jennie is so distraught about being unable to find Steve that, in need of human contact, she succumbs to Dave out of emotional turmoil and total insecurity. He gives her a dose of drugs to "help calm her down," then tries to take advantage of her.

Stoney, meanwhile, who sincerely cares for Jennie, is off searching for Steve. But just as Dave is about to enjoy his seduction, a casual comment he makes reveals to Jennie just how much trouble Steve really is in, having flown the coop from angry creditors. Still under the influence of the hallucinogenics, Jennie rushes off to try and help her brother, though she is clearly in need of help herself, for as she tears through the streets, she sees everything as a kaleidoscope of colors. Steve, freaking out too, locks himself in his house and sets fire to it, trying to torch himself along with the building. Jennie, experiencing a bad trip, wanders along the Golden Gate Bridge, and is just barely saved by Stoney. Dave is not so lucky; he's hit by a car and killed.

Psych-Out seems autobiographical, suggesting Jack's collaborative efforts beyond the mere writing. Sandra did, after all, recoil from the L.S.D. experimentation because she had experienced a particularly bad trip, and this film complements the first one by dramatizing, however fuzzily, a projection of her side of the story. It makes sense, then, that the female lead in each of the films is played by Susan Strasberg; the second movie can be seen as a kind of emotional prequel to the first, showing us the character's bad experience with acid that causes her to be so unsympathetic about her husband's experiments in the first film.

Jack's role also seems close to real life attitudes he has expressed. Actress Sally Kellerman always recalls him not as the dangerously sexy guy many people see but as a

The psychedelic sixties scene was captured forever in the exploitation-cinema of Roger Corman and his cohorts.

The wild life: Stoney wakes up in the arms of a woman he can't quite recall.

One of the film's most intriguing shots visually reveals the way in which the colorful hippie lifestyle not only encourages the romance between Stoney and Jenny but at the same time threatens to entrap them.

brotherly friend; the film reflects this when Stoney—a dangerously sexy rock performer to most of the women who watch him in the club—assumes instead a protective role with Jennie. There's also an unwillingness to be dishonest about the essentially capitalistic nature of one's work. Just as Jack would jokingly admit, "I didn't go into the movie business to be poor," so does Stoney say to his more artistically pretentious friends, "Cut the bullshit, we're in it for the money." And just as Jack would, in his directorial debut, *Drive, He Said*, make a film that refused to romanticize the anti-war youth of a few years later, so did he appreciate that this film did not romanticize the drug culture, instead offering "a pretty accurate" description of the dark side of the love-flower scene.

About that, Jack could speak from experience. Though there are certain drugs he has shied away from ("I've never taken any poppers, I'm afraid of them"), he does confess to "a lot of experiences with acid," some in direct preparation for the scripting of *The Trip*. His first experience on acid, after taking it at a downtown L.A. laboratory one afternoon, resulted in his spending five hours with a therapist, later hallucinating for another five hours back at his home, in the later stages of the experience. But it was the approach of the therapist in dealing with Jack's trip that would haunt the actor. This man blindfolded Jack, which heightened the "dream-like" quality of the imagery he perceived, causing Jack to grow ever more "introspective" when any opportunity to look out at the real world was taken away. "You think it's going to be like getting stoned on grass, which I had done, but all of your conceptual reality gets stripped away and there are things in your mind that have in no way been suggested to you."

Some of Jack's experiences had to do with looking onto the face of God, seeing how the sap moves about in a tree. But in addition to visions of heightened perception of the greater reality, many of Jack's strongest visions had to do with reconciling him to what were then still mysteries about his own identity, trying to put together the pieces of the jigsaw puzzle. So when in the early seventies he confessed to re-experiencing his own birth, one recalls that Jack ultimately would have to come to terms with a long-held secret about his birth.

"Taught me a lot about myself," Jack reflected, insisting that it was "a good psychological experience." Certainly, it focused his awareness that all had not been, in his childhood, what it seemed on the surface: "I became conscious of very early emotions of not being wanted— feeling that I was a problem to my family as an infant"; on another occasion, he has said of the first acid trip, "I got back to a terrible realization I had as an infant that my mother didn't want me." This, of course, before he had any way of knowing who his mother *really* was, or what had actually happened after his birth.

Jennie's search for her brother becomes yet another variation on the search theme basic to so many Nicholson movies. Few would argue that *Psych-Out* offered anything more than a perfunctory view, though, for Richard Rush's direction was characteristically flamboyant yet facile, with whiz-bang imagery ultimately displaying no depth or dimension beyond the surface impact. Even the rock music was second-rate, performed by groups like the Strawberry Alarm Clock who rode the crest of flower-power fame but had no staying power. Jack's performance has not been treated kindly: Critic Derek Sylvester noted that, "Nicholson, who played Stoney, one of the rock group, had to contend with the totally unfocused, underscripted characterization of a nervy hipster with a lean and hungry look." Stoney is, though, a clear-cut Nicholson role in two ways: he's identified by a characteristic nickname rather than his given name, and he is striving to be an artist while realistically aware of his own limitations in a way the other members of his group are not.

The film itself has not been treated particularly kindly, either: "Once again the cameras would zoom in and out of multi-colored inner landscapes," David Downing complained, "and once again the resulting film would prove less than compulsive."

The self-proclaimed hippie Stoney feels the calling and returns to the straight life.

93

Head

(1968)
A RAYBERT PRODUCTION

CAST:

Davy Jones, Mike Nesmith, Peter Tork, Micky Dolenz *(The Monkees)*; Victor Mature *(The Big Victor)*; Annette Funicello *(Minnie)*; Jack Nicholson and Bob Rafelson *(Themselves)*; also featuring Timothy Carey, Logan Ramsey, and Frank Zappa.

CREDITS:

Director, Bob Rafelson (with James Frawley); producers, Bob Rafelson and Jack Nicholson; screenplay, Bob Rafelson and Jack Nicholson; cinematography, Michael Hugo; editor, Mike Pozen; musical director, Ken Thorne; music coordinator, Igo Cantor; running time: 86 mins.

Head is a cult movie, one of the more bizarre undertakings of Hollywood filmmaking. Any film that boasts a pair of personalities as far apart in their frame of pop-culture reference as Jack Nicholson and Annette Funicello deserves special attention.

But to note such iconoclastic casting is only to scratch the surface of a forgotten film that ought to be remembered and revived, if not necessarily for what it delivers (in many respects, it's a mess) but for originality and experimentation. Only two years later, Jack and Bob Rafelson would collaborate on the first classic of the early seventies, *Five Easy Pieces*; in 1968, they were still stuck in the déclassé world of B-budget flicks. The underground was about to hit the mainstream; in the meantime, with *Head*, they managed to take what seemed a less than promising premise (developing an

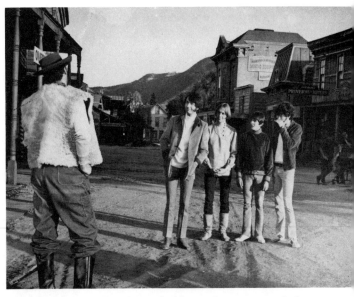

The Monkees' Last Hurrah. Look close, and you can spot Jack and Bob Rafelson on the far right.

exploitation flick for what most people considered a no-talent rock group already overexposed on television) and turned it into a bizarre, offbeat venture.

Jack had, in his screenplay for *The Trip*, already expressed serious interest in the notion of a person who works in the media as a pop hero for his times. The Monkees were the perfect pop stars for the illustration of such a theme. They had been patently, consciously created for television when NBC believed, in the wake of the Beatles and their successful op art movies (*A Hard Day's Night, Help!*) that a watered-down, completely controllable foursome could be developed for the plasticized medium of television, and that undiscriminating teens and pre-teens could be manipulated into buying records, T-shirts, magazines and all sorts of other merchandise plugged by the computerized group. No matter that, at the beginning, The Monkees were unable to do their own singing, much less their own musical accompaniments. They had nothing to do with the emerging

Monkees' mayhem was finally finished on TV, but Jack and Rafelson used the Pre-Fab Four to make a statement about media exploitation.

art of rock; rather, they represented a strategy for homogenizing, packaging, and merchandising the styles that had been revolutionary only a year or two before. Clever young men were needed to create The Pre Fab Four; NBC found them in Bob Rafelson and James Frawley, who became the project's initiators.

By 1968, the popularity of the group had waned, as the kids who'd at first been overwhelmed by the TV blitz grew older and more sophisticated about music. The Monkees remained an item that could be exploited one final time, and it seemed likely the resulting quickie flick would prove inferior even to the slick but superficial TV series, the last leg of The Monkees' downward slide.

It turned out otherwise. Perhaps Rafelson was already uncomfortable with the commercial coup he'd pulled off; perhaps Jack, in writing the screenplay for *The Trip*, had made the Peter Fonda character a combination of Jack Nicholson and Bob Rafelson (the character is guilty over the financial success he's achieved through what he knows is derivative and manipulative use of trendy prototypes). *Head* is the movie that redeemed Rafelson. He decided "to make a picture that would in a sense expose the project" by admitting the vapidness of the series and directly addressing the issue of style over substance as a way of life.

In many respects, the film (its narrative line is literally indescribable) is like those Surrealist experiments of the 1920s, when people such as Salvador Dali and Luis Buñuel collaborated on *An Andalusian Dog*, a film with a title that makes no sense, a storyline that doubles back on itself, symbolism that's rampant but elusive, themes

that are oppressive and obscure. *Head* often looks as though it were stitched together from other people's outtakes, full of imagery that appears unrelated to the film's other imagery or to any central idea. Either one perceives a meaning emerging from the relationship of one strange, startling image to the next, or one gives up trying and writes the film off as an elaborate put-on. The technique is, essentially, to string together a succession of non sequiturs (intriguing but undecipherable images which, at first glance, seem to have little if anything to do with one another, operating as in-jokes the audience seldom understands).

Critical reaction was mixed but, for the most part, surprisingly positive. David Downing tagged the film "a wittily self-conscious exploration of The Monkees' strange rise and fall," while Pauline Kael nervously noted the emerging tendency to convince "kids that they are visually sophisticated when they buy old jokes and black-out routines as mind-blowing, psychedelic, McLuhanite collages"; Richard Combs called the film "the apotheosis of late sixties psychedelia" and "a satire on the solipsism of image-making"; Renata Adler of *The New York Times* found it "dreadfully written by Jack Nicholson." Jack's own opinion? In 1970, he said: "I saw it 158-million times. I loved it! Filmically, it's the best rock and roll movie ever made (because) it's anti-rock and roll. Has no form. Unique in structure, which is very hard to do in movies."

Early in *Head*, The Monkees—out of work now that

Annette Funicello was one of the numerous stars who offered incongruous cameos.

The freewheeling film, which ultimately spoofs all of pop culture, suddenly (and without motivation) thrusts the Monkees into a World War II situation.

The Last Monkeeshine . . . that is, until the band's unexpected resurgence of popularity in the mid-1980s.

their TV show has been cancelled—are lucky to find themselves a job playing flakes of dandruff on the hair of a has-been Hollywood star (Victor Mature) for a commercial. What follows is a film about the making of the film the audience is watching. At one point, Mickey Dolenz unhappily calls to the director: "Bob, I'm through with it!" and wanders off-camera. The film offers not so much a continuation of The Monkees' TV career as an epilogue to it, an attempt to make the audience that thoughtlessly accepted the show aware of the manipulative tendency of modern media. By barraging viewers with relentless images so discordantly yoked together (a conventional cavalry vs. Indians chase is juxtaposed with horrific documentary footage of Vietnam), it made them notice the decisions being made by the filmmakers. Hopefully, the audience would come away from the film "educated"—or at least slightly more conscious—about the essential hollowness of the process by which TV in particular and the media in general plasticizes everything around us.

"The suicide of The Monkees" is the way Jack would later describe the film's basic theme, for he was impressed by the way members of the group blew the whistle on the canned quality of their music. The irony was that this phoniest of all rock groups was composed of four human beings who were unable to live with the way they were employed to exploit the public—they were being exploited, too—and willfully destroyed their still lucrative situation. Many Nicholson characters—including what may be his greatest, Randall Patrick McMurphy in *One Flew Over the Cuckoo's Nest*—are "suicides" in this noble sense of the term, sacrificing themselves to make a point.

The movie also implies Jack's politics through comic sequences. "I like scenes between machines and people," he told *After Dark* in 1969. "Machines baffle me. . . . In *Head*, we had the empty Coke machine in the middle of the desert, flashing EMPTY. Micky (Dolenz) flips out. He's flipping himself against Coca-Cola, business, all of American industry." The lead-in is like a stereotypical British desert movie. Shortly, though, Micky gets into an argument with his own inner voice, and finally tells it, "Shut up!" It does . . . and he's freaked out. His inner monologue just stops. He panics. Then the voice says, "Quiet, isn't it, George Michael Dolenz?" Then the film veers into pure fantasy. The whole Italian army arrives. A sheik rides in across the desert. A tank blows up the Coke machine. Then the picture abruptly whisks away into a big harem number. "At the end, all of the forces of inhumanity are lined up—the army, Victor Mature (as The Jolly Green Giant), and so on—the last threat, at the end of the line, is the Coke machine."

Derek Sylvester wrote that, "*Head* possesses its own built-in defense mechanism to confound potential critics. If one complains that it doesn't make too much sense, the movie coolly ripostes that it isn't supposed to make sense; if one grumbles that it isn't consistently funny, one soon learns that it isn't supposed to be all that funny, and therein lies the real joke. . . ." Once again, Jack had diverted his arthouse aspirations into America's own "alternative" cinema, the youth exploitation flick, and perhaps the film's underlying pretensions is part of why it failed to click at the box-office; at a time when most filmmakers were still celebrating psychedelia and the pop-art scene, this put-down of the greed and avarice that underlined the "cultural explosion" of the late sixties was ahead of its time. One self-styled pop philosopher of the time could boast that young people were turning on to "Revolution for the Hell of It," but in point of fact, moviemakers, record distributors, and other dealers in commercial merchandise were quite willing to peddle Revolution for the Sell of It. This forward-looking film contained, in its strange but appealing combination of silliness and cynicism, an awareness others would not exhibit until the early seventies.

AN AMERICAN ANTHEM:

Easy Rider

(1969)
A COLUMBIA PICTURES RELEASE

Jack Nicholson as George Hanson.

CAST:

Peter Fonda *(Wyatt/"Captain America")*; Dennis Hopper *(Billy/"Billy the Kid")*; Jack Nicholson *(George Hanson)*; Antonio Mendoza *(Jesus)*; Phil Spector *(Connection)*; Mac Mashourian *(Body Guard)*; Robert Walker, Jr. *(Hippie Leader)*; Sabrina Scharf *(Hippie girl)*; Luana Anders *(Lisa)*; Luke Askew *(Stranger on Highway)*; Karen Black *(Karen)*; Warren Finnerty *(Rancher)*.

CREDITS:

Director, Dennis Hopper; producer, Peter Fonda; screenplay, Peter Fonda, Dennis Hopper, and Terry Southern; cinematography, Laszlo Kovacs; editor, Dawn Cambren; music, performed by Steppenwolf, The Byrds, The Band, The Holy Mondal Rounders, Fraternity of Man, The Jimi Hendrix Experience, Little Eva, The Electric Prunes, Electric Flag, and Roger McGuin; running time: 94 mins.; rating: R.

The Underground was about to surface; Beatle-length hair, acid rock, tie-dyed shirts and granny glasses were no longer cult phenomena. In the mid-sixties, the hippies who protested the confusing, ambiguous conflict in Vietnam were still small groups, wandering the country; by early 1969, it seemed as though the entirety of American youth had followed suit. Radio stations which a year before had been hesitant to play drug-inspired lyrics were now fully programmed with them, and moviegoers eagerly awaited the first film to capture the spirit of the times. They read into *Easy Rider* an anthem. If it hadn't existed, there would have been a tremendous

vacuum; its importance as a generational epic transcended any cinematic limitations.

Some critics, like Penelope Gilliatt in *The New Yorker*, gleefully accepted it on this level, claiming "*Easy Rider* is the real thing . . . ninety-four minutes of what it is like to watch, to hold opinions, to get killed in America at this moment. . . . It is beautifully simple. It goes almost like the country's traditional frontier myth, but run backward." Others sensed something more complex, like Dan Wakefield in *The Atlantic*, who felt the film represented "The most powerful artistic statement I have seen about the hostility engendered in this conflict (it might be called the Great Haircut War) . . . sometimes pretentious, sometimes pompous, often overly romantic and naïve, and yet for all its flaws it has raw power, it communicates something vital and real, and it

The young, alcoholic civil rights Southern lawyer wakes up in the local jail; behind Jack is an in-joke, as a real-life pal was apparently there previously.

sets against some of the most beautiful American landscapes some of the ugliest American emotions."

Hailed as an immediate classic, *Easy Rider* was the film of the year in the eyes of everyone but those who voted for the Academy Awards. But Wakefield's accurate description of the pretentious and pompous qualities explain why *Easy Rider* dates so badly. Viewed as an antique—an overly romantic but deeply passionate statement of late sixties angst—it remains worthy of consideration, despite simplification of issues and awkwardness in storytelling. Remove it from the social context out of which it grew—see it simply as a film and evaluate it on a strictly objective level—and the movie seems inadequate, even laughable, today.

The tale is a picaresque, focusing on two California bikers (Peter Fonda and Dennis Hopper) who sell hard drugs to finance their cross-country trip to the Mardi Gras. Along the way, they see "the real America," which has become polarized: communities of free living and life-loving hippies representing the positive elements, rednecks the negative. Naturally, then, the bikers are given food and shelter by the wide-eyed innocents, then shot down in the final moments by a pair of truck drivers. Youthful viewers saw in this stunning climax a dramatization of their darkest nightmare: the film confirmed their belief that the Generation Gap had reached a point at which adults were ready to kill kids.

All of this was neatly (perhaps too neatly!) schematized by the script, which made a sentimental simplification seem so much radical wisdom. But *Easy Rider* had presented evidence of two great talents. Laszlo Kovacs'

stunning photography of the American landscape contained a visual integrity, his camera's eye so unsparing, perceptive, ironic and honest (especially effective considering the remarkable sound editing in which top rock records are neatly set against the images) that the film truly does offer a time-capsule image of the late sixties. And there is one great performance: As George Hanson, the sad-faced lawyer the boys briefly take up with, Jack Nicholson offered the first characterization that caused critics to sit up and take notice of him. In sharp contrast to Fonda's bland pseudo-heroic posturing or Hopper's hysterical grunting and mugging, Nicholson's well-rounded, intricately detailed characterization won an Oscar nomination for Best Supporting Actor.

Surprisingly, though, he hadn't been the first choice for the part. Another fine (and at the time better known) actor, Rip Torn, was scheduled to play George, but wasn't comfortable with Hopper's conception of "direction." After Torn pulled out, Nicholson's pal Bruce Dern was briefly considered, though he was at the time attempting to break through to a greater status in the film industry and refused the relatively small payment producer Fonda offered him. Jack got the part almost by default, though with all due respect to those other actors, it's doubtful the film could have clicked without him. Two old pals of Jack's, Fonda and Hopper, came to Rafelson hoping he might help them bring a concept of theirs to fruition. Hopper had read a magazine article about two hippieish bikers who had been found dead on the side of a rural road, presumably murder victims of straights, and began fleshing the idea out in screenplay

Coming around, George befriends two cellmates, the hippies Billy (Dennis Hopper) and Wyatt (Peter Fonda).

George talks the deputy into releasing Billy and Wyatt in his care; like so many smaller roles in the film, the part is played by a local.

Sobering quickly, George explains to Billy and Wyatt that they are free to go.

form. But neither he nor Fonda had any idea how to get an agency like William Morris interested in the idea, so they approached old friends who had entered the executive end of the business. Roger Corman listened to their idea of doing the first biker movie with a strong social statement, but when he sent them on to the offices of American International Pictures, its titular leader, Sa-

muel Z. Arkoff, was less than convinced Hopper would be the right person to see the project through.

Hopper remembered that pal Nicholson was involved in an independent company that produced projects which Columbia Pictures would release; called BBS, it was run by Rafelson, Bert Schneider, and Steve Blauner. Upon arriving at the offices, Hopper was spirited by Jack to Schneider's office, where, after Jack spoke on behalf of his buddies, a check for $650,000 was handed over to Hopper and *Easy Rider* was on its way. But as soon as shooting commenced, the BBS offices began to wonder if perhaps Arkoff had been right; word trickled back that Hopper was having trouble getting the picture done. Somebody had to rush down to New Orleans and make sure the investment was not lost. Shortly, Jack was dispatched, showing up in an Executive Producer capacity.

Jack has half-jokingly commented that without *Easy Rider*, "I probably would have a major film studio and be directing several acolytes around in Burbank." Certainly, though, it was the remarkable casting that sparked his fading acting career. George Hanson is the only fully realized character in a film full of cultural clichés and self-glorifying stereotypes. A Southern liberal who feels trapped in the small town where he springs the hippie bikers from jail, Jack dominates the picture's most memorable scene: the campfire discussion of America and what has gone wrong with it. "This used to be a hell of a country," George muses. "I don't know what happened." Once, an interviewer asked Jack what Dennis Hopper meant by the campfire scene. "I don't know what he meant," Nicholson replied. "We were both stoned the night we shot it." Perhaps unknowingly, Nicholson spoke not only for his character but for millions of well-meaning, relatively young and relatively straight liberals: intelligent, educated young men and women who filled their expected role in the great American Dream and now saw the Establishment they'd become part of turning sour.

Critics responded as though discovering an actor in his debut role rather than a veteran of some 20 films. In fact, an indication of how little recognition Nicholson received up to that point can be seen in a rave review in *Commonweal* by Philip T. Hartung, who sang the praises of "George Nicholson" who "brilliantly" played the lawyer: so brilliantly, perhaps, that the critic con-

On the Road: George, a holdover from the Kennedy era, joins up with the Wave of the Future to see America firsthand.

The famous campfire sequence, in which UFOs and the identity of America are discussed with equal enthusiasm, while an untold number of joints were purportedly smoked.

fused character and actor by ascribing the first name of the former to the latter. Vincent Canby of *The New York Times* pointed out that halfway through, the bikers "come upon a very real character and everything that has come before suddenly looks flat and foolish," while Jacob Brackman of *Esquire* noted, "The movie felt empty after his death." "Actually," Jerry De Muth wrote in *Christian Century*, "the film comes alive only once. . . . Jack Nicholson gives a tremendous performance as George Hanson, a heavy drinking A.C.L.U. attorney. . . . In highly entertaining fashion Hanson proceeds to tell his fellow inmates a preposterous tale about UFOs from Venus, a planet whose people, he says, have infiltrated the entire world. . . ."

As for that famous speech, Jack has commented that despite the off-the-cuff quality of the scene, it was actually almost verbatim from the script. "It's hidden under that coat you see there. . . . It looks improvised, but most of it was written out in advance. I'd say that, out of everybody in the cast, I stuck closer to the words than anyone—and wound up further away from the character in the script. . . . The cafe scene was completely improvised, but it was three times as long before it was edited down . . . the film changed more in the editing room than from script to film." The speech about UFOs is there because Hopper was, at the time, fascinated with them. He claimed to have spotted a UFO

102

once, when he was tripping out, and made contact with it.

In *The Atlantic*, Dan Wakefield wrote: "George the lawyer, played with perfect wit and style by Jack Nicholson, is the prototype of the sharp but alcoholically self-destructive local lawyer, wanting to break out of his life but unable to make it. . . ." Nothing in the film is as poignant or powerful as the scene in which Wyatt mentions that if George owns a helmet, he is welcome to journey with them; he rushes home, returning not only with his old football helmet but also his college varsity letter sweater. The incongruousness of his wearing this—an unofficial uniform of his idealism from the early sixties—as he sits on the back of a bike driven by a shaggy late sixties hippie, allows us to vividly see the distinction between not only the older and younger generations but also the remarkable future-shock change which overcame American society in a scant five years. "After the gut-level excitement generated by the film had cooled," *Ramparts* would reflect a year later, "it was the image of Nicholson that remained."

The part also captures something of Nicholson himself, communicating fully the ambiguity—the two-sidedness—of the man: the clean-cut boy who has a desire to ride with bikers, the innocent and intelligent young man who enjoys mixing with the counterculture. "Time and time again I wanted to reach out and shake Peter Fonda and Dennis Hopper," Joseph Morgenstern wrote in *Newsweek*, "until they stopped their damned-fool poeticizing on the subject of doing your own thing." But he was quick to praise Nicholson for his "fine, crucial performance as a sly, sad, funny lush of a lawyer." *Time*'s unsigned review noted the same problematic elements, but dismissed them as "minor lapses in a major movie," likewise praising Jack: "But in his first major role Jack Nicholson proves he knows far more about acting than either of his co-stars." "Delightfully played by Jack Nicholson," Roland Gelatt wrote in *Saturday Review*; "wonderfully played" claimed Richard Schickel in *Life*; "a full-blooded, almost Faulknerian character in a southern landscape otherwise inhabited by cartoon figures," Vincent Canby glowed in *The New York Times*; "funny, utterly winning, and quite moving" is the way Stanley Kauffmann summed up Jack's work in *The New Republic*.

"I liked myself in it," Jack told Rex Reed shortly after the film's release. "If I get an Oscar, I won't feel like I've stolen anything. I got to edit my own part, so I picked the best shots and everything. I was the most sensible character in the whole movie. If you read [the script], he was a real hick, saying things like 'Marijuana! Mercy!' I still don't know who wrote what. The writing was confused. Terry Southern (author of the cult novel *Candy*) was brought in as one of the writers so people wouldn't think it was just another Peter Fonda motorcycle flick." But even with the rave reviews, Jack did not win the Best Supporting Actor Oscar. Hollywood was that year too busy acknowledging the last of the old-fashioned films, those big-budget movies they hoped would somehow survive the turbulent era American society—and, necessarily, American movies—was passing through. Jack must have seemed too much like the movie he appeared in: terribly radical and perhaps a passing fancy. Unlike his co-stars, he would grow old gracefully with the audience that had discovered him in this picture, to continue acting as a cultural icon for them long after the self-styled cultural symbols of Captain America and his shaggy hippie companion had passed into the realm of nostalgia. "Right about the time of *Easy Rider*," he has said, "I got myself locked right into the sociological curl—like a surf rider—and I found I could stay right in there, ride this, and cut back against it."

There is a powerful autobiographical element. Enlarging on the sketchy script, Jack added a poignance to the man's alcoholism that can only have come from his own experiences with an alcoholic "father." Cinching the fact that he was, essentially, playing the man he then believed to be his father is the fact that, before the

Jack originally arrived on the set as an executive in charge of production, when rumor had it that Dennis had lost control of the film.

104

The advertisement that became a poster . . . the poster that
became a generational anthem.

cameras rolled on him, Jack sought out a pair of plain round glasses to complete the characterization which were identical to the ones John Nicholson had always worn. "The character was very heavily involved in family conditioning and the small town," Jack tellingly told columnist Archer Winsten. But this was only part of the characterization: He was "in jail because of his own best instincts, not his worst," and Jack lent the part some political shading by copying George's accent from Lyndon B. Johnson, thereby making George something of a symbol for the failed liberalism that was the source of so many of the country's problems then.

How about the legend that Jack smoked 155 joints during the campfire sequence? "That's a little exaggerated," Jack later admitted, "but each time I did a take or an angle, it involved smoking almost an entire joint. . . . Now, the main portion of this sequence is the transition from not being stoned to being stoned. So that after the first take or two, the acting job becomes reversed. Instead of being straight and having to act stoned at the end, I'm now stoned at the beginning and have to act straight, and then gradually let myself return to where I was—which was very stoned. It was an unusual reverse acting problem. And Dennis was hysterical off-camera most of the time this was happening. In fact, some of the things that you see in the film—like my looking away and trying to keep myself from breaking up—were caused by my looking at Dennis off-camera over in the bushes, totally freaked out of his bird, laughing his head off while I'm in there trying to do my Lyndon Johnson [imitation] and keep everything together."

The grass may have been great, but the Acid left a bitter taste. One night, near Taos, Jack and Hopper had some on top of the tomb of their hero, D. H. Lawrence, then talked about art and friendship and what was happening in society. The following morning, Jack woke on top of a 40-foot tree. He has no idea how he got there, but it would be a long time before he would consider experimenting with anything stronger than marijuana.

Many cast members were local people recruited in the small Southern towns they passed through. In the restaurant sequence, the policeman was the actual local deputy sheriff, though he refused to appear in the beating scene once he realized what the movie was about. And there was an actual fight in the restaurant when Fonda casually used some rough language during a phone call and the super-straight owner took offense. The film undeniably captures the tension in the air of America then. Other films of the time (most notably *Alice's Restaurant* and Jack's own *Drive, He Said*) may be better movies, but *Easy Rider* remains, despite its flaws, the focal film of the late sixties.

On a Clear Day You Can See Forever

(1970)
A PARAMOUNT RELEASE

Jack Nicholson as Tad Pringle.

CAST:

Barbra Streisand *(Daisy Gamble)*; Yves Montand *(Dr. Marc Chabot)*; Bob Newhart *(Dr. Mason Hume)*; Larry Blyden *(Warren Pratt)*; Jack Nicholson *(Tad Pringle)*; Simon Oakland *(Dr. Conrad Fuller)*.

CREDITS:

Director, Vincente Minnelli; producer, Howard Koch; screenplay, Alan Jay Lerner, based on the musical stage play by Alan Jay Lerner and Burton Lane; cinematographer, Harry Stradling; editor, David Bretherton; musical direction, Nelson Riddle; running time: 129 mins.; rating: GP.

Ironically, after achieving popularity thanks to the most important of the "new movies," Jack nearly set his career back by winning a role in a huge, sprawling Hollywood extravaganza. Just as he had, in previous films, displayed a tendency to play opposite sides of the coin in pairs of pictures, so did he in *On a Clear Day* portray the complement of what he incarnated in *Easy Rider*. There, he had been a super-straight caught up with hippies; here, he played a hippie caught up with super-straights. This role might have indeed helped to establish him as a counterculture icon had the film been successful, but *On a Clear Day* failed to click as entertainment. As compared to the successful Barbra Streisand vehicle *Funny Girl*, this appeared as empty as

it was elaborate. It was strange to see Jack, who had always been at the forefront of gutsy, experimental pictures, attempting to prop up a lumbering caricature of the big, brassy middlebrow entertainments of the past.

The storyline concerns Daisy Gamble (Barbra Streisand), a quiet and unassuming young woman living in Brooklyn, who visits a psychiatrist (Yves Montand) in hopes he'll be able to help her give up chain-smoking;

In *Easy Rider*, he had played the film's "straight" character, surrounded by hippies; here, Jack played the hippie, surrounded by straights . . . though his director instructed him, ironically enough, to get a haircut for the part!

An odd couple, if there ever was one: Tad and Daisy Gamble (Barbra Streisand) toast one another.

her uptight Establishment oriented fiancé (Larry Blyden) would appreciate having a wife who doesn't light up at company functions. Listening to one of the doctor's seminars on hypnotism, she suddenly realizes she can completely put herself under his spell with great ease; in this state, she has all sorts of strange psychic powers. Daisy can make flowers grow just by speaking to them, can even recall all sorts of previous lives while under his hypnotic power. For instance, she's able to drift back to Britain in 1814 and relive her adventures as Melinda, an exciting independent woman. Though Daisy is a bit of frump who doesn't attract the doctor very much, he does fall in love with Melinda, and is frustrated that he cannot meet this past incarnation. At least they can take solace in the realization that, a hundred years hence, each will be reincarnated again, and those two upcoming incarnations will fall in love.

What did Jack have to do with all this? He played Streisand's neighbor, and they share a mercifully brief scene on the rooftop patio. Director Vincente Minnelli

always insisted he chose Jack not because of the actor's counterculture reputation but because he liked Jack's voice; Jack himself agreed to do the part because "I was fascinated by the idea of someone who doesn't sing doing a song." Ironically, Jack's solo ended up being removed from the final print. "They had the good sense to leave me on the cutting room floor," Jack said several years later. The film's nervous sense of compromise could be seen in the fact that, though he was set to play a hippie character who would hopefully make this old-fashioned film attractive to younger viewers, he was told his hair was too long and he ought to get it cut. Everyone on the set wanted to have it both ways: to make a film that would be hip and contemporary, yet somehow simultaneously create a film that would be inoffensive to older viewers. But in 1970, the Generation Gap was too wide to permit a film to cautiously straddle the chasm, which is why the movie appealed to no one.

Most major critics ignored Jack as emphatically as they had carefully analyzed his work in *Easy Rider*.

Stanley Kauffmann concentrated on the female lead in *The New Republic*: "She has broad abrasive theatricality . . . but since *Funny Girl*, her performances grow repellant. . . . What we are getting from her is the return of the 19th-century stage Jew. This is about as timely and ingratiating as the return of Stepin Fetchit would be." In *Newsweek*, Joseph Morgenstern chose to concentrate on the work of Vincente Minnelli, creator of so many great musicals *(The Band Wagon, An American in Paris)* during the golden age of MGM: "Minnelli and his photographer Harry Stradling whip up some lovely old fluff in the regression sequences, which were shot in England, Brighton's Royal Pavilion. The decor is sumptuous, the extravagance justifiable, the tone lightly self-mocking. . . . But Minnelli and Stradling, custodians of a defunct tradition, bring a negligible sense of style or pacing or humor to those modern sequences which constitute, alas, most of the movie's running time. They, far more than poor Daisy Gamble, are haplessly trapped in the present."

Morgenstern did briefly mention "Jack Nicholson, who seems to have forgotten how to act as he struggles with the small part of Miss Streisand's ex-step-brother." *Time*'s unsigned review perceived Jack as Streisand's "sitar-playing lover," though his part was cut so extensively that it is difficult to figure out what he is doing in the picture and what function Tad is supposed to play in Daisy's life. "Nicholson's part is at once minuscule and a giant trip backward from Easy Rider," *Time* concluded.

The film did have its defenders. In *Saturday Review*, Arthur Knight claimed Streisand "is marvelous in it— deft with her lines as she switches effortlessly from a glamorous British beauty to a drab little New York college girl of today, equally authoritative in her movements and gestures to make both roles convincing and appealing, and in glorious voice." His was a minority opinion. The film is rarely if ever broadcast on television today, even in an era when all the competing cable stations create a huge hunger for old films, especially those with one or more star names. Streisand and Nicholson, in their only project together, would seem to fit into that category, but no one has ever rushed to revive it, very simply because no one would sit still for it. This is best perceived as a footnote to Nicholson's career, one more of the engagingly eclectic film projects he has chosen to involve himself with.

In a March 1970 *New York Times*, Jack spoke with Rex Reed about the as-yet unreleased film, saying: "I'm very frightened about it. . . . I wanted to see what it would be like to be in a big Vincente Minnelli musical. It's a radical departure for me, 'cause he makes a certain kind of movie, you know? I didn't take a step in the whole thing after I walked on carrying my suitcase. From that moment on I'm either leaning on the windowsill or up against a chimney. Once he let me get up to light someone's cigarette and I think my back went *crraccuhcchh*. You can probably hear it on the screen. There was so little—uh—movement. You have to sort of guess what he wants. One day, I said, 'Look, Vincente, I really don't mind being directed,' you know what I mean?"

At that point, Jack took a gulp of Coca-Cola, then admitted: "It was the clearest-cut job of acting for the money I've ever done."

The hippie meets The Establishment, as embodied by Daisy's button-down fiancée Warren Pratt (Larry Blyden); only in Hollywood hokum could their hair lengths be identical!

Director Vincente Minnelli, always known for his strong visual sense in colorful sequences, managed to capture something of the psychedelic sixties in images like this one.

Five Easy Pieces

(1970)
A COLUMBIA PICTURES RELEASE

Jack Nicholson as Bobby Eroica Dupea.

CAST:

Jack Nicholson *(Robert Eroica "Bobby" Dupea)*; Karen Black *(Rayette Dipesto)*; Lois Smith *(Partita Dupea)*; Susan Anspach *(Catherine Van Ost)*; Billy "Green" Bush *(Elton)*; Fannie Flagg *(Stoney)*; Ralph Waite *(Carl Fidelio Dupea)*; Helen Kallianiotes *(Lesbian Hippie Hitchhiker)*; Sally Struthers *(Country Girl)*.

CREDITS:

Director, Bob Rafelson; producers, Bob Rafelson and Richard Wechsler; screenplay, Adrien Joyce (a.k.a. Carol Eastman), based on an original story concept by Adrien Joyce and Bob Rafelson; cinematography, Laszlo Kovacs; editors, Christopher Holmes and Gerald Shepherd; running time: 96 mins.; rating: R.

After *Easy Rider,* Jack needed a strong starring role, a complex, multi-faceted part that would prove George Hanson had been no mere one-shot affair. He found it in the film that represents the culmination of his relationship with Bob Rafelson, allowing their talents and ambitions to reach fruition. The title of *Five Easy Pieces* contained a nod of sorts to *Easy Rider*; it's less than coincidental that, besides Jack, the other great talent to emerge from that film—cinematographer Laszlo Kovacs—was also aboard for this *Easy* film. The key difference, though, is that whereas *Easy Rider* seems confined by its times—watchable today only as a period piece, except for the non-dated contributions by Jack and Laszlo—*Five Easy Pieces* plays as well today as when released. Though it perfectly distilled and communi-

cated the anguish and confusion of the early 1970s, it did not overtly insist on the framework of that time period, as *Easy Rider* had.

So Nicholson's performance as Bobby Dupea can be interpreted, with equal effectiveness, as a symbol of that specific era or seen in more universal terms as a vision of an American loner in search of himself at any time, any place, caught between upper-middle-class culture and values and the lure of an alternative life-style. It emerges as the story of a man—singular and specific enough to make him fascinating as a unique character, but by inference representative of all American men—unable to decide whether he wants to live in a mansion or a trailer, sip wine or guzzle beer, listen to classical compositions or country and western, make love to a cool, elegant, sophisticated woman or a mindless but warm and lovingly responding one. And in his brilliant delineation of the central character, Nicholson established beyond question that he himself was not only a fine actor but an American movie icon as well.

Shouting his alienation, aesthete-turned-redneck Bobby struggles to his feet during a fight at the rig.

Bobby is one more counterculture hero, being beaten by "straights" in business suite; his fallen buddy Elton (Billy "Green" Bush) looks on.

Among other things, this film—released in 1970—proved the awkward period of transition for film was over, as the people who in the mid-sixties inhabited Hollywood's Underground of A.I.P. B-budget pictures had now surfaced and become the mainstream with B.B.S. And it makes clear why Jack, rather than Dennis Hopper, would demonstrate "legs" as a filmmaker. *Easy Rider* preached at the public ("This used to be a great country—what went wrong?"), but *Five Easy Pieces* avoided such overt didacticism, following Jack's longheld belief in the Chekhovian dictum that art should undermine middle-class assumptions not through direct statement but by the implications in its storyline.

On the surface, *Five Easy Pieces* might seem little more than a curious story about a rather unsympathetic man. When we first meet Bobby, he works as a rigger on the oil fields in a stretch of California resembling parts of the deep South more than it does our image of the state containing Disneyland, Hollywood, and Beverly Hills; he might as well be in rural Mississippi, considering pals like Elton (Billy "Green" Bush) and his countrified girlfriend Rayette (Karen Black), with whom he shares a sloppy trailer. The implication here is that it's a mistake for us to typecast sections of the country, to assume in our minds that the South is redneck, California sophisticated. There are plenty of rural types living near L.A. and, conversely, there are doubtless plenty of sophisticates in the South. In suggesting this, the film is a part of Nicholson's socio-political consciousness, making viewers aware (through onscreen situations that do not

Down, but not out, Bobby is forced off the rig . . .

. . .but finds solace in the arms of the uneducated yet warmhearted Rayette (Karen Black).

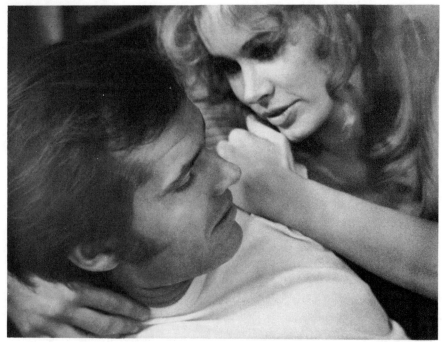

Bowling and beer provide a raw, healthy alternative to the stultifying aesthetic life Bobby must eventually return to.

play to an audience's pre-existing stereotypes but go against the grain of cliché) of the complexity of life in these United States. "I think if what you are doing is too naked," Jack has said, "you will alienate those who disagree and the people who already agree will fall in line with you."

Early on, we sense Bobby has a dimension the other blue-collar characters lack, despite his insistence on spending (wasting?) his time in rural bars and bowling alleys. *"Five Easy Pieces,"* Jack told the *Village Voice* in 1975, "is about a man who is an extraordinary person [but] posing as a common man." In offering this interpretation, Jack himself brings up the notion of double identities that has haunted his public statements as well as the otherwise diverse movies he's chosen to appear in. Bobby wants only to be free, and this working-class environment appears to offer him that. Then, two things happen: Rayette announces she's pregnant and wants him to marry her; word arrives from his sister (Lois Smith) that his father, patriarch of a wealthy, cultured family, has suffered a massive stroke. If Bobby ever wants to see the man again, he must return immediately. Feeling trapped by both events—and caught between the two polar-opposite lifestyles—Bobby begins his journey toward home and a tentative confrontation with self-knowledge.

The film is a picaresque—a road movie—as was *Easy Rider*. But with a difference, for Bobby Dupea is a finely drawn, flesh-and-blood person first, a cultural and generational symbol only by implication. He and Rayette travel toward Puget Sound, encountering other alienated people along the way. But when he arrives, Bobby dumps Rayette in a motel and visits his family alone, where he becomes deeply involved with the fiancée (Susan Anspach) of his brother. His relationship with her seems amoral—Bobby is too complex a character to be viewed as either a hero or a villain—and it's clear that while he desires her, he cannot permanently commit himself to the high-class society she represents any more than he can to the redneck world of Rayette. The movie's power derives from the effectiveness with which Bobby's inability to permanently commit to anything or anyone makes him a figure of tragic stature rather than a hippieish hero: We can simultaneously understand Bobby's rejection of both these lifestyles while pitying the way his alienation finally causes him to stand completely alone, not in any romanticized sense but in a sad, pathetic way. When, at the end, he leaves his home, then abandons Rayette, hitching a ride to some other life on the last frontier of Alaska, it seems not so much an aggrandizement of an adventurer but a sorrowful study of a desperate loser, a man who may for the time being be alone but who will, eventually, be lonely. Above all, though, the movie is magnanimously nonjudgmental

113

about Bobby Eroica Dupea: It portrays him honestly, allowing each viewer to make up his or her mind about the character.

Richard Goldstein observed: "Nicholson's characters do not often fall in love, and never even end up with the women they pursue. He is a loner in a classic cinematic sense—Shane in a pick-up truck." But while that beautifully articulates Bobby, the attempt to make a sweeping generalization about all Nicholson's characters seems misguided, failing to take into account the characters in

On the Road Again: Jack's own earlier experience with a waitress was incorporated into the script by writer Carol Eastman, making for a classic moment.

Back home, Bobby finds himself forsaking country music for Mozart, Rayette for his own brother's woman, Partita (Susan Anspach).

The confrontation between Bobby and his father remains the central moment in a Nicholson film, relating as it does to his own life; remarkably, Jack was never happy with how he was directed to play the scene.

King of Marvin Gardens, *The Shining*, or *The Fortune*. Jack played Bobby so intensely that it's understandable critics would want to portray him as a prototype of a Jack Nicholson persona, but Jack would object to that as much as his idol, Marlon Brando, had a generation earlier resented any attempts to typecast him as the outlaw-biker apotheosized in *The Wild One*. For Brando or Nicholson, the role was merely another interesting character he chose to play.

Two sequences have always stood out. First, there's the remarkably funny confrontation between Bobby, Rayette, and a spaced-out lesbian hippie hitchhiker (Helena Kallianiotes) and a waitress in a diner, who cannot bring Bobby the plate of wheat toast he wants (she can only take orders for items on the menu, and a side-order of wheat toast is not listed), forcing him to order a toasted chicken-salad sandwich on wheat toast while instructing her to hold the butter, lettuce, mayonnaise, and chicken salad. The politics at work are no different than those in *Easy Rider*, where we saw the heroes striving for freedom by standing firm against the ridiculous network of rules that govern our institutionalized world. Here, though, the hallmark is humor; the scene isn't preachy or arch, but cleverly written and delightfully performed, an infectiously funny bit viewers can relate to because it reminds them of their own experiences in a world where an individual's desires crash up against a system insisting on "No Substitutions." The sequence grew out of an actual experience, demonstrating Jack's collaborative input, even when unintentional. Screenwriter "Adrien Joyce" (longtime pal Carol Eastman) once witnessed an infuriated 20-year-old (and

The final image: the movie is marvelously ambiguous about whether Bobby is a hero or a coward for running away to Alaska.

Director Bob Rafelson sets up a scene between Jack and Karen Black.

completely unknown) Jack verbally attacking a snotty waitress in Pupi's, a Sunset Strip eatery. "You say one word," Jack finally told the woman, "and I'll kick you in your pastry cart." Years later, while specifically writing the role of Bobby for Jack, Eastman recalled the incident and transformed it into the classic sequence. No wonder Jack has said: "I think that's what professionalism really is in an actor—when he can function well within a collaborative point of view." Or why Richard Goldstein noted that if "only because he has consistently chosen to work with his friends, Nicholson can be said to have participated more than most actors in the (creative process)."

The other scene is more powerful still: Bobby's final, lengthy monologue to his father rates as one of the great moments in American cinema, deserving a place of honor alongside the Marlon Brando/Rod Steiger taxi cab confrontation in *On the Waterfront* and Montgomery Clift's long-distance phone call to his mother in *The Misfits*. "I guess you're wondering what happened to me after my auspicious beginnings," Bobby says to his stroke-paralyzed father before beginning to sob. Significantly, that dialogue is not in Carol Eastman's script; the day before the scene was shot, Jack crossed out what she had written and penciled in: "Something else?" He improvised that something else as the cameras rolled. Considering Jack's own remarkable background in terms of father figures, the movie takes on a striking autobiographical dimension. This theme would come to domi-

Jack relaxes on the set with writer Carol Eastman and director Bob Rafelson.

An image that sums up a movie: Bobby (Jack) stuck in the modern industrial landscape.

nate films as different from one another as *The Shining* and *Chinatown*.

Jack has explained: "I've been asked whether I was really thinking of my own father and his tragedy during that scene. . . . Of course I was." Jack argued with director Rafelson for an entire night as to how this scene should be played. Rafelson insisted Bobby would break down and cry in front of the paralyzed parent, but Jack always felt that approach was wrong: "This character would never indulge in self-pity," he grumbled. Hemingwayesque stoicism, he felt, would make the scene less a soap opera and more a fullblown tragedy; the less emotion displayed, the more experienced by the audience. "I'm in conflict with Rafelson [during shooting]," he later reflected, "because he fears my lacking 'sentimentality,' afraid I'm going to make the character too tough and too unapproachable for an audience." Jack still feels, despite all the accolades, the scene would have been better—tougher, more unrelentingly honest—without the tears, which only gild the scene's emotional lily: "Everything is not class," he admits, though without bitterness and with full recognition of the need to compromise during collaboration: "This is the professional game."

Bobby is autobiographical in other ways. There is Bobby's obsession with but inability to commit to any one woman. And the fact that, according to co-star Susan Anspach, Nicholson managed to put her into the same situation Rayette finds herself in. When asked by Gene Siskel of the *Chicago Tribune* which of his roles most closely related to himself, Jack immediately referred him to Bobby. "My character in *Five Easy Pieces* was written by a woman who knows me very well. I related the character to that time in my life, which Carol knew about, well before *Easy Rider* when I was doing a lot of (second-rate) TV and movies. . . . So in playing the character, I drew on all the impulses and thoughts I had during those years when I was having no real acceptance." In 1986, he would further reflect that the "hidden dynamic" of his characterization—that is, the key that unlocked the character for him and allowed him to bring the person to full fruition onscreen, even if the audience, which completely believed in the reality of the man, remained oblivious to that key—resided in the fact that "I was playing it as an allegory of my own career: 'Auspicious beginnings.' " The New Jersey boy who earned high grades but turned down a university scholarship to bum around the country and hang out with intriguing characters found a perfect counterpart in Bobby Eroica Dupea; on the surface, different enough from Jack to offer the actor an intriguing challenge; in essential life patterns, similar enough to allow for self-expression.

Five Easy Pieces refused to homogenize radicalism; instead, it employed a radical vision as the undercurrent of a carefully crafted work of art. In *Life*, Richard

Rayette holds Bobby tightly, sensing he belongs to another world.

Bobby hustles girls at the bowling alley. Sally Struthers, shortly to gain fame on TV's *All In the Family*, is to his right.

Director Rafelson was able to create moments that "say" much more than anything the characters verbalize. Here, Partita and Bobby attempt to communicate over the din of society.

118

Bobby and Rayette.

Schickel stated that the central character was "consummately played by Jack Nicholson, who must now be regarded as one of the few truly gifted movie actors we have." Bobby turns out to be "something of an enigma. He refers us to life—to those friends and loved ones whose behavior we can never quite predict or totally explain—instead of to other movies." *Ramparts* analyzed Jack as Bobby this way: "Nicholson plays Dupea as a man who can forget neither his blue blood nor remember his all-American heart." In *Vogue*, John Gruen described the movie as "a quiet, thought-provoking, thoroughly engrossing film that relies on mood, atmosphere, and detailed characterization to make its point," praising the film's protagonist as "a man so unaccepting of himself that no amount of self-awareness can free him from a constant state of psychical torture. Jack Nicholson, so good in *Easy Rider*, is superb." But Stefan Kanfer of *Time* glibly stated: "Jack Nicholson is either a mountebank or a highly gifted actor. Possibly he is both." After making such a lofty claim, Kanfer incongruously went on to criticize: "Amongst mannerisms and quirks, Nicholson rides uneasily. . . . His attempts at humor make him look a bit like a third Smothers brother, and Nicholson's now familiar laconic manner and smile often appear to be a handy substitute for acting." Few critics or viewers agreed.

Time would change its tune: In a 1974 cover story about Jack entitled "The Star With the Killer Smile," *Time* assessed the character this way: "Bobby Dupea, strangled by a sense of his own failed talent, allowed Nicholson not only to turn on his own bursting temper, but to flash the charm that has its greatest single emblem in his smile, cordially unsettling and made mostly of radium." Pauline Kael seemed far closer to the truth when, in *The New Yorker*, she wrote of the character: "Nicholson plays him with a bitter gaiety. . . . It is a striking movie—eloquent, important, written and improvised in a clear-hearted American [idiom] that derives from no other civilization, and describing as if for the first time the nature of the familiar American man who feels he has to keep running because the only good is momentum."

A SUMMING UP:

Drive, He Said

(1970)
A COLUMBIA PICTURES RELEASE

CAST:

William Tepper *(Hector Bloom)*; Karen Black *(Olive)*; Michael Margotta *(Gabriel)*; Bruce Dern *(Coach Bullion)*; Robert Towne *(Richard Calvin)*; Henry Jaglom *(Prof. Conrad)*; June Fairchild *(Sylvie Mertens)*.

CREDITS:

Director, Jack Nicholson; producers, Jack Nicholson and Steve Blauner; screenplay, Jack Nicholson and Jeremy Larner, from the novel by Larner; cinematography, Bill Butler; editors, Pat Somerset, Don Cambern, Chris Holmes, and Robert Wolfe; music, David Shire with a title theme by Louis Hardin; running time: 90 mins.; rating: originally X, changed to R.

Jack's official debut as a director (not counting his contributions to Corman quickies) appeared shortly after *Five Easy Pieces* made Jack a star. Many people have wrongly assumed that direction of *Drive, He Said* was some sort of appeasement, as if Hollywood—thrilled to discover its great new actor/star—was willing to stroke his ego a bit, assuaging his artistic ambitions by allowing him to direct a film in which he would not appear. In fact, nothing could be further from the truth. In the mid-sixties, the novel *Drive* had been forwarded to Jack with the notion he might play one of the leading characters, Gabriel. Jack, at that time, was seriously considering giving up acting. *Drive, He Said* is best looked upon, then, not so much as a film that emerged from his newfound status in Hollywood but as a holdover from the days when B.B.S. was trying to make itself felt as a thinking man's A.I.P.

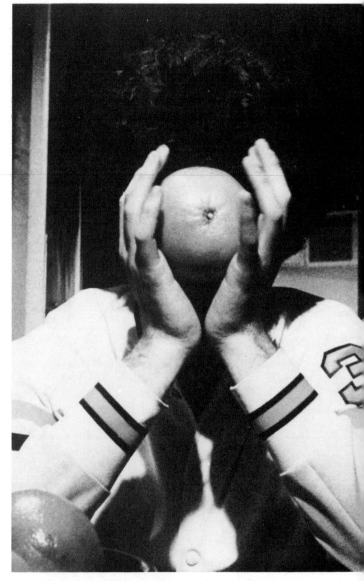

Actor Michael Margotta assumes a pose that communicates the absurdist/Dadaist approach Jack was after.

Jack Nicholson, director, reviews a scene with Michael Margotta, who plays Gabriel, the student turned radical activist, and Karen Black, as the middle-class dropout Olive, one of his teachers' wives.

But the length of time Jack worked on the project was basic to its ultimate failure. It is not out of the ordinary for a serious movie project to take five years in the fermentation process. Society seemingly changed at only a snail's pace, so a film about a subject such as contemporary college life could, back in the thirties or forties, be based on a book written several years before and still rate as relevant when it finally appeared on-screen. But that was not the case in the 1960s, when Alvin Toffler developed his theory of Future Shock to describe the way changes were occurring so fast that society could no longer adjust to a new fashion before it had already become passé. This was hitting every aspect of our lifestyle from music to clothing, but nowhere was it so evident as in the movies, which by their very nature require a longer gestation period than other popular art and entertainment forms. How could a movie reflect contemporary relevance when it took at least two years to make, but society itself turned over a new page every six months?

Jeremy Larner, who achieved notoriety as chief speechwriter for maverick-Democrat Senator Eugene J. McCarthy during his "children's crusade" for the presidency in 1968, had, in 1964, written a novel that effectively depicted the students of the early sixties. They saw their sedate lifestyle challenged as Vietnam became ever more significant and the day of the college letter-sweater, fraternity food fights, homecoming parades and harmless beer blasts gave way to bell bottom jeans and tie-dyed shirts, radical (and occasionally violent) anti-social protests, love-ins and drug use. But as Jack worked on the project he'd been attracted to back in the mid-sixties, he found himself continually having to rewrite the story to make it fit the rapidly changing times, as such radicalism ceased to be a preoccupation of a minority of students (as it is in the book) and emerged as the temporary focus of all campus life. Then, as the film was finally finished and ready for distribution, it unhappily played at a time when campus rebellions were, without warning, over and done with.

Had Jack made *Drive, He Said* several years earlier, it might have, like *Easy Rider*, been a cinematic Bible for the New Youth; had he made it several years later, it might have served as a thoughtful reflection on the period, observed from the vantage point of a calmer time. Unfortunately, *Drive* was shot during the transition, and shows it. This is obviously a story set in the mid-sixties, desperately revamped to look like a depiction of the late sixties, playing in the early seventies. So at the Cannes Film Festival—where *The Strawberry Statement* (a hokey, homogenized white-bread film version of college radical James Kunen's witty journal of the Columbia University student takeover) had been loudly applauded and awarded the grand prize only a year

121

Gabriel becomes hysterical when he's told he must join the service and fight in Vietnam.

Entrapped, Gabriel plans revenge.

earlier—Jack's film was booed and hooted at unmercifully. Recalling the screaming fist-fights that broke out in the audience there, Jack would later recall to Kathleen Carroll of the *New York Sunday News* that, "I thought I was Stravinsky for a moment. I had a major riot, but it hurt the picture. It was a [commercial] disaster; I knew it

was going to set me back." When *Drive* was released in America, influential critic Judith Crist found it "insulting" to her intelligence. But if the film is a failure, it is an honorable one in a way *The Strawberry Statement* is not. For while Jack erratically updated the plot of Larner's book, he did not pasteurize its vision: His film is rough-edged, uneven, occasionally unintelligible, but it is also passionate, intelligent, and (in the best sense of the term) ambitious. The most casual viewing reveals it does not, by any stretch of the imagination, "work." It never panders, like *The Strawberry Statement*, which simplistically attempts to make its audience cheer the freaks and hiss the pigs. Rather, it is clearly the work of a director with great talent, a talent which—perhaps owing to the absolutely dismal reception of the film—has been given little opportunity to develop.

A few observers did sense that *Drive* was far from the superficial youth-groovin' flicks which, to paraphrase Abbie Hoffman, offered Revolution for the Sell of It. In the long-since defunct *Ramparts* (a popular journal of the politically active period), Jon Stewart perceptively noted: "Nicholson has had the courage to populate his story with all the clichéd faces of recent 'revolutionary' movies but then to step back and refuse to deliver on the romantic revolutionary situation." And as William S. Pechter noted in *Commentary*, "During the first few minutes [I had] the sinking feeling of being about to celebrate my first anniversary of having seen *Getting Straight*. 'More drivel,' I said to my companion, but very soon after I realized with surprise that I was wrong. . . .

As subject matter, the campus in turmoil has been so thoroughly travestied by our movies that one is predisposed to dismiss such things out of hand: which makes even more astonishing the film's achievement in imaginatively remaking the campus into an arena of serious human emotions. . . . I don't think one can effectively convey the impact of *Drive, He Said* by any paraphrase of what happens in it. . . ."

That last observation neatly expresses the quality of Jack's direction, for if the screenplay seems awkward, the style with which Jack tells the tale transcends the material. The main characters are Hector (William Tepper), a college basketball star with no strong political convictions, and Gabriel (Michael Margotta), a more intellectual student who finds himself seduced by radical activities and anti-war protests. In the film's opening scene, the two roommates are at odds when Hector plays a basketball game in the gymnasium, running through his ascribed role in the Establishment notion of how college students should behave, while Gabriel is a part of a

guerrilla-theatre group that invades the sporting event to stage a "happening" in hopes of awakening the middle-class observers of the terrible state of the world, those events they ignore while sitting in their hermetically sealed universe. Clearly, this was Nicholson's vision, not Larner's: "The kids on my college campus," the filmmaker would later admit, "said a lot of things about society that I wanted to say."

The story follows Gabriel's attempts to avoid the draft, as he takes enough drugs to be rejected at his physical examination; and, on a parallel track, it considers Hector's brief and unhappy romance with Olive (Karen Black), the wife of one of his teachers. Essentially, Hector is what literary critics might call a "dynamic" character. One way of schematizing the film's dramatic movement is to study his change, his unsentimental education from a mindless accepter of all those statements which emanate from the institutions he's part of (from his specific school to higher education in general) to becoming more like Gabriel. Gabriel is, then, a

Gabriel burns all the files at the local draft board.

123

"static" character: he has, before the film starts, realized what it will take Hector the length of the story to learn. At the end, Gabriel will catch up with Hector, reach a point where he accepts the point-of-view of the old buddy whose radicalism he could, at the beginning, not comprehend. In thusly revamping Larner's storyline, Jack attempted a specific story about two characters who would capture, in representative form, what had happened on college campuses everywhere across the country during the late sixties.

But whereas *Getting Straight* and *Strawberry Statement* are overly schematized—the college rebels are simplistically portrayed heroes, anyone who opposes them is caricatured as Establishment type heavies—Jack softened the edges of all the characters and wisely painted them in shades of gray. Speaking of his characters and what they stood for, but also his own conscious and admirable refusal to accommodate an audience by making one a good guy and the other bad, Jack said: "Hector and Gabriel (initially) represent totally opposed philosophies, but neither is completely wrong or right, neither is meant to be wholly sympathetic." This may explain why *Drive* received considerably less distribution than either of those less impressive films did; as Jack himself has said, "I realized that if you have a drama with two central characters neither of whom is totally right or totally wrong, and the interest is evenly divided between them, you are breaking one of the first rules of financing. The first thing anyone (in Hollywood) asks is, 'Where's the rooting interest?' . . ." Essentially, he was not making a Hollywood film which hoped to exploit the youth-rebellion phenomenon (which was already on the wane when he began working) but to do a European-style art film about such a subject, the very film Bertolucci might have made about this period. He didn't want to create what he calls the "puppy dog" characters of most American films, easily accessible and completely agreeable, "just to get audience identification," but rather takes the approach of the best European filmmakers: "The fact that [the imperfect characters] are human beings is why I'm interested in them."

Drive, He Said seemed, to those few young people still involved in anti-war attitudes who came to the film hoping to cheer idealized heroic images of themselves, confusing and unsatisfying. Which is why it's of far more interest today (and overripe for a revival and reconsideration!) than those naïve-looking features *Getting Straight* and *Strawberry Statement*. The style, as well as the statement, of the film is marvelously untrendy, again revealing Jack as a man at once contemporary and classic: "It's a very old-fashioned movie," he said in March, 1970, before he began shooting. "No zoom lenses or anything." And while that made the film appear visually stodgy at the time of its release, it's what distinguishes it from the facile, flashy flamboyance of those other hippie movies, in which almost every shot is a zoom.

Jack himself refused to admit any desire to depict the larger social scheme, or even to have made a film that would express the point of view of the left. "Politically, I'm a humanist," he said at the time, suggesting that he didn't (like friend and colleague Jane Fonda) want to make movies that would "enlighten" an audience and persuade (some would say propagandize) them toward the artist's own position. Uninterested in and incapable of such simplification, Jack makes even the character least likely to win our sympathy—the macho coach, played by Nicholson's old pal Bruce Dern—a well-rounded human being rather than the cliché villain he, under the guidance of most any other director of that time, might have become.

Time critic Jay Cocks dismissed the film, in an off-hand and off-the-cuff review, as "a bush-league disaster that might have passed unnoticed, and perhaps unmade, but for the participation of Jack Nicholson. . . . While other fledgling directors would be allowed to fail in comparative privacy, Nicholson's reputation makes his failure agonizingly public." Reading this may, at the time, have upset Jack, but he needn't have given it much credence: Cocks is, after all, the same critic who first trashed Jack's pal Warren Beatty's *Bonnie and Clyde*, then a week later swallowed hard and admitted it was a masterpiece. In *Newsweek*, Paul D. Zimmerman revealed a far greater sensitivity: "This is Nicholson's film, transformed everywhere by his irreverence, honesty, and energy . . . [a] serious but ultimately flawed film."

Jack argued that the movie perfectly expressed his attitudes: "I know people are trying to do good things, but I don't see a lot of success. . . . The revolutionaries have created a voice, but I don't see anyone listening. I see them as you see them in the picture. . . . At the end, when the camera drops back, you see all the rest of the people on the campus just kind of looking on while Gabriel is led to the padded truck, and it's just another event that day in that society. That's the way I see it: things just go on."

Not a great deal was known about Jack then, and since the social problems the film addressed were so obvious and important, no one delved into the degree to which Jack also used this story as revelation of his personal, specific history. What stands out when the film is viewed today is the relationship between Hector and the wife of his favorite teacher (writer Robert Towne, in his only dramatic acting role). This prof has become a substitute father figure for the boy, so there's an Oedipal quality to his seduction of the teacher's wife, a violation of the very substitute family he so desperately needed. This adds an implication of classical tragedy to the story, but beyond that, Jack's own confusion about father-figures, about the nature of a mother figure, and about a young person's role within the structure of a family unit are given roughhewn but worthwhile expression here. Consequentially, the concurrent theme of a male character's ambivalent feelings toward women are also powerfully and poignantly communicated.

Asked what he thought of the results, Jack was certainly not humble: "I felt it was a very good first film. Now, I'm swimming upstream, and I'm depressed by it." But there was no confusion about what *Drive, He Said* meant to him: "It's a summing up both philosophically and technically. I put where I am now in the film."

Frustration: Olive (Karen Black) grows depressed with her middle-class existence.

Future die-hard Lakers fan Nicholson appears to be giving Michael Margotta some jump-shot pointers in his role as *Drive, He Said* director, co-producer and co-writer.

THE ONE WHO GETS LEFT:

Carnal Knowledge

(1971)
AN AVCO EMBASSY RELEASE

CAST:

Jack Nicholson *(Jonathan Fuerst)*; Candice Bergen *(Susan)*; Art Garfunkel *(Sandy)*; Ann-Margret *(Bobbie)*; Rita Moreno *(Louise)*; Cynthia O'Neal *(Cindy)*; Carol Kane *(Jennifer)*.

CREDITS:

Director, Mike Nichols; producer, Mike Nichols; screenplay, Jules Feiffer; cinematography, Guiseppe Rotunno; editor, Sam O'Steen; running time: 96 mins.; rating: originally X, later changed to R.

It seemed natural Jack would, at this point in his career, star in a film for Mike Nichols.

The film was *Carnal Knowledge*, and the importance of being a part of it can hardly be overestimated. With a script by Jules *(Little Murders)* Feiffer, ultra-hip cartoonist for the counterculture, and featuring Candice Bergen (most glamorous of the new female stars) and Art Garfunkel (the popular singer-turned-actor), *Carnal Knowledge* emerged—forgetting for a moment any questions of quality—as the film of the year. A measure of how much participation in this picture could affect one's career can be seen in the fact that Ann-Margret had, since her debut a decade earlier, been typed as an energetic sex kitten, able to do little but frug frenetically and sing in a sultry manner; her appearance here earned her an Oscar nomination for Best Supporting Actress and, more significant, drastically changed her popular image. Henceforth, she would (deservedly!) be regarded as a show biz heavyweight.

Jack Nicholson as Jonathan, while an upbeat college student in the film's early moments . . .

126

. . . and, several decades later, as an embittered, pensive adult in the film's second half.

Clearly, *Carnal Knowledge* was a major undertaking, and proper attention was paid to every detail in the production values. In addition to Mike Nichols's painstaking work with his once-in-a-lifetime cast, resulting in performances that left indelible impressions, there was the careful regard for the moods of the changing times, as the film carried its three major characters in a love-triangle story through the decades from the late forties to the early seventies. The striking set designs perfectly captured the evolving styles, while the neatly selected pre-existing popular music (a device Nichols had brought to mainstream moviemaking with *The Graduate*), beginning with Glenn Miller and running to contemporary sounds, made it quite unnecessary for the filmmaker to identify any year with a subtitle or title card. The audience could see and hear what year it was, for the film worked as a visual and aural catalogue of the passing decades.

Yet this film appeared unable to see the forest for the trees; once one had appreciated all these handsome fringe benefits, something was clearly missing at its core. The main character, Jonathan (Jack Nicholson), is a hollow man; the problem is that the movie also seems somehow hollow, without a complex enough point of view on Jonathan's mindless (some would say vicious) womanizing to allow *Carnal Knowledge* to emerge as a moral movie about an amoral type of American male. *Carnal Knowledge* seems as slight as it is, on its surface, scintillating. And the critical reaction of the time caused the beginning of a revision in attitude about Mike

American archetypes: Sandy (Art Garfunkel), the gentle, good-natured side of the American male, and his roommate, the darker, more dangerous Jonathan.

Méange-à-trois: Sandy, Jonathan, and Susan (Candice Bergen).

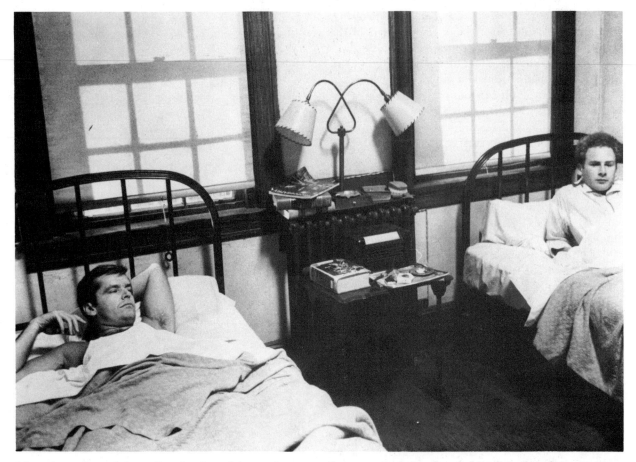

Filmmaker Mike Nichols employs the physical distance between college roommates Jonathan and Sandy in their dorm room to suggest the emotional and intellectual differences between the close friends.

Jonathan finds himself attracted to Susan, though he's
unsure if it is in spite of or
because of the fact that she's
his best friend's girl.

Nichols, as people began to ask whether he was truly perceptive and important or only flashy and facile, technically clever and visually glib.

The storyline begins when Jonathan and Sandy (Art Garfunkel) are college roommates at Amherst. Jonathan is the wisecracking womanizer, Sandy the soft, sweet, sensitive type. Jonathan cannot admit to any emotions and uses women like paper cups, carelessly casting them aside when he's finished; Sandy is desperate to find true love. He believes he has this with the gorgeous blonde Smith student Susan (Candice Bergen), but when she meets Jonathan, she falls in love, and soon they're involved. Afraid Jonathan will never be true to any woman, even one he loves (and he clearly does desperately love Susan, though he can't bring himself to verbally commit himself to her) and unwilling to hurt Sandy by breaking up with him, Susan tearfully goes ahead with her plans to marry Sandy.

Understandably, the marriage ultimately proves unsuccessful. But any reunion between Susan and Jonathan is out of the question, for he's thrown himself into a series of ever less enthusiastic affairs. His ultimate involvement is with Bobbie (Ann-Margret), a mindless, busty woman at first content to be his live-in lover, then—growing older—pathetically begging him to marry her. Jonathan believes that she would leave after trapping him, but when Bobbie attempts suicide, he does grudgingly marry her. And, shortly after, she does leave him. Embittered, Jonathan treats Sandy and his new hippie-ish girlfriend (Carol Kane) to a slide projec-

tor show of all the women he has (as acts of revenge against the female of the species) engaged in intercourse with; Sandy notices a shot of Susan mixed in with the others, at last realizing the betrayal. At the end, Jonathan is impotent and Sandy is into consciousness raising; the polar-opposite archetypal American males have reached their logical conclusions.

The key symbol of the film is a beautiful ice skater Jonathan and Sandy observe at the Woolman Rink in Central Park in New York; as the times around them change, she remains permanently locked in their minds as their mutually beloved romantic vision: the perfect woman, the ideal they will never know and never touch and therefore never be disillusioned with. They will continue to date and be disappointed by an endless string of real women, always comparing them (and finding them inferior to) to the image of perfection in their minds.

Jules Feiffer based his screenplay on several of the "cartoon plays" he originally wrote for performance off-Broadway, where they were greeted as delightful little lampoons of self-consciously hip people, striving to be "deep" but wallowing in self-indulgence. Yet there's a difference between an off-Broadway play, with its non-existent production values and suggestive settings, and a full-scale motion picture. A theatrical will-o'-the-wisp, providing a light, slight and engaging evening of entertainment, can—given the full-scale Mike Nichols treatment—appear overproduced, a slight script burdened by a heavyweight treatment, suggesting that the director is

129

The differences between Sandy and Jonathan are emphasized by their body language in this carefully constructed shot.

Almost every Mike Nichols film contains a sequence in which two characters find their relationship drastically altered while behind the wheel of a car.

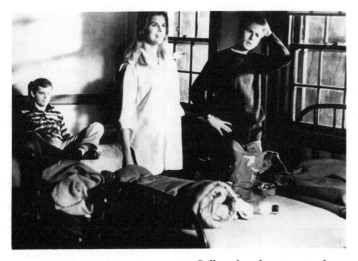

College days draw to an end . . .

more interested in style than substance. Presented as a major movie, the Feiffer script seems unsatisfying, as if one of his sketchy cartoons—good for a good chuckle or two—were done on a multi-million dollar budget. Simply, the flimsy material doesn't call for anything so elaborate. And Nichols's production was nothing if not elaborate.

Many reviews were, understandably, mixed. In *Life*, Richard Shickel praised this as "a beautifully performed film," but added: "I can't say that I like *Carnal Knowledge* very much. . . . One has a sense of director and writer safely high and dry, observing those thrashing about in the water beneath, unwilling to take a nervy, truly exploratory plunge into the depths. . . . In the end, one feels cheated [because] it comes to seem cold, superficial, manipulative."

Other critics took extreme positions. Hollis Alpert, in *Saturday Review*, found it a masterpiece: "Never do Nichols and Feiffer allow a whiff of sentimentality to cloy their tale. If there is sympathy, it is because the people, through all their betrayals of and double-dealings with each other, somehow manage to remain likable. They are struggling with a bewildering change in mores; they are truly the prisoners of sex. And they remain so into their fatuous middle age. A cruel film, perhaps, but an essentially honest one." Joseph Morgenstern of *Newsweek* took precisely the opposite approach: "People swarm to *Carnal Knowledge* . . . to learn what nasty infants American men are, to see Nicholson treating [his] women as objects and moping through half a lifetime of self-ignorance. This isn't too much in the way of original observation, but it's enough for moviegoers and some critics ('What Feiffer and Nichols have given us here is an essay on the impotence of the American male . . .') who take eager refuge in the familiar, and think that cruelty automatically means truth." The mere fact that the film was reviewed twice in succeeding issues of *Newsweek* suggests how controversial it was.

Most of the more observant critics came out against *Carnal Knowledge*. "I was dismayed," wrote David Denby. "The obscenity and abuse of women continued through scene after scene, going way past the point of satire and taking on an obsessive importance of its own. I decided that Feiffer and Nichols had simply devised a way to be as coarse as possible while going through the motions of attacking coarseness. Their 'devastating' exposure of male chauvinism turns out to be a shrewdly commercial piece of work in which the satirical attitudes have roughly the same cynical function as 'redeeming social importance' in a pornographic movie." "Why," *The Atlantic* asked, "do people fall for a movie like *Carnal Knowledge*? . . . when [the educated audience sees] a movie which is not reassuring but is harshly

. . .as the former bohemians find some room at the top, joining the Establishment. This theme clearly ties *Carnal Knowledge* in with the body of Jack's film work.

accusatory and seems to be attacking them, they assume it must be serious; it must be art and truth."

Stefan Kanfer, writing in *Time*, admitted that "the film does glitter with explicit wit, but far too often it is reduced to attitudes posing as people, glimpses pretending to be insights." Pauline Kael, whose habitually acerbic tongue here seemed pointed at the right target, described this as "a grimly purposeful satire about depersonalization and how we use each other sexually as objects and, in Mike Nichols' cold, slick style, it is like a neon sign that spells out the soullessness of neon. This movie doesn't just raise a problem, it's part of it. . . . It's all surface and whacking emphasis."

Essentially, the critical debate centered on whether a film about characters who never learn anything and never grow could sustain itself. Certainly, filmmakers have the right to make a movie about such characters but for the film to hold an audience, it must somehow continue to involve us with those characters even after we have adjusted to the fact that they will not grow and, therefore, are not interesting in and of themselves. The consensus had it that Nichols failed to do this; the flashy

writing and flamboyant direction, initially so intriguing and appealing, lose along the way their capacity to intrigue us. We fidget in our seats, even when getting to see a woman as breathtaking as Ann-Margret appearing nude onscreen for the first time, because as terrific as her torso may be, or as expert as Nicholson's acting is, such elements cannot sustain a film we sense has long since told us all it has to say. It can merely go on repeating itself, not so much doing variations on its single theme of men who relate to women as objects but only hammering home that theme without variation until the final effect is like being lectured at by a Bible-belt preacher. Indeed, as Kael put it, "This show-business fundamentalism is probably perfectly timed: What *The Graduate* was for the generation gap, *Carnal Knowledge* can be for Women's Lib sex-gap arguments."

The single element critics generally agree on is the excellence of acting in any Nichols film. Kael stood almost alone when she complained that, "The actors are badly served" and that Jack "acts up such a tormented, villainous squall that even his best scene—a well-written monologue about the perils of shacking up—seems to be

131

delivered in a full voice against cliffs and crashing seas."
Mostly, though, other critics (even those who hit the
film hard) had nothing but positive things to say about
Jack's contribution. Kanfer wrote: "As for Nicholson, it is
no secret that he can take lines and make them assume
almost any shape. But this is the first time he has been
called upon to age twenty years in the span of two hours.
It is more than merely his hair that thins; it is his amour-
propre, his attitudes, his ego. Feiffer has composed a
cartoon, but Nicholson has created one of the screen's
few straight misogynists." In *The New Republic*, Stanley
Kauffmann claimed that, "Jonathan was evidently conceived as New York Jewish, and Nicholson neither looks
nor sounds it; but Nichols has guided him to a performance so violently-defiantly wretched that the inappropri-
ateness is muted, if never quite lost." Hollis Alpert added
that, "If you thought Jack Nicholson was good before,
you will find him superb on this outing. . . . True, Jack
seems a bit weathered as an Amherst undergraduate in a
few of the early scenes, but the spirit is accurate and he
displays astonishing power as he advances. . . ." Zimmerman commented that "nearly [everyone is] blasted
off the screen by Nicholson's power. It is Nicholson,
more than Feiffer, who makes Jonathan more than a
hapless heel with his charm and his rages. . . ." William
Wolf of *Cue* summed it all up: "He catches the beat of
the chauvinist male's sad immaturity."

Indeed, Jack was so convincing as Jonathan that he
was in danger of becoming closely identified with the
character, emerging as the key screen target of Women's
Lib. William S. Pechter noted, in *Commentary*, the
possibility that this part would become identified with
him: "Here is an actor . . . with a genuine audience
rapport; notice how in the scene in which he brutally
berates Ann-Margret, even though his is the unsympathetic character, his appeal as a screen personality has
the audience in his hands, laughing at his cruel jokes at
her expense."

Besides, wasn't Jack someone who had experienced a
failed marriage and now boasted a reputation as one of
Hollywood's leading bachelor/playboys, who with his pal
Warren Beatty enjoyed (at least according to the scandal
magazines) competing to see which could bed the greater
number of women in a given period of time? Jack,
however, sees himself as a fan of liberated women: "I was
a feminist long before women's rights became a fashionable topic," he has said. Certainly, Sally Kellerman's
insistence (they have always been pals rather than lovers)
proves Jack is capable of a non-sexual relationship with a
beautiful woman. "Jonathan," Jack notes, "is exactly the
opposite (of myself). I don't think he knows any way to
communicate with women beyond screwing them."

As feminist criticism abated, Jack was able to evolve a

more accepting attitude to the character, telling the *New
York Arts-Journal* in 1977: "I can find a certain heroism
in Jonathan; it's tragic, but the man is, after all, within
his own limited perception, doing what he thinks is
right, to the general disapproval of those around him; so
maybe that's what an anti-hero is, someone who's behaving in all the ways that might produce heroic behavior
but he's motivated differently." His defense of Jonathan
went even further in Jack's *Playboy* interview, where he
said: "Jonathan is the most sensitive character in the
picture. He's the one who doesn't recover from the
original sexual triangle. He's never able to really trust
girls after that." And, later still, he told interviewer
Richard Warren Lewis: "In a casual conversation with
me, you could have a certain difficulty in separating my
sexual stance from Jonathan's." Precisely what he means
by that can be seen in a *People* story in which Jack's self-
declaration could easily be a capsulization of Jonathan's
personality: "Basically, I still relate to women by trying to
please them as if my survival depended on them. In my
long-term relationships, I'm always the one that gets
left."

Does that mean Jack approves of Jonathan's casual, compulsive womanizing? Not if one takes note of this admission: "I've had days in my life . . . when I've been with more than four women. I found that to be an internal lie. You're just not really getting it on past a certain point." That comment, coupled with a commitment to a single long-term relationship with Anjelica Huston makes clear that Jack, quite unlike Jonathan, has survived the singles scene and gone beyond it, rather than turning up on its victims list.

Trivia fans will appreciate this sidelight: Jack became hooked on the Monte Cristo number two Cuban cigar, which he has regularly bought in Europe or Canada where they can still be legally obtained, while filming *Carnal Knowledge*. The reason was simple: Nichols felt that smoking grass to relax slowed down Jack's tempo and threw the scenes off, especially for the scenes in which Jack would play a juvenile. The Monte Cristos were a happy substitute.

Jonathan treats Sandy and his new feminist companion (Carol Kane) to a slide show featuring his various (and ever less satisfying) conquests.

If anything sustains Jonathan and Sandy in middle-age, it's their Romantic memories of the good old days, when they innocently enjoyed their friendship with each other and their mutual love for Susan.

A Safe Place

(1971)
A COLUMBIA PICTURES RELEASE

CAST:

Tuesday Weld *(Susan)*; Jack Nicholson *(Mitch)*; Orson Welles *(Magician)*; Philip Proctor *(Fred)*; Gwen Welles *(Bari)*; Dov Lawrence *(Larry)*.

CREDITS:

Director, Henry Jaglom; producer, Bert Schneider; writer, Henry Jaglom; cinematography, Dick Kratina; editor, Peter Bergema; music consultant, Jim Gitter; running time: 94 mins.; rating: R.

Considering *A Safe Place* from the perspective of today, the most interesting question raised by the film is how this self-indulgent mess ever got made. To understand that—especially for younger viewers who did not experience firsthand the turbulent period of cultural revolution which this country experienced during the late sixties and early seventies—one must recall that the movie industry, like the rest of America, was throttling through an era of change.

MGM auctioned off its studio accoutrements and Universal closed down its holdover notion of contract players, because the assembly-line system for making films was clearly gone. Formula films were, for the time being at least, out, and if *Easy Rider* was any indication of what the new audience wanted, then the thing to do was give a movie camera, an ample budget, and complete freedom to some young, apparently gifted filmmaker, and let him do "his own thing," as a popular phrase of the time had it.

But that freedom would prove short-lived. Only a year

Jack Nicholson as Mitch.

Fred (Philip Proctor) and Mitch vie for the attentions of the beautiful blond Susan (Tuesday Weld).

and a half after the smashing success of *Easy Rider*, filmgoers were forsaking Dennis Hopper's follow-up, the aptly titled (and incoherent) *The Last Movie*, instead flocking to a film which revived old-fashioned craftsmanship, Peter Bogdanovich's *The Last Picture Show*. Why did the public veer back to an updated version of the Hollywood product? One reason is that so many awful "experimental" films were turned out that the public recoiled from the lot of them. But while the funding was still available for post-*Easy Rider* "relevant" little movies, into this no-man's-land of free-for-all filmmaking wandered Henry Jaglom, an alumnus of Jack's old BBS bunch. Since *Easy Rider* had briefly convinced Hollywood that the people associated with it were the New Wave and last great hope of the picture business, anyone connected with that film or with that group could easily convince some producer to finance a feature, no matter how fatuous it may have sounded in description.

After all, didn't the great Fellini often go into a film project with nothing more than an idea, a mere blueprint for the film that would take shape during the creative process? Somehow, producer Bert Schneider

became convinced that the intense young Jaglom—who had, remember, been a co-star of Jack's in *Psych-Out*, one of those Cormanesque predecessors to *Easy Rider*, and then helped to edit *Easy Rider* itself—stood at the center of what was happening.

Out of any group like BBS will emerge genuine talents (like Bob Rafelson, Robert Towne, and Jack himself) and the hangers-on who, at first glance, may seem every bit as talented (or, indeed, more so) than the bona fide articles. Henry Jaglom was such a character; even more remarkable than the fact that *A Safe Place* ever got made is that he's managed, over the years, to make several more films, all of them as assinine and unappealing as his first. But in 1970, the bearded, intense Jaglom—who was able to persuade his old colleague, and by then incredibly popular star—could con his way into instant-auteurism.

In David Downing's biography of Nicholson, he quotes Jaglom as describing the film's "creative process" this way: "I came to New York, where I'm from, went to the Central Park of my mind, found Orson Welles, seats, Jack Nicholson, squirrels, Tuesday Weld, chessplayers, Phillip Procter, crackerjacks, Gwen Welles, rowboats,

135

The Queen of the Hippies: Tuesday Weld (seen here with Philip Proctor) had been, since the late 1950s, a talented nonconformist, so the emerging counterculture styles of the late sixties and early seventies seemed made to order for her special screen sensibility.

The aged magician (Orson Welles) helps the strange, seductive Susan understand her magical place in the universe.

Dov Lawrence, merry-go-rounds . . . Friends. Myths. Images . . . I put them all together, juxtaposed the realities, sank into the fantasies, tried to break through the myths, creating anti-myth, feelings, thoughts, vibrations. Painted my movie, changing colors and shapes as I went along, exploring childhood, loss, pain, loneliness, isolation." In other words, wallowed in self-indulgence and then committed the results to film. In our fiscally conservative times, it may be stunning to think that little more than fifteen years ago, such psychobabble-dribble could possibly have been accepted by sane, mature, reasonably intelligent adults as a kind of countercultural wisdom. But let's not forget that this was the era when a book called *The Greening of America* predicted young people would soon save the world by painting peace signs on buildings and practicing free love. A year or two later, it was obvious they were creating only graffiti and an epidemic of venereal disease.

At a time when the Generation Gap was the most popular phrase in our emerging vocabulary and the emphasis of fashion, film, and the media was on youth, it made some sense Jaglom would whip up a simplistic allegory in which the heroine refuses to mature, and her attitude is depicted not as a form of infantilism but a hippie's wisdom. For the female lead, Jaglom chose Tuesday Weld, an actress as brilliant as she is beautiful, though a woman of dubious taste in film projects and an apparent death wish so far as her career is concerned.

Tuesday plays a woman sometimes called Susan, at other moments Noah (why, we never learn, but ambiguity—however purposeless—was *trés chic* at the time), who wanders around Central Park, sensuously experiencing life on a deep level most people are incapable of. There are two men in her life: an incurable, exasperating straight named Fred (Philip Proctor) and a vivacious, exciting fellow named Mitch (Jack). They are clearly not meant to be taken as real people but symbols for the different routes Susan can go: Establishment or Bohemian. But she wants to go her own way or, in the exasperating pop-phraseology of the times, "do her own thing."

Wandering in and out, on an irregular basis, is the fat magician who speaks solemn words of heavy meaning. The most pompous, ridiculous, and oft-quoted bit of pretension in the picture is delivered by Welles: "Last night in my sleep I dreamed I was sleeping, and dreaming in that sleep that I had awakened, I fell asleep." Heavy, man, heavy! But not nearly as heavy as the actor who said it.

Amazingly, the film did receive some positive reviews. In England, *Sight and Sound* marveled at the "delightfully . . . eccentric" quality of the humor. Also in Britain, though, Gavin Millar of *The Listener* complained, "While it is boring you to death, it thinks it is breaking new ground." Derek Sylvester dismissed it as "an indigestible mound of yesterday's lukewarm whimsy. . . . That happiness is something irrevocably lost with childhood and only to be recaptured through fantasy is a retrograde but appealing notion, but the Eden recaptured in *A Safe Place* is also what's known as 'second childhood.' "

For Jack, who refused to do pat pictures, appearing in *A Safe Place* was the risk he had to take. He couldn't know which of his old chums would prove to be geniuses and which would in time turn out to be talentless phonies, and probably didn't care. They were his old friends, trying to get going, and that's what mattered: the loyalty of those who shared the hard times. Part of Jack's appeal is that he's never been self-protective of his "image" in making such decisions. He generously gave of his time and energy. *Five Easy Pieces* was a film that existed in Rafelson's mind, and Jack's participation in it cinched his stardom; had he been more cautious, he wouldn't have done that one, either.

And there is a slight similarity in this film to the thematic thread in Jack's output, since the position of the Tuesday Weld character—balanced halfway between the longhairs and the straights, living in both worlds but belonging to neither—makes her a "double-character" like so many of the men he has played. Jack has rarely been asked to reconsider the film, though he has noted: "Most films you do are written. I've done it all ways. In *A Safe Place*, I improvised the entire part. *Carnal Knowledge* was done word for word. *Five Easy Pieces* had two or three scenes improvised. . . ." Suggesting, quite clearly, that improvisation is perhaps best employed on a limited basis. When asked what he thought of the film in retrospect, he shrugged and with characteristic lack of false humility told interviewer Tom Shales: "My stuff was great." But Jack can be overly hard on himself: "There was a time soon after *Easy Rider*," he confessed, "when I was rude to [old] friends—didn't return phone calls as promptly as I should." Other overnight sensations, however, don't return them at all, and *A Safe Place* is, if nothing else, evidence that even after superstardom hit, he could be counted on to come through for old friends, however temporary a setback it might prove for his own career.

Flower child Susan "does her own thing" with the help of the nature loving magician.

A KAFKA-ESQUE CHARACTERIZATION:

The King of Marvin Gardens

(1972)

A COLUMBIA PICTURES RELEASE

CAST:

Jack Nicholson (*David Staebler*); Bruce Dern (*Jason Staebler*); Ellen Burstyn (*Sally*); Julia Anne Robinson (*Jessica*); Scatman Crothers (*Lewis*); Charles Levene (*Grandfather*).

CREDITS:

Director, Bob Rafelson; producer, Bob Rafelson; screenplay, Jacob Brackman, from a story by Brackman and Rafelson; cinematography, Laszlo Kovacs; editor, John F. Link II; musical supervision, Synchrofilm Inc.; running time: 104 mins.; rating: R.

After the twin failures of *Drive, He Said* and *A Safe Place*, the smart thing would have been to find a surefire vehicle. Certainly, Jack had that option—both the Redford role in *The Sting* and Pacino's part in *The Godfather* were his for the asking. But he passed on them, consciously risking his own stature.

Why? "They were not creatively worth my time," Jack told Gene Siskel. The films were well made, though in his estimation, the contemporary equivalent of the mass-produced Hollywood product of the studio era. "I know the general audience may enjoy those films more than something I might choose, but that's not my concern," he insisted. "I mean, regardless of whoever does those films, those films are going to do well." He wanted less safe roles in less safe projects, which hopefully would turn out to be successes. Rafelson's movies are, in Jack's estimation, "full of departures, they don't relate to other films, they're germinal films." That is, one of a kind,

138

ground-breaking pictures that never play off proven formulas for success, but try to achieve success on their own terms and sometimes (as with *Five Easy Pieces*) succeed.

So he courageously accepted the lead in an off-beat arthouse item, working once again for Rafelson, though this time taking on a part far removed from the romantic hero he'd played in *Five Easy Pieces*. In fact, by playing David Staebler in *King*, Jack appeared to be now repeating in A movies the pattern he'd established in his biker films and westerns: insisting on portraying, in successive pictures, the absolute reversal of the personality he'd most recently brought to life.

As in *Five Easy Pieces*, Nicholson and Rafelson here vividly tell the story of a singular man, bringing his plight to three-dimensional life onscreen in a film rich

A man operating outside of his normal milieu has been a recurring Nicholson theme, and he here handles it handsomely, as David finds himself involved with Atlantic City lowlifes.

As David Staebler, Jack (seen here with frequent co-actor Scatman Crothers) abandoned his new star image in order to play a less than stellar character role as an owl-eyed intellectual.

with the details of reality closely observed. But the ruggedly individualistic quality of the *Five Easy Pieces* character allowed that film an accessibility to an audience hungry for powerful entertainment, while the bookish, reserved personality of the man in *King* does not offer a mainstream audience any such thing, diverting this film directly to college communities and small theaters oriented to the art film crowd. The problem is not that *Five Easy Pieces* was a better film than *King*—they are both excellent—only that this story remained specific, a marvelously told tale that appeared to have none of the popular appeal of its predecessor.

Five Easy Pieces told the story of Bobby Dupea in such a way that it opened up to its audience, suggesting it was really about much more than it at first seemed to be, capturing something of the mood of America in the early seventies, thereby presenting the audience with a generational saga; whether Rafelson and company intended that, or if they merely told an interesting and worthwhile story as well as they could and their popular success was the result of lucky timing and what the critics and audiences happened to read into the film, is hard to say. *King*, on the other hand, seems more narrow, a beautifully rendered and completely believable story that is self-contained, failing to stretch beyond its boundaries and become an "important" picture that can move an audience to feel they've discovered not only the truth about the man onscreen but also about themselves.

In fact, Rafelson conceived of doing *King* while he was still working on *Five Easy Pieces*, when he realized that the *Pieces* script would have to be tightened, preventing him from developing the relationship between the two brothers which he'd looked forward to exploring. The answer was to save that part for his next project. When *Five Easy Pieces* was behind him and he began writing a film based on his own awkward and ambivalent relationship with his real-life brother, Rafelson decided to add another autobiographical element based on his experiences, in Japan, as a free-form radio announcer.

This, then, is a complementary piece to *Five Easy Pieces*. The story that emerged is as cold and East Coast oriented as *Five Easy Pieces* is warm and West Coast: *King* is set in Atlantic City during a chilly week, Atlantic City before the renovations began, when the once grandiose buildings were crumbling and the boardwalks were in disrepair, a site peopled mainly by the aged and the infirm. It is a tawdry place caught at a melancholy moment when David shows up. Early in the film he reveals his frustrations to us. Though he's achieved some success and notoriety as a late-night radio talk show host, he's terribly unhappy about never having lived up to his own expectations for himself by becoming a serious novelist. Like Bobby Dupea, he is in his own estimation a failed artist; psychologically speaking, he is Bobby's city cousin. What has brought David to such an unlikely setting for an ambitious, embittered intellectual is a call from his older brother. Jason (Bruce Dern) is the opposite of David, working for a gangster named Lewis (Scatman Crothers), and has amassed some money with which he wants to buy a Hawaiian Island, then turn it into a resort area.

The pattern that their attempts to crash the big time together takes is not unlike that of a game of Monopoly (they rapidly make and lose great amounts of money, continually are sent back to Go, even once Go Directly to Jail), an ironic underscoring to the story since they are darting about the city that inspired the game in the first place. The owl-eyed David hops along behind Jason, getting caught on the spiderweb of huge ambitions, petty greed, and complex interpersonal relationships that also include Jason's aging but attractive girlfriend Sally (Ellen

David, the radio talk show host, interviews a beauty queen.

Burstyn) and her stunning daughter, Jess (Julia Anne Robinson). In fact, Sally becomes so terrified Jason may dump her for her own daughter that, in a fit of rage, humiliation, and fear, she shoots the man she loves. At the end, David brings his brother's body home to Philadelphia, puts his momentarily-cherished dreams of financial bonanzas behind him, and goes back to his midnight "novelizing" on the radio.

This is a film about losers, but they lack the glamorous aura of the losers in *Five Easy Pieces*. If anything, that makes this the more honest and demanding of the two films, but those very qualities are what dimmed its moneymaking potential. Jack himself seems to have been aware this had to be approached as one from the heart, for, at a time when he could easily have commanded $500,000 per picture (a sizable amount in those pre-inflation times), he chose to work for scale so the film could be brought in on a tight budget. In many ways, *King*—though almost completely unknown and rarely revived—is truly the film B.B.S. was formed in order to produce: the perfect "little" picture, an alternative to Hollywood hokum, past or present, offering an American equivalent of the noncompromising and noncondescending European pictures turned out with something other than the pocketbook primarily in mind.

The film even included direct address by Nicholson to his audience, reminiscent of that technique in the films of Ingmar Bergman. There is a complicated narrative

140

technique, as we're made aware that on one level David is talking directly to us, the moviegoing audience, while on another level he's speaking to his radio listeners; the entire film must ultimately be understood as a visualization of one of his on-the-air monologues in which he at length weaves confessional tales, verbal novels for the illiterate. Adding to our confusion and the film's complexity is the fact that we can never quite grasp how much of what David tells his own audience (and us) is true: he relays a terrible memory of his boyhood in which he and Jason purposefully allowed their grandfather to die on a fishbone that had become caught in his throat, though we must reconsider our reaction when we realize, later on, that the grandfather is in fact alive and well. Or is he? Is perhaps the grandfather we see in David's home, when no one else is around, meant to be perceived by us as the grandfather, alive and well (implying David was merely making the story up for his audience), or an imaginative reconstruction of a man

who did indeed die? Though most of the film has, like *Five Easy Pieces*, a realistic on-location look to it, the ellipses of the storyline lead us to understand why Jack would, in describing the film, proudly call it "Kafkaesque."

At least with this film Nicholson had some nice notices to show for his effort, though not all critics agreed on its merits. As Derek Sylvester noted, the movie was "greeted with enthusiasm mingled with mild perplexity" when it opened at the New York Film Festival, and has often been written off as an ambitious, ingenious near-miss. The great danger with such an esoteric work was that it could sink into ersatz existentialism, rendering it pretentious rather than profound, and that was essentially the conclusion of Robert Hatch in *The Nation*: "The film proceeds by set pieces. . . . I wondered . . . was it necessary to invent so many tableaux of loneliness and rootlessness? However, a Fun Pier in February can be counted on not to let the

Jason (Bruce Dern), David's risky brother, tries to calm down a creditor; though he had emerged as the bigger star, Nicholson here happily took a back seat to old friend Dern, who was given the more flamboyant role.

141

cameras down." Likewise, in *Life*, Richard Schickel voiced a similar opinion: "Jacob Brackman's script is rueful and ironic and as aware of its own literacy as Rafelson is of how photogenic his shots are of everybody running and walking and even riding horses. . . . In fact, that's the trouble. . . . [The filmmakers] are so damned aware of the whole tradition of modernist despair, so smugly pleased to be allowed to be joining in, even if they are (or were) just humble commercial movie people, so proud to match the essential bleakness of their vision with all them fancy writers."

Stanley Kauffmann took an even tougher stance: "My biggest grievance is that they have wasted Jack Nicholson. Melancholic resignation is not his strongest suit. He needs strong tensions, not necessarily loud (though he's good when he's loud) but deep and certainly tense. When he's being quiet about something—which means, with the threat of explosion even if he never explodes—he's arresting. Here, he simply stands around most of the time, observing and reflecting, occasionally wrinkling his nose bunny-style to adjust his glasses. It's quite a negative achievement to flatten Nicholson, but this picture does it."

While numerous critics and viewers agreed the film missed true power by slipping into portentousness, few agreed with Kauffmann's assessment of Jack's offbeat acting. "Rafelson may be too detached and dispassionate," Jay Cocks wrote in *Time*, "but Dern and Nicholson never are." Defending the film as "odd" and "irresistibly fascinating," Cocks wrote of Jack's work in a way that seemed almost a direct answer to Kauffmann: "Nicholson has already displayed remarkable range. David, so thoroughly introverted, so tentative, is the most demanding role he has had so far partly because it does not give him the chance to do what is easy for him—display

sudden rage, ruthlessness, a casual, cunning kind of cool. Here, wearing a slowly unraveling cardigan and squinting nervously behind a pair of glasses forever smudged with fingerprints, Nicholson invests David with real turmoil and vulnerability." In *Saturday Review*, Arthur Knight hailed the performances of Jack and Bruce Dern as "fabulous," and went on to defend the film: "As any devotee of Monopoly must know, it is a game. *The King of Marvin Gardens* is the superb metaphor for the American dream—the dream of getting rich quick, with a minimum of effort and a maximum of manipulation."

Though the film is clearly autobiographical for Rafelson, it also provides Jack with plenty of elements he must have taken on a most personal level. The film is about a strange family situation, one Jack could certainly relate to: "Everybody's got a weird family, and in that way we're all average," he once kidded. The death of a parent or parental figure ties this film in not only with *Five Easy Pieces* but many of Jack's other choices as well. There's also the vision of a man-woman relationship as dangerous, though it's Dern, not Nicholson, who is killed by his lover here; in most of the films, it will be Jack himself who is in danger, a theme that reaches full fruition in *Prizzi's Honor*.

"In order to continue to have your choice of roles," Jack has admitted, "you have to have a success every once in a while." No matter how personally satisfying *King* and, before it, *Drive* may have been, a schedule of movies exclusively of this order would have been a ticket into oblivion. He needed a film that would recapture the public's interest, and like some of the cunning characters he has played, he shortly found just the right item, though in a film intriguing enough that it was worth his while to do it.

The Last Detail

(1974)
A PARAMOUNT RELEASE

CAST:

Jack Nicholson *(Billy "Bad Ass" Buddusky)*; Otis Young *("Mule" Mulhall)*; Randy Quaid *(Larry Meadows)*; Clifton James *(M.A.A.)*; Carol Kane *(Young Whore)*; Michael Moriarty *(Marine O.D.)*; Luana Anders *(Donna)*.

CREDITS:

Director, Hal Ashby; producer, Gerald Ayres; screenplay, Robert Towne, adapted from the novel by Darryl Ponicsan; cinematography, Michael Chapman; editor, Robert Jones; music, Johnny Mandel; running time: 105 mins.; rating: R.

By luck, ingenuity, destiny, or some canny survival instinct, Jack turned up in precisely the kind of role the public most enjoys seeing him in: Billy "Bad Ass" Buddusky may be the most finely etched portrayal in Nicholson's entire spectrum of characterizations, and while the film was not a box-office smash, it proved a solid enough moneymaker to re-establish Jack as the reigning and representative male movie star of the 1970s. Best of all, it allowed Jack—who at this point nervously had one eye on the box-office and one on his own serious ambitions as an actor—to approach a role he knew would satisfy on both levels: "It's a strong character," he would later say, "but it's also one I knew audiences would immediately like."

The storyline is deceptively simple: two career sailors (Nicholson and Otis Young) make the five-day trip from their base in Norfolk, Va., to the prison compound in Portsmouth, N.H., in order to deliver a 17-year-old

Mr. Macho: Jack Nicholson as Billy "Bad Ass" Buddusky.

The pathetic misfit Larry (Randy Quaid) receives lessons on life from his cigar-chomping protector/guard, Billy.

Mr. Macho shows his tender side: Billy confronts a whore (Carol Kane).

144

recruit (Randy Quaid) who will begin serving an eight-year sentence in the brig for petty theft. Initially, the lifers are happy to get the assignment because it will allow them plenty of time to get drunk and go whoring before returning: it is, in their initial estimation, a paid vacation.

Until they meet their prisoner, that is. This boy, the two men quickly realize, is a born loser: He had the bad luck to get caught pilfering petty change from the favorite charity of the commanding officer's wife, for otherwise he would never have received such a severe sentence for such a minor infringement. Indeed, Larry Meadows is such a sad sack that the lifers can't see the need to maintain strict discipline; he's so sorrowful they're touched into believing it's their unofficial duty to show him a good time before he goes in. So there's a beer blast in Washington and a brawl with Marines in a Penn Station men's room. A bond forms between the three, as the career sailors realize the youth is still a virgin and decide to initiate him to broads as well as bars, which they do in Boston's seamiest brothel. In the companionship of the two swell fellows, the youth enjoys the wild and seedy side of life for the first time.

Ironically, though, their kind treatment has a tragic result: Larry, at first so nonchalant about being confined in prison, has now had a taste of honey, and can't stand the thought of being confined behind bars. Desperate at the thought, he makes a mad dash for freedom. While the two career sailors have come to care deeply for the youth, they are locked into a code of behavior which they follow religiously: they could allow the youth to escape, but that would mean doing his time, so instead they recapture him, reluctantly turn him over to the authorities, then march back into the grim, unfair world, knowing they have done what they had to do, however distasteful it may have been.

In summation, this may sound more like a dead-end episode than a full-blown drama, more an equivalent to a short story than a film with the sweep and depth of a novel. But that first impression is misleading. For *The Last Detail* is a picaresque perfectly poised between comedy and drama; we laugh throughout, then leave sensing we've just witnessed a tragedy. In part, that derives from the growth of Quaid's character. At the beginning, he is a total victim, treated shabbily by the world but, in a sense, deserving it because he accepts and

One last lark before prison: Larry, Billy, and Mule (Otis Young) on the town.

evokes it. The first thing the sailors notice is that he unhappily accepts an overcooked cheeseburger in a diner they stop at. But their presence—and their friendship—change him. It is a subtle, rather than overt, change; there are no big, phoney melodramatic fireworks here. Yet just before "Bad Ass" Buddusky and "Mule" Mulhall surrender him, Meadows sends back an order of fried eggs that haven't been cooked to his specifications. The movie's moral complexity comes from the fact that we don't know whether to cheer or cry at his growth. If we had seen the man he was five days earlier incarcerated, we might have shrugged and admitted he was probably better off on the inside; but he has at last become a self-respecting man, and while such a dynamic turnabout is usually to be applauded, it makes him precisely the kind of person who can least suffer imprisonment. He's been freed from his self-imposed psychological prison only to be locked away in a real one.

In a less obvious way, the lifers have grown, too: though they have not changed in any clear-cut, easily definable ways, the look on their faces after surrendering their prisoner suggests their anger at the system they are a part of; they will never be able to completely enjoy their naval careers again. Understandably, Jack has described this as the story of "a trip and a search at the same time." The movie, then, is anti-institutional by implication rather than direct statement, making it "political" in the subtle way Jack much prefers to the easier but less effective approach of direct statement of the movie's message.

The three-man ensemble is perfect. Quaid manages to make Meadows a totally believable innocent without turning him into a stereotyped, sentimentalized saint; Young is quietly powerful as the strong but softspoken black sailor. Yet there is never any doubt as to who owns this movie, and the reviews made that clear. "Nicholson dominates," Paul D. Zimmerman wrote in *Newsweek*. "His special blend of cockiness and charm keeps us constantly entertained. Whether he is brandishing a pistol before a bartender reluctant to serve the young sailor a beer or perched half-drunk on the edge of a bed listening to Quaid . . . relate the one moment in his life when he got angry, Nicholson distracts us. . . ." Cynical on the surface but sensitive underneath it, physically burly but emotionally bruised, arrogant and angry and alienated, he is a remarkable characterization, and Nicholson brings this downscale decent man to life every bit as convincingly as he did the upscale slime in *Carnal Knowledge*. If Jonathan was so superficially appealing that it took us the entire movie to realize how detestable he in fact was, Buddusky immediately puts a middlebrow audience off with his vulgarity and swaggering, so it takes us the entire film to understand how fundamentally worthwhile a human being he really is.

Writing in *The Nation*, Robert Hatch put it this way: "Buddusky is a fellow I've been avoiding off and on for as long as I can remember . . . now, in the person of Jack Nicholson, you can spend two hours with him." Nicholson managed to correctly embody an entire type of male behavior while, at the same time, creating a character who was as specific and real as an individual as he was convincing when taken as an archetype. Jack "redeemed" Buddusky, making an audience see the positive side to a most questionable character without ever stepping over the line and whitewashing him.

In *Time*, Richard Schickel noted that "Nicholson's bluster only partly masks his insecurity as he moves through the excess of options presented by the civilian world." Stanley Kauffmann claimed: "Here [Jack] has a part that is exactly right for him—a rough romantic, innately furious, frequently gentle but knowingly cruel. . . . Aside from the faint air of virtuoso occasion, he and the role are perfect for each other, and together they galvanize the film." Pauline Kael of *The New Yorker* hailed him this way: "Jack Nicholson can make his feelings come through his skin. . . . Other actors might communicate a thought or an emotion with a gesture, but Nicholson does it with his whole body . . . his specialty [is] a satirical approach to macho [and] Buddusky is the best full-scale part he's had." Jack remains confident that Buddusky rates among his best work: "*Last Detail* was very satisfying," he has said. "I felt I fully realized what I wanted to do in that film."

One of the few critics to attack Nicholson's work here was John Simon. Writing in *Esquire*, he argued: "Nicholson gives what many consider a superlative performance, and what strikes me as yet another example of his customary turn—one cannot get around the feeling that the basic pigment of all Nicholson performances is an impasto of smugness." That seems unfair, attacking Jack for what he has accomplished: after all, Nicholson is here (as in certain other performances) defining and describing a brand of male smugness for us through his dramatic creations.

Simon chose to trash not only Nicholson's performance but also the film containing it. "Ashby's direction is plodding, always settling for the obvious shot, and betraying not a hint of personal vision."

Far more intriguing is William Walling's assessment of the film in *Society*, where he analyzed it not so much as a movie about vulgar-mouthed career sailors but as a study of the plight of the American workingman, the blue-collar worker who has remained essentially unchanged in our century even as the world around him has experienced various "revolutions," sexual and otherwise. "The plot of the film," Walling wrote, "reflects almost uncannily that schizophrenic separation between work and pleasure we've come to recognize as one consequence of the way most large-scale jobs are organized in an industrial society—especially for those workers whose functions must be performed somewhere near the bottom of a bureaucratic or technocratic hierarchy . . . we view the constant pursuit of pleasure against the backdrop of a work assignment. . . ."

Walling's fascinating if debatable social-inequity interpretation is undercut somewhat by the limitations of all narrow approaches to film. He ultimately argued that the realistic ending, which in fact is the hallmark of this movie's integrity, was actually a weakness, and that *The Last Detail* would be far better if Nicholson and Young were depicted as rebelling against the system they were a

part of, changing it for the better or destroying it. That might have made *The Last Detail* more attractive to a strict Marxist, but it would also have diminished the honesty and replaced it with idealistic propaganda, for the two men do what in fact they would do: accept the world, with all its inequities, and move on with the business of living. Stanley Kauffmann put it this way: "The real agony comes from the fact that, after temptations to go somewhere else, the script gets right back where it was heading—into reality, habit, fear and compliance. The result is not ironic; it's flatly truthful." And, to a degree, tragic. As Gerald Forshey wrote in *The Christian Century*, "*The Last Detail* exults in the repli-

Billy introduces Larry to a madam in hopes that the virginal boy may have a good moment or two before the inevitable incarceration.

147

Though in the late sixties and early seventies, Jack was frequently cast as a symbol of the counterculture, he resented that label, and enjoyed having a hippie serve as a foil for his Establishment character in *The Last Detail*.

death, chances are it's better because death is [too handy an] answer. But Buddusky is killed in the book. . . . I was for ending it as the book did, I was taking an easier way out—I know dramatically what a cheat that is . . . and I think the movie might have had a greater commercial success had that been done. Towne felt that was a cheat so I went along. . . ."

A behind-the-scenes story was as intriguing—and tragic—as the tale told in the film. One of the many admirable qualities of *The Last Detail* is that while "Mule" is played by a black actor, there is little in the script that identifies him as such. Jack thought it would be marvelous to have old friend Rupert Crosse, a black actor, play a man whose race is never identified, a breakthrough bit of casting at that time. But just before shooting commenced, Crosse began behaving strangely. When shooting was scheduled to start, the actor couldn't be found. At last, Jack located him and initially thought Crosse had suffered some sort of nervous breakdown. Then he realized the man had a terminal illness. They held up production for a week, in hopes that Crosse might yet do the film as his farewell gesture as an actor, but he could not work, and Otis Young was brought in as a replacement. At the end of filming, Jack congratulated Young "on being the first member of his race allowed to play just a human being."

cation of reality." That is, any "changes" are not introduced into the larger social structure, but take place internally, within the make up of the men. "Their commitment to each other is much greater than their commitment to anything in the outside world. The navy protects them, and yet even the navy is no longer sufficient when it can tolerate the injustice being visited on Quaid."

Jack has defined "Bad Ass" as "a master of his profession, so to speak. I like that aspect of the character . . . he has his own personal code. He loves the Navy and in line with that he does things that he doesn't love with as little muss and fuss as possible." He has also noted: "A guy my age in the Navy is an old man in his profession. I like to play young-old men. They have depth."

Jack acknowledged both the similarities and differences between himself and this character when he told Robert Kerwin: "Buddusky was the closest of all the roles to the merging of my feelings and personality, to myself being superimposed on one of my characters. Buddusky was close to me in gut reaction, but where was he intellectually? He couldn't think like I do, see things in my mental terms." Interestingly enough, Jack admits to having argued with Towne about the film's ending, and (surprisingly!) come down (perhaps because he needed a hit just then) on the side of commercialization for the sake of a bigger sell: "One of the rules of dramaturgy is that if you can resolve a dramatic situation without a

The moment of truth: Billy and Mule drag Larry in to prison.

148

WATERGATE WITH REAL WATER:

Chinatown

(1974)
A PARAMOUNT RELEASE

CAST:

Jack Nicholson *(J. J. Gittes)*; Faye Dunaway *(Evelyn Mulwray)*; John Huston *(Noah Cross)*; Perry Lopez *(Escobar)*; Dianne Ladd *(Ida Sessions)*; Darrell Zwerling *(Hollis Mulwray)*; John Hillerman *(Yelburton)*; Roman Polanski *(knife-wielding punk)*.

CREDITS:

Director, Roman Polanski; producer, Robert Evans; screenplay, Robert Towne; cinematography, John A. Alonzo; editor, Sam O'Steen; music, Jerry Goldsmith; running time: 131 mins.; rating: R.

Chinatown was (at least on the surface) a genre piece, a throwback to the kinds of stories Dashiell Hammett and Raymond Chandler had written during the 1920s and thirties and which, in their screen versions, most often starred Humphrey Bogart. Jack had spoken of trying to balance his more demanding projects with things his audience (and he himself) would find a bit easier to take, and an occasional well-wrought genre piece seemed a perfect project for such an off-season entry. Only something special happened with *Chinatown*: while it does effectively evoke the private-eye picture of the past, it also manages to transcend the genre. This is no simple escapism exercise in nostalgia but a movie that employs a period from the past to comment on the political climate of the present.

The opening is deceptively charming, as the titles appear in black and white art deco format, suggesting the bygone film noir style. The initial plot set-up is, like-

Jack Nicholson as J. J. Gittes.

149

J. J. falls into an affair with the elusive, enigmatic Evelyn (Faye Dunaway).

wise, reminiscent of *The Maltese Falcon* and *The Big Sleep*: Detective J. J. Gittes, a former cop who once patrolled the Chinatown district, now specializes in messy divorce cases. As the film opens, he presents a distraught client with evidence (photographs Gittes has taken or acquired) of the man's wife in adulterous situations, and we note a coolness, a distance, a removal from any emotional involvement on Gittes's part. He is a man who needs to have his human and moral sides reawakened, and, by the picture's end, he will.

Shortly, we see him begin work on a case he mistakenly believes will be one more routine excursion into the sleazy side of moneyed people's lives. A supposed Mrs. Mulwray (Diane Ladd) asks that her husband's possible extra-marital affair be looked into. Gittes opens an investigation, then is stunned to learn the woman who hired him is not Mrs. Mulwray at all. He meets the real lady (Faye Dunaway) at about the same time the actual Mr. Mulwray is murdered.

Gittes is smart enough to sense he's been set up, used as a chess piece in some larger plot. But because his interest has been piqued, and he's more than a little

Director Roman Polanski did a cameo bit as the cheap hood who cuts J. J.'s nose.

J. J. is disfigured by the hoodlums working for the corrupt Establishment.

attracted to the widow Mulwray, Gittes doggedly continues his investigation on his own time, even after a maniacal punk (director Roman Polanski in a cameo role) cuts his nose open during a late-night encounter. As it turns out, Mulwray was the head of the city of Los Angeles' water Authority, and a drought is currently putting a premium on that commodity. People in power want the water diverted to certain areas, so all sorts of dirty deals have transpired. Gittes finds himself in much the same position of a reporter who has followed what he thought to be a routine story and instead uncovered nearly endless layers of corruption, reaching to people at the pinnacles of authority.

The similarity between reporters and detectives was not lost on the filmmakers of the mid-1970s. It hardly seems coincidental that the private eye genre was revived. By the time *All the President's Men* reached the screen a year later, the public had already been treated to numerous characters going through escapades similar to those of Dustin Hoffman and Robert Redford, playing Carl Bernstein and Bob Woodward. Hollywood had found, in the 1930s private eye film, a model for the significant 1970s exposés of cover-ups. The detective film was the natural genre for the Watergate era, and no

other so effectively employed that roundabout approach to contemporary problems as *Chinatown*.

The movie also captured the mood of Hollywood in the mid-seventies. What audiences hungered for were films achieving a delicate balance between the time-honored traditions of entertaining formula films and the modern 1970s sensibility. *Little Big Man* as a western, *M*A*S*H* as a service comedy, *The Three Musketeers* as a costume film, *The Godfather* as a gangster flick, and *Chinatown* as a private eye picture were not flat, flaccid genre pieces, but rather revisions with a cynical and ironic point of view toward things previously taken at face value, but nonetheless recapturing the entertainment qualities American audiences always demand.

Yet even today—removed from all such considerations—*Chinatown* plays perfectly, reaching beyond the limitations of the time and place either of its setting or creation, achieving an almost tragic stature. Gittes comes in contact with Evelyn Mulwray's chilling father Noah (John Huston), a jovial monster who is the movie's symbol for the grinning, genial face of omnipresent evil in the world. If he is immoral, then the Chinatown where the movie ends represents the vast amorality of the modern world, and Jake—who has by this time believably transformed before our eyes into a moral creature—finds himself impotent in the face of abiding and accelerating darkness. The movie ends as night descends on Jake, and it is not just the specific night following this particularly gruesome day but a metaphoric night of moral darkness descending on Jake, on L.A., and on the world at large. As Ron Rosenbaum would reflect in 1986: "The shattering discovery Gittes makes at the end—that beneath the deepest levels of political corruption is something even darker and more frightening, the ineradicable corruption of the human heart—gave that 1974 film the added dimension of being a kind of farewell to arms for 60s idealism."

Towne's screenplay is responsible for much of this. Though the film is set in 1937, the incident which inspired it was the 1908 Owne River Valley scandal, one of the great blights on Los Angeles' history. The Civic Leaders of Southern California used their trusted positions to make themselves multi-millionaires. And the essence of this is captured in the movie, when acres of parched land near L.A. is purchased by Noah and his cohorts, aware it will make the rich and powerful more rich and powerful still.

Yet Towne was not interested in a docudrama approach; he did, after all, reset elements of the real-life situation a quarter century later. Throughout, Jake senses Mrs. Mulwray (who has become his lover) is hiding something. He also believes that when he forces this information from her, he will know why and how he was set-up. But when (as he hits her again and again in an excruciating scene that causes the ugly facts to pour out as her emotional dam breaks) she at last confesses her secret, Jake realizes it has nothing whatever to do with money and water. Her child, we realize, is in fact the illegitimate offspring of a rape by her own father, lending the film a sense of familial confusion of identities basic not only to the films of Jack Nicholson, but also to the most terrifying of human drama. Desiring only to help her shield the child from Noah (but always wondering, at least on some level, if Noah's protestations of innocence are in fact true, that Evelyn is the paranoid schizophrenic Noah claims her to be), Gittes inadvertently leads Noah directly to the child. In a freak accident, Evelyn is killed, and Gittes—dragged away by a friend—can only look back at evil triumphant, as Noah takes his granddaughter/daughter and leaves.

This dark vision derives from Polanski's point of view. In the first draft of the script, Towne had Evelyn shoot her father and spirit her daughter out of the country, suggesting the screenwriter's own characteristic belief in a cautious hopefulness. Polanski opted for the grimmer approach. Towne chastized the ending for being "relentlessly bleak," but in fact it's worth noting that Gittes (who

is, after all, our focal character) does not die, but has been transformed from the superficial cynic of the film's opening to a profound pessimist; he has stared into the face of evil and survived. The movie is the story of his moral and emotional journey, and Polanski seems correct in sensing the power inherent in this approach.

Whether the symbolism of the final Chinatown setting stems from Towne or Polanski (or, most likely, the tense collaboration of the two), it works. Early on in the film, we learn that Gittes—while working as a Chinatown cop—loved and lost a woman there. When he loves and loses Evelyn in the same spot, there's a terrible sense of coming full circle. It's carefully schematized yet played with a natural flair that makes it believable, a ritualistic action that comes off as realistic. "Do as little as possible," the police take as their creed in this alien world where they always feel like outsiders; it is the new non-involvement of the 1970s imposed on the period setting, a philosophy of life Gittes will reluctantly subscribe to as, unable to help the forces of good in any way, he staggers from the scene. "Come on, Jake," his former partner (Perry Lopez) reminds him. "It's Chinatown." But Chinatown is, symbolically speaking, where we all live today. And Noah, who holds court here, has a simple, terrifyingly convincing credo of his own: "Politi-

A risk few superstars would dare to take: throughout most of the film, J. J. wears an ugly bandage over his wounded nose . . .

152

cians, ugly buildings, and whores all get respectable if they last long enough." From the final version of *Chinatown*, we fear Noah will last forever.

A few critics failed to recognize the levels and dimensions of *Chinatown*. In *Commonweal*, Colin L. Westerbeck dismissed it as "just a pretty, kinky period film." Indeed, Polanski himself admitted that his admiration for the stereotypical private eye films he saw in his youth drew him to the project: "Anyone who loves the cinema wants to make each of the genres," he claimed. The more perceptive critics noted that Polanski did not merely mimic the timeworn clichés but played surprising variations on the themes. "*Chinatown* is a thriller for grownups," Penelope Gilliat explained in *The New Yorker*. "It is exempt from the usual exile filmmaker's romanticism about Los Angeles, is obviously steeped in knowledge of older Hollywood thriller-masters, but is full of young verve, bowing to no one."

An "exotic and cunning entertainment," Jay Cocks wrote in *Time*, with "a sort of edgy placidity that breaks into moments of sudden violence . . . No [contemporary] film has even succeeded quite so well in conveying the ambience of Los Angeles before the war—sun-kissed, seedy and easy." Paul D. Zimmerman, in *Newsweek*, called it "lurid, spellbinding . . . with cinematographer John A. Alonzo, Polanski creates a moral midnight in the solar glare of Los Angeles. The result is a brilliant cinematic poem in the style of Poe circa 1974, a highly atmospheric portrait of evil-doing promoted by official power and big money, and unchecked by the agencies of law enforcement—Watergate with real water." For Gerald Forshey, Polanski was not so much investing the detective genre with undercurrents of 1970s social comment but imposing an autobiographical vision on the period-picture format: "Polanski, still possessed by the memories of the Manson family massacre in his home, is exploring . . . depravity." *Christian Century* insisted that the film's power and importance derived from a combination of the two: "Polanski . . . merges Manson with Watergate as elements in the substance that now pervades and stains all of society."

Jack's performance also received rave notices, even from critics who carped about the overall success of the film: In *Time*, Cocks wrote: "Nicholson's Gittes is a

. . .though Evelyn apparently does not find him any the less sexy.

J. J. makes a strange odyssey through the haunts of Los Angeles, discovering corruption everywhere; here, he is beaten by farmers who misdirect their anger at him.

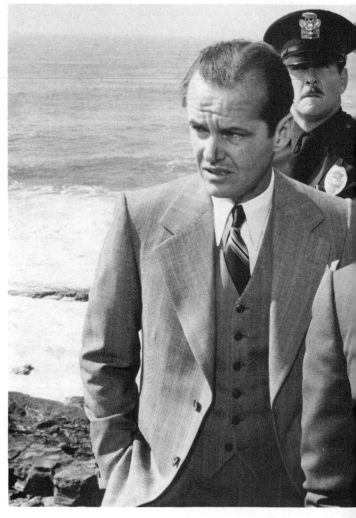

As the world around J. J. grows ever blacker owing to his comprehension of corruption, director Polanski effectively darkens the film's lighting to convey the character's perception of the moral darkness of his world.

Irate farmers protest the construction of a new dam, disrupting a city council meeting by parading their sheep through the room; the incident, like the film itself, was based by writer Robert Towne on an actual L. A. scandal.

Police officer Escobar (Perry Lopez) leads J. J. on a grand tour of the scene of the crime.

"She's my sister . . . she's my daughter . . . she's—" The moment of truth between J. J. and Evelyn.

No wonder one critic called Jack "Bogart in the age of rock 'n' roll."

Jack, as J. J., learns the terrible truth at the end: "Remember, J. J. . . . it's Chinatown!"

clever piece of acting, funny and winning, but Polanski and Towne do not give him the chance to get any depth." Others, however, saw considerable depth: "As soon as you see him in the role of J. J. Gittes," Robert Hatch wrote in *The Nation*, "you realize it was inevitable that Nicholson would one day have a shot at the West Coast 1930s genre of adultery, larceny and homicide. . . . He is absurdly foolhardy, cynically idealistic and very lucky." Significantly, though, Hatch added: "Being one of the smartest actors around, Nicholson does not attempt to look, speak, or drink like Bogart."

John Simon drew an even sharper distinction between Gittes and the film noir heroes to whom he bore what Simon saw as only a superficial, even misleading, resemblance: "The hero . . . is played by Jack Nicholson as an emblematic man of today. Unlike the Bogartian hero, he is not coolly sure of himself all the way down the line. . . . Nicholson has never trod with greater assurance the fine line between professional cynicism verging on sleaziness and a still untarnished self-respect and concern for at least the less demanding decencies of life." Jack must have appreciated that comment, for in describing his role, he saw Jake this way: "I depart from previous characterizations. . . . I'm a detective, but a lousy one, who handles divorce cases and screws everything up."

Stanley Kauffmann of *The New Republic* was most impressed that Nicholson was willing to spend half the

This advertisement for *Chinatown* captured the film noir quality of
Hollywood in the 1940s; after too many self-indulgent hippie-era films
like A *Safe Place*, moviegoers were eager for more traditional entertain-
ment genres if only they were given a contemporary angle:
Chinatown may have been set in the past, but seemed to be about
Watergate.

John Huston as the charming but corrupt Noah Cross.

Faye Dunaway is the anguished Evelyn Mulwray.

J. J. and Evelyn move ever closer to the final confrontation.

film's running time with his face largely covered: "Nicholson either has a big bandage on his nose or, later, some stitches showing fuzzily. It's a neat mockery of the way heroes were/are supposed to look." It also served as a reminder of just how willing to take risks Jack was, allowing the usual veneer of star glamour to be so completely cut away; instead of suffering from this, he emerged as a more glamorous figure and greater star for his daring.

The results were great, but the process of getting the picture done was sometimes troubled. Asked if Polanski was difficult to work with, Jack replied: "He's an irritating person whether he's making a movie or not making a movie." A terrible fight erupted on the set one day: hysterical, Jack tore all his clothes off, at which point Polanski threw Jack's TV onto the ground. Each man screamed at the other and furiously left the set. Jack jumped in his car, drove off, halting at a light. On the corner, he spied Polanski standing, grinning at him. The grin was infectious: Jack smiled back, got out of his car, and they stood in the middle of the street for a while, laughing, then returned to the set.

"I was tremendously confident about the material," Jack said of Towne's script, "why I was doing it and what it would mean to me. But I had the feeling there was something that was better that was being lost in the actual creative process." Intriguingly, Nicholson—purportedly less interested in the script than what the director would do with it—worried that Polanski might produce something less powerful than what the writer supplied the potential for. But as soon as he viewed the rough cut of the film, he knew different. "Mogul," he said to producer Robert Evans, "we got that hot one. Get those checks ready—we're on our way!"

Though Jack would not learn of his own familial confusion for several more years, Chinatown hints at the identity crisis he would eventually face. Our hindsight knowledge lends an added poignancy to the scene in which Evelyn desperately tells Jake about the young girl: "She's my sister . . . she's my daughter . . . she's my sister and my daughter." There is the parallel of his onscreen and offscreen relationship with one co-star: "One of the secrets of Chinatown," he would reflect, "is that there was a kind of triangular offstage situation. I had just started going with John Huston's daughter, which . . . actually fed the moment-to-moment reality of my scene with him" ("Are you sleeping with her?" Noah demands of J.J. in the film.) There is an element of the myth of Sisyphus—Jack's favorite archetypal storyline—as J.J. undertakes a great chore, clearly beyond him, but achieves dignity in the walk back down the mountain: the effort, not the effect, is everything.

Scoffing at the more vulgar aspects of commercial moviemaking, Jack has steadfastly refused to do sequels that would merely milk a hit for more money. But J.J. Gittes was a character he would have liked to return to at regular intervals in his career, not in some slapdash Chinatown II, but rather as part of a trilogy dealing, through the fictional character, with the actual history of Southern California. Jack had been the precise age of Gittes when he did Chinatown, and the idea was to set the second story (dealing with the petroleum issue) in 1948, eleven years after Chinatown, actually shooting Two Jakes eleven years after they'd shot Chinatown; the third film would be shot (and take place) seven years after that. Adding to the autobiographical element, the first film takes place the year when Jack was born, the third at the time when Jack and Towne first met. Which explains why Jack and Towne had written into their original contract that the studio could steamroll no immediate follow-up to the film, nor could they turn it into a TV series. Sadly, though, things didn't work out: intricate problems kept Two Jakes from being made on schedule, causing Jack to move on to other available projects. So what might have been one of the most fascinating trilogies in American movie history will, apparently, never reach fruition.

A man from the wrong side of the tracks meets a woman with a touch of class.

NOWHERE MAN:

The Passenger

(1975)
A METRO-GOLDWYN-MAYER FILM

CAST:

Jack Nicholson *(David Locke)*; Maria Schneider *(The Girl)*; Jenny Runacre *(Rachel Locke)*; Ian Hendry *(Martin Knight)*; Stephen Berkoff *(Stephen)*; James Campbell *(Witch Doctor)*; Ambroise Bia *(Achebe)*; Chuck Mulvehill *(David Robertson)*.

CREDITS:

Director, Michelangelo Antonioni; producer, Carlo Ponti; screenplay, Mark Peloe, Peter Wollen, and Michelangelo Antonioni; cinematography, Luciano Tovoli; editors, Franco Arcalli and Michelangelo Antonioni; musical advisor, Ivan Vardor; running time: 119 mins.; rating: R.

Jack chose whenever possible to work with the European directors whose work most inspired him. Among them was Michelangelo Antonioni, whose purposefully dispirited, slow moving approach to storytelling earned him a reputation as the prime purveyor of chic cinematic existential ennui. At least up to the landmark *Blow-Up* (1967), when Antonioni grafted his vision of hollow lives in a post-meaningful world to plots that sounded like the kind of suspense thrillers Alfred Hitchcock would concoct.

The Passenger is just such a film, featuring Jack as TV reporter David Locke, on assignment in Africa where his job is to procure an interview with some elusive guerrillas, men actively challenging the status quo of a trouble-torn country. That may sound like an exciting sidetrip on a fascinating career, but not the way Antonioni presents it. David feels himself stuck in a remote backwater removed from everything of importance (if, indeed, anything at all remains important anymore), feels frustrated and impotent that he has no luck at all in making contact with the people he's supposed to capture on film, even considers himself a passive parasite, forever observing events rather than making things happen. David Locke does not like the person he is.

"He's a real nowhere man," the Beatles sang some years earlier about just such a modern character, and that's precisely what David believes himself to be. The African natives look through him as though he's invisible, and his guides walk away, losing interest in him as well as the project. When David's jeep gets stuck in the desert, he tries to hail down a ghost-like nomad on a

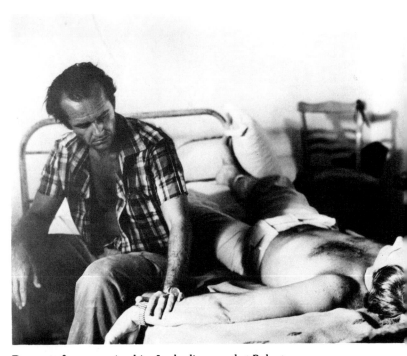

Desperate for companionship, Locke discovers that Robertson has died of a heart attack.

Locke finds himself in the heart of a desert that proves as hostile to him as civilization will, in turn, later prove.

camel but the man does not even acknowledge his existence. David can't help but wonder if the nomad is right: maybe he isn't even there.

At his hotel, David has struck up a friendship with an Englishman named Robertson, there on some undefined business. Returning after a particularly depressing day ("I don't care," Locke earlier screamed at his useless vehicle) and seeking Robertson's company, David is surprised to find the man dead, apparently of a heart attack. We at once notice the two men look strikingly similar, and a flashback reveals they share the first name "David." Even their rooms are identical, further defining their similarity through environment. Impulsively, Locke takes off his shirt and puts on Robertson's, then changes the pictures in their passports. This accomplished, he convinces the hotel manager it is David Locke who has died; taking David Robertson's datebook, plane tickets, and luggage, he then embarks on a new life.

First, though, he heads home to London where, hiding outside his house, David sees his wife (Jenny Runacre) and adopted child adjusting to his "death," telecast on TV. Then he's off to Munich and Spain and places Robertson was supposed to visit. Only David—Locke or Robertson, for it becomes harder and harder to separate the two—discovers his alter ego was anything but what he appeared to be. No simple "businessman," he was a gun-runner, supplying weapons, ironically

161

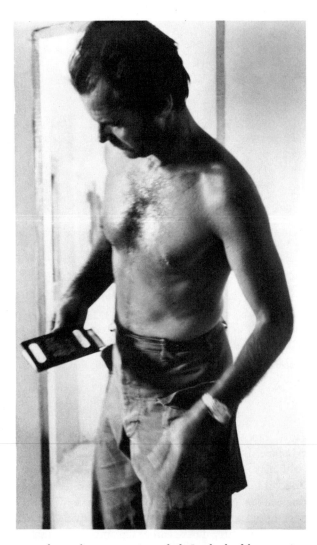

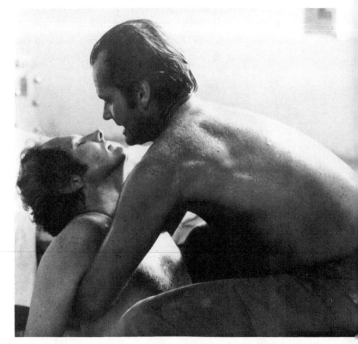

Locke trades identities with Robertson . . .

. . . then moves the man's body into his own room.

enough, to the very native rebels Locke had been trying to interview. That cinches the connection between the two men, while casting Locke in the role he always wanted to play: the man of action.

Locke's wife meanwhile senses something is wrong and sets out to search for Robertson, supposedly the last man to see her husband alive. Locke has in the interim picked up a hippieish architectural student (Maria Schneider, of *Last Tango in Paris* fame), who combines a bohemian lifestyle with an interest in the relationship of people to places essential to all Antonioni films. Also pursuing David are agents of the government under siege by the rebels, who eventually kill him.

When Locke's wife—who has become aware of the altered passports—is asked to identify the body, she merely sighs and says, "I never knew him." The police take this to mean that the man in front of them is Robertson, not her husband; what she in fact means is that she never really knew her husband at all, as his strange, inexplicable (at least for her) recent charade proves.

But what is this: Intriguingly ambiguous or intentionally obscure? Truly important or merely pompous? Profound or pretentious? A serious message-movie with a significant vision of our world, or only an overinflated thriller paying lip-service to trendy themes? Some critics and moviegoers, who had found the earlier Antonioni films as emotionally insufferable as they were aesthetically impressive, welcomed the new direction of his work. Others, who believed the earlier pictures to be pure expressions of a serious artist, felt he was capitulating to broad popular tastes. While the smashing box-office success of *Blow-Up* had swept such critical considerations aside and the devastating failure of *Zabriskie Point* led to that film's curt dismissal, *The Passenger* was caught in a middleground: occasionally panned or praised, it was more often heatedly debated within the context of single reviews.

"*The Passenger* is Antonioni's most beautiful cinematic canvas and certainly one of the most stunning visual voyages ever filmed," Paul D. Zimmerman commented in *Newsweek*, though he then complained: "[An-

162

tonioni's] handling of the film's melodramatic elements is clumsy and obvious," adding that the English language text "ranges from flat to awkward to laughable," and that "Antonioni occasionally uses didactic stretches of dialogue to carry the film's meaning, a device other directors, not fit to carry his camera, know enough to avoid." Jay Cocks of *Time* applauded the use of "eerie and voluptuous imagery to define a condition of spiritual paralysis," but also noted that "[Antonioni] lets go of the thriller elements midway and starts to concentrate on the growing relationship [between Locke and The Girl]," though "the change of focus does not deepen the picture" but instead "diverts it while saying nothing new about Locke."

Stanley Kauffmann, in *The New Republic*, asserted "It is all plot motion on which meaning has been painted," and complained of a narrative "fuzziness," citing one example in particular: "Why does [Nicholson] pass Schneider in a London park before he later accidentally meets her in Barcelona?"

In fact, though, there's an answer to that question: part of the impact of the film is that while the title may refer to Nicholson's character (who is a symbolic passenger on the journey of life, also a passenger on another man's itinerary with fate), it's more likely intended as a reference to The Girl, whose ambiguousness—she lacks even a name—suggests she's the mystery woman all men seek to comprehend but never really know, the passenger who rides along with Nicholson/Locke/Robertson, the love child presumably able to give the kind of support his

Enjoying his new identity, the once up-tight Locke frolics with the seemingly innocent hippie girl (Maria Schneider).

Locke and the girl use Robertson's notebook to plan their "passage": director Antonioni subtly suggests the sexual tension by having Nicholson squeeze a fruit held provocatively close to Schneider's breasts.

more conventional wife never did, but also quite possibly his betrayer.

Indeed, one possible interpretation of the seven-minute, single shot travelling-camera ending (the most celebrated set-piece in the film, and quite rightly so) is that she's set him up. Though their initial meeting is quite possibly a casual one (in which case their initial near meeting was an ironic visual indication to us they will meet when fate is ready for them to), it could also suggest she is in league with those conspiring against him, spying on him for some time, and that his "passenger" is in fact his angel of death.

If one likes one's movies to be wrapped up neatly at the end, Antonioni certainly frustrates that desire, but he has managed to transform the thriller into a vehicle for modernist sensibility while transcending genre limitations by ultimately breaking the rules we at the outset expect him to follow, gradually forcing us to see that the

163

old notions of order don't fit today's suspense film any more than they did life itself in the mid-1970s.

The much-debated finale, more than an example of technical virtuosity, is a visual delineation of theme: seven full minutes without a single edit in which the camera begins in the room where Locke and The Girl have made love, progresses out to the courtyard and searches endlessly for some explanation as to what has happened as each of the major characters in the drama come and go, finishing finally in the room again. At the time, serious movie buffs were fascinated by the seeming impossibility of what they saw: how the devil did Antonioni manage to make his bulky camera pass through the tightly barred window and then back in again? More important, the meaning of the entire movie is contained within that shot: By refusing to edit, and therefore fragment, the action, Antonioni visually tells us life is a continuum—that characters who throughout the tale appeared to have nothing in common are in fact related in ways they perhaps cannot understand—and that, study the surface events as much as we will, we can never quite grasp the entirety of the reason why Locke must die. Casual occurrences may have simply piled up in such a fashion that they have doomed him; a vast conspiracy may have been operating against David. There is no way of knowing who is innocent and who is guilty because the characters themselves are unsure. No matter how many times we watch the film and concentrate on the performance of Maria Schneider, we will never determine absolutely whether Locke's "passenger" was indeed a well-meaning pick-up or the key element in a plot to destroy him. Antonioni is not being murky or obscure; he is sharing with us his vision of modern man's inability to ever comprehend anything completely.

As for Jack's performance, critics tended to have trouble with Locke having been written as an Englishman, then played by an American; in the script, this is quickly explained by a line or two insisting Locke was educated in America. In *America*, Lauder begrudgingly complimented the stars for their work in a film he didn't care for: "Jack Nicholson and Maria Schneider are as good at underplaying their roles as the project allows."

"Is this your husband?" Rachel Locke (Jenny Runacre) studies the body of the man before her.

Cocks acknowledged that while Antonioni "tends to depersonalize actors," Nicholson "manages a certain level of bleak intensity."

In fact, it is that quality of Antonioni's which—considering Jack's usual favoring of directors who put their greatest creative energy into their work with actors—once caused Jack to quip: "Working with Antonioni has its ups and downs." In other contexts, though, he's spoken more enthusiastically: "Working with him is the outside pole of filmic idiosyncracy. Once you've been through a production with Antonioni, no one is going to ever throw you with strange moves again. He's fully in control of what he's doing, but he really does it his own way. We'd probably still be shooting if he wasn't locked in by contracts. I mean, he lay down in front of the plane to keep Richard Harris from leaving *Red Desert*. The guy just kept shooting and shooting and shooting 'cause he loves making movies, and that's why he's great. He drives you crazy. The guy throws two tantrums a week. They tell me I'm the first actor in 25 years he got along with, but that was because I wanted to do an Antonioni movie."

Fans of the film cited Jack's presence as essential to its success. Bea Rothenbuecher wrote: "Nicholson's natural aura of alienation . . . has a universal appeal. He brings a touch of our world to Antonioni's world." Zimmerman claimed: "Nicholson provides a crucial ballast of realism to this calm nightmare vision." Hatch concurred: "Nicholson plays a resourceful man who has exhausted his resourcefulness with the easy eloquence that characterizes his acting. Since the early performances of Brando, no American screen actor has had Nicholson's almost hypnotic gift of being absolutely present. As with Brando, it is almost impossible to take your eyes from him, even when he seems to be doing nothing." Gilliatt added: "Nicholson's performance is a wonder of insight. How to animate a personality that is barely there? He does it by cutting out nearly all the inflections from his voice, by talking very slowly, by making random movements. One particular gesture is oddly expressive and impassioned. A slight flapping of the arms, as if he were trying to fly."

Considering the film from our present perspective, it not only seems a far greater work from the artist Antonioni than critics at the time acknowledged but also one that expresses the star/actor as much as it does the director/co-author. Jack's life has turned out to be a search for his self, an attempt to understand his identity and grasp who he is. Also, while Locke is as different from Bobby Dupea and David Stauber as they are from one another, all three men see themselves as failures in their profession. And while in those earlier films, Jack played out his "double identity" theme by portraying opposites in successive pictures, here he in one film got to portray a man who fulfills that famous statement of his: "I know people who have managed to live out double lives. . . ."

Tommy

(1975)
A COLUMBIA PICTURES RELEASE

CAST:

Ann-Margret *(Nora Walker)*; Roger Daltry *(Tommy)*; Oliver Reed *(Frank Hobbs)*; Elton John *(The Pinball Wizard)*; Keith Moon *(Uncle Ernie)*; Jack Nicholson *(The Doctor)*; Eric Clapton *(Bizarre Character)*; Robert Powell *(Strange Man)*; The Who *(Themselves)*.

CREDITS:

Director, Ken Russell; producers, Ken Russell and Robert Stigwood; screenplay, Ken Russell from the rock opera by The Who; cinematography, Dick Bush and Ronnie Taylor; editor, Stuart Bird; musical direction, Pete Townshend; running time: 111 mins.; rating: R.

It figured that sooner or later Nicholson would work with Ken Russell, whose visually dazzling if thematically incoherent movies struck Jack as intriguing, even exceptional. Russell's was a kind of way out avant-garde sensibility somehow managing to exist within the mainstream moviemaking industry. He had, in particular, always been interested in the creative experience, especially the musical end of it, and his films *(Women in Love, The Music Lovers, Savage Messiah)* were often inspired by serious works of literature, music, or graphic arts, or by the lives of those special people who produced them. But rather than doing straight biographies, he went in for subjective, outrageous, intellectually simplistic and visually surrealistic interpretations, imposing his own manic vision on those pre-existing people or works. More recently, he had demonstrated some interest in popular music, filming that pleasant 1920s homage *The*

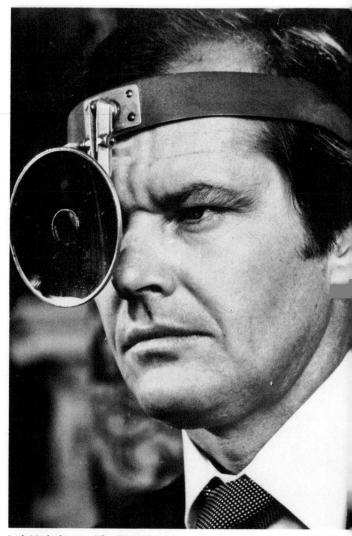

Jack Nicholson as The Doctor.

In their first film together since *Carnal Knowledge*, Jack plays the doctor who attends to Nora Walker (Ann-Margret) at the height of Tommy-mania.

Sonny Boy Williamson. The film version had a technical plus going for it, since the recently developed quintaphonic sound track allowed a mega-audio experience for the young viewers the film was aimed for.

If the technical process was complex, the story it told was simple enough, about a British lad who is struck deaf, dumb, and blind when witnessing the stepfather he holds accountable for the death of his real father (though the man may have died innocently in World War II) making love to his mother. After calling out "See me . . . feel me . . . touch me . . . heal me . . ." endlessly, Tommy in time becomes a celebrity by defeating The Pinball Wizard, then emerges as a new messiah. The film's ostensible theme is that pop culture icons are, in our secular society, usurping the role once played by religious leaders; understandably, then, at one point in the movie, people worship at a statue of Marilyn Monroe as if she were the Virgin Mary.

Whatever one thinks of all this, Russell's connection with the project is dubious. Upon first suggestion that he

Boy Friend in such a way that it appeared as if he hated all the nostalgic tunes and Busby Berkeley style production numbers people expected him to salute.

Yet despite his looking like an aged hippie, Russell knew nothing and cared nothing for rock music. But Robert Stigwood—who'd previously been the driving force behind the filming of one rock opera, *Jesus Christ Superstar*—knew a bad thing when he saw it, and decided a no-holds barred sensibility was necessary if *Tommy* were to be successfully translated to the screen.

A rock opera implies, presumably, a musical play in which rock songs are the means by which the drama is carried; there is no spoken dialogue, any more than there is in a traditional opera. The *Tommy* album was released in 1969, at the height of the rock-youth-counterculture craze, and its success led to live performances by The Who. For the necessarily longer film version, the original numbers were expanded by composer Pete Townshend to include two songs by John Entwistle and one by Keith Moon, both of The Who, along with another by

A great screen team in a less than great vehicle for their substantial talents: Jack Nicholson and Ann-Margret.

167

The magnificent Ann-Margret is forced into vulgar gyrations by director Ken Russell; as one critic put it, "Pry open Ken Russell's brain, and toads would pop out."

Ann-Margret, as the mother of Tommy, with her son (Roger Daltry).

should make the film, his initial reaction after hearing the *Tommy* album was to call it "Rubbish." Later, when he'd been persuaded to sign on as director, he loudly announced that Tommy was "the greatest art work of the twentieth century." Such (extreme) hedging suggests either a fickle mind, an uncertain vision, or absolute dishonesty. Or perhaps a combination of the three. Russell's approach has always been excess for the sake of excess, not only in this film but before *(The Devils)* and after *(Valentino)*. It's as though he naïvely believes that to shock with a gross-out will change for the better the social consciousness of anyone who has the misfortune of viewing one of his films.

Fanatics, with or without cameras, are often mistaken for seers, and a number of critics unaccountably treated the ugly, insipid film with groveling respect. Jay Cocks, in *Time*, called it "weird, crazy, wonderfully excessive," though his single adjective is highly debatable. Cocks insisted Russell was "a film maker who glories in the kind of heightened visual absurdity that *Tommy* both invites and requires," and that he also was "among the boldest of contemporary film makers. He fears nothing, including being bad, and he has often been. He is bad occasionally here, but it does not matter. . . . His unceasing visual

imagination gives the movie an exhilarating boldness, a rush of real excitement."

Of course, bear baiting and cock fighting can give one a rush of real excitement, but that does not mean they are to be admired and respected and treated as legitimate spectator sports. For many viewers, it does matter that Russell is bad here and more than occasionally so. Claiming that he "is not concerned with the usual standards of good taste, except to mock and outrage them" may seem a fitting defense of Russell from up-tight superstraights, but it could also be used to defend someone who flagrantly passes wind in public places. *Tommy* was, likewise, flatulent in its own way.

Cocks attempted to defend the film by suggesting Russell was not so much interpreting Townshend's rock opera as undermining it: "What is best in this movie version is Ken Russell's attempt to comment upon and satirize a culture where a shaky totem like *Tommy* could attract such worshipful respect. . . . Townshend wavered

Roger Daltry as Tommy, a pop-savior crucified by the modern media.

crazily between satire, science fiction and sanctimony, Russell mocks the very seriousness of the piece. . . ." Even such an ardent defender had to admit, though, that "the movie ultimately fails . . . because all of Russell's invention exposes but does not defeat the daffy banality of *Tommy* itself."

But others, in no way taken with anything about the film, had little trouble in coming to terms with it. Ironically noting the lack of dialogue, Penelope Gilliatt wrote in *The New Yorker* that "it doesn't talk, it yells," adding: "*Tommy* does exactly what it pretends to criticize. It seems to be parodying commercials and modishness, but the film itself is a commercial to try to keep alive the modishness of The Who. It seems to be parodying belief in pop stars, but it's actually asking you to believe in The Who and Ken Russell to break box-office records. That's not a criticism of false idols, it's a paroxysmally sincere ad for idolatry." Demolishing what is supposed to be Russell's strong point, she insisted, "It wasn't energy, it was delirium," calling it "deeply unmusical . . . peekaboo for thugs."

In *The New Republic*, Stanley Kauffmann wrote that "Ken Russell seems to be the man for high school students of the '70s. His style is ultra-cinematic in the least demanding way—it can be called the TV commercial in excelsis, all split screens and star bursts and swiftly changing colors and anything else that's handy, all the time. For the adolescent, both young and old, who thinks that filmmaking virtuosity is all of filmmaking, he is ideal."

The movie did at least reunite Jack and Ann-Margret for the first time since *Carnal Knowledge*. That marvelous actress transcends the trashiness of the material, revealing both her considerable beauty and acting/singing gifts as Tommy's mother. Her talent as well as her terrific torso is shown off to great advantage in one scene featuring her in a peekaboo jumpsuit that shrinks as she watches a TV ad for soapsuds and is deluged by them. Jack has little to do as a doctor who cares for her, and his role was small enough that few bothered to comment on it. Cocks mentioned that the film "is acted with appropriate verve by all, including . . . Jack Nicholson playing a physician who represents a bit of high-class lowlife." Michener commented that "Nicholson is slick New Hollywood as a Harley Street physician," whatever that means.

When asked what he thought of his singing in this one, Jack flashed the killer grin and said he felt he sang "better than Oliver Reed." And it's understandable Jack would be impressed by a filmmaker as iconoclastic as Russell, who (if nothing else) certainly doesn't turn out formula films. Jack's casually risking his star-level career to accept a cameo in a film by a director who at least is adventurous enough to be daring ("I thought it might be fun to do a Russell picture," Jack has offered as his explanation for being in *Tommy*) only makes Jack all the more interesting. But his favorite directors—Nichols, Hellman, Rafelson—are those who study human behavior and avoid flashy pyrotechnics; that is, they are the opposite of Ken Russell, whose films are all pyrotechnics and reduce characters to living cartoons.

WHY A CHICKEN?:

The Fortune

(1975)
A COLUMBIA RELEASE

CAST:

Jack Nicholson *(Oscar)*; Warren Beatty *(Nicky)*; Stock-ard Channing *(Freddie)*; Florence Stanley *(Mrs. Gould)*; Richard Shull *(Head Detective)*; Tom Newman *(John the Barber)*.

CREDITS:

Producer, Hank Moonjean; director, Mike Nichols; screenplay, Adrien Joyce (pen name for Carol Eastman); cinematography, John A. Alonzo; editor, Stu Linder; music, David Shire; running time: 88 mins.; rating: R.

Along with Richard Lester (*A Hard Day's Night, Petulia*), Arthur Penn (*Bonnie and Clyde, Little Big Man*) and Stanley Kubrick (*2001: A Space Odyssey, Dr. Strangelove*), Mike Nichols was one of the most rele-vant—in terms of theme and technique—filmmakers of the sixties. But by the early seventies, he—like those others—began to lose his hold on the national con-sciousness, on the direction in which filmmaking was moving, and on the temper of the mass audience that only a short while before had responded so strongly to his directorial sensibility.

If *The Fortune* had been a hit, it might have restored Nichols's reputation and dignity. But it was a lame, slight farce that boasted only one single honest-to-good-ness laugh: Jack's inspired moment when, his frizzy Afro (he looks more like another Nichols alumnus, Art Gar-funkel, than his usual self) practically stretching to the sky in abject fear, he hysterically confesses to a murder that was never committed. Except for that brief moment,

Jack Nicholson as Oscar.

Oscar and Nicky find themselves in trouble with the
law.

Oscar, in a rare happy moment before the world begins to close
in on two losers who mistakenly believe themselves to be winners.

the film is flat, humorless, uninvolving and tasteless, but
never intriguingly so.

The plot concerns one of those buddy-buddy teams
that were, along with natural disasters, so popular
throughout the 1970s—in this case, Jack and Warren
Beatty, two real-life chums who finally got together for a
film. This period piece, set in the mid-1920s, casts
Beatty as Nicky, with greased-back hair and an ultra-thin
mustache, looking like what were in those days referred
to as lounge lizards or local Sheiks, slimy romantic types
who drew their personas from the popular movie stars of
the day. Jack is Oscar, his somewhat dim-witted companion in crime, an innocent on the order of Stan
Laurel. To a degree, the story that unfolds is an attempt
at situation comedy in the original sense of that term,
with all its (intended) comedy based on the premise of
the Mann Act: the illegality, so significant at that time of
America's first sexual revolution, of transporting a
woman over state lines for "immoral purposes."

Early in the picture, Beatty sneaks into the mansion
where a privileged American aristocratic princess (Stock-
ard Channing) lives with her rich father, and makes off
with the delirious girl, who is clearly madly in love with
him. Why such a con artist would court an overweight,
unappealing young woman other than her father's fortune (the unrelentingly awful sensibility of the picture
has her the heiress to an inheritance based on the sale of
sanitary napkins) is the question we can't help asking, so

we assume his displays of lust are all as insincere as his phony demeanor. But when they reach the Justice of the Peace, she marries not Nicky but his pal Oscar. The reason, simply, is that Nicky is already married, and he can't elope with the lady without risking arrest. Nicky, a crooked bank teller who's been caught with his hand in the till, can be blackmailed into making the runaway legal.

The film then turns picaresque, as the trio zips across America by train, Oscar the husband unable to approach his bride, Nicky the "best man" who is in fact her lover.

Buddy-buddy team or the new Odd Couple? Warren Beatty as Nicky, Jack as Oscar.

Once in Hollywood, they set up housekeeping in one of those cottages usually inhabited by future stars waiting to be discovered or has-beens on the skids. Officially, Beatty is (to their neighbors) her brother. By now, though, her "husband" wants to be that in more than name only, and starts wooing his "wife" when his friendly rival is away, going so far as to buy her (of all things) a chicken for a pet. But when the two men start openly fighting over her, the airhead—in a moment of rare perception—realizes each man is only after her money and impulsively decides to give her entire inheritance away. Before she can do that, the men decide they must murder her, patching up their friendship in order to accomplish that deed, and afterwards split the financial rewards. They throw a rattlesnake in to bite her, but the chicken kills it. They dump her in a birdbath and in the ocean, but she survives both.

Up to this point, the film has been tiresome, but here the audience picks up hope; there's a stirring of energy, a suggestion the film is suddenly going to take off and fly, that everything we've seen (suffered through would be a better description) will be worth it as a slow but necessary prelude to a fabulous finale. Instead, in an embarrassingly unbelievable ending, the heiress embraces them both, forgiving them their trespasses against her. At that point, the movie doesn't so much end as just stops.

What begins as situation comedy, then fitfully turns into a screwball picaresque, somehow transforms into a broad bedroom farce and then opts for black humor, ending as sentimental tripe. All of those comedy genres have great potential for fun, and certain rare filmmakers (like Preston Sturges in his classic *Sullivan's Travels*) were indeed talented enough to jump from comic subgenre to subgenre, milking each for all it was worth for a quarter-hour before dumping it and proceeding to the next, then entertaining us in a very different mode for the following fifteen minutes before successfully changing directions once again. But *The Fortune* has none of that film's charm. The only thing one can say for it is that it's consistent in terms of quality (or lack thereof): each subgenre of comedy is handled as poorly as the last and the next; Nichols shows himself to be no better at farce than screwball.

Nichols is unable even to make anything of some fascinating thematic possibilities that present themselves but are never tapped for their potential. Oscar and Nicky, while struggling over the girl, appear to us to be at least a little in love with each other; they nickname her, of all things, "Freddie"; Oscar is only attracted to Freddie when he happens to notice her wearing some of Nicky's clothes. This could have been a film about confusion of sexual identities; it might have worked not merely as another buddy-buddy film, but a comment on those

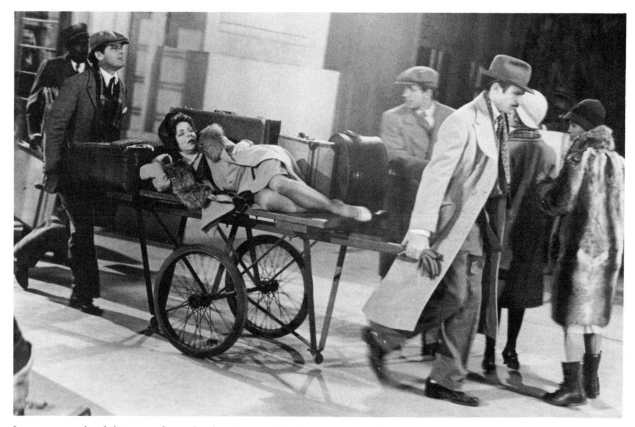

In a sequence that fails to provide any laughs, Oscar and Nicky transport the sleeping Freddie (Stockard Channing) out of a busy building.

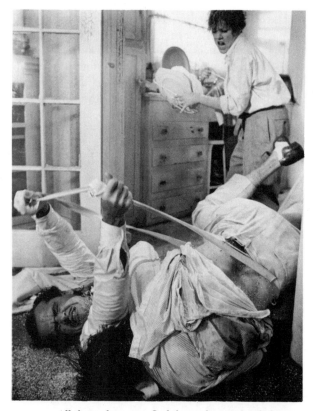

All three characters find themselves embroiled in a messy fight; lots of fury for the characters, not much fun for the audience.

films and the homoerotic elements under the surface in all of them. That would have made it a most intriguing film for Jack, who—when asked by *Playboy* what he experienced during his acid trips of the late sixties—talked not only about castration fears but also the fear that "you're going to come mush-ass to face with your own homosexual fears." But Nichols rushes past all this as if uninterested in it; if only he were clearly interested in something else, that would be fine, but we never do figure just what he's getting at. Was the film supposed to be "about" anything? If so, we never figure out what. Was it intended as merely escapist entertainment? If so, it's failed fluff, for it isn't funny.

Understandably, the critics unanimously trashed the film. In *The New Republic*, Stanley Kauffmann claimed that the screenplay "is simply bad: a complete misconception of the very idea of farce. . . . In farce we laugh at the protagonist's frustrated attempts to do something we want him to succeed at. That's flatly impossible here." As for Nichols's direction, it was, simply, "not very funny. . . . Where were Nichols's wits?" In *The Nation*, Robert Hatch complained that "it is noisy, improbable but not original and messily sexy; the exuberance and surprise of farce are nowhere in sight. . . . *The Fortune* is tasteless: to be more precise, its content is stale and its tone is rancid."

Hatch was one of the few critics who extended his criticism to Jack, complaining that, "Nicholson, for all that he is made to look a little like Stan Laurel, is incapable of sustaining Laurel's innocence; his leer is for real." That's a bit too tough: Jack does about as nice a job at sustaining a charming idiot's affable approach to evil actions as any actor since the estimable Stanley has managed. Cocks had a rough time with the performances, too, insisting that, "Instead of being funny—which requires some degree of seriousness—Nicholson and Beatty act funny." That is, they self-consciously try to be humorous rather than (in what makes for great screen comedy) merely playing the character as believably and honestly as possible, letting the funny situations that the character finds himself in draw laughter from the audience.

In fact, though, most critics took time out, in their unhappy reviews, to pat Jack on the back, finding his work the best thing in a bad lot. While Zimmerman offered nothing more than to point out Nicholson's "frizzy hair and sneaky clown's face," Kauffmann went much further. Despite his despairing review of the film itself, he wrote that "Nicholson's strengths, as he has shown them so far in his career, lie in a wide range of the American rural . . . experienced and hardbitten but something of a victim and a dupe. Now he is back in the

Easy Rider vein, amplified to the farcical . . . Nicholson fixes the quality with charm." Praise Jack himself would not approve of, for it's one more attempt to delineate a clear-cut characteristic running through his work, when what he desires is to do the most diverse parts possible. One can imagine him shrugging at the impossibility of ever convincing anyone there's no single Jack Nicholson persona when a critic can see George Hanson from *Easy Rider* and Nicky from *The Fortune* as essentially the same character!

Perhaps Jack was attracted to *The Fortune* because of the chance to team with Beatty, or maybe the lure of a twenties period piece (when *The Great Gatsby* had just recently eluded him) had something to do with it. When *Viva* asked him why he signed on for *The Fortune*, he unhesitantly answered: "I like working with Mike Nichols. . . . He's really good for actors, because his attention is on them—as opposed to some other facet of filmmaking. He goes for the performances and you get a feeling that you're being well watched over. That's what's best when you're acting—relaxation, freedom." And part of the appeal must have been getting to do a zany character, something entirely different from anything he'd done since *Little Shop of Horrors*, and a real departure from his other work in the mid-seventies; asked how he chooses to do a part, he insisted the key was: "How interesting is my character and is it something I haven't already done?"

Oscar begins to develop lascivious ideas about his best friend's girl. Mike Nichols appears to be redeveloping his *Carnal Knowledge* theme, only this time with Jack Nicholson in the Art Garfunkel role.

175

One Flew Over The Cuckoo's Nest

(1975)
A UNITED ARTISTS RELEASE

CAST:

Jack Nicholson *(Randall Patrick McMurphy)*; Louise Fletcher *(Nurse Ratched)*; William Redfield *(Dale Harding)*; Will Sampson *(Chief Bromden)*; Brad Dourif *(Billy Bibbit)*; Marya Small *(Candy)*; Louisa Moritz *(Second Hooker)*; Sydney Lassick *(Cheswick)*; Scatman Crothers *(Mr. Turkle)*; Danny DeVito *(Inmate)*; Dr. Dean Brooks *(Dr. Spivey)*.

CREDITS:

Director, Milos Forman; producers, Saul Zaentz and Michael Douglas; screenplay, Lawrence Hauben and Bo Goldman from the novel by Ken Kesey; cinematography, Bill Butler and William Fraker; editors, Lynzee Klingman and Sheldon Kahn; music, Jack Nitzsche; running time: 129 mins.; rating: R.

Few films have had as long or troubled a journey from conception to release as this, which ranks along with *Gone With the Wind, Jaws,* and *The Godfather* as a classic case of a popular novel being turned into a film no one believed could possibly succeed. Yet somehow, some way, everything turned out right in the end. *Cuckoo's Nest* swept the Oscars the spring following its release, becoming the first film to take all the major awards since *It Happened One Night* some forty years earlier.

That, of course, had been during the studio days,

whereas this independently produced feature from Fantasy Films was the brainchild of Saul Zaentz (who would later turn out the equally admirable *Amadeus*, also directed by Czech Milos Forman) and Michael Douglas, son of superstar Kirk Douglas and soon to emerge as a major producer/star on his own, one of the rare examples of second-generation Hollywood equalling his impressive parent in prestige, power, and performance. Michael had inherited the *Cuckoo's Nest* property from his father when, after leaving the popular TV police series *Streets of San Francisco*, the younger Douglas expressed interest in moving into the development and production aspects of motion pictures. Kirk had tried, unsuccessfully, to get a film production of *Cuckoo's Nest* off the ground since 1962, when he'd first optioned the Ken Kesey novel and appeared in a Broadway version.

But certain elements in society had changed drastically during the preceding decade, making an exact filming of the book a questionable undertaking. Kesey's novel concerned a rebellious man named McMurphy who wreaks havoc in the asylum for the mentally ill in which he's interred, specifically focusing on his conflict with The Big Nurse who has assumed control of the place from the higher-ranking doctors. The McMurphy of the book is very much a Kirk Douglas character: a broad-shouldered, brawling redheaded cowboy/lumberjack/biker, clearly a mythic incarnation of all the American legendary larger-than-life symbols of personal freedom; The Big Nurse is a grotesque caricature, a creature with Jayne Mansfield's bustline and Joan Crawford's cold killer smile. She represents a misogynist's nightmare vision of the female as castrator.

That theme may have gone unchallenged in 1962, but by 1975, the Women's Movement had replaced civil rights and Vietnam as the key social issue of the time.

Hoping to get away from the hard work details at the prison farm, McMurphy willingly allows himself to be incarcerated in the state mental institution . . .

. . . where he must try and convince the nurses that he's insane.

177

McMurphy's card-shark antics quickly prove him to be anything but crazy.

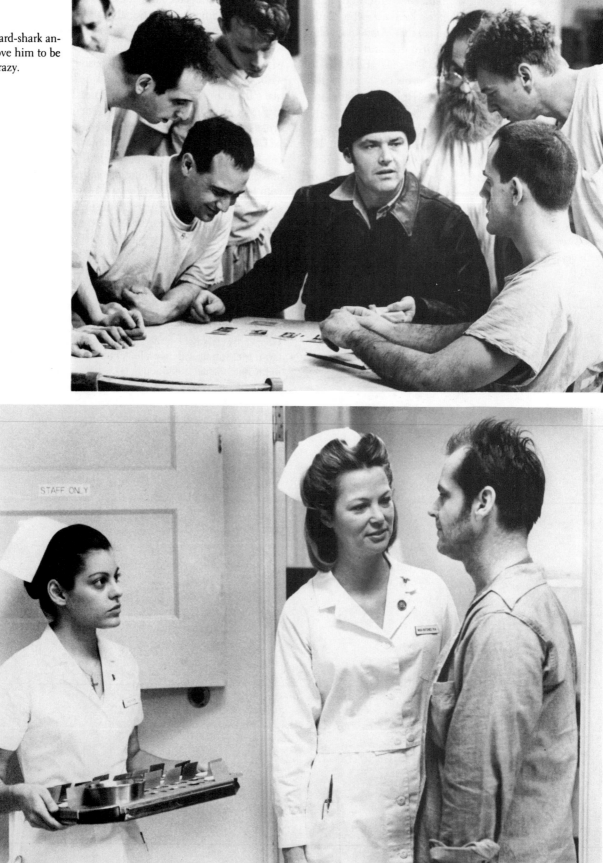

Nurse Ratched (Louise Fletcher) and McMurphy immediately find themselves in sharp conflict.

Being good liberals, Douglas and Zaentz didn't want to make a film that would offend a cause they in fact admired; at the same time, they wanted to bring this powerful story to the screen. How to resolve the situation? They realized there would be big problems when such stars as Anne Bancroft, Faye Dunaway, Jane Fonda, and Ellen Burstyn all passed on the role of the nurse, recalling that the celebrated book had recently acquired a reputation for being "sexist." At the same time, Douglas and Zaentz realized that their hero, McMurphy, was as written no longer relevant. Cowboys had all but disappeared from our popular art, TV and the movies; people had, in the cynical seventies, turned their backs on the western loner as our national hero.

And there was a third major problem: Kesey had written *Cuckoo's Nest* based on his actual experiences as an asylum guard in the early sixties, but while under the influence of certain mind-expanding drugs he'd taken while a creative writing student. The book, told from the point of view of an Indian inmate, perceived the events in surrealistic terms: characters changed shape and form, time stood still, the walls sprouted monstrous arms which tried to grab inmates walking by. There had been an attempt, in the Broadway play by Dale Wasserman, to

hint at this by featuring an expressionistic set design and having Chief Bromden (believed deaf and dumb by the hospital staff, though in fact faking both those handicaps) continually slip upstage, confiding to the audience in asides. But anyone who knows anything about films understands how difficult it is to make such effects work in a commercial Hollywood picture.

For less ambitious people, these seemingly unsurmountable problems may have been incentives to scrap the project. Instead, Douglas and Zaentz (along with screenwriters Lawrence Hauben and Bo Goldman) rethought the piece, reconsidered its elements, and came up with a script that restructured *Cuckoo's Nest* for a contemporary audience. They eliminated the battle-of-the-sexes theme by altering the controversial characterization of Big Nurse so completely that her nickname never once appears. Their Nurse Ratched is a softened (rather than overtly menacing) person, who could have been played as either a male or female nurse since there is no mention of gender here. (In fact, a number of the name actresses who turned thumbs down later commented that there was nothing offensive about the portrayal of the nurse in the film version, and felt they'd missed out on an Oscar-winning role). The book is

Charlie Cheswick (Sydney Lassick) proves to be a McMurphy supporter on the issue of whether the men will watch the World Series or the afternoon soap operas.

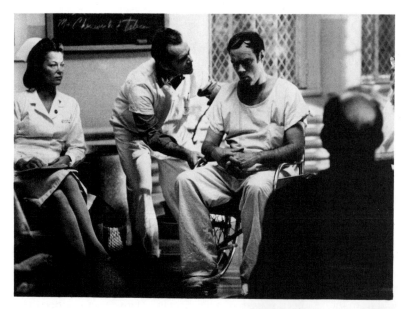

In open defiance of Nurse Ratched, Mc-Murphy attempts to convince the other inmates to assert themselves.

McMurphy pretends to be enjoying the World Series, even though the Nurse refuses to turn on the TV; his excitement proves infectious, as the other inmates join in the antics.

McMurphy sprays the other men to calm them down when tempers run high.

about the conflict between a man and a woman, and their battle comes to symbolize the greater battle of the sexes; the movie is about the conflict between two strong-willed people who just happen to be a man and a woman, and their conflict has nothing to do with men and women at all.

What the filmmakers instead concentrated on was the other thread running through the novel: the vision of McMurphy as a symbol of freedom and the nurse as a representation of institutional attitudes. They likewise eliminated the narrator's voice and the surrealist style it necessitated, reducing The Chief to one more character in the drama, thereby freeing themselves to do the film in a near-documentary fashion. The movie was shot not on a Hollywood set's reconstruction of a mental hospital

McMurphy teaches the Chief (Will Sampson) how to play basketball.

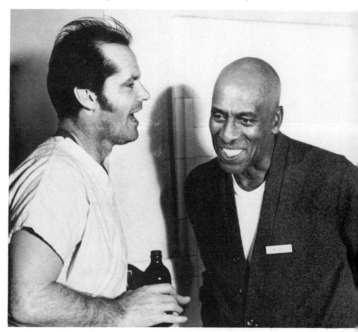

McMurphy fights one particularly brutal black guard . . .

. . . but befriends a gentle one (Scatman Crothers).

but at Oregon's state hospital at Salem; except for the central characters played by the top-billed stars, the inmates, guards, and physicians seen in the background are real, including hospital superintendent Dr. Dean Brooks as Kesey's muddled if well-intentioned Dr. Spivey.

The ultimate choice, though, had to do with picking the actor who would play McMurphy. The image of him strolling with heroic nonchalance into confrontations with the authorities like a cowboy heading for a *High Noon* gun duel would have had audiences on their feet and cheering back in the early sixties, but by the mid-seventies would have seemed silly. So all McMurphy's western style brag-talk was eliminated, along with his cowboy boots and a biker's cap that made him appear a second cousin to Marlon Brando's "Johnny" from *The Wild One.* Instead, he was transformed into a 1970s street person. "Nicholson is far more appropriate for today [than Kirk Douglas]," co-star William Redfield observed. "He's a four-letter-word star."

And that he was: the film rightly earned him his first Oscar and proved a solid hit at the box office, reestablishing Jack at mid-decade as the reigning representative male star of his time. So it's disorienting to realize that at the time of release, most national reviews were negative.

In *Time,* Richard Schickel saw the film as "faithful to the external events of the novel—no complaint there." (In fact, it drastically changes and reorders those events). "The trouble is that it betrays no awareness that the events are subject to multiple interpretations. . . . The fault for this lies in a script that would rather ingratiate than abrade, in direction that is content to realize, in documentary fashion, the ugly surfaces of asylum life." To a degree, the complaint is legitimate; the movie does indeed take a single theme from the far more complex book, concentrating exclusively on it. Whereas the McMurphy in the novel could be interpreted (for starters) as an individual against the Establishment, a Christ figure attempting to create disciples for a radical approach to life, or the American male standing up against dominating women, the McMurphy in the film is only the first of these things. Yet the ambiguity that made the book so rich rarely plays within the context of a movie, oftentimes causing a film that attempts such an approach to appear ambiguous and unfocused. Besides, the approximately two-hour running time for a commercial film allows for considerably less levels of meaning than a book that may require twenty hours to carefully read and completely absorb.

Still, most national critics shared Schickel's approach. In *Newsweek,* Jack Kroll admitted Forman and company had "simplified" Kesey's book "with clarity and shape," but lamented that, "What's lost is the powerful feeling at

The sheet of glass separating the Nurse from McMurphy comes to represent the coldness of feelings between them.

the center, the terror and the terrifying laughter. . . . By opting for a style of comic realism, Forman loses much of the nightmare quality that made the book a capsized allegory of an increasingly mad reality." Judith Crist, in *Saturday Review*, acknowledged the movie's impact while sharing such reservations: [This] "is one of those films that are better in the watching than in the retrospect. It is a finely made film, perhaps the most honest to date to deal with a mental hospital. . . . But its subsurface rewards are minimal, its insights as naïve as its thesis is obvious." In *The Nation*, Robert Hatch commented that, "Forman's superb dance of fools . . . leads to nothing beyond its immediate and entirely justifiable goal of superior crowd pleaser. It's impossible not to whoop it up for *Cuckoo's Nest* while watching, but afterwards, what is one to think?" In *The New Republic*, Stanley Kauffmann went even further: "The film as a whole is warped, sentimental, possibly dangerous."

Intriguingly enough, Pauline Kael of *The New Yorker*—usually the first to seize upon such simplification as justification for demolishing a film—rushed to the defense, calling *Cuckoo's Nest* "a powerful, smashingly effective movie—one that will probably stir audiences' emotions and join the ranks of such pop-mythology films as *The Wild One*, *Rebel Without a Cause*, and *Easy Rider*." Noting that the film seemed more natural, less carefully schematized than the book, she wrote that "even when there are clashes between Kesey's archetypes and Forman's efforts at realism there's still an emotional charge built into the material. It's not as programmed a mythic trip, yet . . . this movie achieves Kesey's mythic goal."

Kael also noted that much of the film's impact derived directly from Jack's remarkable performance: "Nicholson is no flower-child nice guy," she asserted, "he's got that half smile—the calculated insult that alerts audiences to how close to the surface his hostility is. He's the people's freak of the new stars. His speciality is divided characters. . . . Nicholson shows the romanticism inside the street shrewdness."

Even those critics who thought less of the film than Kael did were quick to point out the power of Nicholson's work in it. Kroll wrote that, "McMurphy is the ultimate Nicholson performance—the last angry crazy profane wise-guy rebel, blowing himself up in the shrapnel of his own liberating laughter." In the middle of her string of criticisms, Crist paused long enough to acknowledge that this "may well be the vehicle to win Jack Nicholson his long-deserved Oscar. . . . Nicholson's persona is irresistible, the machismo tempered by a kindliness, the worldliness by a lower-class simplicity." Even Kauffmann admitted "Nicholson is tremendous . . . in that blue-wool hat and those lounge-lizard sideburns, his eyes smiling; withdrawing; threatening."

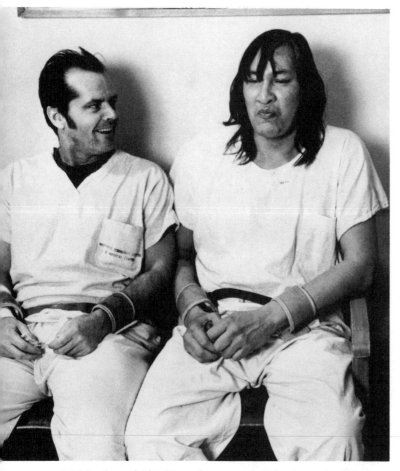

McMurphy and Chief Bromden are readied for electro-shock therapy.

Only Schickel, among the key critics, abstained from praising at least the performance. "Jack Nicholson plays McMurphy," he wrote, "as an unambiguously charming figure, a victim of high spirits, perhaps, but without a dark side or even any gray shadings." In fact, the McMurphy of the film is far darker than the agreeable cowboy we met in the book. Kesey's McMurphy was clearly a wonderful, if rough-hewn, hero; there was no room to doubt he was the good guy, or that the snivelling, castrating, uptight, sexually terrified woman he opposed stood as a figure to be ridiculed and, in the end, raped.

In this sense the movie is, despite the catcalls of many critics, in fact more complex than the novel. Though the producers attempted to eliminate the sexual nature of the McMurphy/Ratched conflict, Jack personally felt that it was still there, only in a manner that was less glorifying to the male, less detrimental to women: "It's not in the book," he reflected for the *Times* in 1986, "[but] my secret design for it was that this guy's a scamp who knows he's irresistible to women and expects Nurse Ratched to be seduced by him. This is his tragic flaw. This is why he ultimately fails. I discussed this only with Louise, that's what I felt was actually happening—it was one long, unsuccessful seduction which the guy was so pathologically sure of."

In other respects, the movie offers the darker vision: We're never quite sure if this soiled, often unsympathetic McMurphy is as fundamentally decent as he likes to tell the other men on the ward he is, or if the nurse—sweet, quiet, seemingly sympathetic—may emerge, at the end,

McMurphy sneaks a prostitute onto the asylum dorm after the Nurse has left for the night.

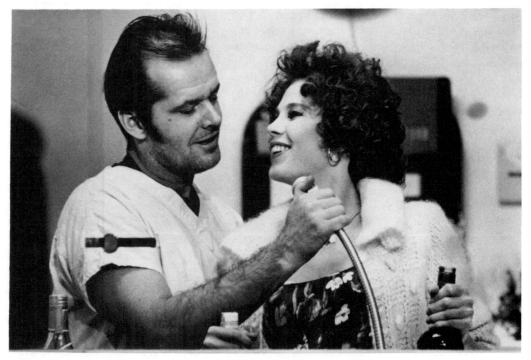

as a decent and misunderstood person. She is not anything of the sort, we finally realize, when she shows her true colors by making Billy (Brad Dourif), the virginal and impressionable self-committed inmate, so guilty about having experienced and enjoyed sex with a prostitute that he takes his own life. Even the ending is darker: The book concluded with McMurphy's lobotomy (at the hands of the nurse, who manipulates the operation to destroy his vitality) and death (at the hands of his friend Bromden, who engages in an act of mercy killing), which sparks the remaining self-committed inmates to go out into the world, where they will try to make it on their own. In the film, Harding and the others are still incarcerated in the hospital after all this has transpired, suggesting McMurphy's sacrifice may have achieved little.

Jack's personal attraction to the vision of Zaentz and Douglas can be seen in this comment: "It's traditional that an American literary personage be in conflict with the authority of some kind or another, and that that conflict is noble. This is what's indigenously interesting about American work. This is traditional literature for America." Perhaps surprisingly, Jack was not specifically referring to *Cuckoo's Nest* when he offered that remark, but it clearly reveals his affinity for the material. Also relating McMurphy to the canon of Nicholson's films is Kael's comment about the two distinct sides of McMurphy's personality: he is, in that respect, yet another of Jack's varied characters tied by the common thread of establishing double identities. Intriguingly, then, Jack revealed to Helen Dudar that he almost passed on the project: "The starting problem with *Cuckoo* was that everybody thought I was born to play the part, and in my mind it was going to be very difficult for me. I felt, 'They already think I'm supposed to be great in this, and I'm not sure.' Really, that was almost the main motivation

The morning after the orgy, the Nurse discovers Billy has spent the night with a whore.

185

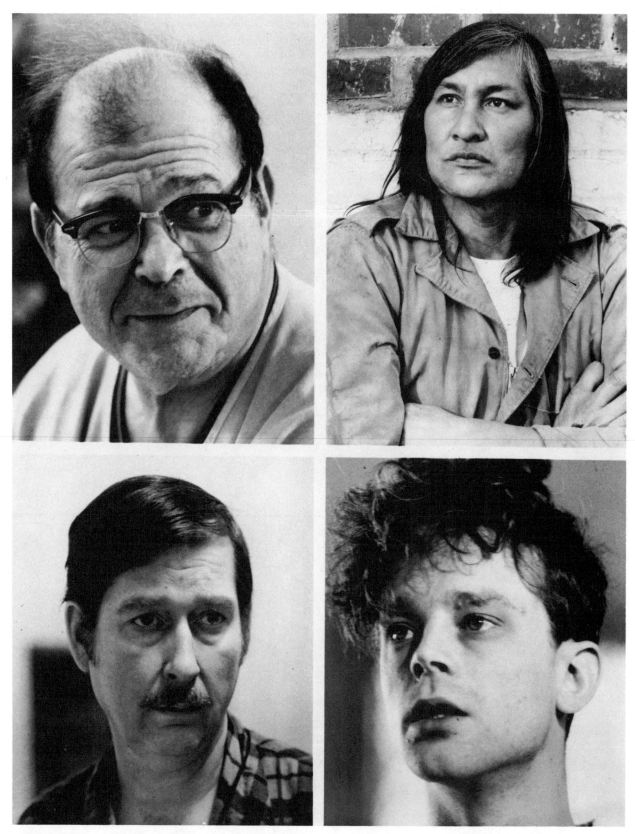

McMurphy's disciples and his Judas: clockwise, from top left, insecure pal Charlie Cheswick (Sydney Lassick); silent but dignified Chief Bromden (Will Sampson); pathetic boychild Billy Bibbit (Brad Dourif); and the ineffectual intellectual Dale Harding (William Redfield).

for doing the part. . . . I wanted to allay it, to put it aside."

While shooting the film, he described his view of the character to interviewer Bob Lardine, making clear he saw McMurphy less as a rebel-hero than as a fascinating case study of a death-wish psychotic: "The character I play feigns insanity, and he must be seen through by the audience. Yet this character has a definite mental disorder himself. He behaves in such an anti-social manner that he eventually forces them to kill him."

Jack researched the role by showing up at Oregon State Mental Hospital in Salem two weeks before he was required, where he persuaded hospital authorities to let him mingle with the most disturbed patients, eating in their mess halls and closely observing their speech patterns and body movements. He even watched patients undergoing the same shock treatments McMurphy would be subjected to in the film, in order to make his depiction more authentic. "Usually, I don't have much trouble slipping out of a film role," he admitted, "but here, I don't go home from a movie studio. I go home from a mental institution. And it becomes harder to create a separation between reality and make-believe." That intense association with the character is evident in the remarkable work onscreen. "He is absolutely McMurphy," Milos Forman commented. "Based on this picture, Nicholson is unique among actors in the world today. Nicholson does not exist when he steps before the camera." But Jack modestly credited this actor-oriented director with much of the character's convincing quality: "Milos's angle, which I agreed with, is that the film had to be more real, the behavior less theatrical," than his previous performances.

He understood, though, the controversy their interpretation would provoke among fans of the novel. While making the movie, Nicholson tersely admitted: "Kesey probably won't like the film."

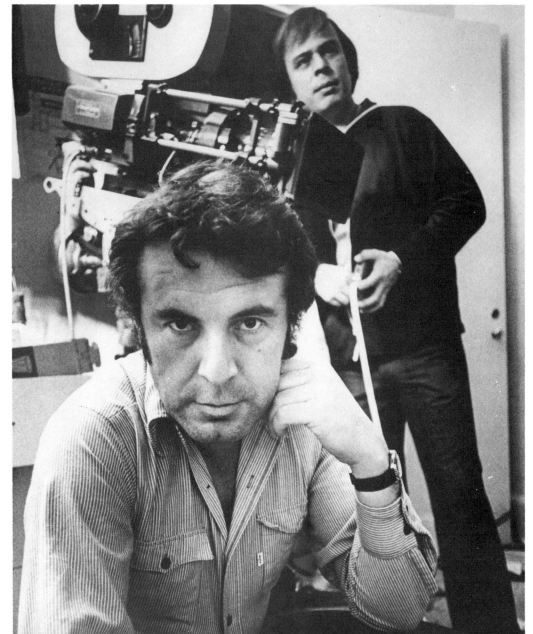

Director Milos Forman.

187

THE GUY ON THE HILL:

The Missouri Breaks

(1976)
A UNITED ARTISTS RELEASE

CAST:

Marlon Brando *(Robert E. Lee Clayton)*; Jack Nicholson *(Tom Logan)*; Randy Quaid *(Little Tod)*; Kathleen Lloyd *(Jane Braxton)*; Frederick Forrest *(Cary)*; Harry Dean Stanton *(Calvin)*; John McLiam *(David Braxton)*

CREDITS:

Director, Arthur Penn; producer, Robert M. Sherman; screenplay, Thomas McGuane; cinematography, Michael Butler; editors, Jerry Greenberg, Stephen Rotter, and Dede Allen; music, John Williams: running time: 126 mins.; rating: PG.

"The western," Jack has said, "is the closest thing to class theater that America has." Considering that remark, it's surprising Jack had not appeared in one since his pair of arty experiments in the late sixties. For appearing in *The Missouri Breaks*, Jack was paid a cool million. No matter that he received second billing, or that Marlon Brando—onscreen for less than half the time—received top billing and a million and a half. Jack had, like most actors of his era, revered Brando as the most significant screen personage to emerge during the postwar era, and being in the same picture with him would in itself be a thrill. Jack had, for some time, been a neighbor of Brando's, often referring to him in conversation with friends in almost awesome terms as "the guy on the hill."

So when Arthur Penn—the much admired "New American Cinema" director of *Bonnie and Clyde* and

Little Big Man—agreed to direct a kinky, controversial, unconventional western to be written by the acclaimed cult novelist Thomas McGuane, how could Jack resist signing on? Once, Jack claimed: "When I read a script, the only standard I use as to whether I do it or not is: 'Would I pay money to go into a theater to see it?' " A fine standard, to be sure, but one he apparently did not apply in this case; it wasn't the strength of the script but the lures of Penn, a director he admired, and Brando, an actor he idolized. Indeed, one of the reasons he had passed on *The Godfather* was, in his own words, "I figured sooner or later Brando and I would do a film together, and I didn't want to blow it on one in which we'd have almost no scenes together." That dream had finally come true, and Nicholson has charmingly admitted: "I was up very early in the morning [the first day] I worked with Marlon Brando. It was like a [giddy teenag-

Logan and a cohort are ambushed by the rancher's hired gun.

er's] first trip to New York." (Afterwards, he would admit to being irritated at learning the great Brando relied on cue cards, when Jack showed up every day fully prepared.) So he found himself in a film he might otherwise not have agreed to do, one that drastically divided audiences and critics; *The Missouri Breaks* landed on almost as many critics' Ten Worst lists as it did Ten Best.

The dramatic situation is the stereotypical range war that's permeated western literature since *The Virginian*. Being a Watergate-era western in sensibility if not time frame, *The Missouri Breaks* presents us with a God-abandoned universe that is as crazed and unyielding as the stretch of land where the Missouri River breaks over rough, uninhabitable hills in Montana. Here, the good guys act like bad guys and the bad guys like good guys, until it becomes impossible to tell them apart, difficult to determine where our sympathies are supposed to rest.

But if the basic story is familiar, the presentation is anything but. The drama concerns a big-time rancher named Braxton (John McLiam) who grows tired of rustlers cutting away 7 percent of his annual profit and hires a "regulator" named Robert Clayton to come in and rid the area of such elements. But Clayton (Brando) is more than anyone bargained for. An eccentric, grotesque character wearing strange costumes (at one point, he inexplicably dresses up like a little old lady), he carries weird weapons (including a vicious-looking hand-thrown device with which Clayton can bring down rabbits for his dinner and men he's assigned to eliminate), and speaks in ever-changing accents. In comparison, the head rustler, Tom Logan (Nicholson), seems an absolute gentleman: relatively well-mannered and rather harmless, at least until Clayton kills off all his best friends. At that point, Tom uses a razor to slit the throat of his sleeping enemy, then rides off into the sunset with the daughter (Kathleen Lloyd) of the very man who hired Clayton.

Everything about the film radiates its mid-1970s mindset. Jane Braxton is a post-Women's Lib revisionist portrait of a frontier woman, assuming the initiative in her forbidden affair with Logan, casually flaunting convention by refusing to remain a part of The Establishment represented by her father and his corrupted combination of great wealth and great culture (he owns more horses, and more books, than any one else in the territory). The outlaw hideout is reminiscent of the hippie commune in Penn's earlier *Alice's Restaurant*, with its lovably scruffy misfits who strike us as being far more appealing than the stiff, straightlaced people inhabiting nearby mainstream society. Heroes and villains are no longer easily identifiable; the capitalists who economically won the west are here portrayed as unsparingly as were the bloodthirsty cavalry in Penn's *Little Big Man*.

They are westerns that would not be made during the Reagan years, when America turned its back on such depressingly shadowy visions, opting instead for a return to reassuring simplistics in film as well as politics.

The vision of life imparted by *The Missouri Breaks* is out of touch with that of most moviegoers of today. The relevant question is, was it a good film of its time? But that's not so easy to answer. Many critics found it a twin tour-de-force for its stars, allowing them to dance about like sparring partners, doing so in a ring that proved unsubstantial to hold the heavyweight opponents it contained.

In *Time*, Richard Schickel noted Jack was "the man regarded as Brando's likely successor as the best and most powerful actor in films," and that in contrast to Brando's bout of "excess," Jack played his part in this bizarre balancing act with "restraint," creating a convincing portrayal of "a man moving almost unconsciously from raunchiness to respectability." In the end, though, Schickel declared Brando the winner: "The crazy daring, the reckless bravado of his work simply overpowers everything else on the screen. . . ."

Brando himself, by the way, admitted he'd only taken on the project because he needed money to finance a vacation resort in the South Seas (the place went bust after one season) and because he felt he might twist the film into a political statement about the oppression of native Americans (there is little evidence onscreen that

Logan runs horses across the breaks . . .

. . . and, Jesse James style, robs a train . . .

190

he managed anything of the sort); when asked by a *Time* reporter about working with Nicholson, Brando insensitively claimed that in his mind, Robert De Niro was actually the brightest star among the young up and coming actors. "Poor Jack Nicholson," Brando said of the difficult position Jack allowed himself to be placed in, carrying the bulk of the screen's running time but necessarily doing so in a low-key manner conceding Brando, however briefly glimpsed, the big impression. "He's right at the center, cranking the whole thing out while I'm zipping around like a firefly."

Jack Kroll of *Newsweek* saw the outcome of the acting duel as more of a draw, also offering praise for the picture containing it: "Brando vs. Nicholson—obviously a great shoot-out, dominating any film and any director. . . . Brando has become a symbol of lost innocence; Nicholson radiates a new kind of beleaguered innocence, grinning hedonistically amid the moral confusion of our time . . . they face off against one another, not only as characters but as magic icons of our lives." Noting the vividness with which the rough countryside was portrayed, the offbeat approaches to western movie clichés, and former theatrical director Penn's inspired work with supporting actors, Kroll concluded that the filmmakers made "an intelligent, entertaining Western, nicely balanced between the protagonists and the well-woven, colorful tapestry in which they're placed."

. . . but finds himself seriously wounded.

191

In *The Nation*, Robert Hatch took a similar opening approach to that of Kroll: "Brando and Nicholson on the same screen! It must have struck the publicity minds at United Artists as the coup of the decade. Pit the old bear against the young fox and the citizens will storm the arena crying for blood." But he exhibited no such appreciation for the film itself, continuing: "In their infatuation with this idea, however, the proprietors neglected to supply any reason other than box-office glamour." Referring to the material as "thin," he scoffed at Brando's absurdist play-acting ("Old Father Marlon does everything but balance eels on his nose to make the occasion lively") and also panned Jack's more serious portrayal of his character: "In this company of loons, Nicholson's Logan is restfully sane, but for the same reason rather unexciting."

Critic Alan Lelchuk insisted that "Nicholson as the horse thief is thoroughly miscast"; William S. Pechter claimed, "Nicholson is fine, but he is stuck in the somewhat blandly written starring role of hero . . ."; Stanley Kauffmann insisted, "Nicholson, bearded, manages at least to flex his fairly featureless role to his persona," though Jack himself would certainly consider that intended compliment an unintentional insult, since he's attempted throughout his career to avoid any such set persona.

Much criticism of this movie has centered around the script, and it's worth noting that in interviews granted afterwards, Jack himself viewed this as a basic problem: "The storyline wasn't tied together enough," he said, "so inside the individual episodes you lose the progression because the episodes are too protracted." Simply, the movie is a succession of intriguing scenes, in which two remarkable actors either work together or singly and in contrast to one another, guided by a gifted director; but those scenes, however powerful (even stunning) to watch in isolation, do not ultimately add up to anything but a movie that, at its center, is hollow. If one agrees this is the film's flaw, then it can be traced directly to the writing style of Thomas McGuane, known also for *Rancho DeLuxe* (essentially, the very same story of charming outlaws and despicable capitalists re-set in the contemporary west). Penelope Gilliatt of *The New Yorker* complained about his "joltingly smart-aleck" attitude, finding both *Rancho Deluxe* and *Missouri Breaks* to suffer from "varying tone, mixing genuinely felt expression and flippant epigrams rank with the odor of cool . . . the plot lines become muddied, and the actors seem to

be decking out an otherwise characterless Western. . . ."

In *America*, Tom Allen complained: "*The Missouri Breaks* is a mess. And not just a small mess, but a large-scale, plushly upholstered, repellently violent mess that is crammed with more disoriented, high-cost talent and made with more virtuoso film technique than will probably be assembled for any other American film this year." Kauffmann viewed McGuane's point of view as "the latter-day pretentiousness and patronization" of a novelist "who has come to films to show those movie boobs how to 'class up' things. All he lacks is the ability; all he does is make us long for some competent old screenwriting craftsman."

Love the film or hate it, Jack at least got to work with both Brando and Penn, and escaped with no permanent damage to his reputation. When things were not going right on location, the actor who once had trouble paying the rent threw up his hands in mock dismay and, a self-conscious caricature of a good working man, sighed: "Another day, another 20,000 dollars!"

Yet witnesses insist he always gave the film his all, as when he and old pal Harry Dean Stanton sat up all night discussing the possible motivations (not even hinted at in the script) for their characters becoming rustlers in the first place: "Who are we as a gang?" Jack's diligence impressed Penn: "Jack is the hardest working actor I've ever known," he claimed, "and I've never seen anyone with more of a responsibility to fellow performers."

Jack was able to tap his personal interests, thereby adding the element of autobiography he claims is inherent in all his work. The difficult relationship of an outlaw in love with a daughter of the Establishment bears a certain parallel to the notion of outlaw-actor Nicholson, who began as a part of Hollywood's Underground, involved with Anjelica Huston, daughter of one of the great established directors. A number of the gang members are played by people like Stanton, who were in fact part of Jack's crowd before he became a member of the Establishment, as his character here seemingly does at the end. Most of the characters lead double existences, including Jack's, half-time settler and half-time rustler. And as for the film's politics, they may have fallen from popular favor, but they are as basic to Jack's attitudes today as they were when he was Hollywood's first hippie in the mid-sixties: the scruffy redneck-hippie outlaws seem far preferable, in their life-loving camaraderie, to the cool, elegantly empty lords of the corporate state.

The outlaws: clockwise, from top left, Cary (Frederic Forrest),
Si (John Ryan), Calvin (Harry Dean Stanton), Little Tod
(Randy Quaid), and Tom Logan (Jack).

GETTING EVEN:

The Last Tycoon

(1976)
A PARAMOUNT PICTURE

CAST:

Robert De Niro *(Monroe Stahr)*; Ingrid Boulting *(Kathleen Moore)*; Robert Mitchum *(Pat Brady)*; Jeanne Moreau *(Didi)*; Jack Nicholson *(Brimmer)*; Tony Curtis *(Rodriguez)*; Donald Pleasance *(Boxley)*; Ray Milland *(Fleischacher)*; Dana Andrews *(Red Riding Hood)*; Theresa Russell *(Cecilia Brady)*; Leslie Curtis *(Mrs. Rodriguez)*.

CREDITS:

Director, Elia Kazan; producer, Sam Spiegel; screenplay, Harold Pinter from the novel by F. Scott Fitzgerald; cinematography, Victor Kemper; editor, Richard Marks; music, Maurice Jarre; running time: 125 mins.; rating: R.

Instead of shopping around for a proper vehicle to solidify his position in the New Hollywood, Jack instead chose yet another cameo role in a movie he found intriguing: an adaptation of F. Scott Fitzgerald's unfinished novel about the Old Hollywood that Jack, ironically enough, had helped to bring the final curtain down on with *Easy Rider*. Now that the studio system was at last finished, it seemed a fit subject for appraisal.

The Last Tycoon, based on the author's own firsthand experiences in Hollywood and loosely derived from the personality of boy genius Irving J. Thalberg, seemed an appropriate vehicle to present an epic vision of the picture making industry of the past. Fitzgerald's on-the-spot observations could now be rounded out with hindsight perceptions added by esteemed playwright Harold Pinter. The movie, intriguingly enough, would be di-

Jack Nicholson as Brimmer.

194

rected by Elia Kazan, who more than any other filmmaker had served as a bridge between the Old Hollywood and the New: his postwar films (*Pinky, Boomerang, On The Waterfront*) continued the craftsmanship developed during the preceding decades but introduced a social consciousness that was part of the emerging 1950s sensibility, along with heightened visual realism through on-location shooting. If Jack and his cohorts had been rebel filmmakers of the 1960s, then certainly Elia Kazan had been their counterpart and predecessor back in the fifties.

But the work of Jack and his director friends had made the vision of a previous generation of innovators look old hat. *The Last Tycoon* is just such a work: a sincere film by an intelligent, well-intentioned director who failed to create an organized interpretation of and coherent expansion of Fitzgerald's fragment. The moviemaking is

Two reigning superstars together at last, if briefly. The remarkable thing about both Jack Nicholson and Robert De Niro is the insistence of each on maintaining the right to play small character roles, despite the achievement of full superstar status.

flat and uninvolving; the picture does not appear to have been directed, in the sense that the camera tells the story, but only photographed, with stationary set-ups, resulting in aloof, arbitrary depictions of conversations between an odd assortment of actors. It is as if *The Last Tycoon* had not been reinterpreted for films but dramatized theatrically, then dutifully recorded for prosperity. All the acting is good, but the diverse amalgam of performers were working in different styles of performance that didn't jell. Worse still, the individual scenes never add up to a complete sense of story; like the

195

Brimmer, Monroe Stahr
(De Niro), and Cecilia Brady
(Theresa Russell) momentarily
clown around, though strong
emotions will shortly erupt.

unfinished novel it's based on, the film plays as a series of scenes from a work in progress. If the motivations for making the movie were undeniably commendable, the style is stale and uninspired.

Like *The Great Gatsby* and all of Fitzgerald's best work, *The Last Tycoon* attempts to take a romantic man and turn him into a modern tragic hero. In this case, it is Monroe Stahr (Robert De Niro), doomed by the bad timing that makes him an anachronism in Hollywood: the last of the producers who want to create great art, existing in an era when the studio systems are moving further and further into formula filmmaking. Like Thalberg in real-life, Stahr believes great art can be created within the commercial moviemaking industry, and the innocence of this belief will set him up for destruction. He is at odds with Pat Brady (Mitchum), a Louis B. Mayer type producer who wants to move on with the Big Business approach of turning out a product for public consumption.

Stahr can fight to maintain integrity so long as he singlemindedly pursues his career. But when he spots a breathtaking, ethereal beauty (Ingrid Boulting) who reminds him of his deceased first wife, his interests (and energies) are diverted. Like Gatsby, Stahr believes he has a second chance at happiness with the woman he loved and lost, who is his vision of the ideal; like Gatsby, his subjective, idealized vision of the woman's greatness is out of proportion to the attractive but vulgar woman we

see her as. Like Gatsby, his admirable if over-aggrandized love for her will serve as his tragic flaw, as his weakness for a woman who is, in fact, unworthy of his attention causes him to lose the empire he has amassed. Yet his romantic vulnerability is what lends him tragic stature.

Unlike *The Great Gatsby*, which in 1974 had been filmed as an unrelentingly bright and upbeat version of Fitzgerald's vision, *The Last Tycoon* was done as a dark, dim film, a kind of lifeless waxworks approach to the novel. Perhaps in appreciation of the sincerity of this film in comparison to the commercialized travesty of *Gatsby*, in deference to Kazan's long and oftentimes impressive career, and in awe at the willingness of top young stars like De Niro and Nicholson to lend their talents to the project, most critics reacted with gentle reviews. In *Time*, Jay Cocks called the film "a reasonably scrupulous adaptation . . . a flawed, divided movie, sometimes full of cool, funny insight, sometimes crippled by the flyaway myths of movietown." In *Newsweek*, Jack Kroll commented that the film rated as "by far the best attempt yet to translate F. Scott Fitzgerald to the screen. . . . It's an exceptionally well-made movie. But something is missing . . . a certain vital incandescent fusion of style and feeling" that might have communicated "the graceful poignance" of Fitzgerald's prose. In *Saturday Review*, Judith Crist was considerably less sparing but far more on-target, calling this "a faithful, lavish, and bloodless transcription . . . of Fitzgerald's literary fragment," insisting everyone involved mistakenly undertook "the roles of literary executors rather than of filmmakers" and, in the process, turned an epic vision of Hollywood and a modern tragic vision "into an insipid little love story."

Stanley Kauffmann of *The New Republic* concurred: "Only occasionally did I get from the screen any Fitzgerald feeling. . . . This picture [jostles] along in chunks that elbow one another out of the way . . . if I had to choose the celebrated director least suited to both Fitzgerald and Pinter, I might well pick Kazan." That observation is keen: Kazan's serious, solemn approach can be remarkably powerful in a project like Budd Schulberg's *On The Waterfront*, but seems all wrong for Fitzgerald's subtle, elegantly understated style. In *The New Yorker*, Pauline Kael argued with the choice of screenwriter: "The film needed a writer who would fill in the characters and clarify the conflict. . . . But Pinter doesn't supply what's missing; Pinter's Art is the art of taking away. . . . The film is bewilderingly mute and inexpressive." Indeed, Pinter's best known work for the theatre *(The Homecoming)* and film *(Accident)* makes clear that his talent is for suggesting the endless in-depth resonances reverberating beneath the mundane everyday small-talk, whereas Fitzgerald worked for a kind of heightened poetry.

In *The Nation*, Robert Hatch compared *The Last Tycoon* with the far more heralded (and, indeed, overhyped) version of *The Great Gatsby*, insisting this was "the more scrupulous work, but both are failures and for the same reason: they cannot make visible the magic that

Monroe Stahr presides over a movie empire that includes a
fading superstar (Tony Curtis), his bored wife (Leslie Curtis), a pair of old hacks (Ray
Milland and Robert Mitchum), a Garboesque beauty (Jeanne
Moreau), and the boss's daughter (Theresa Russell).

197

Fitzgerald convinced us he felt in his two central characters . . . as with *Gatsby*, when Stahr is reduced to human stature, the (effect) deflates. . . ."

The failed *Gatsby* film helps explain Jack's participation in *Tycoon*: He was first considered, then passed over (in favor of Robert Redford), for the lead in what ultimately emerged as less a movie than the centerpiece for a vast marketing empire of Gatsby era products. When asked about the role, he admitted his love for Fitzgerald's work and for the book *Gatsby* in particular, explaining: "I would like to have played Gatsby. . . . I would not like to have played him in the film they made." But why the penchant for Gatsby in the first place? "The role that's been hung on me since I was 20," Jack has said. Consider the parallels between Jack and the part, and it makes sense. Jack did manage—like that character—to transform himself into a wealthy figure of mystery, and do it by sheer will power. Gatsby's father is described in the book as "shiftless" and "unsuccessful"; Gatsby's imagination, Fitzgerald tells us, never really accepted his father or mother as parents at all. "I was righter for it than Redford," Jack insisted after losing out on the project. "He looks like a privileged person. He wouldn't worry about chopping his way up."

Appearing in *The Last Tycoon*, then, had a certain quality of vengeance to it, allowing Jack the fun of getting even by aligning his own romantic sensibility to that of Scott Fitzgerald's without being exploited as the centerpiece in a marketing promotion for Gatsby shirts and cuff-links.

Jack's brief role was singled out, by many critics, as one of the film's high points. Hatch felt the roster of big-name stars did little but lend the film a sense of "celebrity glitter," that the actors "have the fault of reciting their Fitzgerald dialogue as though they had memorized passages from some sacred text," but singled out Jack as an exception: "Nicholson is arresting as the Communist labor organizer with whom Stahr chooses to tangle at a bad moment in his life." Cocks considered Jack "very canny as a Communist union organizer." Kauffmann commented that "Jack Nicholson tries to juice up the thin role of the Communist, in an episode that is even thinner than the same episode in the novel." Crist, in her pan, took time out to note: "In the aridity of the screenplay and the unfocused plotting, it is small wonder that when at last Jack Nicholson appears for a much too small cameo as a writer's union organizer (and little is done to give meaning to the political backgrounds or significances of the time), the screen lights up—all too briefly, alas, and even Nicholson is reduced to schtick. But the effect of his appearance points up the lackluster quality of the other performances, the total absence of charisma and of conviction."

A MIME ON AN ACID TRIP:

Goin' South

(1979)
A PARAMOUNT PICTURE

CAST:

Jack Nicholson *(Henry Lloyd Moon)*; Mary Steenburgen *(Julia Tate)*; Christopher Lloyd *(Frank Towfield)*; John Belushi *(Hector)*; Veronica Cartwright *(Hermine)*; Richard Bradford *(Sheriff Andrew Kyule)*; Jeff Morris *(Big Abe)*.

CREDITS:

Director, Jack Nicholson; producers, Harry Gittes and Harold Schneider; screenplay, John Herman Sharer, Al Ramus, Charles Shyer, and Alan Mandel; cinematography, Nestor Almendros; editors, Richard Chew and John Fitzgerald Beck; music, Van Dyke Parks and Perry Botkin, Jr., with additional musical material written and performed by Ry Coorder; running time: 109 mins.; rating: R.

The Missouri Breaks whetted Jack's appetite to work in the western form again, while the mixed reactions that major movie elicited persuaded Nicholson to try his luck with a more modest exercise in the genre. From that big (some would say overblown) oater, he shifted to a modest (some would say minor) one, while returning to directing for the first time since he'd been burned by the less than enthusiastic response to *Drive, He Said* in 1970. *Goin' South* is a "romantic comedy of character" set in the west; as such, it features a minimum of satire on such western forms as the shoot-out and the chase, emphasizing instead laughs that grow out of an unlikely relationship.

The story takes place in the town of Longhorn, Texas, where Henry Moon is about to be hanged for the

Jack Nicholson as Henry Lloyd Moon.

199

In a posed publicity still, Moon prepares to meet his maker . . .

irascible, mangy bank, horse, and cattle thief he is. But there is a curious law in this particular stretch of territory stating that a man can be saved if any single woman in the community will step forward and accept him into her house as a husband. The prim and proper Julia Tate (Mary Steenburgen) does just that. But if Moon initially jumps for joy, he will have time and reason to reconsider his reaction. Theirs is to be a marriage of convenience in which he will be reduced to a virtual slave, working for Julia without benefit of wages or her bed. But as he helps Julia work the gold mine her late father has left to her, then rises to heroic proportions as he aids Julia in protecting her small piece of property against the approaching railroad, he wins her heart as well as her hand, and the stirrings of romance are at last felt between them.

This theme of the individual fighting against encroaching corporate mentality was supposed to lend the film a sense of social significance, hopefully underscoring the lightheartedness of the interplay between the two main characters. This appeared to be an attempt at an updating of the warmly-remembered Humphrey Bogart/Katharine Hepburn *African Queen* depiction of opposites who are at first repulsed by, then attracted to, each other, finally changing one another for the better. The scruffy Moon, like Bogie's Charlie Allnut, at last begins to clean up his act and class up his attitudes and appearance, while Julia (much like Kate's Rosie Sayer) finally lets her hair down, shedding both her inhibitions and apparent frigidity. But to compare the two films in

. . . but is rescued, at the last possible moment, by a marriage of convenience.

Thinking he has it made, Moon strolls off with the woman who has rescued him from the gallows, Julia Tate (Mary Steenburgen), not realizing he's in for a wild west version of *The Taming of the Shrew*.

terms of storyline is hardly to suggest they are similar in quality, for this gentle misfire is certainly no classic on the order of *The African Queen*.

The film—a surprisingly dispirited and charmless attempt at whimsy—is not the sort of thing that divides critics and audiences the way *The Missouri Breaks* had. No one, apparently, could work up much anger or excitement over this halfhearted, softboiled film. Noting Jack's exalted position in the Hollywood hierarchy at that particular point, Frank Rich of *Time* labelled this "a peculiar choice. *Goin' South* is not likely to be a commercial smash, but neither is it artistically ambitious. The film is just a small inconsequential frolic: always eccentric, sometimes wonderful," noting that this "two-character sketch" started well enough but soon wore "thin" and turned "predictable." The majority of the movie's scenes were filmed at a tepid level of near-inertia, while the performances are out of control. The resultant movie is a bizarre paradox: overenthusiastic

acting contained within the context of a film that seems dull, lethargic, listless.

Even Jack's own acting appeared broad and undisciplined, perhaps explaining why he has never directed himself again, and why—whenever he talks of possible future directorial projects like *Moon Trap*—he consistently insists he will not appear.

In *Goin' South*, he received some of the most negligible reviews of his later career. "Nicholson in full flight," Robert Hatch wrote in *The Nation*, "is no jogger. He leers, slaps his thigh, mumbles his lips, cavorts, exults, sues for mercy, pleads for understanding and scratches himself with the abandon of a mime on an acid trip." Even before the film was completed, Jack told a visitor to the set that "It is difficult directing yourself in comedy, because you have no idea whether you are going over the top."

To be fair, the role and his portrayal of it has its defenders. In his less than enthusiastic review, *Time's* Rich nonetheless praised the part as "the funniest—and possibly most enjoyable—role he's ever had. . . . Nicholson's repertoire of dumb grins and crazed laughs is as amusing as ever." *Newsweek's* David Ansen was equally generous to Nicholson, calling his performance "delightfully cantankerous."

Pauline Kael of *The New Yorker* (ordinarily a champion of Jack's onscreen work) proved unsparing in her assessment of Nicholson's acting in this: "His face is given over to full-time ogling: he bats his eyelids, wiggles his eyebrows, and gives us his rooster-that-fully-intends-to-jump-the-hen smile. . . . In most of his roles, Nicholson saves his grin for a few devastating flashes; each time we see it, it's a revelation of the demon he's got bottled up. Here there's nothing hidden and nothing hell-bent or sinister; he grins all the time—he's just a fatuous actor, a leering leprechaun. . . . Nicholson keeps working his mouth, with the tongue darting out and dangling lewdly; he's like a commercial for a porno film."

The comments may border on cruelty, but they also provide a pretty fair assessment of Jack's performance. Kael clearly attributed all the failures of his acting here to his decision to direct himself. "When movie actors also direct," she complained, "they're rarely able to bring anything new to their own performances, but with Nicholson it's not just that we don't get anything new— we get the old in an unrestrained form." In fact, watching Jack in *Goin' South* is very much like watching a Frank Gorshin style celebrity-mimic run through an overdone parody of Nicholson at his rangiest.

No matter how good-natured the film wants to be, or how innocent Jack's desire to act and direct in a single project may have been, the film nonetheless does appear

In a montage of action shots, the relationship between Moon and his new wife develops tumultuously, as a marriage of convenience gradually metamorphoses into a meaningful relationship.

more of a "star-turn" than anything he has done before or since. Nicholson allows himself full rein: he dances and prances, shouts and squirms, giggles and grunts, howls and hops about like a man with a hotfoot. It's all supposed to be wildly entertaining, but it's a strange sight to see an important actor making something of a silly spectacle of himself. In fact, few actors could have gotten away with it; careers have been ruined by just such stuff. Fortunately, Jack's deserved reputation as a gutsy risk taker allows him to fail on occasion in a way other stars would be wise to avoid.

Outside of the total lack of control over his own performance, Jack's direction seems uncertain, uneven, and unconvincing. It is overly restrained when it needs to work up some excitement, then desperately tries for

some wild fun just when it ought to slow down and allow us some consideration of the developing romance. Jack hired the remarkable Nestor Almendros to photograph the film, but instead of the kinds of fabulous vistas that cinematographer achieved for Terrence Malick on his visually breathtaking if dramatically minimalist turn-of-the-century western *Days of Heaven*, Almendros here was reduced to photographing the wide open spaces as though they were but a bleak backyard. That might be forgivable if it in some way related to the thrust of the piece: The distinct look of a film, no matter how unappealing, can be justified if it appears necessary and proper for the directorial approach to the story. But *Goin' South* apparently wants to be rambunctious, a cross between a folk fable or tall tale we see rather than hear and an observant comedy of manners and morals. With that in mind, the listless imagery seems incongruous and, quite simply, wrong.

The best scene in the film (and the one that, in the trailers, was used to sell the picture) features Nicholson's escaping outlaw riding across the Rio Grande and, once on the Mexican side, turning to hoot and holler at the pursuing posse. The sequence is enjoyable, based not only on an audience's familiarity with old movie clichés, but also a recognition that the character of Moon himself is aware of those clichés, seemingly senses he is in a movie and mistakenly thinks that it's going to be an old-fashioned formula western. Thus, when the posse continues to ride at him without stopping to notice the sacrilege of crossing the Mexican/American border, the look on Moon's face rings with a beautiful sense of exasperation. Don't they know that posses aren't allowed to do that? Because of that purposeful violation of myth and cliché, the sequence—and Nicholson's reaction in

it—is hilarious. We laugh, too, as he scrambles to escape, but his horse—the trusted pal of western film fugitives from William S. Hart to John Wayne—only manages to trip and get his master caught. We laugh because Henry Moon is a movie outlaw caught in a real west. If only the remainder of the film played off that paradox which the opening sets up, this might have been something special. But such an approach is never again used throughout the entire picture.

"No one extracts the serious plot from *Goin' South*," Jack complained in 1986. "The characters were once all members of Quantrill's raiders, the original guerrilla warfare unit in America. And what do you do with these people once they're now home? The fact that this wasn't even touched on critically was disappointing to me." But that point hardly seems raised by the film. True, Jack has always followed the Chekhovian concept that art ought to suggest, rather than insist on, ideas. In *Goin' South*, though, the implications are not explored deeply enough

Moon celebrates his second chance at life with a dance reminiscent of Anthony Quinn's famous footwork in *Zorba The Greek*.

203

to make us understand and acknowledge that they are indeed intended as a subtext to the romantic story. Quantrill's Raiders seem presented as a passing plot device on the film's surface rather than as cross reference to returning Vietnam vets.

While the film is mellow, it also seems mainstream: unintriguing and unadventurous in a way that's uncharacteristic of Jack, or at least his popular image. What it most clearly lacks is a strong directorial sensibility, just the sort of thing Jack suggested he had with *Drive, He Said*. "So why do I want to direct? Well, I think I have a special vision." Undoubtedly this intelligent, creative person does, but if *Goin' South* contains that vision in his own mind, the film failed to communicate it to his fans. If anything, the writing is what allows us some insight into Nicholson. The film is, however incidentally, political in terms of his own point of view: the villains are representatives of the conglomerate that would like to swallow up the mine these decent individuals run. "Our country is becoming corrupted little by little by conglomeration and conglomerate thinking," Jack told interviewer Fred Schruers in 1986. He was referring to the takeover of movie companies by mega-corporations like Coca-Cola, run by people with little understanding of cinema art but much knowledge of bottom line moneymaking strategies. By implication, though, he was talking also about *Goin' South* and many of his other projects as well.

The difficulty of the man-woman relationship—and the ultimate worth of their romance following all the fights—is close to Jack's own stated attitudes. Certainly, Henry Moon leads a double life: the scraggly, sloppy outlaw without apparent values; then the clean-cut man who risks his life to defend the land of the lady he loves, and in so doing rises to heroic proportions. Still, the movie tries to be wild and woolly but is only mild and minor, as slight as it is silly. For Nicholson's careers as actor and director, *Goin' South* was in fact goin' nowhere.

JACK THE RIPPER:

The Shining

(1980)
A WARNER BROTHERS RELEASE

CAST:

Jack Nicholson *(Jack Torrance)*; Shelley Duvall *(Wendy Torrance)*; Danny Lloyd *(Danny Torrance)*; Scatman Crothers *(Dick Hallorann)*; Barry Nelson *(Stuart Ullmann)*; Philip Stone *(Delbert Grady)*; Joe Turkel *(Lloyd)*.

CREDITS:

Director, Stanley Kubrick; producer, Stanley Kubrick; screenplay, Stanley Kubrick and Diane Johnson, adapted from the novel by Stephen King; cinematography, John Alcott; editor, Ray Lovejoy; music, conducted by Herbert von Karajan; running time: 142 mins.; rating: R.

Jack has consistently avoided the movie-star trap of appearing in a string of safe, conventional movies by involving himself with films made by off-center creative artists involved in honest efforts to put something new and daring on the screen. Certainly, Stanley Kubrick and *The Shining* rated as just such a director and film. The movie infuriated as many viewers as it satisfied. People who approached this as fans of the Stephen King novel (ardent aficionados consider King the rightful heir to Edgar Allan Poe) saw the film as a disastrous misrepresentation of his finest book, a big, cold, empty movie missing all the emotional horror; those who considered King's novel nothing more than upscale pulp argued that the directorial genius of Stanley Kubrick transformed a clever if negligible book into a major work of the cinema. People who love horror films in general and ghost

Jack Nicholson as Jack Torrance.

205

Stuart Ullmann (Barry Nelson) and a colleague interview Jack about the job of caretaker.

stories in particular were put off by the movie, which in fact pulls the rug out from almost every convention associated with such tales; people who scoff at such stories as simple-minded tripe were delighted by what they perceived as Kubrick's devilishly unorthodox approach, satirically undermining the absurdities of the storyline.

That story begins as Jack Torrance (Nicholson), a former teacher and aspiring writer, applies for the position of caretaker at the vast Overlook Hotel, located in an isolated mountainous section of Colorado. A buzzing resort during the summer months, the place is kept closed during the winter; the general manager (Barry Nelson) confides to Jack that one previous caretaker, apparently driven quite mad by the isolation and emptiness, murdered his two small daughters with an axe. Then again, the man's flight into murderous action may have had less to do with psychological causes than the hotel's location, as it was unknowingly built over an ancient Indian burial ground; endless rumors abound that the ghosts of those native Americans still haunt the place, possessing the people who live there and spurring them on to awful deeds.

Jack, though, pays little attention to such information and is happy to be awarded the job, as it will allow him both the economic base and quiet solitude he desperately needs if he is to finish his great American novel. So he moves his wife (Shelley Duvall) and small son Danny (Danny Lloyd) into the enormous place. At first, everything seems fine: Danny whisks around on his tricycle, Wendy becomes a kind of caricature of the dutiful housewife and mother, while Jack pours himself into his writing with manic intensity. But there is another element, a supernatural side, to their life at Overlook. Each of the family members is subject to visions of spirits: the ghosts of the two murdered daughters, spooky images of tattered and terrifying creatures, walls that drip blood which eventually floods its way over everyone and everything. In time, Danny uses his unique clairvoyant gifts for seeing through space and time (an ability to "shine," in the words of an elderly black cook, played by "Scatman" Crothers) to make connection with an imaginary friend named Tony, who has long been with him and now introduces Danny to the horrific forces hovering everywhere. Danny sees that his own father is surrendering to the evil in this place ("You are the caretaker," a dark voice tells Jack, "and you have always been the caretaker!"), hinting that he is merely the latest incarnation of the hideous presence which previously took the lives of innocents.

Certainly, the cinematography and editing (along with the precise musical scoring) is dazzling, and some critics were overcome by Kubrick's technical accomplishments. "The first epic horror film," Newsweek's Jack Kroll claimed. "[Kubrick] not only gets the horror, he gets the perverse beauty of horror," praising Kubrick's "love for the technical and formal sides of filmmaking." In Time, Richard Schickel likewise praised Kubrick's "stylistic mastery and rigorous intelligence," congratulating him for "flouting conventional expectations of his horror film," and insisting "it is a daring thing the director has done."

Those reviewers able to accept Kubrick's approach to King's novel also admired Jack's acting. Kroll claimed that for "all [the film's] brilliant effects, the strongest and scariest element in The Shining is the face of Jack Nicholson undergoing a metamorphosis from affectionate father to murderous demon." Kroll also noted that Jack's famed "killer smile," so often an element in his various characterizations, here became the basis for the character: "The smile is the facial barometer by which we read the state of his soul as it's sucked deeper and deeper into demonism by the black forces that infest the huge hotel. You suspect Kubrick cast Nicholson in the part chiefly because of" that smile. Kroll was likewise able to accept the sudden flights into self-parody (in both Jack's performance and in the film containing it) as basic to the directorial vision: "Nicholson's Jack Torrance is a classic piece of horror acting: his metamorphosis into evil has its comic sides as well—which makes us remember that the devil is the ultimate clown." Schickel concurred: "[Kubrick] has asked much of Nicholson, who must sustain attention in a hugely unsympathetic role, and who responds with a brilliantly crazed performance."

Others, however, found the performance to be one of the least disciplined and most mannered ever delivered by Nicholson, usually a remarkably "realistic" actor. For such critics, the "gags" were offensively unfunny: the visual discovery by Wendy that Jack's "novel" is nothing more than the single phrase "All work and no play makes Jack a dull boy," endlessly repeated but in diverse typographical arrangements; Nicholson's extended Richard Nixon imitation; Jack's delivery of the famous Tonight Show opening ("Heeeeeeeere's Johnny!") as he axes his way through a door to kill his wife. They constituted not an acceptable, even important, aspect of the film's iconoclasm, but the ultimate proof that this was an immense and elaborate but empty film existing only to share a few strained, paltry gags, as such making an absolute travesty out of a workable horror novel. "Jack Nicholson," John Simon of the National Review wrote, "hams atrociously from the outset." Pauline Kael, often a Nicholson admirer, wrote in The New Yorker that, "There's no surprise in anything he does, no feeling of invention. . . . Axe in hand and slavering, with his tongue darting about in his mouth, he seems to have stumbled in from an old A.I.P. picture."

In Commonweal, Colin L. Westerbeck, Jr., pointed out: "The plain truth is that [Kubrick] has let Jack Nicholson run riot. Jack is made to seem dangerous and crazy before the family even moves to the Overlook Hotel," which of course cuts away the edge of psychological thriller from the plot: We need to see him gradually go bonkers for the suspense to mount, but he's clearly bouncing off the walls even before their encounter with the evil in this place. King carefully hinted at the character's predisposition for madness, then put him into precisely the situation that would step-by-step logically lead him down a dark path to just such a terrible state. Kubrick, apparently uninterested in such niceties of characterization or plot but fascinated by the newest developments in camera technology and sound editing, paid little attention to any narrative elements.

Or, as Kael wisely observed, "If The Shining is about anything, it's tracking." Simon argued the film's failure grew out of Kubrick's "basic inability to deal with people. . . . In two and a half wearying hours, The Shining fails to establish a single man, woman, or child." Of course, this is where the film most markedly differs from the approach found in King's novel, where he delineated the personalities and psychologies of each protagonist, then created a drama in which their actions are true to what we know of them.

In the novel, for instance, we clearly understand Jack, not as some twisted tour-de-force for a great actor gone over-the-top but as a vulnerable, frustrated, confused, self-interested but not entirely unsympathetic man. The Jack of the book, hungry to create a great novel, becomes convinced the previous crime is the source of the masterwork he was predestined to write, so he understandably becomes obsessed with that crime. Yet there's the problem of his modest gifts. Which is why, when Jack Torrance cannot get the story down on paper, he must objectify the problem; knowing deep down it's his own failure as a writer but unable to squarely face this, Jack searches for a scapegoat or, in his case, scapegoats. His family, in his mind, is the reason for his being unable to complete the masterwork. Combine this with the obsessive attention he has paid the past murders, and it makes a horrifying sense that the current caretaker would eventually follow the pattern established by his predecessor.

Wendy Torrance (Shelley Duvall) begins to suspect her little boy Danny (Danny Lloyd) is not behaving normally . . .

. . . then fears for her writer/husband's sanity.

What happens, then, can be interpreted either as a ghost story or as a tale of psychological horror.

In the film, such intriguing ambiguousness gives way to arch horror antics. The flamboyant filmmaking does not function to communicate King's ideas, but glides around them, just as Danny's tricycle glides around the maze-like corridors of the hotel: moving fast but going nowhere. It rates, therefore, as style without substance, technique presented on attention-getting level. There is no content, in terms of character or drama, but rather the form becomes (for Kubrick, and those who can stomach his approach to film) the content. As Pauline Kael observed, "Kubrick loves the ultra-smooth travelling shots made possible by the Steadicam." More, apparently, than he loves his characters. Kubrick—as critic Henry Bromell correctly stated—"simply makes Jack an exaggerated, highly stylized boogeyman rising from the shadows to frighten children."

Jack, apparently, was gleeful at that possibility: "Within the next six months," he announced in May 1980, "I will be something petrifying in between 10 and 100 million dreams." He has, moreover, claimed he wanted the character to be even nastier than what we see, if that's possible: He'd "have been a lot worse if I'd had my way. . . . What I liked about that guy was that he was so nuts that even before he was doing anything, he liked scaring people. . . . Grand Guignol was that story's classification for me." On the other hand, he's also stated that, at various points during the shooting, he would stop a take to nervously ask: "Jesus, Stanley, aren't I playing this too broad?"

Certainly, the experience of shooting this film was unique. Jack learned that Kubrick shoots the simplest of sequences over and over again until somehow, some way, something special happens, lending an otherwise mundane scene a unique edge. Afterwards, co-star Crothers recalled: "He had Jack Nicholson walk across the street, no dialogue. Fifty takes. He had Shelley, Jack and the kid walk across the street. Eighty-seven takes, man. He always wants something new and he doesn't stop until he gets it." The film was preceeded by a string of stories detailing the difficulty on the set between Nicholson and Kubrick. "I'm a great off-stage grumbler," Jack later told *Newsweek*. "I complained that he was the only director to light the sets with no stand-ins. We had to be there even to be lit. Just because you're a perfectionist doesn't mean you're perfect."

But Nicholson's own preference for people movies (and directors who do them with a minimum of visual flamboyance and a maximum of concentration on characterization) suggests he must on some level have been aware of the essential hollowness of *The Shining*. He was not specifically speaking of Kubrick (though he might well have been) when he told Gene Siskel in 1974 why he loved doing *The Last Detail*: "I think we've had a long period in the movies where fancy editing and tricky camera movements have been the fashion. I suspect and hope that very soon the only unusual element in a movie will be its characters. After the audience has been sufficiently shocked by special horror effects, explicit sexual fantasies, and endless brutality, what you're going to have is what you used to have, which is unusual people behaving in interesting and hopefully illuminating ways." In *The Shining*, he appeared in the kind of

fancy/tricky film he had five years earlier condemned.

Yet Jack's attraction to the part was understandable, considering its autobiographical element. Jack Torrance marks the first time Nicholson has shared the first name with one of his characters, and Torrance serves as a kind of doppelgänger for Nicholson, a nightmare vision of what he himself might have become had his career not gone so well. The image of Torrance with his phoney grins as he tries to get the job doubtless derives authenticity from Nicholson's memory of how demeaning it felt to go out on casting calls as an unknown actor, smiling ingenuously at people who would probably reject him. The intensity of Torrance's frustration as he tries to write something worthwhile, and his enormous anger at his family when they disturb him, grew from Jack's oftentimes frustrated attempts to write while still married to Sandra Knight. "That's the one scene in the movie I wrote myself," Jack confided to the *New York Times* in 1986, "that scene at the typewriter. That's what I was like when I got my divorce. I was acting in a movie in the daytime and writing a movie at night and my beloved wife walked in on what was, unbeknownst to her, this maniac—and I told Stanley about it and we wrote it into the scene. I remember being at my desk and telling her, 'Even if you don't hear me typing it doesn't mean I'm

Jack begins to erupt violently . . .

. . . as Wendy recoils in horror.

"Here's Johnny . . ."

not writing.' I remember that total animus. Well, I got a divorce."

The joke concerning the worthlessness of Torrance's "creative" work may be viewed as Nicholson's (and, for that matter, every author's) deep-down fear that what he turns out at the typewriter is thin and insignificant: "I used to write, so I understand this guy's writer's block." And the difficult, demanding role of father is basic not only to this film but to so many of the projects Jack (with his lifelong ambivalence about father figures) has been drawn to. Jack confesses to having had an imaginary playfriend as a child, just as Danny does here.

Jack's vision of the ultimate evil as appearing in the guise of Richard Nixon reflects his own politics ("Personally, I impeached Nixon long ago," he said during Watergate). Even the fact that many of Torrance's visions in the hotel are from the 1920s ("spectral revelers right out of *The Great Gatsby*," Kroll commented) adds to this autobiographical element, for Jack has always been personally "haunted" by *The Great Gatsby*. Torrance's drifting through life can be viewed as a parallel to Jack's own earlier inclinations in that direction, while "Daddy" Torrance's hinted-at problems with alcohol struck a chord for Jack, having been brought up by a father-figure who suffered from drinking problems. Finally, Torrance is the ultimate example of the character who leads a double-existence: loving father and axe-murderer; middleclass provider and struggling artist; caretaker and writer; Jack Torrance and some other man from out of the past.

For trivia buffs, one further bit of information is imperative: Love it or hate it, the "Heeeeere's Johnny!" line was Jack's (ever the collaborator!) idea. "Stanley lives in England," Nicholson once said, "so he didn't really know what it meant."

Danny's moment of terror . . .

The Postman Always Rings Twice

(1981)
A PARAMOUNT PICTURE

CAST:

Jack Nicholson *(Frank Chambers)*; Jessica Lange *(Cora Papadakis)*; John Colicos *(Nick Papadakis)*; Michael Lerner *(Katz)*; John Ryan *(Kennedy)*; Anjelica Huston *(Madge)*; Jon Van Ness *(Motorcycle Cop)*.

CREDITS:

Director, Bob Rafelson; producers, Bob Rafelson and Charles Mulvehill; screenplay, David Mamet, adapted from the novel by James. M. Cain; cinematography, Sven Nykvist; editor, Graeme Clifford; musical director, Michael Small; running time: 123 mins.; rating: R.

One might guess a major movie star would have little problem bringing a screen project to fruition, especially if that project contained all the elements usually considered "commercial": sex and violence, a thriller plot, period trappings of the sort nostalgia-inclined audiences are enamored of. But that's not always true. If there is a single film Jack had, from the early seventies on, been interested in doing, it was a remake of James M. Cain's pulp fiction turned film noir classic, *The Postman Always Rings Twice*.

At one point in the mid-seventies, the film was set for production, but the sponsoring studio insisted Raquel Welch (then still considered a hot item) be cast as the female lead. Jack, who was living with Michelle Phillips at the time, saw the film as the perfect co-starring vehicle for them. Indeed, Phillips did come much closer to

Jack Nicholson as Frank Chambers.

Cain's vision of Cora than did Welch, but the studio was less interested in casting correctness than in box-office potential, and held firm. So did Jack, and the project lay dormant. "It's the role every actress in Hollywood wanted to play," Jack claimed. "The woman is really the instigator, her subconscious is the designer of the crime." Then the Nicholson-Phillips relationship deteriorated, but Jack was already involved in other film roles, so the movie did not "happen" until 1981, when Jack finally got to make it with a remarkably varied group of talents: director Bob Rafelson, who had guided him through two of his finest vehicles; screenwriter David Mamet, Pulitzer Prize-winning playwrite and author of such trendy and controversial works as *Sexual Perversity in Chicago*; cinematographer Sven Nykvist, responsible for the world-class imagery of Ingmar Bergman's best films; co-star Jessica Lange, who was already establishing that she was in fact a heavyweight actress.

For such a remarkable blend of talents to come together for a film is a rare occurrence. Jack must have felt assured the wait was, this time out, worth his while, that *Postman* would be done far better for all the delays. That was not the way it was to be. *Postman* rates as a decided disappointment, a dreary dud lacking the impact not only of Cain's novel, but even of the previous film version, which has always been considered a considerably compromised vision of the book: "Classic in that the memory of it is huge compared to the film itself," Jack has said of Tay Garnett's version. Specifically, what Jack objected to was the sentimentalization of Cain's characters: "Whereas [Frank] has been played very charmingly, the fact of the matter is he's a sadist who solved every problem he ever had in his life with violence."

On the surface, this film follows the basic story pattern. Frank Chambers (Nicholson), a drifter with a prison record, is hitching cross country during the dark Depression days and is dropped off near an isolated gas station and eatery. Shortly after his arrival, he meets not only the Greek owner (John Colicos) but also his sexy wife Cora (Jessica Lange), and there's an immediate sexual chemistry between them. The two sleep together whenever Nick is out of town, and in time, their affair turns into an obsession: They can think of nothing but each other, so much so that they'd kill to maintain their relationship. Frank and Cora concoct an elaborate plan to murder Nick and make it appear an accident, but small details trip them up, and they are arrested. In court, a clever lawyer gets them off; it appears they are free, but the two grow mistrustful, especially after Cora discovers Frank is still a womanizer. They grow ever more bitter and resentful, but just as they are on the verge of recapturing their romance, Cora is killed in a freak automobile accident.

The biggest mistake with the film is that it ends at this

Almost immediately after arriving at the sleazy diner, Frank is consumed by a horrible surge of lust tinged with contempt for Cora (Jessica Lange), the wife of his boss . . .

213

. . . which he shortly satisfies in the most violent manner possible.

Following their affair, Frank and Cora gradually realize they are going to kill her husband.

Cora's husband, the Greek Nick Papadakis (John Colicos), applauds a friend at a party while Cora, unimpressed, looks on.

point: viewers unfamiliar with the novel or the earlier film version barely noticed the sound of police sirens in the background. The filmmakers trusted that this sound implicitly suggested Frank—who the police always knew was a killer, even if they couldn't prove it—would now be arrested for the "murder" of Cora. This doesn't come across. What we need is what we had in Garnett's version. There, the audience sees one additional scene in which Frank, sitting in a jail cell and considering his impending execution, laughs with grim irony at his situation: having gotten away with a murder he had in fact committed, he's now about to be executed for one he didn't do. There's a terrible rightness to his fate, a pulp-level poetic justice even he, in his primitive way, can comprehend. For just before being led to the gallows, Frank mutters: "I guess the postman always rings twice. . . ."

In Garnett's film, Frank's final utterance not only explains the title but also serves as a fabulous punch line. Watching the newer version is like listening to an elabo-

Sex and the desire to murder grow inseparable for Frank and Cora . . .

. . . until finally, they commit the murderous act.

rately set-up gag with no pay-off. This time, more than one pundit commented, the postman only rang once. What was meant as a more subtle approach failed to click; the sense of an abiding destiny hanging over people who mistakenly believe they operate on the principle of free will was never effectively implied. Despite the sordid settings and the sleazy characters, Cain was writing a modern variation of Greek tragedy (no wonder, then, his choice of ethnicity for Nick) in which a man kills his adopted father-figure to sleep with a substitute mother, setting a terrible fate into motion for himself. Cain's sense of inexorability is completely stripped away, reducing this to a grimly realistic episode without resonance. As Colin Westerbeck wrote, "For things to turn out this way seems not inevitable, as in the novel, but arbitrary." Instead of fated, Cora's death appears random, as if Mamet didn't know how to end his story and so killed off the heroine.

There's another problem as well. The very nature of the relationship is altered in this film, and with it, the meaning of the story. In Cain's book, the first sexual embrace between Frank and Cora is accompanied by her screams of "Bite me! Bite me!" To that, first-person narrator Frank tells us: "I bit her. I sunk my teeth into her lips so deep I could feel the blood spurt into her mouth. It was running down her neck when I carried her upstairs." Theirs is a sado-masochistic relationship, based more on animosity than attraction; even before he touched her, Frank made clear from his first view of Cora that he didn't find her particularly attractive ("she really wasn't any raving beauty") but that he was moved to seduce her out of a viciousness she inspired in him ("her lips stuck out in a way that made me want to smash them in for her").

216

The re-creation of period detail is strikingly conveyed in this scene featuring Frank and Cora attempting to escape from their sleazy surroundings; sadly, the filmmakers could not see the forest for the trees, failing to capture and communicate the essential meaning of James Cain's story.

Afterwards, they celebrate with a candlelit dinner.

Cora and Frank are incarcerated for the crime.

The book is a brilliant case study of the intense bond that can grow between two people who despise each other, how such a relationship can prove more obsessive than one based on love. So there's a carry over from the violence in their sex to the violence they then perpetrate: They kill Nick less so that they can spend their lives together than as a result of their violently-inclined sex. In the book they are so turned on by killing him that they uncontrollably rush into the bushes to fornicate, an

The attorney Katz (Michael Lerner) attempts a desperate defense, as Cora looks on.

Frank awaits his trial: Nicholson brings a sense of existential world-weariness to the character.

abrupt change in their plans that leads directly to their eventual demise.

"Both people are pathological," Jack said of Cain's characters. "They are not the boy and girl next door." But like the earlier version, his film suffers because of the Hollywood belief that audiences will not stick with characters unless they are at least somewhat sympathetic. In the 1946 version, sex is left offscreen; here, it's vividly portrayed. But in both cases, the S & M aspect is gone, and what we see is an irresistible romance. The killing of Nick seems considerably more justifiable, done only to eliminate the one man who stands in the way of their sharing of their lives. Whether it is Garfield and Lana Turner or Nicholson and Lange, we see a charismatic screen couple, doing what they have to do to be together, and it's impossible not to secretly hope they will get away with it.

"I did *Postman* because I hadn't come down the middle with the fastball about sex in a movie," Jack said. "The whole reason for that movie is sex, and that's why I wanted to do it." What hurt the first film version was the fact that the diner and gas station never looked as sordid as Cain had described, while Lana Turner (in her starlet's white shorts and turban) was not Cain's sluttish nymphomaniac but an MGM love goddess. Certainly, Rafelson improved on that, making the settings as grimy as they need to be. And Lange, a remarkable actress as well as a remarkable beauty, willingly toned down her natural glamour to better approximate Cain's Cora.

Despite that, the more graphic sex results not in a turn-on but in a movie that's too clinical and considerably *less* sexy than the Garnett version. Richard A. Blake complained in *America* that far from the eroticism the film's advance word promised, the movie only offered "a good example of *anti*-erotic sex as spectacle . . . there is little if any nudity." This was a conscious choice: "I like the idea there is not a speck of nudity in *Postman*," Jack claims, "another stylistic thing we did." To make this a film about an obsessive sexual relationship that cannot be tagged pornography because, despite a graphic tone, it refuses to go for the easy, expected sensuous stereotypes of bodies in action, but sordidly shows two people having it out amid the onion peelings.

But despite this integrity of approach, the initial sex scene misrepresents Cain's vision: Instead of the mutually acknowledged sado-masochism, there is a rape by Frank which Cora initially repels, then succumbs to and encourages. The film, made by the most sophisticated talents in Hollywood, ended up embodying the offensive stereotype that women really want to be raped, which is far from what Cain was getting at. "Now don't throw me in with Larry Flynt—that all women are looking to get raped," Jack told *Rolling Stone* in 1984, "but in this area, *Postman* did clarify this for me. I'm not talking about everybody, but those two people in that movie liked it." That they did, but the characters James Cain created liked something else entirely. So the stated *raison-d'etre* of the film—to finally shoot the love scenes as Cain had wanted them—is not what emerged.

Damaging the film even more was an unexpected comparison: At the same time *Postman* was making the theater rounds, so was writer-director Lawrence's Kasdan's *Body Heat*, that filmmaker's homage to Cain's two finest works, *Postman* and *Double Indemnity*. Kasdan did not set his film in the past but shot it more cheaply by updating such a *film noir* tale to the present. The lack of vestiges from the late thirties/early forties does not interfere with *Body Heat* fully capturing the essence, the spirit, the vision of Cain. In *Postman*, Cain's period is brought to life with careful and vivid reconstruction, but for all the perfection of detail—from big objects like cars to small ones such as the labels on cans—it somehow fails to convey the proper tone. Proud of the authenticity that had been achieved, Jack tagged his film "Depressionesque," but added: "I hope no one really goes away from this movie saying how great the thirties were recreated." That, in fact, is precisely the problem. Rafelson and his colleagues apparently couldn't see the forest for the trees; while getting every "tree" right, they missed the "forest."

To be fair, some critics did appreciate the picture. James M. Wall of *Christian Century* praised its "cinematic artistry," noting that *Postman* "is not a film to be enjoyed, but one to be admired." *Horizon*'s Diane Jacobs hailed it as "the best thing that's happened to *film noir* since *Chinatown*." In *Time*, Richard Corliss first praised *Postman* as "a purposefully paced retelling of Cain's story," then pounced on Rafelson's direction as "too handsome, too careful." *Newsweek*'s David Ansen revealed no such ambivalence: "They haven't pulled it off," he wrote. "Just when Mamet's script should be tightening the screws, it grows diffuse." Pauline Kael put her finger on the film's failings: "It's overcontrolled and methodical in its pacing . . . Rafelson takes the grandaddy of hot tabloid novels and treats it with dedication and concern. . . . He has too much at stake in each frame. . . . The camera stays at a chilling distance and never heats up."

Following his out-of-control performance in *The Shining*, it is not surprising that many critics (even those who didn't care for the film) praised Jack's work in *Postman*. James Wall argued that "Nicholson once again shows himself to be one of our finest actors, willing to present himself unattractively as a desperate man." Richard Corliss was as ambivalent about Jack as he was about the film itself: "Nicholson's performance as Frank is studied . . . the dashing star of a decade ago has dared to inhabit the molting seediness of the character actor." Ansen, however, did not like Jack in the role and found him basic to the film's failure: "The problem(s) may be traced to the miscasting of Jack Nicholson as the obsessive Frank Chambers. Not only is he a bit too old for the part, but one lift of those sardonic eyebrows and Chambers's raw passions are dissolved in ironic distance. He's too innately sly an actor to be playing a victim of passion." Stanley Kauffmann, in *Commentary*, showed no mercy: "He looks a good deal of the time as if he hadn't recovered from the *Cuckoo's Nest* lobotomy. . . . The role of the stud vagabond, as written here, is stock; and Nicholson makes not one move to nudge it past platitude." Kael likewise found little to like: "Nicholson appears to be working very seriously, yet he doesn't come up with anything fresh, and he doesn't seem to know how to do anything simply. . . . His performance could have been given by a Nicholson impersonator."

Perhaps Jack didn't supply the proper poetry; then again, Kael may not have seen the poetry he was showing her. As to a lack of freshness, Jack has commented on how he tried to bring new shades to what had been an overly-romanticized character: "In the first scene, I steal cigarettes from the guy who's giving me a free meal." In addition to adding such bits of unsympathetic business, there was once again his famous "against-the-grain-of-cliché" approach, refusing to lose weight for the role to embody the stereotype of a gaunt

Depression era deprived drifter: "Rafelson kept trying to slim me down . . . [if] this guy gets hungry, he'll just steal your food. He might be a bum, but he didn't miss no meals."

It's not hard to understand why Jack has always been attracted to this tale, for in addition to its "love" story there is Cain's implied political attitude. Discussing the protagonists brought down by a big, ugly system beyond their comprehension, Richard Blake wrote that "they run into the corruption of dishonest lawyers, rigged courts and the merciless rich and powerful. In depression fiction, the cards are always stacked against the little people." In the films of Jack Nicholson as well. Projects as diverse as *Cuckoo's Nest, Easy Rider,* and *The Last Detail* deal with individuals unable to realize their desires owing to entrapment in a system that abides no freedom of will, strangling those who try to achieve.

Whereas most major stars would recoil from the film's graphic scenes, Jack hoped to take them further: "There was a shot I wanted to do when he first makes love to her, when he backs her off the chopping block—a reverse angle with my clothes on, but I wanted to have a full stinger, because they'd never seen that in [mainstream] movies. I just knew this odd image would be a stunner. Well, I went upstairs and worked on it for forty-five minutes, but I couldn't get anything going because I knew everyone was waiting down there to see this thing. Somebody else might have said I was a pervert, but in my terms, this would've been extremely artful."

The remarkably talented Jessica Lange brought a moral complexity to what might have been, in lesser hands, a stock femme fatale, showing both Cora's sluttish side . . .

. . . and also her gentler, more vulnerable qualities.

OF COMRADES AND LOVERS:

Reds

(1981)
A PARAMOUNT PICTURE

CAST

Warren Beatty *(John Reed)*; Diane Keaton *(Louise Bryant)*; Jack Nicholson *(Eugene O'Neill)*; Edward Herrmann *(Max Eastman)*; Jerzy Kosinski *(Grigory Zonoviev)*; Paul Sorvino *(Louis Fraina)*; Maureen Stapleton *(Emma Goldman)*; Nicolas Coster *(Paul Trullinger)*; Ian Wolfe *(Mr. Partlow)*; Bessie Love *(Mrs. Partlow)*; Gene Hackman *(Pete Van Wherry)*.

CREDITS:

Director, Warren Beatty; producer, Warren Beatty; screenplay, Warren Beatty and Trevor Griffiths; cinematography, Vittorio Storaro; editors, Dede Allen and Craig McKay; music, Stephen Sondheim; running time: 200 mins.

Long before Nicholson's pal Warren Beatty first tried his hand at directing with this 1981 release, Jack had directed two films, each receiving mixed critical and mild commercial reaction. But Jack was not yet ready to tackle The Big One: a huge, heavyweight, heartfelt expression of everything in life most dear to him. That's precisely what Beatty delivered his first time out.

For ten years before the premiere of *Reds*, Beatty had been researching, considering, reconsidering and attempting to define the approach he would take to a biographical story he committed himself to someday telling on film: the life of socialist writer John Reed. When *Reds* finally hit the theater screens in 1981, there was no question Beatty was putting his reputation as experienced actor/producer (*Bonnie and Clyde, Heaven*

Gene drifts into a love affair with Louise Bryant (Diane Keaton), despite the fact that she's his best friend's girl; though the story is based on fact, there are striking parallels to similar situations in many other films Jack has chosen to appear in.

221

Can Wait) as well as debuting director on the line. With a budget officially recorded as $35 million (though many insiders insist it ran higher than $50 million), a 3½ hour running time, and a title that seemed a slap in the face to an American public which had just elected one of the country's most famous red baiters as president, this was clearly no safe film, no easy sell. *Reds* attempted an intimate love story set against the turbulent times of the 1910s and twenties, when the emerging socialist movement took fire not only in Russia but also in the U.S.

Here, many intellectuals were won over by the Marxist theories of a working-class revolution. Reed, himself the product of a middle-class home in Portland, Oregon, joined the fervent idealists of New York's Greenwich Village arts-and-politics circle, where he and others like Emma Goldman were inspired by the belief that a new

and fairer order of things was about to emerge. As a "romantic reporter" (making no bones about objectivity, Reed openly aligned himself with the revolutionaries while serving as a journalist for such political publications as *The Masses*), he covered Pancho Villa's struggle in Mexico, then produced his masterwork—*Ten Days That Shook the World*—when he happened to be at the right place at the right time; the perfect meeting of the man and the moment allowed him to report first-hand on Lenin's takeover of the Russian government.

But there was another side to his life: Reed's strained, ongoing relationship with Louise Bryant, the brilliant, talented, self-interested and thoroughly irresistible woman who left her comfortable station in life as the wife of a dentist after hearing one of Reed's speeches, becoming his companion in radical politics and an

Jack Nicholson as Eugene O'Neill.

important early feminist writer. Though Bryant shared most of Reed's political views, she did not share his compulsive, consuming commitment to politics. Though he initially inspired her to desert her middle-class existence, Bryant proved no mere disciple, instead reaching her own conclusions and establishing her own values about the possibilities of achieving any lasting good through politics. Essentially, her views were more realistic, less romantic than Reed's. She understandably found herself attracted to Eugene O'Neill, the brilliant writer who supported the same causes as Reed even while scoffing at his friend's wide-eyed idealism. Essentially, Louise was caught between them; while her own realistic attitude drew her to O'Neill, her love of Reed's romantic idealism made him irresistible.

One significant aspect of the film, then, had to be the triangular relationship, and Beatty wisely chose to enlist his close friend for the part. It proved a brilliant bit of casting. Once again, Jack's refusal to approach his career with a star's options as the basis for decisions allowed him to accept a supporting role and, in the minds of many, steal the show. John Simon of *The National Review* didn't care for the casting: "Nicholson, as O'Neill, is more restrained and to the point than he has been in a long while; but he is too laid-back, unintellectual, wise-guyish of voice, aspect, and manner for this tormented, complicated, much deeper figure."

Colin L. Westerbeck of *Commonweal* complained: "This movie isn't really about the romance between John Reed and Louise Bryant, but something far less significant, far less engaging: the romance that Beatty found in Keaton." But he is right and wrong at the same time—right in that Beatty allowed his own love for Keaton to become a subject of the film, wrong in claiming that this damages the end result. Much of *Reds'* power grows directly from the way in which it is clearly autobiographical as well as biographical, as sociological as it is historical.

Beatty is playing Beatty as well as Reed, and that can be said of Keaton (her post-*Annie Hall* image as screen representation of the modern woman provides us with the easy access to Bryant a mass audience absolutely needs) and Nicholson as well. On the level of love story, what informs the film with its curious impact is this double vision: its basis in historical fact but also the common knowledge that Beatty and Nicholson have often competed for attractive women. The projection of their long-held friendly rivalry onto the evolving canvas of this fictionalized account of a factual incident adds a remarkable edge. One watches, trying to decipher what is actual and what is acted.

When asked by *Rolling Stone* in 1984 if he truly did develop a crush on Diane Keaton during the filming,

Ultimately, Louise forsakes Gene for the more idealistic John Reed (Warren Beatty).

Jack explained: "During the production, that's the way it began to feel . . . 'My God, I've got a real crush, and this is my best friend and his girlfriend.' But that's also what the movie was about. . . . I'm focused on my job all the time . . . during the work, I would allow myself to get overinflamed about it with Warren right there—just to see what would happen." In other words, for the scene to play "true" onscreen, it must—to a degree—literally *be* true. "That poem I give to Miss Keaton," he admitted to *The New York Times* a year later, "was not some verse by O'Neill. "I wrote a real poem that was extremely revealing." For a serious actor, dedicated to making the scene absolutely real, "It's the kind of thing no one else sees but you know it's there. And believe me, I did not misplace that prop." Only by fully collaborating on the project, creating a character who was halfway between a biographical sketch of Eugene O'Neill and an autobiographical image of Jack Nicholson, could a third man— a dramatically real characterization who partook of both—emerge. To offer that, Jack had to discover aspects of O'Neill that were true also for himself: "I understand him," he would later say, "the way he approached women."

Which is why Jack could use his characterization as an expression of atttiudes closest to him. Stanley Kauffmann of *Commentary*, who generally approved of the film, hit Jack hard: "Jack Nicholson, as Eugene O'Neill, is Jack Nicholson. His role is written blandly, without individuation, and Nicholson does nothing to supply colors—he just floats through. He's too healthy-looking, anyway, for the gaunt O'Neill." But movie stars—by the very nature of their being—are invariably more attractive than the real-life people they play. If Nicholson plays Nicholson, that may be less the criticism Kauffmann intended than an acute observation.

For once again, Jack the writer gets to play a writer, embodying onscreen the particular glories and anguishes of the profession he's a part of. Not only O'Neill's politics but his early cynicism about the ideals of the movement he supported without idealistically embracing (as compared to his colleagues who would in time realize he'd been the perceptive one) are perfectly parallel to Jack's, who has said: "You can't be radical; if the people vote you in, then that means you are approved by the majority. Then what kind of a radical are you?" Robert Hatch complained in *The Nation* that: "As always, [Nicholson] is fun to watch, but O'Neill was a morose and drinking man, and Nicholson has played that character so often he fell into the trap of giving us the type instead of the man." Few who watch his work would agree: his O'Neill is an intense, burning intellectual-cynic who appears jealous of Reed's infantile idealism, seducing Reed's woman in part to prove to himself the superiority of his own cynicism.

And there are hints of the moroseness and the drinking, as much as time would allow a supporting character. Once again, Jack was able to draw on memories of that morose and drinking man he knew firsthand, John Nicholson. Pauline Kael seems closer to the truth when she comments in *The New Yorker*: "The jitters and freak exhilaration of Nicholson's recent performances are gone. He isn't just throwing off sparks here. His mannerisms have been straitjacketed, except for the bare minimum—the lurking malevolence, the eyes rolling back, one leering high-flying eyebrow . . . he sinks down into himself and plays a quiet, deeply bitter man."

Others also caught the special quality Jack brought to the role. "Actor-directors often bring out the best in their colleagues," David Ansen wrote in *Newsweek*. "Nicholson, as the cynical, boozing O'Neill, plays the devil's advocate to the romantic revolutionists—and almost steals the picture. He has three razor-sharp scenes with Keaton in which hostility and lust mingle with caustic menace. It's his best work in years." Richard Corliss of *Time* agreed: "Under Beatty's direction, Jack

Nicholson proves how resourcefully sexy an actor he can be. His O'Neill stalks the shrouded Provincetown beach in search of the eloquence of fog people; lounges lynxlike and purrs out a denunciation of political commitment; walks slowly toward Louise and waits as she steps up into their first illicit kiss—and most erotic moment in a movie that is as much about comrades as about lovers."

The political situation in the film has a double meaning. On the one hand, *Reds* features an accurate (if necessarily simplified) rendering of the radical politics of the 1910s and twenties; on the other, it employs that historical period for the purpose of commenting on the more recent wave of American radicalism in the 1960s and early seventies, which Beatty, Keaton, and Nicholson all participated in. Like Reed with his heroes, Beatty supported Eugene McCarthy and George McGovern in their presidential campaigns, wholeheartedly believing that "the new politics" was about to take root; like O'Neill in his time, Jack supported both those candidates but scoffed at the notion that any long-range good would come of it. The film finds, in history, a

Warren Beatty as John Reed must balance his time between being a social activist and a subjective journalist.

means of appreciating and understanding our own times: it sees in Reed's life a bitter but necessary coming to terms with the inability to accomplish one's more idealistic goals, the importance of fighting the good fight for the cathartic quality of its Sisyphian struggle.

That's why, at the end, Reed appears to die less of typhus (as he did, three days short of his 33rd birthday, in real life) than for symbolic reasons: this is, after all, a drama drawn from history, not a docudrama. So there's a marvelous ambiguity about the death scene: We're not sure if he passes away because he's finally faced the terrible truth O'Neill has always divined or if he wills himself to, so he will not have to face that ever more ominous and obvious reality. This is a movie about disillusionment with the political process. By continually emphasizing the anti-war attitudes of the American socialists, Beatty indicates that they are meant as stand-ins for the anti-war youth of his own time. That fabulous moment when John and Louise march through the streets of Petrograd, with banners waving as the "Internationale" is loudly, fervently sung, looks (as presented here) remarkably similar to the TV news images of the

At the height of the Russian Revolution, Reed finds himself in the center of the action, a journalist who does not merely report the news but helps make it.

225

student takeover of Columbia University. But what appears to be the beginning of a brave new world turns out to be a magical moment that somehow slips through their fingers.

Beatty must have been—during the same years he was developing his Reed project—trying to understand why the youth movement of his own time evaporated before his eyes, even when it appeared on the edge of success. His political conversations with Jack affected him much the way O'Neill's cynical statements do Reed in the film. And however unconsciously, Beatty fashioned a film which sees in the souring, in the early 1920s, of the dream from the late 1910s a clear parallel with the souring, in the early 1970s, of the dream from the late 1960s.

John Simon was characteristically tough on the film: "War and Revolution," he scoffed, "are mostly an exotic background to spice up the screwball comedy of battling, wisecracking lovers . . . political thought and action are grossly oversimplified if treated at all." But he was unfair as well as unkind, simply missing the whole point of the movie.

For this is not an "educational film" from *Encyclopedia Britannica* or an underground movie with revolutionary attitudes and purpose. It is a commercial Hollywood picture, though one with the loftiest of ambitions.

While some critics carped about the "trivializing" inclusion of romantic comedy (the pet dog who always interrupts any attempts at lovemaking by Reed and Bryant, as if they were characters in a Neil Simon comedy), this is absolutely essential to the movie's impressive impact: it is why the characters come off not as cardboard figures in a dull, plodding, purposeful recreation of exciting times, but as contemporary, rounded people an audience can immediately relate to. Beatty wants to entertain, with romantic drama and comedy relief, certain such a crowd-pleaser is the best way to make his thematic points, which are slipped in subliminally.

For the movie is, despite lapses, quite monumental; "alternately rambling and riveting," James M. Wall called it in *The Christian Century*. Among other things, it combines the best qualities of the two extremes of Hollywood moviemaking: the all-star historical epic of *Gone With the Wind* with the intellectual analysis of a complex man found in *Citizen Kane*. Those polar extremes of the classic American movie are awkwardly but effectively yoked together here. *Reds* deserved the Oscar for Best Picture that unaccountably went to the agreeable but forgettable *Chariots of Fire*. Beatty can be proud of his accomplishment; what remains now is for his pal Jack to return to directing, and give us a Big One of his own.

The Border

(1981)
A UNIVERSAL RELEASE

CAST:

Jack Nicholson *(Charlie Smith)*; Valerie Perrine *(Marcy)*; Harvey Keitel *(Cat)*; Warren Oates *(Big Red)*; Elpidia Carrillo *(Maria)*; Shannon Wilcox *(Savannah)*.

CREDITS:

Director, Tony Richardson; producer, Edgar Bronfman; screenplay, Deric Washburn, Walon Green, and David Freeman, from a story by Deric Washburn; cinematography, Ric Waite; editor, Robert K. Lambert; music, Ry Cooder; running time: 107 mins.; rating: R.

As if to confound those critics who hope to discover and define a Jack Nicholson "persona," Jack chose as his next lead a role as different as possible from the crazed, dangerous hero of *The Shining* or the corrupt, self-interested man in *Postman*. In *The Border*, he played an idealist, but not one who hides behind a cynical front, like his wisecracking crusader in *Chinatown*. J.J. Gittes wore smart suits and acted hip, though we soon learned he had a heart of gold deep down, much like those mythic men—Sam Spade and Philip Marlowe—played by Bogart in the film noirs *Chinatown* paid homage to. In *The Border*, Jack played not another marvelous turn on a stock figure from pulp fiction, but a decent, flawed man with believable problems (like paying the bills racked up by a spendthrift wife) few movie heroes worry about.

People magazine once tagged Jack "an icon of ordinariness," and no role he has played more closely associates him as a representative man of the people than this one:

Jack Nicholson as Charlie Smith.

Charlie Smith rises to heroic proportions when he unconsciously, instinctively assumes an idealistic approach toward life. When we first meet him, Charlie works as an Immigration Services investigator in Los Angeles, specializing in the problem of "wetbacks": Mexicans illegally entering the country. The job is menial and unrewarding, and while Charlie makes a decent living, he feels unfulfilled, sensing he can do little to stem the tide of people slipping in, feeling as if he's persecuting rather than prosecuting those few pathetic souls he does manage to apprehend. What Charlie would love is to return to the Forest Service, suggesting he symbolizes an environmental, ecological mentality: There he could believe he was accomplishing something worthwhile— that his life had meaning—by protecting the forests and the wildlife contained in them. But his snippy, social climbing wife Marcy (Valerie Perrine) will hear none of that.

In fact, it is she who browbeats Charlie into transferring to El Paso, Texas, joining the United States Border Patrol. That organization similarly serves the function of restricting the illegal entrance of people desperate to cross the Rio Grande. Marcy wants to move to El Paso because her favorite girlfriend is married to one of the patrolmen (Harvey Keitel), and he can get Charlie a position as his partner. At first, it seems this may at least be a more exciting variation of Charlie's old job, as he will be working in the field, cowboy style, packing a gun,

Following a raid on a group of distraught people illegally crossing the border, patrolman Charlie Smith meets the Madonna-like Maria (Elpidia Carillo) for the first time.

Having come in contact with the purity of Maria, Charlie cannot stand to be around his beautiful but ultra-materialistic wife, Marcy (Valerie Perrine).

zipping around in a car. Very quickly, though, Charlie learns the reality of the situation: His partner, like their officer (Warren Oates) and most other members of the force are totally cynical about the possibility of achieving their aim. Instead, they cruelly hassle the hungry, poverty-stricken wetbacks, hustling them into custody and then back over the border; they casually take bribe money to turn their backs while high-powered entrepreneurs smuggle paying customers across in vans. Problems arise only when a rare officer refuses to take such a bribe, and inadvertantly signs the death warrant of any wetbacks being illegally transported. For to avoid capture and incrimination, the smugglers are quick to kill all the Mexicans in their custody rather than allow them to remain alive as potential witnesses in court.

For a while, Charlie seems likely to remain one of those honest (if unintentionally dangerous) patrolmen, at first refusing the hints of offers coming from his new partner. But when his wife ceaselessly complains she doesn't have the money necessary to maintain the kind of lifestyle her girlfriends enjoy, Charlie begins accepting bribe money like most of his colleagues. He soon hates his job, and he hates himself for succumbing to the worst kind of acquiescence to wholesale corruption: He feels he's worse than the others, for they don't care about or consider the morality of what they're doing, and he does. He should, he knows, maintain a morality—a sense of decency—and his inability to do so causes a kind of soul-sickness.

Then, he spots Maria (Elpidia Carrillo), a Madonna-like Mexican woman who, with her child (she is widowed) and baby brother sits in a dirty border camp on the far side of the Rio Grande, hoping to cross over to what she believes is the promised land. The Virgin-like sense of innocence Charlie sees in her face touches something in him, stirring not lust but protectiveness. He senses that if he can save this woman and her wards, he will have accomplished something decent in an ugly world, will have—like a Hemingway hero—created a clean, well-lighted place, no matter how small. For what matters is not the enormity of the accomplishment but the rightness and goodness of the intent. It is clear that Charlie will be able to look in the mirror again if he only manages to pull this off, to protect not the multitudes he sees in their pain and fear and agony, but only these three.

So it's difficult for Charlie when he has to arrest them as part of a large group. While under custody, Maria's child—who for Charlie is now a miniature Mexican Christ—is torn from her by a group of thieves, paid by the smugglers, who regularly sell such babies to upscale childless couples. It's at this point that Charlie acts in the most moral fashion possible, moving outside the law but into the value system he believes in as he attempts to find

the child and return it to Maria, then spirit the three of them to safety.

Sadly, things don't work out as planned. The brother is killed, Maria seriously hurt. Yet this only further arouses Charlie's wrath. Steadfastly, he pursues the missing child. At this point, he rises to full heroic stature as he takes on both his partner and their boss, who—as part of the kidnapping ring—stand against him. And it is here, sadly, that the film goes awry. Clearly needed is an ending that somehow resolves the complex issues and socially significant themes that have laced the film. Instead, The Border supplies us with nothing more impressive than a routine (and less than convincing) shoot-out, lifted from any bygone B-western. When Charlie fights it out with two adversaries, swapping shots as if he were Wyatt Earp taking on Ike Clanton and Johnny Ringo, the filmmakers have to grope to contrive a means by which he beats them both, and what began as a movie with large ambitions breaks down into a routine potboiler. We can't help but come away wondering, is that all they were leading up to?

Stanley Kauffmann noted this problem when, in The New Republic, he complained: "It's a 'subject' script. That is, it seems to have started with a topic, then was fleshed out . . . the authors dreamed up people and entanglements to exploit the situation, and, in doing so, burdened themselves. . . ." The "subject" he refers to is, of course, illegal immigration, and the treatment of it resembles one of those problem-play films of the 1950s (racism in The Defiant Ones, nuclear holocaust in On The Beach, etc.), often appearing more interested in conveying a message than in developing characters as believable people or drawing situations with a sense of accuracy and immediacy.

Another problem was the choice of Tony Richardson as director. Like America's Mike Nichols, England's Richardson has a way of making movies that seem imposing and important while one looks at them, but tend to recede in the consideration. The Border had an intense, vivid imagery; one was immediately convinced that this was among the year's important pictures. Why else would the visuals appear so belaboredly beautiful? But such a striking style is only valid if supported by the script; if it ultimately boils down to nothing more than a melodrama with a timely message, than the word to describe that style has got to be "pretentious." Early on, The Border mutely promises (through its overwrought look) more than it can deliver. Added to this problem was the fact that Richardson, best remembered for British films both heavy (A Taste of Honey) and lighthearted (Tom Jones) seemed something of an outsider, more familiar with (and influenced by) old western movies than a firsthand knowledge of the new west.

Some critics were kind, though: In Time, Richard

Searching for Maria and hoping to redeem himself by saving her, Charlie gets beaten up in a Mexican bar.

Charlie grows ever less patient with his partner and old pal Cat (Harvey Keitel), who has totally succumbed to the numbing senselessness of their impossible job.

Corliss called Richardson's approach "a successful invasion of Peckinpah Country," adding that "the film's mercuric feeling is heightened by Ric Waite's supple zooms, pans and tracking shots, and by the whining chords of Ry Cooder's music." But such qualities, however impressive, finally seem bogus, first-class accoutrements designed to disguise a third-rate script. *Newsweek*'s David Ansen recognized both the qualities and the ultimate failure of the film when he referred to it as a "rousing but problematic movie," noting that while the issue of illegal aliens was worthy and capable of serving as the basis for a devastating film, "it's the kind of subject that gets financed in Hollywood only if it's twisted to fit a commercial genre. *The Border* has a lot going for it: tension and anger, a fine sense of the hot, dusty milieu. . . . But in its eagerness to supply sure-fire Hollywood thrills . . . ultimately succumbs to sentimentality and contrived melodramatics. . . . [The film] doesn't resolve the issues it has raised. *The Border* has the air of a project marred by studio compromises. . . ."

Surprisingly, the film had a fervent supporter in *The New Yorker*'s often acerbic, occasionally cruel Pauline Kael, who complained that *The Border* was unfairly "unheralded." Though she ultimately tabbed it, neatly and correctly, as "muckraking melodrama," Kael insisted that it rated as "a solid, impressive movie [willing to] lay out—very graphically—the essential irrationality of government policies, and the cruelty that develops out of them." Mostly, though, Kael was impressed with the star's work. "Jack Nicholson may still have plenty of surprises in him. . . . He gives a modulated, controlled performance, without any cutting up. Except for his brief appearance in *Reds*, this is the first real job of acting he has done in years. . . . The movie might have been disastrous if anyone else had played the part."

Indeed, Nicholson's sturdy, unsentimental portrait is what gives the film what conviction it has. Though Stanley Kauffmann had a considerably less impressive reaction to the film than did Kael, he too praised Richardson's work with Jack: "He gets the best performance from Nicholson since *One Flew Over The Cuckoo's Nest*. The macho lethargy, or lethargic machoism, that has come into Nicholson's work *(Reds)* or the unbridled exaggerations *(Goin' South, The Shining)* are gone; in their place, much of the best Nicholson returns. He doesn't quite have the threat of fire that he used to have, but he shows again his gift for authenticity, for implied susceptibilities, for suggestions of depth beneath the mundane. . . ." Ansen concurred: "Watching Jack Nicholson work is a pleasure again . . . and in *The Border* he's mesmerizing . . . in fact, greater than the script intended." Yet Ansen couldn't help noting how the very quality of Jack's work hurt the film's final effect, by inadvertently pointing out the weaknesses in the context containing it: "The complexities of his performance demand a more morally ambiguous climax."

Which is why *The Border* is not a great film, despite a great subject, a great vision of the landscape, and a great Nicholson performance. What makes *The Last Detail* or *Cuckoo's Nest* rate as great movies is that the script is, in each case, carefully thought out: the endings are not desperate attempts to tie up all the loose ends in the fastest, most facile manner possible, but logical conclusions to the drama that precedes them. Those films, like Greek tragedies, have been moving toward a preordained ending all along. Such a script supports a performance,

and here we can't help feeling that Jack is contributing a characterization worthy of Eugene O'Neill or Arthur Miller to a work of drama that ultimately seems so much contrived pulp. A measure of how simplistic (and, for that matter, retrograde) the film ultimately is can be seen in its portrayal of the women: Madonna and monster. While the two actresses play those parts with, respectively, conviction of total innocence and a sharp sense of satire, they are not well-rounded, flesh-and-blood people but symbols for the ultimate in good and evil, existing not as approximations of real people but as the polar extremes Smith—the ordinary man—must choose between. Compare them with, say, the two imperfect but extraordinary women in *Carnal Knowledge* or *Prizzi's Honor*, and the inability of this film to realize women (or any of the other supporting characters, for that matter) as complex human beings rather than chess pieces becomes all the more obvious—and disappointing.

"You can't change the world," Jack has said of the political impact of movies on audiences, "but you can make them think." His best movies—like *Cuckoo's Nest*—do just that, but *The Border* has a pre-digested quality; it attempts to do the audience's thinking for it. It works far better on the level of personal expression, for while Smith may be the closest Jack has ever come to playing an American Everyman, he managed to slip in more than a little of his own interests and attitudes. Smith leads a double existence: the homebody who is secretly involved in a complex (though intriguingly non-sexual) relationship with a woman other than his wife. A peasant with the soul of a poet, he has a difficult time with women, especially those who want a prefabricated American Dream delivered to their door as part of the marriage agreement. Jack's favorite (and most oft-quoted) myth, Sisyphus, comes into play, as Smith embarks on a desperate job that cannot be successfully completed, but which confers dignity in the attempt. Nicholson made Charlie Smith a believably modulated character, an expression of his own deepest anxieties, and a symbol of the ordinary American. That is indeed a major accomplishment with a single characterization: almost—though not quite—enough to carry the picture containing it.

AN OLD SEX WARRIOR:

Terms of Endearment

(1983)
A PARAMOUNT PICTURE

Jack Nicholson as Garrett Breedlove, in a staunchly serious mood . . .

CAST:

Shirley MacLane *(Aurora Greenway)*; Debra Winger *(Emma Greenway Horton)*; Jack Nicholson *(Garrett Breedlove)*; Jeff Daniels *(Flap Horton)*; Danny DeVito *(Vernon Dahlart)*; John Lithgow *(Sam Evans)*; Betty R. King *(Rosie Dunlop)*; Kate Charleson *(Janice)*; Lisa Hart Carroll *(Patsy Clark)*; Troy Bishop *(Tommy Horton)*; Huckleberry Fox *(Teddy Horton)*; Megan Morris *(Melanie Horton)*

CREDITS:

Director, James L. Brooks; producer, James L. Brooks; screenwriter, James L. Brooks, from the novel by Larry McMurtry; cinematography, Andrzej Bartkowiak; editor, Richard Marks; music, Michael Gore; running time, 132 mins.; rating R.

The summer of 1983 was not a good time for adult moviegoers: slob comedies and sci-fi epics intended for the teen audience glutted the screen. Then came fall, the kids went back to school, and adults hoped that their kind of movie might once again be available. They were not disappointed, for along came *Terms of Endearment*. It proved not only the most intelligent entertainment of the season, but the film against which adult-oriented movies would be judged for the remainder of the decade; when such pictures as *Places in the Heart* (1984) and *Nothing In Common* (1986) were released, the nicest compliment any critic could think of was "this year's *Terms of Endearment*," though such films rarely lived up to the comparison.

Terms is a terrific situation-comedy that, in mid-

Though at first Aurora Greenway (Shirley MacLaine) treats
her neighbor with scorn . . .

. . . after years of surviving on a less-than-cordial level, a romance
suddenly flickers between easygoing ex-astronaut Garrett and the
haughty Aurora . . .

. . . and in an alcoholic stupor, demonstrating once again
how effective Nicholson is at playing characters with a Jekyll/
Hyde double life.

. . . leading to a sophisticated (and sexy) lunch date . . .

movie, successfully transforms before our eyes into a morbid melodrama, ending on the most tragic note possible. The film's focus is on the relationship between Aurora Greenway (Shirley MacLaine), a Boston-bred/Houston-based matron, and her independently minded daughter Emma (Debra Winger), carrying them through a 30-year relationship filled with ups and downs, happy encounters and terrible misunderstandings, pleasant reunions and painful departures. At the very beginning, we see the youthful Aurora leaning over the crib where her baby happily sleeps, suddenly becoming convinced the child is about to succumb to crib death, attempting to revive Emma, only waking the peaceful infant. Their

lifelong relationship emerges as an extension of that moment—the well-intentioned but exhausting Aurora (long since widowed) interfering with Emma's life, destroying the daughter's peace of mind for reasons that are always above reproach.

The basis of their greatest conflict is Emma's decision to marry Flap Horton (Jeff Daniels), a congenial loser who makes a living as a nearly itinerant English professor, kicking around the country from one junior college to the next, never earning tenure but always emerging as the heartthrob of the young women in his classes. Aurora is convinced Flap will never make enough money to support her daughter in the manner to which

... culminating in the film's best-remembered moment, when Garrett and Aurora frolic in the ocean, as her inhibitions begin to disappear.

A healthy, happy sexual relationship follows . . .

she has become accustomed ("You're not special enough to survive a failed marriage," Aurora insists), and while time proves her right about Flap's shortcomings, she underestimates her daughter, who does grow as a result of the adversity she faces.

Emma's greatest regret, however, is not Flap's lack of earning power but that Flap is compulsively and consistently unfaithful. She has an affair of her own with a nice loser (John Lithgow) who works at the bank in their Iowa college town, not so much out of revenge for Flap's infidelities but because the sweet, sad man needs some warmth terribly, as does she. But whether Emma and Flap can resolve their differences and concentrate on the proper raising of their children becomes a moot point when Emma discovers she is dying of cancer.

At that moment, the tone of the film changes drastically. Few approaches are as risky as altering styles in mid-movie, but *Terms* is one of those rare pictures that breaks the rules and gets away with it. The transformation is so gradual the viewer thinks, for a moment, this can't be happening: the film was too much fun in its first half for anything quite that awful to happen. But it does, and the audience is deftly manipulated into willingly going along with the change in content and style.

The concept of a much-loved character dying of cancer has been used endlessly, not only in weeper movies but on TV medical shows and afternoon soap operas, and would at first appear a trite, familiar device,

only it doesn't play that way. Instead of going for cheap surface sentimentality, the film opts for a rich, deep sensitivity. One feels as if such a story has never been told before, so uniquely and powerfully is it told here. And the characters reach so far beyond cliché, are so clearly specific individuals with flaws as well as strengths, that we never associate what happens to Emma (and, as a result, to everyone else in the story) with the patterns of such previous potboilers.

James L. Brooks, the TV producer who created such exquisite sitcoms as the original *Mary Tyler Moore Show*, had plenty of experience blending the comedic and the dramatic in the best of those human interest half-hour series, but his big-screen debut nonetheless rated as a remarkable achievement. There was heavyweight competition for the Best Picture Academy Award—*The Big Chill* and *The Right Stuff*, most notably—but no one was surprised when *Terms* walked off with the top statuette and numerous other Oscars as well. Shirley MacLaine, previously passed over for such deserving work as *The Apartment*, finally won Best Actress. And Best Actor in a Supporting Role went to Jack Nicholson for his perfect portrayal of Garrett Breedlove, the brash, breezy former astronaut who moves in next door to Aurora and, after a cool relationship of several years, is suddenly informed by the spirited, willful, self-admittedly haughty lady that he will have the honor of being her lover.

235

His very acceptance of the part indicates the icono-clastic attitude Jack has always assumed toward the movie business: no other big name star was willing to take the role (and several, including Paul Newman, were offered it before Nicholson), owing to the fact that Breedlove remains on the sidelines. Other stars may take cameo roles for the sheer lark of it, but few if any willingly take character-roles in other people's pictures. Jack has always been less interested in discovering vehi-cles for his ego than projects to collaborate on: "I've always wanted to protect my right as an actor to play a short part without everyone thinking my career is over," he's claimed, "and so I've always intermittently done them."

In truth, though, Jack may have agreed as much out of necessity as choice. Every one of his previous starring vehicles for the past five years had failed at the box-office, and he was no longer considered bankable. Still, many other performers, finding themselves in the same situation, would have desperately clung to star status by accepting leads in lesser films, rather than facing what they might have considered the humiliation of taking not only a character role but third billing. But Jack liked the script, the role, and the director, so he took the kind of

. . . though Garrett also proves to be a fine friend when he helps Aurora survive the death of her daughter.

risk others avoided. It paid off with a great part and his second statuette.

And some of the best reviews he'd received in years. In *Time*, Richard Schickel complimented him for giving "a joyously comic display of just the kind of wrong stuff that appalls and attracts" Aurora. "Garrett Breedlove," David Ansen noted in *Newsweek*, "is not a starring role. But he's a scene stealer, and Nicholson obviously relishes the opportunity. He takes daring farcical chances with this character and pulls them all off. Nicholson may be unique for a star of his stature: he hasn't the usual leading man's vanity; indeed, he seems to revel in playing the slob, exhibiting his paunch." That willing-ness to be unglamorous yet appealing also touched Lawrence O'Toole of *Macleans*: "Nicholson is superbly rambunctious in his nonstarring role, displaying a spirit as big as his paunch and uncovering a sensitivity beneath the playboy veneer." Stanley Kauffman wrote in *The New Republic* that, "The idea of the Nicholson charac-ter—an ass-chasing, heavy-drinking, pot-bellied ex-as-tronaut, with charm that is more overbearing than insinuating—is itself a ten-strike. All that remained was for it to be written well and acted well, and it was." Even John Simon, who trashed the film in *National Review*, had kind things to say: "What real merit the film has [rests in the] sporadic fun contributed by Nicholson and, in some cases, improvised by him." Pauline Kael, in *The New Yorker*, observed that, "The years have given Nicholson an impressive, broader face, and his comedy has never been more alert, more polished. He isn't getting laughs because of his lines; he's getting them because of his insinuating delivery . . . There's a charge of fun in his acting; it isn't just the flab hanging out that makes him funny—it's that he stands like a dirty-minded little kid who hasn't yet learned to suck in his gut, an old sex warrior who can't be bothered."

A little kid and an old sex warrior: that is, two men living inside one body, and thus one more of those "double-existence" characters that make up Nicholson's canon of roles. As a man of great sexual experience ("a lifer as far as womanizing goes," Jack has said of Breedlove, though he might have been talking about himself) who finds himself involved in an ongoing, awkward relationship with a world-class lady who loves him but may not be willing to marry him, Jack certainly found a role in which he could assess his own parallel relationship with Anjelica Huston. To a degree, he based his portrayal of the role on his brother-in-law, a test pilot after World War II, as well as on astronaut Russell Schweikert, a high school friend. Jack has his own interpretation of the part, and why his playing of it touched so many people: "One of the things that moti-vated me with that character is that everyone was starting

Jack relaxes on the set with co-stars Shirley MacLaine and Debra Winger, who emerged from the film a budding young superstar.

to make a total cliché out of middle age crisis, they were dissatisfied, they hated their job. I just went against the grain of the cliché. I just wanted to say, 'Wait a minute, I happen to be this age and I'm not in any midlife crisis. I'm not an object of scorn and pity by anybody ten years younger than me.' There's got to be other people like me, so I'd like to represent that in this movie." Once again, Jack was a full collaborator in the filmmaking process, able to add the element of personal expression even to another person's picture.

It's worth noting that the character didn't exist in the book, where a half dozen different men served the function of Aurora's male companion at various points. But that would have been too confusing for a film, and Brooks wisely decided to coalesce all those characters into a single one, eliminating the appealing discursiveness of the novel by supplying the kind of tight, developing comic/dramatic relationship that works far better in the context of a film's structure. Often, though, such composite characters don't play; because their situations and dialogue are bits and pieces of the various characters in the original, the composites emerge as awkwardly assembled patchwork-quilt characterizations. Not so here: Brooks and Nicholson created a man as convincingly specific as he is impossible to neatly analyze.

The movie itself had a deservedly marvelous reception. "*Terms* comes to at least glancing terms with almost every problem a person is likely to encounter," Schickel wrote, "within the context of lifelike randomness." Ansen compared the picture to the other occasional adult-oriented films that somehow still managed to get made, finding it superior to those exalted Oscar winners: "Though *Terms* may find itself linked with movies like *Kramer Vs. Kramer* and *Ordinary People* because it appeals to the same audience, it's never locked in the grip of a thesis. Its characters—happily—don't represent a Social Problem, only themselves."

There were occasional mixed reactions; O'Toole admitted this was "one of the most memorably acted movies in years. Unfortunately, it lacks an underlying design which would have made an exceedingly good movie a great one." This criticism gently lodged by O'Toole was more stridently stated by Simon: "By what sort of artistic integrity does a film go from freewheeling farce about seemingly invulnerable comic-strip characters to sudden troweled-on tragedy, from Mel Brooks to Erich Segal?" But of course few would agree that the characters are, in the first half, written or played on a comic strip level like those in a blazing Brooks burlesque; rather, they resemble the characters in a Neil Simon

237

comedy, very close to real life people, exaggerated slightly for comedic effect. The ending, rather than on a par with *Love Story*, in fact avoids easy emotions, going instead for a sensitive, rather than sentimental, approach.

Kauffmann seems closer to the truth when he compliments the film for that very quality: *"Terms* does have a highly emotional conclusion, but it comes about quite arbitrarily, as highly emotional occurrences do in life." Kael took a kind of middleground on the film, finding it blatantly manipulative but apparently enjoying every moment: "This is a real-life-tragedy movie that leaves you no choice but to find it irresistible," insisting Brooks was merely "extending half-hour gag comedy to feature length by the use of superlative actors who can entertain us even when the material is arch and hopped-up."

There is an underlying strength underscoring the surface sense of sweetness. The film's style does not jump out and grab the viewer, but is invisible in the way the styles of some of the finest (though self-effacing) directors of the Studio era (Howard Hawks, Michael Curtiz) were. Though the movie's visual scheme does not draw attention to itself, it's nonetheless functional and, in a subtle way, demanding, for there are intriguingly unexpected points of view and rather daring ellipses in the editing.

Still, we remain unaware of them while watching *Terms* for the first time, which is the way it should be; they are subtle enough so that they add to the film's aura of a unique story, effectively and intriguingly told, while always diverting our attention away from the technique and toward the people and the plot. Brooks is, then, much like the directors Jack has previously announced he most admires—Rafelson, Hellman, Ashby—in that this filmmaker is more interested in people than in pyrotechnics, inspiring the actors to deliver even the more conventional lines of dialogue in such an unconventional but convincing manner that we come away feeling life has been distilled to its essence, then shared as art.

"One of the things about my character," Jack has said of Breedlove and his approach to the man, "is that about 40 percent of his occupation has died. They were sun gods and at that point in aviation (the early 1950s), there just weren't any other people who could show up in Long Island and say they'd just arrived from Cairo . . . [but in the eighties] it just isn't there any more, so the comic adjustment of this character is that he's a little squeamish." The key similarity between himself and Breedlove is that Garrett is "very nonjudgmental, he has a fatalistic sense of humor about other people and doesn't try to change them very much. I don't think he was always that way. He's changed, grown." In talking about the character, Jack is clearly talking about himself. Then again, in delineating such a character dramatically, he is in another sense always "talking about himself," or some aspect of himself.

THE BORGIAS OF BROOKLYN:

Prizzi's Honor

(1985)
A 20TH CENTURY-FOX FILM

CAST:

Jack Nicholson *(Charley Partanna)*; Kathleen Turner *(Irene Walker)*; Anjelica Huston *(Maerose Prizzi)*; William Hickey *(Don Corrado)*; John Randolph *(Angelo "Pop" Partanna, Charlie's Father)*; Lee Richardson *(Dominic Corrado, Maerose's Father)*; Robert Loggia *(Eduardo Corrado, Maerose's Uncle)*; Michael Lombard *(Filargi "Finlay")*.

CREDITS:

Director, John Huston, producer, John Foreman; screenplay, Richard Condon and Janet Roach, from the novel by Richard Condon; cinematography, Andrzej Bartkowiak; editors, Rudi Fehr and Kaja Fehr; music, Alex North; running time: 129 mins.; rating: R.

When *Prizzi's Honor* opened, some viewers sat in stunned silence, amazed at what transpired onscreen: a deadly-dull, emotionally empty, detached and distant, aloof and ugly, longwinded and unlovable film, based on a script for a zippy dark comedy but done with the deliberate pace of a grand opera. The film was bland, bleak, and boring, eliciting an emotional response from such an audience only twice, when two beautiful women are gruesomely, graphically murdered: an innocent bystander in an elevator killed by the female lead, herself ultimately done in by the male lead. The tone for their killings is cool, clinical amorality, each drawing an anguished groan from the audience.

But there was an alternative view. Some people perceived *Prizzi* as a brilliant black comedy, a remarkably

Jack Nicholson as Charley Partanna.

subtle work distinguished by an unsparingly cynical sensibility on the part of 79-year-old director John Huston, rating as his masterpiece of old age, the film that perfectly summed up the dark view of humanity so basic to his work during the past half century.

The dichotomy of reaction was drawn along tight lines: those who defended the film could think of its detractors as unsophisticated boobs who missed the understated dark humor and mistakenly tried to interpret this admittedly offbeat farce as a drama; those who attacked it believed the film's fans had come determined to like it, no matter what, pretentiously finding ways to congratulate the nasty movie for its mistakes.

The film that caused all this uproar is based on a novel by Richard Condon, whose best work *(The Manchurian Candidate)* treads a thin line between serious international thriller (in the same general genre as Hitchcock's *Notorious*) and a broad burlesque of high-level bureaucracies (not unlike Stanley Kubrick's *Dr. Strangelove*). *Prizzi's Honor* is intended as a combination gangster genre-piece and satire on such serious gangster film/ books as *The Godfather*. The key character is Charlie Partanna (Jack), a none-too-bright hit man for the Prizzi family, an East Coast organized-crime dynasty dominated by a wizened, wicked patriarch, Don Corrado (William Hickey). Having once been engaged to Corrado's granddaughter Maerose (Anjelica Huston), and not quite fully recovered from the failure of that seemingly perfect match, Partanna attends a family wedding and is absolutely enchanted by a West Coast lady, Irene (Kathleen Turner), he meets. They couldn't be more wrong for each other: he's sloppy and rumpled, she slick and chic; he's as Italian as can be, while she's Polish; he's dark and she's blond; he's a part of the traditional male-oriented view, while she's a liberated lady who runs her own business firm; he's New York grungy and she's L.A. casual; he's a romantic and she's a realist; he's dumb and she's smart. Somehow, though, the opposites attract; before long, Charlie is endlessly flying back and forth across the country to court her.

What he comes to realize, in time, is that she's also a hit person, a cold-blooded killer who has sometimes subcontracted for the Prizzi family but just as often worked against their best interests. Confused about what he should do ("Do I marry her or do I ice her?"), Charlie turns to Maerose, his former lover turned confidante and best pal, and (seemingly) the stereotype of the Mafia princess who never ventures out of the house, purposefully knowing nothing about the family business. Indeed, it's Maerose who convinces Charlie he ought to go through with the marriage, which (in the film, as opposed to the book) he does. But Maerose is in fact a spiritual descendant of Lucrezia Borgia, so no matter

how cold-blooded the elegant Irene may appear, Maerose outdoes her, plotting this woman's eventual demise. Maerose is in no rush, perfectly willing to let Irene have Charlie (in all senses of the word) for some time, knowing that with patience and diligent manipulation, he will someday once again belong to Maerose.

And he does. The family "honor" (the term is, of course, employed ironically here) ultimately demands Charlie kill his wife, when it's clear that she has wheedled away a huge pot of the organization's earnings, also causing the police to clamp down on organized crime owing to her sloppy accidental killing of a police chief's wife. Charlie would seem to be the vulnerable one here, but when he and Irene finally do face off for their duel in the sun, he appears considerably sharper than anyone might have guessed, killing Irene (with a gruesome knife to the throat) before she can shoot him. In the end,

family loyalty wins out over romance.

For Jack, the role offered yet another unique acting stretch: He'd never really played a dumb lead before, having done so only in supporting parts *(The Raven, The Fortune)*, and was intrigued by trying to make a less than sharpwitted character a romantic hero. At the same time, though, he found yet another character which, as different as Charlie may appear from previous Nicholson parts, nonetheless offers a unique variation on some recurring themes: the concept of family; family allegiances vs. romantic relationships; the love/hate bond of a man and a woman; the difficulty in making a long-standing commitment; characters who lead double existences; men dealing both with their immediate father-figure substitutes and their more elusive actual fathers.

Jack has admitted some serious problems with playing

. . . only to discover that she, like him, is a "hit person," leading to a decision that they'll share professional as well as personal lives.

The urban, ethnic Charley is charmed when he meets a cool, elegant West Coast lady, Irene Walker (Kathleen Turner) . . .

Charlie during the initial read throughs. "Initially, I did not understand it," he said of the material in a *Film Comment* interview. "I did not know it was a comedy, [despite] having read the novel." The first thing John Huston said was, "It seems to me, Jack, everything you've done is informed by intelligence. And you can't have that with this film. It's got to be dumb, very dumb." Huston actually believed Jack should wear a big, bad wig for the role, to make the character look even tackier than the costumes would present him as being. The wig did

241

not come about, but Jack was entranced when Huston said: "I think we have a chance here to do something *different*." He touched Jack's favorite nerve: *different* is one of the key things he's always after as an actor. "The fun of doing it is in the *difference* of it," he always says. So the work came about, in Jack's words, when "I put my not understanding the material together with the character's dumbness into a kind of dynamic on how to play him." Perhaps because of the lack of understanding, the dumbness looks both strange and strained; because of the mock-humorous approach (never really the forte of this realistic actor), we can constantly see the intelligent Jack Nicholson acting dumb as Charlie Partanna. That is, we can see the mechanism at work, destroying any illusion of believability. Jack is *playing* dumb, not *being* dumb. He never completely disappears into Charlie: we can always distinguish here the actor from the character.

Not everyone agreed with that judgment. In *The New Yorker*, Pauline Kael praised Jack's work: "Nicholson's performance is a virtuoso set of variations on your basic double take and traditional slow burns. . . . Nicholson doesn't overdo his blurred expressions or his uncomprehending stare; he's a witty actor who keeps you eager for what he'll do next." Richard Schickel of *Time* hailed this as "one of his boldest performances," noting that "in Nicholson, [Huston] has an actor whose subtlety and nerve match his." In *Newsweek*, David Ansen explained

Anjelica Huston as Maerose Prizzi, the stay-at-home Mafia princess who turns out to be the Lucrezia Borgia of the Bronx, quietly manipulating everyone to her own ends.

Between two women: Charley is torn between the icy, aloof Irene (top) and the intense, concerned Maerose (bottom).

that "Nicholson takes wild chances: assuming a deceptively dumb Brooklyn accent, he plays this hilarious anti-hero as if he were a schizo who couldn't decide if his role in life was Bogart's or Elisha Cook's. It's a masterful turn." Ansen, of course, touches on the double existence of this latest Nicholson characterization, in comparing him to two diametrically opposed performers who graced Huston's earlier films: the Bogartian jaded romantic hero and Cook's creepy little sleazeball of a scene stealer.

There were other accolades for his work in *Prizzi*: "Nicholson speaks in a Brooklyn palooka's accent that is perfectly sustained yet flexible enough to suggest shades of feeling we didn't think could possibly be there," David Denby wrote in *New York*. "Nicholson is indeed very funny. He can look completely out of it—a dumb thug with nothing going for him but instinct—until, suddenly, something switches in his brain, his eyebrows drop like twin semaphores, and his whole face comes back into focus. In a world governed entirely by force and guile, his Charley is stupid enough to fall in love, and where that leads him is both pathetic and funny."

Others agreed it was pathetic, though in a less complimentary sense of that term, and not particularly funny at all. "Nicholson sports a marvellous Brooklyn accent, but his character is too limited for his talents," Lawrence O'Toole complained in *Macleans*. Tom O'Brien of *Commonweal* argued: "Nicholson brings the hit-man to

Back at his job, but with a new purpose, Charley continues his life of crime even as he finds himself being forced to kill the woman he loves.

Mafia chieftan Don Corrado Prizzi (William Hickey) confers with the blond "independent" female-killer, Irene, then addresses a family gathering with sons Dominic (Lee Richardson, left) and Eduardo (Robert Loggia, right); the theme of family ties and inter-familial betrayal, a common thread in Jack's films, reaches its apex in *Prizzi's Honor*.

243

half-life; not just with perfect idiomatic Sicilian American, but with well-timed dumbo gestures and a pair of eyebrows arched to resemble a mini-Satan's. . . . But Nicholson's hit-man is never allowed to grow, or even to feel real conflict. Huston's main character is finally a puppet, and the satire, accordingly, skin deep." Stanley Kauffmann added in *The New Republic* that, "Jack Nicholson . . . gives such a designedly stupid performance that he's incredible as a crown prince, and he wallows so utterly in Brooklynese—with a paralyzed upper lip—that he sounds less acclimated to American than his father" in the film (John Randolph).

The critics' attitudes about Jack's performance directly paralleled their feelings for the film containing it. Kael praised its "daring comic tone," claiming it was "*The Godfather* acted out by the Munsters" and "a baroque comedy about people who behave in ordinary ways in grotesque circumstances." That last phrase, incidentally, may suggest why Jack was attracted to the part (in addition to working with the legendary Huston and Huston's daughter, Jack's longterm girlfriend): He has often used similar phraseology to describe the kinds of projects he most enjoys. "I found myself laughing all the way through," Kael said, also admitting "some people don't respond to the movie at all." As one who did not, this critic rather agrees with O'Toole, who argued that the film "tries for sophisticated black humor" but is "only modestly amusing, and its humor is much too precious . . . The characters in *Prizzi's Honor* are never complex enough to be surprising, nor quite human enough to be tragic."

"Director John Huston has tried to treat raucous, burlesque material with serious subtlety," O'Toole concluded. "Unfortunately, he has used kid gloves when brass knuckles would have done the job." O'Brien agreed: "*Prizzi's Honor* is curious," he complained, "though filled with echoes, it lacks resonances." By echoes, he meant the similarities to earlier Huston film noirs like *The Maltese Falcon*, with its tough guy hero who must stick by his code and turn his lover over to the cops. "Despite all the parallels, however, one thing is missing" from *Prizzi*, in O'Brien's view: "a representation of genuine humanity at the core of the plot. . . . Huston is so intent on debunking sentiment that he winds up impoverishing emotional content, which is quite another matter. The director seems to dare us not to care . . . it feels, in the last analysis, like an empty work."

For Jack, part of the appeal of making *Prizzi* was in being part of a family, both in front of and behind the cameras. The film "had the flavor of a family project," he admitted of this experience which called for him to work with his girlfriend and her father, adding that this couldn't help but inform the picture since "*Prizzi* is *about* a family." As for working with a Hollywood legend as compared with the younger directors, Jack stated: "John camera cuts. If you only do one take you don't really know what you did. You don't get to refine it. You come home and think of the 35 things you might've thrown in the stew. When a director shoots several takes, you eventually find his rhythm. . . . But with John Huston everybody's got to be ready to go right away." Even some of Jack's most devoted fans feel this approach did not lead to his best work.

Director John Huston oversees the production of *Prizzi's Honor*.

Jack's elegant co-star, Kathleen Turner, who thanks to this and a series of offbeat and risky projects (*Crimes of Passion, Romancing the Stone, Peggy Sue Got Married*) emerged as the most talented and glamorous female movie star of the late 1980s.

THE MELLOWING OF JACK NICHOLSON:

Heartburn

(1986)
A PARAMOUNT PICTURE

CAST:

Meryl Streep *(Rachel)*; Jack Nicholson *(Mark)*; Jeff Daniels *(Richard)*; Maureen Stapleton *(Vera)*; Stockard Channing *(Julie)*; Richard Masur *(Arthur)*; Catherine O'Hara *(Betty)*; Steven Hill *(Harry)*; Milos Forman *(Dmitri)*; Natalie Stern *(Annie)*.

CREDITS:

Director, Mike Nichols; producers, Mike Nichols and Robert Greenhut; screenplay, Nora Ephron, based on her novel; cinematography, Nestor Almendros; editor, Sam O'Steen; music, Carly Simon; running time: 108 mins.; rating: R.

Heartburn reunited Jack with Mike Nichols while allowing him to act opposite Meryl Streep, generally regarded as the most significant actress/star to emerge in the preceding decade. Once again, Jack demonstrated his cavalier attitude toward traditional star-status by playing what was clearly the "second-lead" (this is, essentially, the woman's picture) and accepting second billing to an actress who had still been a child when Jack was breaking into pictures. For most Hollywood people, such a career move would have presented a decision that would be painful at best. For Jack, it wasn't even worth considering: he admired the project, the director, and the co-star, so there was no hesitation about going ahead; conventional attitudes about billing and the size of the role did not enter into the picture. Jack was not even bothered by the fact he hadn't been the first choice for his role, but came into the project when Mandy *(Yentl)*

At an upscale wedding, Mark (top) notices an attractive woman while all about him are concentrating on the wedding; Rachel (Meryl Streep) and friends (Susan Forristal, Jeff Daniels) are more intent on watching the bride and groom (bottom).

Washington columnist Mark meets New York food-writer Rachel (Meryl Streep) and love blossoms almost immediately.

At first, the marriage moves along smoothly, though minor annoyances are created by a house contractor Rachel tries to accommodate (top); later, she restrains Mark from attacking the incompetent contractor (Yakov Smirnoff) and his assistant (Luther Rucker).

Tension fills the restaurant as friends (Karen Akers and John Rothman) drop by the table to say hello to Arthur (Richard Masur), Mark, Rachel, and Betty (Catherine O'Hara).

Patinkin stormed off the set.

But Pantinkin left, it's worth noting, with good reason. *Heartburn* was based on Nora Ephron's bestselling novel, a catty revenge-motivated roman-à-clef (it read like the *National Enquirer* for literati) about her tumultuous marriage to *Washington Post* journalist-superstar Carl Bernstein, at first seemingly one of those made-in-heaven matches which rapidly unwound when she (seven months pregnant) discovered he'd been involved in a long and tawdry series of affairs with other women. Bernstein had been portrayed, by Dustin Hoffman in the mid-seventies, as an American hero, fighting the wicked Nixonian Establishment in *All the President's Men*; ten years later, he was to be portrayed as an insensitive, sex-crazed, near villainous male chauvinist pig ("a man capable of having sex with a Venetian blind," Ephron's autobiographical narrator said of her thinly disguised husband) in the upcoming film of *Heartburn*. As for his virtual silence when the book came out, Bernstein later explained to *Playboy*: "I didn't want to get up and have a big match, saying, 'Well, this is what happened, this isn't.' I made a decision: 'Don't say a thing about it.' " But Bernstein apparently felt he'd suffered enough, and had no intention of quietly sitting back as the film further extended the negative image through the mass media. After all, a film would reach a hundred times larger audience than had the novel; afterwards, there would be the videocassette release, and cable TV, then network movie-of-the-week presentation. . . . If this were not nipped in the bud, Bernstein might emerge not only as the laughing stock of a tight little literary crowd but of the entire nation, perhaps even the world. "I said, 'Enough, that's it,' " Bernstein later recalled. " 'We've reached the limit. From now on, I'm going to be real hard-assed about this, about what can be in this movie and what can't.' "

They ended up settling through negotiation rather than going to court. Bernstein won the right to review any script for the movie and confer with the director. The end result was that in the film, the character based on Bernstein could not be portrayed as savagely as in the novel: he had to repeatedly be shown as a loving father, ultimately had to be seen as a sympathetic man. "I was surprised," Bernstein admitted, "that [Nora] agreed to certain of the conditions," for by agreeing to them, Ephron insured—before day one of shooting—that the film would be a failure.

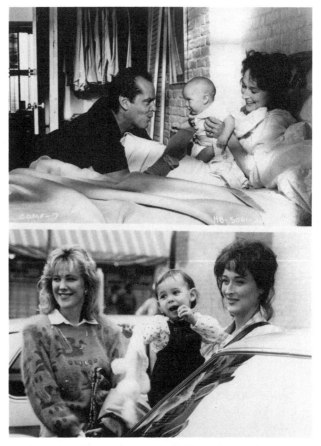

A calm before the storm, as Mark and Rachel enjoy their newborn child (top); shortly therafter, Rachel learns about Mark and his many women from her "friend" Betty (bottom).

Rachel discovers the evidence of Mark's infidelities (top), leaving him to try and patch up their fading marriage (bottom).

Rachel attempts to forgive her philandering husband (top); Mark remains unruffled by it all (bottom).

247

Her novel was wonderfully wicked, irresistibly vicious. In Bernstein's own words: "It had a Joan Rivers sensibility, a nasty tone, a smarmy edge. . . . Nora wrote a clever piece of gossip that owed its success to who we were publicly. . . . In that regard, I think *Heartburn* is truly a book for our time. It is absolutely the perfect book for the eighties. It is prurient. It obliterates everybody's dignity. . . ." Certainly, Ephron told the truth if not the whole truth: she pulled no punches, so the reader clearly saw the rise and fall of this relationship not necessarily as it was (in any objective sense), but as it appeared to her (a precise subjective presentation through one character's eyes). Allowing Bernstein input into the film meant it would be softened and compromised; the very qualities that made *Heartburn* an irresistible read would be gone, making it a most resistible film.

In fact, Bernstein was a friend of Nichols; when the journalist/celebrity learned the director had decided to helm *Heartburn*, he arranged for a lunch date at the Russian Tea Room, where Bernstein complained about what the film would do to his reputation and privacy. "I am your friend," Nichols assured him, "and somebody's going to make this movie, and you're much better off if I make it." That turned out to be a truthful statement. Ironically, in Nichols's film version, Mark, as played by Jack Nicholson, is so charming and likeable the audience cannot understand why Rachel, played by Streep, would be foolish enough to leave such a fabulous husband and father over a minor momentary indiscretion.

But if Bernstein had no reason to complain, everyone else did. The public "complained" through a surprisingly unenthusiastic box-office response to a film with such a striking star combination, while critics nearly unanimously panned the picture. In *Vogue*, Molly Haskell rightly tagged it an "oddly blurry and uninvolving adaptation. . . . Ephron's book is ill-served by the movie: Nichols doesn't do justice to its funny/anxious point of view and, probably inadvertantly, exposes its underlying complacency." *Newsweek*'s David Ansen noted that the movie, which initially seems to allow equal time and rooting interest for the two characters, failed when, in the second half (following the revelation of infidelity), it limited itself almost exclusively to the woman's point of view. "Why was he unfaithful if everything was so rosy?" Ansen asked. "It becomes just another generic story about a suffering wife." In part, that was due to the fact that director Nichols deemphasized the roman-à-clef aspect by casting performers who didn't look like the real-life participants (thereby automatically eliminating some of the possible exploitive/voyeuristic appeal) but did not, at the same time, make his fictional story interesting in its own right.

"The frustration of *Heartburn* is its triviality," Ansen complained. "It's doesn't seem to be *about* anything." The film is not about the break-up of the Ephron-Bernstein marriage, but it is not about the problems of modern marriage in general, either. It lacks both specificity and universality; it does not, cannot satisfy on either level. In *MacLean's*, Lawrence O'Toole wrote: "The chronicle of a disastrous marriage is less a cohesive narrative than a series of small . . . vignettes . . . the film leaves a slightly bitter aftertaste: as audiences exit from its ambiguous ending, its theme of failed love echoes disturbingly . . . *Heartburn* is a maddening film." Indeed, almost everyone found the film "slight": "Nichols has given the film a freshness of composition," Stanley Kauffmann complained in *The New Republic*, "that implies comedy-drama of more import than we get. . . . All very intelligent filmmaking, all wasted on flimsy material." David Denby of *New York* concurred: "A skillfull movie, but very, very small, and often precious—told with great knowingness but very little real understanding. . . . *Heartburn* is perhaps the most naggingly detailed view of an American upper-bourgeois marriage ever put on film."

Rachel is a food writer in the film, and if the movie itself resembles anything, it's nouvelle cuisine: elegant looking little tidbits of nothing that fail to add up to a satisfying meal. Another level on which the film fails is in its refusal to portray the ambience Ephron knew firsthand, observed perceptively, and wrote about wittily: the upper-middle-class Jewish lifestyle. Nichols's decision to de-emphasize this, and have his *Heartburn* be a story about Jewish characters only by implication, may have been intended as a means of lending it broader appeal, but in fact had the opposite effect; by eliminating a sharply observed culture, he only added to the vagueness of orientation as well as of purpose that causes the film to curdle.

Even on the level of plot-structure, the movie fails: Maureen Stapleton is often on view, presented in such a way that an audience assumes she's a close friend or relative, perhaps a beloved aunt. When, toward the end, we realize she's in fact Rachel's therapist (in a long, unnecessary, and unfunny sequence during which Rachel is followed to the therapy session by a mugger), we're thrust into the awkward position of mentally rethinking everything we have assumed about Stapleton's character. Likewise, Rachel's editor (played by Jeff Daniels) is impossible to comprehend: We never have any sense whether he is a sexually shy man in love with Rachel but so intimidated by her he can't propose, a man who respects her but is unattracted to her sexually, or a homosexual who likes and respects her as a friend but has no sexual interest in her or any other woman. In other words, he is not a character in the true meaning of

Rachel, pregnant, returns to New York and shares her problems with her therapy group (Maureen Stapleton, Christian Clemenson, Rich Thomas, Mercedes Ruehl).

that term but only a cipher, a generic "male editor" without any sense of written characterization, coming to life only thanks to what the actor brings to the role.

The movie's best moments tended to be only peripherally related to the central story: Mark and Rachel, enjoying a pizza in their uncompleted home, coming up with as many songs that feature the word "baby" (she has just revealed she's pregnant) as possible. The scene is an oasis in the trite, tiresome tale of one modern woman's problems that plays more like any of the TV *Movie of the Week* approaches to such a subject than it does the stinging, sharpwitted, unique "voice" of Ephron's novel. When, at the film's end, Rachel realizes (after a pathetic and halfhearted attempt at reconciliation) that Mark is cheating on her again, she lets him have it in the face with a key lime pie. The intended effect was to manipulate female viewers into leaping to their feet, cheering on their screen representative as she symbolically struck a blow against upscale male chauvinism. Instead, the scene seemed embarrassing: an obvious, uninspired, simplistic act of cinematic wish-fulfillment that came off as unconvincing.

Jack generally received better reviews than the film itself. In *Time*, Richard Corliss observed that, "Nicholson has a tough assignment . . . [he] reveals the charm that hides the folly. You can hate Mark for his cruelty or love him for his robust grace and fine, sharp humor." *MacLeans* likewise insisted that, "Nicholson

invests the treacherous husband with warmth and humanity," though Lawrence O'Toole wrote: "Nicholson, with his mischievously reptilian eyes and two of the wittiest brows in show business, is often amusing despite the limitations of his cartoon-villain role." Haskell took a similar line: "Nicholson is engaging but he has nothing to work with, no transition from the charmer he shows signs of being in the beginning to the skulking shadow of villainy he becomes." Kauffmann was a tad tougher: "Nicholson is miscast as Mark. First, he is too old. . . . That and the fact that he is gentile would have aroused some comment from [Rachel's] friends. . . . Nicholson seems to be having a harder time these days with non-intense moments. He can handle the anger and passion; for the rest, which is most of the time, he seems merely to be making faces." Denby added: "What are we to make of Nicholson's performance? He glowers and raises his eyebrows in santanic glee, and when he stands on the bed and sings, John Raitt-style, a cornball Rodgers-and-Hammerstein tribute to his unborn child, he's so fierce he's almost scary. Brilliant in a darkly imposing way, Nicholson doesn't look or sound like a man who churns out three columns a week. . . ."

What appealed to Jack about the role? "Actually," he said after filming *Prizzi*, "I'm trying to be the sex symbol of the eighties, now that I've hit mid-life. I've always held that club back out of my bag. Now I'm going to be just a sweet, outrageously appealing guy." Indeed, the period in his career beginning with *Terms* might be thought of as "The Mellowing of Jack Nicholson," as he teed off the ball and entered a new game.

Once again, Jack picked his role in large part to face a new challenge. Yet, simultaneously, *Heartburn* allowed him to approach themes that have been basic to most of his mature work: the difficulty of maintaining a monogomous relationship within the institution of marriage; the unique qualities of craziness, charisma, and creativity that make up a writer. His character is a "lifer," so far as women are concerned, involved in an ongoing love/hate relationship with the opposite sex. The pressures of such a relationship—and the family unit which stems from it—cause Mark to necessarily develop a "double existence," at once a family man and a ladies' man. Rachel's problems in the film version stem mainly from her inability to comprehend which is the "real" Mark: the devoted husband or the compulsive cheat.

After filming had been completed, Jack ran into Carl Bernstein in a restaurant. Jack threw up his arms in a theatrical gesture and said, "Well, buddy, I sure as hell wasn't going to call you during the shooting—I didn't want to know anything more about you than I already know." The statement reveals a great deal about Jack and his approach to the part: he had no intention of mimicking Bernstein—his look, his mannerisms, his attitude—but instead wanted to create a totally unique character for the story. Who this character called Mark was derived from seemed at best an incidental concern to the actor. He was not, so far as he was concerned, doing docudrama; the movie had to have a life, a reality, a vitality all its own, and that's the way he approached it. Sadly, *Heartburn* proved one more case of the film not supporting his performance.

DAT OL' DEBIL JACK:

The Witches of Eastwick

(1987)

A WARNER BROTHERS RELEASE

CAST:

Jack Nicholson *(Daryl Van Horne)*; Cher *(Alexandra Medford)*; Susan Sarandon *(Jane Spofford)*; Michelle Pfeiffer *(Suki Ridgemont)*; Veronica Cartwright *(Felicia Alden)*; Richard Jenkins *(Clyde Alden)*; Keith Jochim *(Walter Neff)*; Carel Struycken *(Fidel)*.

CREDITS:

Director, George Miller, Producers, Neil Canton, Peter Guber, Jon Peters; screenplay, Michael Cristofer, from the novel by John Updike; cinematography, Vilmos Zsigmond; editors, Richard Francis-Bruce and Hubert C. De La Bouillerie; music, John Williams; running time, 118 mins.; rating: R.

At first glance, *Witches of Eastwick* would appear to have little in common with *Heartburn*, Jack's summertime vehicle of one year earlier. Whereas that was a realistic melodrama requiring him to give a controlled, restrained reading of the part, this is a fantasy necessitating one of his more baroque portrayals. Still, there are key similarities. Like *Heartburn*, *Witches* is based on a bestseller, and some critics again found the film wanting in comparison to a book which all but defied successful screen adaptation. Likewise, Jack again played a horny little devil whose sexual profligacy gets him in trouble. The difference is, here he's a devil with a capital D.

As in John Updike's novel, three smalltown New England women find themselves involved in individual and group encounters with a chap who appears to be the devil incarnate. But all resemblance between book and

The publicity shot that captured the movie's mood: Jack, as that devil with women Daryl, surrounded by his lovely coterie of feminist-witches: Cher as the sensual Alexandra Medford, Susan Sarandon as the emotional Jane Spofford, and Michelle Pfeiffer as the intellectual Sukie Ridgemont; during the course of the film, these three symbols for different types of American women all surrender to Daryl.

The two sides of Daryl Van Horne allowed the actor playing him to reveal the two sides of Jack Nicholson: dapper and quite elegant when he wants to be...

film ends there. Updike's women know precisely what they're doing: having enjoyed a string of affairs before purposefully summoning up Daryl, They've consciously cursed their more Puritanical townsfolk with a succession of plagues; in the film version, they are nice, normal, sweet but sexually frustrated ladies who half-kiddingly perform an invocation one night after drinking too much wine, then are stunned when, as a result of their little joke, a Satanic visitor actually appears. All this happens today; Updike, however, had firmly set his book in the late sixties, employing this specific story as an allegory for (and delicate, whimsical satire on) the then-evolving Women's Liberation Movement. Importantly, then the women were all middle-aged; their "coven" equated to one of those "encounter groups" so (briefly) popular during the late sixties and early seventies.

But like *One Flew Over the Cuckoo's Nest*, *Witches* was a book that, to be relevant today and successful with a modern moviegoing audience, had to be stripped of its theme. The film appears less a satire on 1960s-style feminism than a parable (presented entertainingly in the form of a sex comedy) about the eternal battle between the sexes and, in particular, the unique variation of this universal issue present in the post-Women's Lib area. As Cher, very much a woman of the eighties, told me on the eve of the film's release: "We're in a state of flux. The late sixties and early seventies changed everything, which

...but just as often dangerous and terrifying. Jack, who has played characters living double lives throughout his career, found the ultimate Nicholson role in Van Horne.

had to be, but things have not settled yet. Men are disoriented, don't know their position anymore, or how they're supposed to relate to the 'new women'. As a film, Witches is about the awkward state of imbalance in American society today, and how that effects the way men and women relate."

Her on-target interpretation helps us understand the film's marvelous balance. For Witches is remarkably evenhanded, an entertainingly rendered objective overview that refuses to take either side. We are immediately charmed by the three lovelies and their fantasizing about how they would like to see an ideal man enter their lives, as in a bodice-ripping romance novel. But we can't resist Daryl any more than they can, with his impish grin and Pan-like abandonment to the senses. His seduction of Cher's character (the first to succumb) is a key to what the film is saying about men and women: she laughs at his suggestion they go to bed, catalogues in detail all his deficiencies—physical, emotional, intellectual—concluding that he even smells bad; but when he smilingly counters by asking if she prefers to be on top or on the bottom, she's amazed to find herself succumbing. She is simply, a modern woman seduced by a man representing everything she loathes, because he is very much a man—natural, sensual—as compared to the macho jerks and liberated wimps who surround her. We understand why the three women must, after temporarily enjoying the emotional bondage of complete surrender to his power, snap out of their pleasant dream state, reasserting their own power by destroying his; yet we can't help but appreciate his howl when, as he senses himself being coldly, clinically cut down by a rite they're performing to make him powerless, Daryl stumbles into the church and rails against the fairer sex: "Women—a mistake, or did He do it to us on purpose?"

To be appreciated, Witches must be understood not as a film adaptation of Updike's book, but rather as a separate artistic entity that, for a jumping off point, employs the book's basic plot premise. But during the period when Witches was being shot in a Boston suburb, inside word had it that all was not going well. Both Michael Cristofer (Pulitzer Prize-winning playwright for The Shadow Box, previously a screenwriter on Falling In Love) and Australian director George Miller (The Road Warrior) constantly attempted to adapt to the ever-changing whims of their producers, who never seemed certain what they wanted Witches to be: a cute comedy or a flat-out sex farce; a believable story with fantastical overtones or a special-effects spectacle. One early draft of the script featured explicit sex scenes but no special effects at all; the final version of the movie, contrarily, features bizarre visuals by Rob Bottin (The Thing), while all the sexual bouts have been eliminated, apparently because the producers feared it would be ill-timed to release a graphically sexual film when America was gripped with a fear of an AIDS epidemic running rampant through the vast heterosexual community.

Cher and Michelle Pfeiffer both told me that, having eagerly campaigned to win roles in Witches so they'd get to work with Jack, each regularly considered walking off the project, weeping at the thought that their movie was being torn to pieces by conflicting currents, like some rudderless craft in the Hollywood seas. They even admitted that, along with co-star Susan Sarandon, they took a cue from their characters and half-jokingly performed something of a Satanic rite, designed to give their producer Herpes. The only thing that kept them from walking was Jack. "We were all Jack's girls," Cher said, "and we would always go to him when we couldn't take any more. He would listen to us, lovingly, and then go fight our fights for us. As a male superstar, he could stand up to the Hollywood Establishment in a way we couldn't, and he never once failed to take our part." Pfeiffer added: "On most movie sets, you get close with people and then never hear from then after the shoot is finished. But each of us regularly receives cards and little packages from Jack. He still takes care of his witches."

Miller, meanwhile, on his first major American assignment, attempted to cling to his approach, a vision of Satan not as a symbol of evil or cruelty, but as a Natural Man. As Miller told me: "My Devil had to be a Pan. He's the mythological figure with a cloven hoof whose antisocial act was moving from community to community, causing all women to abandon themselves sexually to him and so enraging the menfolk, this despite the fact he is not conventionally handsome. The men can't understand why the women do it, and neither for that matter can the women. But his total self-confidence is what allows him to enjoy their favors, impregnate all the women, then move on. To a degree, Christian concepts of chastity for women were created by a male dominated society to protect themselves from such a presence."

With such an approach in mind, Miller did not initially take to the casting of Nicholson. "My first instinct was, in getting someone for the devil, you need an actor who is totally unlike the devil, and Jack clearly has an impish quality. Fortunately, I had a friend who pointed out to me what a gracious person Jack is. Then, I realized he is like a 200-year-old child: very wise in many ways, even beyond his years, but with a certain innocence and naïveté we expect from someone younger. The moment I saw that, I knew he was the only actor to bring a humanity to the role, to pull the devil out of stereotype." To appreciate how completely Miller and Nicholson succeeded, one only has to watch the dreadful (and completely clichéd) image of the devil Alan Parker and Robert DeNiro settled on for Angel Heart earlier in the year.

Miller also explained that, owing to the uncertainty about what the producers wanted, he and Jack needed to do eight takes for each and every scene, beginning (on take one) with a low-key and realistic approach, in which Daryl is very clearly an ordinary mortal, then giving it just a bit more pizzazz (and making it ever so slightly larger than life) on take two, going all the way to take eight, where Daryl is less a man, more the incarnation of a myth. "That allowed us," Miller explained," to decide, later in the editing room, what kind of a tone we would have for our film." In essence, than, they shot eight separate films—each a distinct interpretation of the material—afterwards picking the film they would share with the public. "The movie you see," Miller continued, "is made up almost exclusively of the eighth takes. Simply, we sensed, in retrospect, that the broader takes were the ones that played best." An actor with Jack's courage was imperative. "Most male American movie stars," Miller insists, "are absolutely dedicated to maintaining and protecting an image before the public. What's so wonderful about Jack, in addition to his enormous talent, is that he never even considers this. He'll take the wildest risk without hesitation. That's the fun of it for him, and the public sees that, and loves him for it."

Generally speaking, critical reaction to the film was mixed. David Edelstein of The Village Voice commented that "It's florid, cartoony, and infantile, like a Disney movie by Ken Russell. Miller is a good comic-strip filmmaker, and Witches has a crisp, pop-out look to it—storybook colonial, with Day-Glo skies and lawns. But Miller's conception of character is, to put it kindly, archetypal [and] to put it rudely, boorish." David Denby of New York noted that "The movie is very broad—a barrelful of monkeys let loose in every scene—yet horribly clouded in meaning, a cross in style between Fellini and a home movie of Jack Nicholson romping with friends."

But even critics uncertain about the movie found much to admire in Jack's work. In Macleans, Lawrence O'Toole wrote: "Hair pulled back in a pigtail, Nicholson has a dandy time as the diabolical Daryl." Jagr. of Variety praised his "ferocious magnetism" in describing Nicholson's "no-holds-barred performance,"adding that "he is larger than life, as indeed the devil should be." Denby, observing that Jack was dividing his time between understated realistic portrayals (The Border, Postman) and purposefully overblown bravura ones (Tommy, The Shining), correctly tagged this as one of the latter: "Van Horne is one of Nicholson's extroverted, Kabuki performances—all forehead, eyebrows, rump, and teeth. We've seen those fangs quite a lot in recent years, but Nicholson hasn't gotten his voice up like this since his famous big blast in Carnal Knowledge. His rage feels good—a gusty

wind full in the face." Pauline Kael of The New Yorker commented on the actor's tendency, in recent years, to approach his parts playfully: "Jack Nicholson entertains himself in Witches, and damned if he doesn't entertain us, too." "He might have been rehearsing for this role ever since The Shining," Richard Corliss of Time added. "If he was over the top there, he is stratospheric here." Peter Travers of People likewise noted the relationship to that earlier picture, insisting Nicholson had "been working toward playing Satan since he filmed The Shining. It's a helluva performance." David Ansen of Newsweek also observed the similarity: "The tone is set by Nicholson, who does a full-throttle, high-lechery variation on his eyebrow-arching diabolism in The Shining. He's magnetic, of course, but on the edge of self-parody: how can an audience be surprised and alarmed by Horne when we're so instantly indulgent of Nicholson?"

Perhaps he's right, in that we're clearly conscious this is not Jack Nicholson attempting to convincingly delineate a character but instead providing a kind of addendum to everything that has gone before, carer-wise; then again, perhaps to complain about this is to miss the point. Ansen's observation can instead be taken as an apt description of the autobiographical aspect of Witches, the way in which this far-fetched fantasy, seemingly so different from anything Jack has done before, is actually a logical extension of the actor's entire body of work. Daryl/Jack's final shrieking at the church expresses the eternal male's inability to ever fully comprehend women: the man who delivers precisely what they secretly pray for will be rewarded by destruction at the hands of those sweet, smiling ladies, who according to female logic (quite incomprehensible to men) must punish him for fulfilling their wildest fantasies. But this is not a nasty misogynist point-of-view (at least not the way Jack plays it), because, even during his final rage of frothing-at-the-mouth hysteria, we still sense he loves those women who are even then pushing pins into his effigy. This male position has been expressed by Jack in pictures as diverse as Carnal Knowledge and The Shining; with its double image of Daryl as both a real man and Satan incarnate, Witches represents a fascinating combination of the two.

Jack has described himself, in interviews about his personal life with women, as the one who gets left; Daryl gets left by all three of the lovelies who earlier expressed—singly and collectively—their undying devotion. Jack once said he'd never been to an orgy with more than three people; that's precisely how many women he enjoys an orgy with in Witches. Jack, attempting to explain Postman, admitted he wanted to throw us a hardball on sex; when asked why he was willing to do a supporting role in Terms, he explained he thought it would be fun to be a middle-aged sex symbol. In Witches, he furthered and fulfilled both ambitions. The devilish side of himself, which has been surfacing since the earliest screen work, was finally allowed full rein here. In that sense, *Witches* seems less a haphazard choice of a vehicle than it does the necessary tying-together of thematic threads which have run through Jack's career as an actor-collaborator, a performer who manages to inject a sense of personal expression into the most seemingly diverse and random selection of projects. Daryl is, in a sense, the ultimate Jack Nicholson role. For as Jack once said—seemingly casually, though in fact pointedly so—everything he has ever done as an actor has, in a manner of speaking, been autobiographical.

Daryl dances the night away with Jane Spofford in a wild phantasmagoria, certain that he is in control.

Broadcast News

(1987)
A 20TH CENTURY FOX RELEASE

CAST:
William Hurt *(Tom Grunick)*; Albert Brooks *(Aaron Altman)*; Holly Hunter *(Jane Craig)*; Robert Prosky *(Ernie Merriman)*; Lois Chiles *(Jennifer Mack)*; Joan Cusack *(Blair Litton)*; Peter Hackes *(Paul Moore)*; Christian Clemenson *(Bobby)*; Robert Katims *(Klein)*; and, unbilled, Jack Nicholson *(The Anchorman)*.

CREDITS:
Director, James L. Brooks, Co-producers, Brooks, Penney Finkelman Cox, and Polly Platt; screenplay, Brooks; cinematography, Michael Balhaus; production design, Charles Rosen; editor, Richard Marx; music, Bill Conti; Running time, 131 mins.; rating: R.

Though Jack's participation in this movie was purposefully small (he is not even billed in the film's credits, nor does he appear in any promotional photographs or materials circulated at the time of release), his willingness to lend himself to the project once again proves the anti-star mentality of this major star. James L. Brooks had warily approached Jack (who enjoyed one of his greatest successes in Brooks' *Terms of Endearment*) with the brief role of "The Anchorman" (part Dan Rather, part Walter Cronkite) at a TV network's news division, knowing full well that a supporting role—however well-written—was unlikely to attract a heavyweight, whose name meant more at the box office than those of the three top-billed "stars" combined. Nicholson, however, loved the script, loved the film's theme, and had loved working with Brooks.

So, with his supremely relaxed attitude toward such intricate niceties of show business, Jack readily agreed to do the role just so long as his brief participation was not

Now fiftysomething, Jack Nicholson had reached a point of prestige and power in the film industry (and in audiences' minds) wherein the onetime rebel-outsider could comfortably convey a leader of the Establishment. (Photo by Jean Pagliuso)

exploited—that is, if his name and presence were not made a part of the advertising and promotional campaigns. Since Brooks—a sincere, serious filmmaker—wanted Nicholson the actor, not Nicholson the box office draw, he quickly agreed, and the project was set.

Part sitcom, part satire, and part behind-the-scenes melodrama, *Broadcast News* tells the story of a romantic triangle with important social implications, as Jane Craig (Holly Hunter), an intelligent and ambitious news producer, tries to choose between two men who love her: brilliant, decent, intellectual (but ultra-frumpy and sadly non-sexy) Aaron Altman (Albert Brooks, no relation to the film's writer-director, though an accomplished if finicky filmmaker himself), and charming, charismatic, totally superficial and supremely successful Tom Grunick (William Hurt). Aaron and Tom are transformed into a bizarre buddy-buddy team of news broadcasters: the informed and perceptive Aaron remains off-camera, feeding the confident looking (but embarrassingly empty-headed) on-camera Tom all the latest information through an earphone. In the modern media, success is determined not by substance, but style, which is why Tom continues to climb the network ladder while Aaron's career stumbles, doomed because his particular pigmentation doesn't photograph well and, worse still, he sweats under the hot lights.

Variety summed up the general critical reaction: "Enormously entertaining for most of its 131 minutes . . . Stronger on character and nuance of behavior than on·the ethics of TV news, [James Brooks] has provided enough brilliant dialog, beautifully realized by Hunter, Brooks, and Hurt, to carry the film over some thin patches and an ending that sputters to a less-than-satisfying conclusion. Nonetheless, picture should delight a sizable audience looking for a thoughtful night out as well as a good laugh." That it did, *Broadcast News* providing the treat of the Christmas '87 season, and long considered a frontrunner for the Best Picture Oscar, though that prize finally went to Bernardo Bertolucci's *The Last Emperor.*

One of the film's (many) great moments occurs when Cusack, desperate to impress this deity, the Anchorman, runs through a litany of all their previous encounters, while Nicholson silently stands by, nodding with mild enthusiasm and feigned recognition. Finally, Cusack—certain she has scored big with the brass, thereby saving her job—giddily turns and rushes back to work, whereupon Nicholson coldly glances over to a network executive, whose rolling eyes reveal the poor girl is not going to survive the current series of staff cuts.

Jack's subdued but pointed playing of such scenes resulted in a series of highly positive reviews. *America* remarked that "Nicholson, in a cameo part as the dour and hugely pompous network anchorman, says more about the self-importance of the television news industry than any critic since Peter Finch went mad on-camera in Sidney Lumet's *Network*." Expounding on the old notion that there are no small roles, only small actors (Jack clearly not being one of them), *Commonweal* put it this way: "Director Brooks shapes the best comic performance in some time by Jack Nicolson [sic] as the main network anchor in the New York studio. Brooks has the wit to keep Nicolson [sic] under wraps most of the time; he must have only ten lines, but because of their held-in quality and the match between verbal understatement and his shrewd, ever active, radar-like eyes, the lines come across as far more convincingly egomaniacal than in most of Nicolson's [sic] blowhard performances. This is wry without the ham."

Even the occasional critic who was tough on the film itself, like Lawrence O'Toole of *MacLean's*, had kind words for Jack: "The performances—including an uncredited supporting role by Jack Nicholson as the network's main anchorman—keep the movie purring along in the absence of any real story." David Ansen of *Newsweek* praised the picture lavishly, adding: "for the frosting on the cake we get Jack Nicholson's deliciously droll cameo as the network's gravely self-important anchorman (reportedly modeled on Chet Huntley). Usually seen on a TV screen, Nicholson makes one 'live' appearance in the Washington newsroom, and it's a beaut. In a couple of minutes, Nicholson tells you more about his character with his puffed-out chest than many actors accomplish in two hours—and makes you howl."

The team, Albert Brooks, Holly Hunter and William Hurt, watches as one of their award-winning reports is broadcast.

A TRAMP AT THE WINDOW:

Ironweed

(1988)
A TRI STAR PICTURES RELEASE

CAST

Jack Nicholson (*Francis Phelan*); Meryl Streep (*Helen Archer*); Carroll Baker (*Annie Phelan*); Michael O'Keefe (*Billy*); Diane Venora (*Peg*); Fred Gwynne (*Oscar Reo*); Margaret Whitton (*Katrina*); Tom Waits (*Rudy*); Jake Dengel (*Pee Wee*); Nathan Lane (*Harold Allen*); James Gammon (*Reverend Chester*).

CREDITS

Director, Hector Babenco; Producers, Keith Barish and Marcia Nasatir; screenplay, William Kennedy, from his novel; cinematography, Lauro Escorel; production design, Jeannine C. Oppewall; art director, Robert Guerra; editor, Anne Goursaud; music, John Morris; Running time, 144 mins.; rating: R.

Jack spent several months in 1987 filming *Ironweed* in Albany, New York, home of novelist William Kennedy, on whose critically acclaimed book the movie was based. Kennedy, who had labored hard and long with little recognition (sales of his novels were so slight that he had to teach college English courses to support himself), had recently and suddenly been thrust into the forefront of American letters when, in the early eighties, his nearly forgotten novels (*Legs, Billy Phelan's Greatest Game*, and *The Ink Truck* among them) were republished in paperback, causing the literary-intellectual Establishment to reconsider his career—and transform a longtime minor writer into a cause célèbre and cult novelist.

The notoriety which had so long eluded Kennedy now caused director Francis Ford Coppola and producer Robert Evans to choose him as their screenwriter for *The Cotton Club*, an ambitious and expensive project about the golden age of Harlem jazz clubs. Despite accolades for its lavish production values and authentic musical score, however, *Cotton Club* received only lukewarm reviews owing to the disappointing quality of the script,

Jack Nicholson as Francis Phelan, life's loser—and, perhaps, Jack's artistic rendering of the father he never knew.

little more than recycled melodrama from B movies of the thirties, presented in a style halfway between loving spoof and belabored imitations of such superficial cliches. Nonetheless, *Ironweed* was optioned for a major movie, with Kennedy himself brought on board to do the screenplay.

Visiting the set, Kennedy was heard to comment that he considered the look achieved for the movie version "properly seedy," which it certainly was. *Ironweed* is a downbeat, depressing tale about a 1930s alcoholic; for Jack Nicholson, such a story allowed him a return (following his baroque portrayal of The Devil in *Witches*) to his alternative style, the more realistic form of acting. Moreover, he again was able to immerse himself in that period which so clearly appeals to him, judging from his work in *Studs Lonigan, Chinatown,* and *The Postman Always Rings Twice.* But if the thirties has always been a recurring subject for Jack, so too has the concept of family, especially the ways in which a father can unconsciously betray his own child. No surprise, then, that *Ironweed* begins with a father who, owing to his drunkenness, has accidentally but fatally dropped his infant son, and as a result degenerates into a state of unabated alcoholism. Once again, Jack chose a project which, if not specifically autobiographical, certainly seems to be highly personal in nature. Perhaps he—in his role as Francis Phelan—was, however unconsciously, portraying his own father—or, more correctly, his imaginative construction of the father he never actually knew.

But Phelan has another reason for drinking: During a strike by trolley workers, a scuffle with a scab inadvertantly led to that man's death. Jack's character, then, has killed two people, his own son and an unknown man who died owing to Phelan's disastrous attempt to turn political ideology into positive action. Phelan stands as an American second-cousin to the existential anti-hero of Albert Camus' *The Stranger*, a man who never thought to harm another soul but, through circumstances beyond his control, inadvertently committed the ultimate act of nihilism. Following a lifetime of avoiding the implications of what he has done, Phelan finally faces the truth while also dealing with his one-time wife Annie (Carroll Baker) and his current companion, Helen Archer (Streep), the well-meaning but alcoholic woman who wishes to help him but has her own values, sensibility, and troubles.

Once again, then, Nicholson was featured in a story dealing in part with the imperfect ways men and women attempt to relate and communicate with one another. Additionally, there was the opportunity of working with yet another director whose previous films he'd admired—Hector Babenco, the Brazilian filmmaker of such powerful pictures of underdogs surviving the urban blight as *Pixote* and the Oscar-winning *Kiss of the Spider Woman*.

Apparently, the two stars enjoyed their personal as well as professional time working together in *Heartburn* so much that they were anxious to reteam, here playing drastically different kinds of characters in another genre of film. "I couldn't wait to work with Jack again," Meryl said on the set. "I really admire him, because he isn't afraid of anything"—as compared to so many superstars who choose their roles "protectively," always worrying about how a performance will effect their image. In *Witches*, Jack had proven he was not afraid to go way over the top; in *Ironweed*, he'd need to courageously pull in tight and create an unpleasant, smaller-than-life portrait of a loser.

Important too is the way in which the two projects Nicholson and Streep have done together reveal the lack of ego on the part of each star. In *Heartburn*, the focus was on Streep's character, with Nicholson (though the bigger name) supremely comfortable in allowing Streep to assume center-stage; in the case of *Ironweed*, Jack's character was the natural lead, so Streep (though herself now firmly established as a superstar) happily assumed a secondary role.

Ironweed has integrity—but, in the minds of many critics, that simply was not enough. Like so many other cerebral novels adapted to the screen by serious-minded filmmakers—Malcolm Lowry's *Under the Volcano*, James Joyce's *Portrait of the Artist as a Young Man*, Marcel Proust's *Swann in Love* come to mind—*Ironweed* was a book that all but defied being turned into a satisfying motion picture. Almost nothing actually happens in Kennedy's novel, its value deriving from the writer's ability to share with his reader, in intimate one-on-one fashion, the inner workings of a unique but fascinating mind. The narrative form allows us to slip inside another person's being, coming to better understand that person's humanity and limitations through the literary experience of inner monologue. But movies are another medium entirely, and to merely watch as those same characters walk through their dreary lives is to be left standing on the outside, peering in at an unpleasant (and unrewarding) sight. The rule of thumb is that the very sort of plot situations which make for the most memorable books are not particularly well suited for the screen.

Which is why most critics praised the film's honesty and authenticity while noting that it was anything but successful or satisfying. *Variety* tagged the film "unrelentingly bleak," adding that it was "without an audience and no reason for being except its own self-importance... [*Ironweed*] only occasionally approaches the wistful, elegiac tone it's desperately searching for.... It's not the poverty that ultimately puts one off, [but] the failure of the filmmakers to use the material to open up this world" [to us, the viewers]. Also problematic was the fact that in the book, Phelan constantly comes in contact

Helen (Meryl Streep) joins Francis for a drink in an Albany, N.Y., bar, where they are served by a singing bartender (Fred Gwynne).

with the presences of people from his past, who exist as apparitions in his mind—ghosts of his own making only he can see and hear. But when Babenco attempted to visualize this by having actors appear in white makeup, the unintentionally comic effect proved, in *Variety's* words, "an all-too-explicit externalization of the internal workings of [Phelan's] mind." *America* magazine correctly added that the "worst failure of artistic judgment is having the scab conductor appear with his brains bulging through his shattered forehead. This is an apparition so close to third-rate Hollywood horror that it could be mistaken for parody."

In *Time*, Richard Corliss added that the novel's "sour, allusive poetry—part James Joyce, part James T. Farrell—[was] lost in translation to the screen.... Francis' life is significant not for what he does but for what he dreams and fears. But a movie like this, which concentrates on mundane plot, can only show, not reveal ... [the film] lurks outside Francis' soul, like a tramp at a suburban window, permitting only dumb speculation on his fertile inner life ... the movie provides a mug shot instead of an X-ray." Joy Gould Boyum of *Glamour* perceptively noted that "on the page, Kenneday's Pulitzer Prize-winning novel had an enlivening humor" noticeably missing from the grim, dreary film version, adding that this was "an extremely literal rendition of the novel—one that sticks to its bleak, slimly plotted surface rather than exploring its bracing, resonant spirit."

Still, most critics had only praise for Jack's performance. Boyum lauded the "stunning characterizations," adding that Nicholson "brings enormous empathy" to his role. David Ansen wrote in *Newsweek*: "playing a grungy,

alcoholic bum with a head full of booze and guilt-driven hallucinations, Jack Nicholson commands the screen with the quiet, weathered authority one associates with the great stars of the past—the Bogarts and Tracys. His charisma isn't about glamour, it's about soul. He's the perfect actor to play ... a homeless man scraping for survival and redemption on the cold, bleak streets of Albany." And that he was; if in *Witches* Jack had proved both his daring and skill as a larger-than-life performer, here he likewise proved his daring and skill at ultra-realistic Method acting.

Part of the film's problem, though, is that Phelan never finds that much-sought-after redemption, appearing—at least in the screen version—the same sad bum he was at the beginning. Though this may add to the film's integrity—thankfully, there is no contrived happy ending—the lack of an arc for the character keeps *Ironweed* from achieving true tragic dimension, as other contemporary works about life's losers—Arthur Miller's play *Death of a Salesman*, Sidney Lumet's film *The Pawnbroker*—have done. This initially impressive movie is emotionally gloomy, intellectually murky, and dramatically unrewarding. *Ironweed* is depressing without being enlightening; true tragedy—Greek, Shakespearean, or modern—rubs our nose in the dark side of existence but redeems that unpleasant experience by leaving us with a sense of exhilaration. *Ironweed* forces us to view people in the gutter, slice-of-life fashion, but is unable to redeem this by providing any larger meaning or rewarding theme. The result is turgid kitchen-sink melodrama. Like the central character, *Ironweed* is not tragic, only pathetic.

Francis and Rudy (Tom Waits) join in the singing of a hymn at a soup kitchen; the film rubbed its audience's collective nose in the bleak life-style without redeeming the unpleasant experience—or the characters.

Helen and Francis attempt to forget their problems and eke a little enjoyment from life as they dance for the other assorted alcoholics.

A tender moment for Francis, as he gives his only object of value—a prized baseball—to his grandson (Ean Egas).

OVER THE TOP:

Batman

(1989)
A WARNER BROS. RELEASE OF A GUBER-PETERS
PRODUCTION

Jack Nicholson as The Joker.

CAST:
Jack Nicholson (*Jack Napier/The Joker*); Michael Keaton (*Bruce Wayne/Batman*); Kim Basinger (*Vicki Vale*); Robert Wuhl (*Knox*); Pat Hingle (*Commissioner Gordon*); Billy Dee Williams (*Harvey Dent*); Michael Gough (*Alfred*); Jack Palance (*Grissom*); Jerry Hall (*Alicia*); Lee Wallace (*Mayor*); Tracey Walter (*Bob the Goon*).

CREDITS:
Director, Tim Burton; producers, Jon Peters and Peter Guber; screeplay, Sam Hamm and Warren Skaaren, based on the DC Comics character created by Bob Kane; cinematographer, Roger Pratt; editor Ray Lovejoy; music, Danny Ellman, with additional songs by Prince; Running time, 126 mins.; rating: PG-13.

A film based on a popular comic book would hardly seem a ripe source for controversy, but that's precisely what occurred once producers Guber and Peters announced *Batman* as their next project. Caped Crusader purists came crawling out of the woodwork, snarling about the casting of Michael Keaton and insisting an actor known for his off-the-wall comic turns would not bring the proper sense of dignity to the part—sounding ("DC Comics Fundamentalists," Keaton sardonically labeled them) like a lunatic fringe parody of those equally annoyed protestors who, a year earlier, complained about *The Last Temptation of Christ* without having seen the final product. Most mainstream movie lovers, however, patiently waited to see if *Batman* would be a virtual replay of the campy 1960s TV series, a companion piece to the recent quartet of *Superman* films, or (hopefully) something totally out of the ordinary.

Happily, *Batman* proved a case of the latter, a dark and somber film, blending drama with black humor while combining an Existential attitude with an Expressionistic look. If the *Superman* cycle of the seventies and eighties effectively caught the mood of sunny optimism characteristic of the Reagan era's early years, *Batman* proved the perfect counterpoint for the decade's end: a glum, mean-spirited but strangely seductive film, visually encapsulating the look of an urban landscape demolished by a decade of benign neglect, portraying raw capitalism gone completely out of control—the sordid greed mentality of the eighties exaggerated to the point of near-cartoon. Indeed, the movie that 30-year-old Disney-animator-turned-director Tim Burton (*Pee-wee's Big Adventure*, *Beetlejuice*) brought back from the sound stages of Pinewood Studios outside London was so self-consciously unpleasant in its approach, unsparing in its portrayal of the American Dream degenerating into ugly nightmare, and uncompromising in its bleak vision that Warner executives held their breath on the eve of the film's release, privately wondering if their much-hyped $35 million-plus investment might provide a colossal cinematic disaster on the order of *Heaven's Gate*, *Howard the Duck* and *Ishtar*.

Instead, *Batman* hit a public nerve, the nasty squalor of menacing modern Manhattan (under the guise of Gotham City) brilliantly visualized onscreen as a retro-future netherworld: part negative nostalgia, part contemporary commentary, part sci-fi dystopia. All such ideas were neatly suggested in what we saw rather than didactically stated in the dialogue. Still, audiences implicitly understood the fundamental (if frightening) truth of what they experienced.

National Review, choosing to interpret the film as a defense of rather than attack on the Reagan era, reported: "The public loves the movie for all the same reasons liberals hate it. This *Batman* is a criminologist in the Pat Buchanan mode. He does not attempt to 'understand' evildoers—he throws them off skyscraper roofs. This is a Batman who believes in the death penalty and practices it. [In comparison,] Superman . . . is definitely a Dukakis liberal, a Green. Batman, however, has a less rosy-eyed view of life. 'It isn't a perfect world,' he tells Vicki. . . . Like that other Wayne, John, Bruce knows that 'a man's gotta do what a man's gotta do.' Here is an unreconstructed Reagan Republican if ever there was one." As for Jack, the fact that rock star Prince's music was reserved for the Joker's appearances caused the *Review* to comment: "Rock is the handmaiden of nihilism and chaos," so in finally killing off The Joker (atop a religious edifice at that!), Batman should be understood as a conservative Christian necesarily eliminating a grotesque parody of liberal thinking gone out of control. Though his review was less politicized in nature, David Denby of *New York* magazine noted, in a similar vein: "Preening and twirling, the master of revels [Jack/The Joker] embodies a truly frightening nihilistic idea—that a completely witty man, who sees everything as absurd and lives only for his own amusement, would have to be a killer."

Whatever the reasons (and whither the film's politics), *Batman* rated as the commercial hit of the year, perhaps the biggest box-office success of all time. Which proved happy news for Nicholson, who had accepted a smaller up-front salary than a star of his magnitude could demand in exchange for a hefty portion of profits earned by ticket sales and merchandising of everything from T-shirts for trendy Yuppies to toys for small tots. When that loot started rolling in, it swiftly became obvious this would be the single most lucrative performance by an actor in history! Yet the public didn't grow resentful, sensing that while dozens of actors might have successfully played the title character, only Jack could properly do The Joker. Also, there existed a general good

will for this man, who takes his craft seriously and his image with a grain of salt, genially enjoying the financial fruits of superstardom while picking his projects with such sincerity that he never seems a sell-out. In a perceptive article for *Gentleman's Quarterly*, Joe Morgenstern later noted: "Most people still think of Nicholson as a regular guy. They don't even begrudge him the $60 million or so [he earned from *Batman*]; it's all part of the cosmic joke. But they're also starting to see him as someone who belongs to the ages, like the guys up on the granite screen at Mount Rushmore. And the ranks of Nicholson fans have now been swelled by hordes of kids who know little or nothing of his thirty-year career but went wild for what they saw in *Batman*—the face of loony evil for our time."

Simply, Jack had become, to older viewers, a screen legend of Spencer Tracy/Humphrey Bogart/Clark Gable/Gary Cooper stature; for youthful moviegoers, he had again managed to (in his own words) "ride the crest of the pop-culture wave," deftly placing himself as the centerpiece of a movie project which touched the popular nerve of an emerging post-MTV audience. For this adult, upsetting *Batman* owed as much to recent illustrated novels *(The Dark Knight Returns)* by Frank Miller, *The Killing Joke* by Alan Moore) as to Bob Kane's original comic strip conception.

In general, reviews were positive if reserved. *Commonweal*'s mixed notice claimed that "*Batman* does dazzle the eye and numb the brain in a pleasing fashion." *Time* tagged this "a tricky but deft attempt to fuse fantasy and reality, pastiche and put-on." *Variety* claimed this "uneven release treats its thin plot too reverentially," predicting *Batman* would "find admirers and detractors in equal numbers," adding that "what keeps the film arresting is the visual stylization" (part art-deco, part German Expressionism, part contemporary punk) and that "Danny Elfman's eerie score is also a big plus," rightly qualifying that by noting "Burton and his superlative tech staff are undercut by the common failing of so many contemporary pix, the story." Indeed, the plot did, at mid-movie, turn ludicrous, off-putting, even incomprehensible. The Writers Guild strike, which began as the film was being readied for production, didn't help matters. Besides, there's a glaring flaw in the plot: reporter Vicki Vale spends the first half of the film attempting to learn Batman's true identity; but when she's finally confronted with the truth, the key issue is inexplicably dropped rather than dramatically developed into a satisfying climax. Yet the movie's striking ambience and undeniable energy managed to rein in viewers before they could drift away, so the momentary lapses ultimately seem pretty insignificant in light of the overall impact.

Most reviews noted that, the title notwithstanding, this was clearly Jack's movie. As David Denby put it in *New York*: "As characters, [Batman and Joker] aren't equals, and that's a big problem. *Batman* is out of balance." "*Batman* suffers from too much Joker and not enough straight men," Paul Baumann complained in *Commonweal*. "Nicholson needs someone as wantonly charismatic as himself to fight the camera for."

Yet while such comments are essentially true, they should serve more as analysis than criticism; to complain about this imbalance makes as much sense as arguing that Milton's *Paradise Lost* suffers because Satan is the character we find most intriguing. While Keaton offered a subdued, realistic portrait of a disturbed but believable man, Jack was allowed (even encouraged) to usurp the film by playing it big. ("Every actor always worries if he's going over the top," he smilingly said, "but you couldn't do that in this part—there was no top!") In one of his most dazzling moments—simultaneously frightening and funny—his Joker grinningly announces: "I'm the world's first fully functioning homicidal artist!"—a line that works thanks to Nicholson's maniacally on-target delivery and the fact that performer and persona merge, making this as much an expression of Jack Nicholson's dark side as of Jack Napier's whitefaced alter-ego. "Nicholson parodied himself as never before," Morgenstern noted, "but he also transcended himself by creating a deep-fried lunatic who seemd to have studied all the great Nicholson screen roles."

Perhaps the most memorable (and, for middlebrow audiences, subversive) moment occurs when Jack's Joker dances through an art museum, defacing the greatest paintings in our culture. But if the sequence proved threatening to older, civilized viewers, it endeared Jack to the post-Letterman crowd, that portion of the public for whom the notion of old-fashioned respect now seemed passé. Only a freaked out work by Francis Bacon is allowed to remain intact as The Joker's vicious orgy of anti-art destruction is unleashed on more polite portraits. The Joker is the logical extension of that impluse first portrayed in Stanley Kubrick's *A Clockwork Orange*, then burlesqued in *The Rocky Horror Picture Show*—a surreal image of the American suburbanite's ultimate fear, as the emerging street culture gleefully trashes everything carefully preserved by self-appointed guardians of the best in mankind's history.

About his role, Jack said: "When I was a kid, what I liked about *Batman* was that it was the only comic book that took place at night. What I liked about The Joker is that he has no taste in his humor." Anyone who thought Jack had already taken the grand guignol/Satanic side of his dual career as far as it could go now realized *Witches* had been a mere predecessor to this. *Variety* noted: "he makes a glorious style of playing the most extravagantly psychotic characters. Even his maniacal writer in *The Shining* and his Devil in *Witches* were opportunities for underplaying next to The Joker. Nicholson embellishes the most fascinatingly baroque designs with his twisted features, lavish verbal pirouettes and inspired excursions

Capitalism gone mad: taking over the TV airwaves, the Joker hawks his line of Smylex toiletries, which are in fact lethal, to a public no longer guarded against such raw greed owing to the deregulation of standards during the Reagan years . . .

. . . and then, as part of Gotham's 200th anniversary celebration parade, reduces the public to a screeching mob when he throws fake dollar bills and gleefully watches as the greedy folks scramble for the dough.

High atop an ancient Cathedral, the men of dual identity
finally face off—and discover each is the other's
doppelganger.

into the outer limits of psychosis. It's a masterpiece of
sinister comic acting." *Commonweal* called him "over-
whelming"; *New York* tagged him "scarifyingly brilliant";
National Review claimed that "The Joker is the ultimate
Nicholson role, the performance he has been groping
toward for two decades." John Simon, who tagged the
film "trash," nonetheless admitted that "Nicholson gives
an inspiredly comic epic performance as the cackling
sadist"; in *The New Republic*, Stanley Kauffmann was
less than kind to the movie, but praised "Nicholson's
richly overripe performance as The Joker." Only *The
New Yorker's* Pauline Kael found fault: "He's all entertainer, a glinting-eyed cartoon—still springing gags after
he's dead. This interpretation is too mechanical to be
fully satisfying. And is Nicholson entertainer enough?
He doesn't show the physical elegance and inventiveness
we may hope for."

Part of Jack's attraction to the project had to be the
single theme that consistently runs through his films: the
character who leads a double life. His own Joker is two

men, the suave if corrupt businessman Jack Napier and
the demented phantom with a white face he is transformed into; the hero, Bruce Wayne/Batman, is likewise
a duality. Batman and Joker, then, serve as each other's
doppelgangers, the bright and dark sides of what's essentially a single coin. At the film's end, when they confront
each other in a duel high atop an ancient neo-Gothic
cathedral (the sequence is lifted whole from Fritz Lang's
1926 silent classic *Metropolis*), the two finally realize
they have created each other, the secret/synthetic identities of Wayne and Napier being mutual responses to the
man who embodies the opposite side of his own psyche.

As filmmaker Burton explained: "He has no agenda,
like Superman's Truth, justice and the American way. If
this Batman knew so specifically why he was doing it, he
wouldn't be doing it. Everybody has a bit of the split
personality—that's the audience hook." Burton may be
right about this theme being an audience hook; certainly,
it was the hook that landed Nicholson.

CHINATOWN REVISITED:

The Two Jakes

(1990)
A PARAMOUNT PICTURE

Jack Nicholson as J.J. Gittes—1940s private eye.

CAST:
Jack Nicholson (*Jake Gittes*); Harvey Keitel (*Jake Berman*); Meg Tilly (*Kitty Berman*); Madeleine Stowe (*Lillian Bodine*); Eli Wallach (*Cotton Weinberger*); Ruben Blades (*Mickey Nice*); Frederic Forrest (*Newty*); David Keith (*Loach*); Richard Farnsworth (*Earl Rawley*); Tracey Walter (*Tyrone Otley*); Joe Mantell (*Walsh*); James Hong (*Khan*); Perry Lopez (*Captain Escobar*); Jeff Morris (*Tilton*); Rebecca Broussard (*Gladys*); Tom Waits (*Cop, Unbilled*).

CREDITS:
Director, Jack Nicholson; Producers, Robert Evans and Harold Schneider; screenplay, Robert Towne; cinematography, Vilmos Zsigmond; production designers, Jeremy Railton and Richard Sawyer; editor, Anne Goursaud; music, Van Dyke Parks; Running time, 137 min.; rating: R.

The Two Jakes was originally to have been distributed during the 1989 Christmas season, then pushed back to Spring '90, finally rescheduled for a mid-August release—at a time when the summer's box office blockbusters (*Dick Tracy*, *Die Hard 2*, *Total Recall*) were finally waning, leaving the field open for more adult-oriented cerebral fare. Naturally, the repeated postponements led to a plethora of conflicting reports, some insiders insisting the delay stemmed from director/star Nicholson's impressive perfectionism and Paramount's admirable willingness to allow him the time and resources necessary to transform an already good film into a great one during post-production, others claiming the film (like such other big, ballyhooed, bloated projects as *Old Gringo*) was a disaster, plagued by a multitude of unsolvable problems. The nay-sayers point to the casting

Nicholson as director.

266

of Harvey Keitel, a perseverant if limited actor lacking the charisma to become a major star, as the film's other "Jake," rather than another heavyweight name (say, Dustin Hoffman or Robert De Niro, either of whom would be fascinating to watch in tandem with Jack) as proof that this cinematic vessel was cursed with an invisible albatross from the word "go."

Sadly, it turned out to be a case of the latter. At the last minute, Nicholson added a voice-over narration in which Jake explains to the audience what's happening—perhaps necessary to make the long-winded and convoluted story understandable, but lacking the wit and irony characteristic of the best voice-overs; what we hear spoken is a storytelling crutch, not an artistic addition to the tale. Jack, of course, once again played Jake ("J.J.") Gittes, private eye, the character he created in *Chinatown*. Nicholson told me shortly after the release of the original that "it would be nice to have a character I could return to, at various points in his fictional life and my actual one, so as to express through him what I learn. But I would neer do something on the order of a routine series, like the James Bond movies, where the character goes through an assortment of experiences that should teach a man something, yet at the beginning of the next film, he's the same guy (as before). No sequel for me, no picking up where we left off to exploit the popularity of the first, provide some additional entertainment, top ourselves with bigger stunt sequences, make more money. I said I'd play Gittes again only if we could come up with a unique script about the same character at some other point in his life, when he's living a totally different existence. Like what Shakespeare did, writing two separate plays about Mark Anthony at specific junctures. I mean, nobody thinks of Anthony and Cleopatra as a sequel to Julius Caesar. It's a different play featuring the same character."

The concept of further Gittes films was viable immediately after *Chinatown* first proved successful in 1974. But a decade passed before Jack and his *Chinatown* cronies—producer Robert Evans, screenwriter Robert Towne—sat down in the study of Evans' Beverly Hills home, seriously planning a picutre that would be shot precisely eleven years after the first, likewise picking up on Gittes eleven years later (set in 1948, shot in 1984) after Jake (like America itself) has survived World War II (returning a war hero, more socially acceptable and middleaged), now suffering through the postwar recession. According to Jack, "It's 'Let's Get America Moving Again' time; Gittes now belongs to a golf club and has a respectable fiancée." However, internal bickering caused endless delays, so the idea of precisely paralleling Jack and Jake was forever lost. In 1986, a disgruntled Nicholson announced, with some bitterness, that he considered it unlikely the film would ever be made.

Jack eventually relented, if never completely comfortable with the fact that the perfect parallels between his art and his life were lost. What went wrong? Towne initially intended *Two Jakes* to be the second installment of an ambitious trilogy that would, through the eyes of the fictional Gittes, study the social, political, and cultural decline of Southern California. The idea was to create a three part epic, with the installments set some eleven years apart, detailing and dramatizing the gradual corruption of L.A. by big money interests: water in the 1930s, oil in the forties, and some yet to be named element (perhaps the expansion of the highway systems) in the fifties.

The deal was that with Roman Polanski having fled the country on a morals charge, Towne would direct as well as write (he had helmed a dismal misfire about lesbian athletes, 1982's *Personal Best*, later being responsible for superficial, lightweight crime drama called *Tequila Sunrise*); Evans, who had begun his film career as an aspiring actor (he played the young bullfighter seduced by Ava Gardner in *The Sun Also Rises*) would both produce the film and play the role of Jake Berman, rising to prominence and power by instigating the building of tract homes in the postwar boom. The idea was to form a mini-United Artists that might not continue beyond this single project, but would allow Evans, Towne and Nicholson to make their dream movie without studio interference. In retrospect Evans would recall: "None of us was going to take any money and we'd own a good percent of it ourselves. We all put our hands together and swore no agents or lawyers were going to screw us up."

They didn't need to: In fact, this was one film devastated not by lawyers, agents, or studio brass—all of whom lent their support and kept their respectful distances—but by flaws in the coterie of supposedly loyal and trusting friends. Everything appeared to be fine, until it became clear that Evans was growing terribly tense at the thought of appearing before a camera again. A mere three days before shooting commenced, Towne realized that Evans was not up to handling such a demanding role. Nicholson claims to have told Towne: "It's a moot point because [Evans] doesn't have to work for another two weeks. So let's ruthlessly shoot for two weeks [other scenes, without the Jake Berman character] and get Paramount on hook for the picture, then let Bobby shoot a couple of days; if he's no good, I'll support you in terms of replacing him." Though the director is ordinarily considered the centrifugal force and ultimate arbiter on a movie set, Jack—well aware that the basic rule in Hollywood is to get the movie made—assumed that mediator role, hoping he could either persuade Evans to drop out if indeed his work was not up to par or, if that seemed impossible, then induce Towne to make the best of a bad situation. If that sounds like patent dishonesty, manipulation, and compromise, it's actually the strategy of survival in the always heady, often

In a role originally to have been played by Robert Evans, Harvey Keitel is "the other Jake"—Berman, a real estate agent exploiting postwar L.A.

hysterical film business. But Towne refused to budge, and Evans—learning of Towne's doubts about him—grew even more tense but flatly refused to quit, even though he could not sum up the courage to come out of his trailer and work.

As Joe Morgenstern chronicled the situation in *Gentleman's Quarterly:* "All hell broke loose. Production ended before it began when Paramount pulled the plug. A million dollars' worth of sets was destroyed. All three parties were sued by creditors; a mountain of dirty linen was washed in public, and the partnership dissolved into acrimony and dissilusionment."

More than 3.5 million had already been squandered, and the project lay dormant for several years. But, Jack remained intrigued enough by the prospect of playing Gittes to eventually approach three world-class directors—Bernardo Bertolucci, Mike Nichols and John Huston—about taking over, finally agreeing to direct himself only after every major international director (perhaps sensing the still hovering presence of that albatross above this well-intentioned but doomed cinematic craft) passed on it. Though an attempt was made to patch up the personal rifts, it's worth noting that during the actual shooting, writer Robert Towne was not on the set to help with any rewriting that might prove necessary (the usual situation for a major movie), but purposefully flew off to Bora-Bora for a vacation, leaving Jack to improvise dialogue where Towne's proved untenable, as well as

patching together the voice-over narrative.

The $19 million film proved to be slow-moving and tedious; if the original Chinatown featured a fascinatingly complex plot, *The Two Jakes* was merely convoluted. Worse still, it absolutely demanded that the audience be completely familiar with *Chinatown*, though even fans of the original admitted certain key plot elements and character names had faded in their memories, while the younger audience had never even heard of it. While Jack had always claimed he wanted to play Jake as a man who had learned from his experiences in the first story, Gittes—despite his upscale life-style—was still portrayed as working on adultery cases, the very sort of situation that had led him to such tragic trouble in the first movie and, as such, the kind of case we would assume he'd steer clear of.

Jake Gittes is hired by slick, sleazy real estate agent Jake Berman to spy on his wife Kitty (Meg Tilly) to see if she's having an affair. Gittes does, even creating a wire recording (a forerunner of today's audiotape) of a tryst; then, Berman—seemingly in a burst of uncontrollable anger—kills his wife's lover. He seems likely to get off easy (a crime of passion) until Gittes learns that the dead man is in fact Berman's business partner, and Berman will prosper now. Gittes suspects he's a patsy, that the entire thing is a set-up—and, worse still, the recording mentions the daughter of the woman he loved and lost in the first film. Naturally, he relentlessly searches for the

268

truth, drawing him into a labyrinth of capitalist greed and corresponding political corruption.

While the production values and period atmosphere were outstanding, the movie never suggested that Jack, as director, had the compelling sense of tone toward his material, or the distinct and consistent point-of-view so characteristic of Polanski's approach in *Chinatown*. Great detective movies, including John Huston's *The Maltese Falcon* and Howard Hawks' *The Big Sleep*, are often difficult to follow plot-wise, but make up for that in various ways. One is the inclusion of memorable little comic/dramatic vignettes, like the famed bookstore sequence in *The Big Sleep*, but *Two Jakes* offers few such moments. Another is the presence of fascinating villains (Sidney Greenstreet and Peter Lorre in *Maltese Falcon*), but here, *Two Jakes* also disappoints: compare Richard Farnsworth's oilman in this film to John Huston's villain in *Chinatown* and we see the difference between a lightweight and a heavyweight heavy. Also, a great detective story demands a knockout ending, whereas *Two Jakes* just fades away.

Understandably, the reviews were mostly negative. "A jumbled, obtuse, yet not entirely unsatisfying follow-up to *Chinatown*" was how *Variety* characterized the film. "*Two Jakes* is no great shakes," Duane Byrge claimed in *The Hollywood Reporter*, adding that the film was "weighted down by a gummed-shoe narrative that folds under the burden of its heavy-bottomed plot and unravels with it tangled threadlines." Mike Clark of *USA Today* did hail it as "a surprisingly rich movie" considering the difficult production circumstances, though noting "*Jakes* is lacking the sense of pervasive evil" that characterized *Chinatown*. Vincent Canby of *The New York Times* seemed to be desperately searching for something nice to say when he called it "an enjoyable if clunky movie," and Sheila Benson of the *L.A. Times* gave it a highly positive review, praising "a lovingly assembled cast in a brilliantly detailed production." Most critics had respectable things to say about Jack's performance: "No living actor is more equal to the task than Nicholson, who brings charisma and world weariness to his reprise of Jake" (*Variety*); "intermittent flashes of Nicholson's pearly gleam" were appreciated by *The Hollywood Reporter*; "a subdued by whoppingly good performance" (*USA Today*). As for Jack's direction, *The Hollywood Reporter* said: "though Nicholson has a fine and devilish eye for against-the-grain flourishes, his pacing is obsessively slow." Canby observed: "Nicholson is a competent but not exciting director—the movie never seems to have a life of its own."

The twin themes of adultery and voyeurism relate *Two Jakes* to Jack's previous work, as does the concept of a doppelganger—two men named Jake who find themselves drawn into a tenuous relationship, secret sharers discovering that by gazing into each other's psyches, both come to better understand the brutal truths about their own souls. Dual identities is the essence of the tale: Jack's Jake is the Nicholson hero incarnate, a one-time lowlife now striving for respectability, but irresistibly drawn back into the tawdry world he has never completely lost his taste for; Keitel's is a seemingly posh man who leads an unpleasant private life. Take the theme of *Batman* and make it the subject of a low-key realistic drama rather than an over-the-top cartoon, and you have *The Two Jakes*. Then again, you have most of the movies Jack has appeared in—fascinating variations on a single theme, that being, of course, the life of Jack Nicholson.

Gittes encounters some unexpected muscle who try to discourage him from pursuing a lead. On the left is tough guy Mickey Nice (Ruben Blades) and on the right, Liberty Levine (Paul A. DiCocco, Jr.).

269

Man Trouble

(1992)
A 20TH CENTURY FOX RELEASE

Jack Nicholson as Harry Bliss, one more of the edgy and seductively devilish characters he has played so often.

CAST:

Jack Nicholson (*Harry Bliss*); Ellen Barkin (*Joan Spruance*); Harry Dean Stanton (*Redmond Laylis*); Beverly D'Angelo (*Andy Ellerman*); Michael McKean (*Eddy Revere*); Saul Rubinek (*Laurence Moncrief*); Viveka Davis (*June Huff*); Veronica Cartwright (*Helen Dextra*); David Clennon (*Lewis Duart*); John Kapelos (*Detective Melvenos*); Lauren Tom (*Adele Bliss*); Paul Mazursky (*Lee MacGreevy*); Gary Graham (*Butch Gable*); Mary-Robin Redd (*Nurse Sonya*); Rebecca Broussard (*Hospital Administrator*).

CREDITS:

Director, Bob Rafelson; producers, Bruce Gilbert and Carole Eastman; executive producers, Vittorio Cecchi Gori and Gianni Nunnari; screenwriter, Eastman; cinematography, Stephen H. Burum; production design, Mel Bourne; editor, William Steinkamp; music, Georges Delerue; running time: 100 mins.; rating: PG-13.

Nicholson stumbled badly with his next venture; *Man Trouble* may have begun with the noblest of intentions, but what finally landed up there on-screen was nothing more than a muddled, off-kilter stab at sociocomedy. Though Jack was reunited with writer Carole Eastman and director Bob Rafelson, who had collaborated with him on the 1970 classic *Five Easy Pieces*, this uncertainly written, awkwardly directed dud suggested that their memorable movie of more than two decades earlier had been a happy accident. Nicholson's star quickly rose after the release of their early work together, but neither Rafelson nor Eastman was ever able to follow up with anything of passing, much less lasting, value, the two working on important movies only when they were lucky enough to get Jack to agree to join them for a project, a tendency that once again attested to his basic loyalties to old friends from the early days.

However, *Man Trouble* certainly appears to be the end of the road for their once-promising triad. It was the second release from an Italian-funded filmmaking company called Penta Pictures, which had already fumbled notably with its first effort, *Folks!*, a so-called comedy teaming Tom Selleck with Don Ameche. *Man Trouble* proved to be strike two: As Stanley Kauffmann wrote in *The New Republic*, "[Jack's] appearance in this scrawny turkey can be seen as an act of loyalty to old friends. So, if you want to pay tribute to that loyalty, buy a ticket to this film. But don't go in." Kauffmann was not alone in this assessment; *Man Trouble* was rudely dismissed by critics and barely made the Top Ten box-office lists during its opening week, then swiftly disappeared from sight, not surprising since its studio, 20th Century Fox, released the film without fanfare, and understandably so. Nicholson's energetic performance occasionally enlivens this lumpalong attempt at serious social humor, but *Man Trouble* is so distasteful and ill-conceived that there is little reason for any but a die-hard Nicholson completist to catch it.

In *Variety*, Lawrence Cohn put it this way: "Jack Nicholson fans should feel cheated by *Man Trouble*, an insultingly trivial star vehicle. After some initial business attracted by his name on the marquee, film is fated for pay-cable use." But anyone hoping a video rather than theatrical screening might help is in for a rude awakening; *Man Trouble* plays no better on the small, intimate television screen than it did in the theaters. The concept certainly sounds ripe with potential: Ellen Barkin—briefly enjoying full flavor-of-the-month star-status following her offbeat-sexy role opposite Al Pacino in *Sea of Love*—plays Joan Spruance, an opera singer who, like most everyone else in America today, has been subjected to the horror of a break-in at her home, and desperately desires to find some way of keeping that from ever happening again.

She makes the mistake of contacting Harry Bliss (Nicholson), an erstwhile dog trainer who convinces her that what she really needs is a menacing-looking German shepherd; he has one, named Duke, who will respond only when spoken to in German, an okay gag that does elicit a laugh or two but is never milked for its full potential. But as Harry attempts to make Joan's home intruder-free, the unlikely two—she classy, he crass—become romantically involved, even though Joan begins to suspect Harry may himself be a possible intruder. So the film addresses not only the current issue of people feeling unsafe in their own homes but also every modern woman's concern that the pool of available men is shrinking; it may be time for even world-class women like Joan to lower their standards if they are going to avoid ending up all alone.

If only the filmmakers had been able to make a movie that pays off on these ideas, using currently significant concepts as the basis for a clever topical comedy, they might have turned out a contemporary gem instead of a flat, forced farce, which is all *Man Trouble* is. Their woe-begone project combines the predictability of a bad TV sitcom with the awkward, amateurish, rough-around-the-edges feel of a film school production. One of their biggest mistakes was the inclusion of various compli-

cated though less than appealing subplots, including one in which Joan's sister (Beverly D'Angelo) writes a kiss-and-tell book about a Howard Hughes-ish billionaire she's been seeing on the sly, causing him to become increasingly nasty as he tries to halt publication. That might have made for a screenplay in itself; in *Man Trouble*, the idea does not enrich or round out the material so much as it plays as mere padding, suggesting that Eastman and Rafelson were unable to develop their basic plot and character relationship in any depth. Instead they relied on the disastrous technique of trying to fill out the movie with as much peripheral material as possible, in the vain hope that this might prevent it from dropping in its tracks.

Sadly, that's precisely what *Man Trouble* does do. Having Joan be menaced by a slasher—who may be her estranged husband (David Clennon) or, for that matter, her new shaggy-dog of a lover, Harry—trivializes a frightening issue by reducing it to a crude plot point in a third-rate film. Still, there's no denying that Nicholson's role fit in perfectly with his choices for past performances. Harry Bliss is the kind of edgy character Nicholson has often opted to play; with his raised eyebrows, devilish demeanor, and unshaven face, he certainly is of a type with the eccentric, oddball roles associated with him over the years. Even the fact that Joan is uncertain as to how she should take Harry—he may be her salvation or the ultimate threat—fits in neatly with a theme that Nicholson has, in his performances, returned to regularly.

He certainly lends this film any distinction that it has; it's impossible to totally dismiss any movie in which we get to watch him roll his eyes as he considers the new lady in his life, playing as he does here a married wom-

Ellen Barkin, hyped as an offbeat sex symbol after her starring role opposite in Al Pacino in *Sea of Love*, was cast with Jack in *Man Trouble*. As Joan Spruance, a modern woman unable to find a suitable man and menaced by rampant crime, she is unsure whether Harry Bliss will be her salvation or her downfall.

The world's richest man, Red Layls (Harry Dean Stanton), draws the seedy Harry Bliss into his complicated schemes.

anizer with an Asian wife, a role that may be more than a tad autobiographical. But most critics were less than kind: *Variety*'s Cohn called this "a role that's way too comfortable for him," arguing that "Nicholson's patented ne'er-do-well persona seems on automatic pilot." Perhaps the problem is that he never decided whether this was to be one of the realistic Nicholson roles or yet another Grand Guignol performance; as Leah Rozen noted in *People*, "Although Nicholson ekes a limp chuckle or two out of double entendre lines . . . he seems alternately muted and over the top (even by his own fairly extravagant standards), mussing his hair and waving his arms frantically, as if he were Leonard Bernstein conducting the *Fidelio* overture."

Despite the fact that this was a Nicholson film, *Time* didn't even bother to honor it with a full-blown review, however negative; *Man Trouble* was deemed worthy

only of one of the magazine's "short takes." Entitled "Dog Tired," and unsigned, the piece claimed that "It's tough on a woman when the best man around is a philandering dog trainer who had to change his name to avoid creditors. *Man Trouble* wants you to believe that it's less tough on the woman when the man is Jack Nicholson. But Jack is looking too creased and rusted to play a romantic lead. And the story, about predatory men from all social strata lurking in the cobwebbed corners of a modern woman's life, gets neither the zest nor the sick thrill it could use. This is an enervated, despondent entertainment."

It seems unlikely that either Eastman or Rafelson could manage a comeback after this fiasco; Jack, however, was off and running with a pair of major-league movies—*A Few Good Men* and *Hoffa*—that would quickly eclipse this disappointing detour.

Bob Rafelson, who had shot to fame with the 1970 classic *Five Easy Pieces*, attempted to reclaim some of his lost glory as a director by guiding Jack through this considerably less successful venture.

QUEEG REDUX:

A Few Good Men

(1992)
A CASTLE ROCK PRODUCTION/A TRISTAR RELEASE

CAST:

Tom Cruise (*Lt. (j.g.) Daniel Kaffee*); Jack Nicholson (*Col. Nathan R. Jessep*); Demi Moore (*Lt. Cdr. JoAnne Galloway*); Kevin Bacon (*Capt. Jack Ross*); Kiefer Sutherland (*Lt. Jonathan Kendrick*); Kevin Pollak (*Lt. Sam Weinberg*); James Marshall (*PFC Louden Downey*); J. T. Walsh (*Lt. Col. Matthew Markinson*); Christopher Guest (*Dr. Stone*); J. A. Preston (*Judge Randolph*); Matt Craven (*Lt. Dave Spradling*); Wolfgang Bodison (*Lance Cpl. Harold W. Dawson*); Xander Berkeley (*Captain Whitaker*); John M. Jackson (*Captain West*); Noah Wyle (*Cpl. Jeffrey Barnes*); Cuba Gooding Jr. (*Cpl. Carl Hammaker*); Harry Caesar (*Luther*).

CREDITS:

Director, Rob Reiner; producers, David Brown, Rob Reiner, Andrew Scheinman; coproducers, Jeffrey Scott, Steve Nicolaides; executive producers, William Gilmore, Rachel Pfeiffer; screenplay, Aaron Sorkin, based on his play; cinematography, Robert Richardson; production design, J. Michael Riva; editors, Robert Leighton, Steve Nevius; music, Marc Shaiman; running time: 138 mins.; rating: R.

Based on the critically acclaimed 1989 Broadway play by Aaron Sorkin, transformed into a screenplay by Sorkin himself (with, reportedly unacknowledged aid from William Goldman of *Butch Cassidy and the Sundance Kid* fame), *A Few Good Men* told the fact-based story of a trial that rocked the American military establishment. Two marines, stationed at the U.S. Navy

Colonel Jessep bolts from the witness stand when the questioning by Lieut. (j.g.) Daniel Kaffee (Tom Cruise, right) becomes too intense.

base at Guantanamo Bay, stood accused of allegedly murdering one of their own, a perennial screw-up named Santiago. They had, under the unofficial, much-denied but all-too-real "Code Red" credo, been hazing the young malcontent (supposedly on their own though in fact under orders from their superior officer), during which time they shoved a poison-dipped rag into Santiago's mouth. He, suffering from a weak heart, died.

Santiago, as it evolves, had been a problem-case for some time. Realizing that he could not, in his physical condition, handle the oppressive tropical climate in

273

The two sides of Nathan Jessep: In *A Few Good Men*, Jack Nicholson played one more of his antiheroic characters who have Jekyll-Hyde personalities. His Marine commander can be stern and ungiving (left), but also dangerously seductive (right).

which they were stationed, he had literally begged his commanding officer, Col. Nathan Jessep (Nicholson), for a transfer. But Jessep, believing that such an attitude denoted intolerable weakness and lack of true character, refused to sign the transfer papers, despite the fact that his adjutant (J. T. Walsh) recommended he do so. By this time the desperate Santiago had, in hopes of arranging for his transfer through some other means, written to his senator in Washington, explaining that he knew about a highly illegal "fence-line shooting" at a Cuban watchtower sentry, and would gladly tell all if the senator would only arrange for his transfer.

That is the complex tapestry of the past; now, a young lieutenant (j.g.) named Daniel Kaffee (Tom Cruise), son of a renowned navy lawyer and himself a recent Harvard Law School grad, has been assigned to defend the two accused marines, a none-too-bright white private, Louden Downey (James Marshall), and a rah-rah black marine, Corporal Dawson (Wolfgang Bodison). Young Kaffee, easygoing cockiness notwithstanding, already has a reputation as an extremely clever plea bargainer, so it's simply assumed that he'll deftly employ his skills to get as light a sentence as possible for the two men, then move on to bigger and better things in his planned illustrious career. Kaffee himself feels that he probably won't have to go as far as an actual trial, since none of his previous cases has ever reached the courtroom. He is a genius at wheeling and dealing, always in the end opting for the convenient compromise.

Initially that appears to be the approach Kaffee will take; he blithely accepts the assignment as a kind of technical exercise, assuming his charges are guilty and planning to put just enough energy into the case to whittle down their sentences, while lavishing as much time as possible on his enjoyment of sports in general, softball in particular. However, one of the lawyers assigned by Internal Affairs in Washington to work with him, Lt. Cdr. JoAnne Galloway (Demi Moore), technically Kaffee's superior, believes the men are part of an elaborate cover-up to protect the truly guilty party. Galloway makes it quite clear that she's offended by Kaffee's glib, mechanical, at best moderately committed approach to this case.

Moved as much by her physical attractiveness as by her impressive idealism, Kaffee gradually transforms during the process of preparing for trial. With their third team member, expert researcher Lt. Sam Weinberg (Kevin Pollak), they gradually realize the two marines are guilty in the same limited sense that, as the Jewish Weinberg puts it, oven attendants at a Nazi concentration camp were guilty of war crimes. The truly responsible party is the one who gives the immoral orders, and the three lawyers in time become convinced that the marines were acting under orders from Jessep and his by-the-book minion, Lt. James Kendrick (Kiefer Sutherland).

Jessep, therefore, is ultimately responsible—the buck stops there—and is the man they want to get, the problem being that Jessep is not on trial. The only way to turn the proceedings against him is to call arrogant Jessep as a witness, then—essentially, doing the job that fairminded prosecutor Ross (Kevin Bacon) is trying to do—manipulate Jessep into incriminating himself while on the stand. If Kaffee can only pull that off, he will be a true lawyer, worthy of standing proudly alongside the memory of his father, rather than remaining in the great man's intimidating shadow.

The film, which received generally positive reviews, proved an immense crowd-pleaser during the Christmas season of 1992. Despite Nicholson's brief screen time, most critics waxed rhapsodic in describing his work. Typical was Peter Travers of *Rolling Stone*: "Jack Nicholson figures in only a few scenes [but] his presence electrifies the film. Nicholson is a marvel—fierce, funny, and coiled to spring. Oscar is bound to salute." Well, not exactly bound: the Motion Picture Academy chose not to salute the man with the killer smile and cobra eyes this time around, although he—and the picture—were nominated. But Travers spoke for most other reviewers with his twenty-one-gun salute to the cagey old scene-stealer; most felt that, in his few ripe scenes, Nicholson deftly pilfered the show from its nominal, youthful, less-experienced stars.

Not everyone agreed that he prevailed. Stanley Kauffmann in *The New Republic* wrote that Nicholson "certainly does not walk through the part; but a man of his talent with a lesser conscience could have done so. Because of different positions in the plot, Nicholson works in the shadow of Tom Cruise." The *New York Times*, however, offered a different appraisal, reporting that "Mr. Cruise and Ms. Moore make formulaic noises, but both are in the shadow of Mr. Nicholson, standing extremely tall as the sly, broiling Col. Nathan R. Jessep."

A Few Good Men dominated the box office for months to come. *Time* critic Richard Schickel wrote that Jessep was "not so much played as demonized by Jack Nicholson—a wickedly smart psychopath, utterly self-confident and self-righteous. Nicholson sees the humor in this dark character but then freezes each potential laugh with a gaze that is hostile to anything not on his own agenda." Of course, That Old Devil Jack has done such things before, and done them brilliantly, in the many frightening characterizations he has offered in a wide variety of projects. The role of Jessep serves as an extension of the flamboyant villains Nicholson has done so often, in films as diverse at *The Shining, The Witches of Eastwick,* and *Batman.*

Though these roles have always existed in fascinating tandem with the sympathetic, decent men Nicholson has proven just as adept at playing (*The Border, The Last Tycoon, Chinatown*), there is no question that Nicholson's occasional heavies have all but redefined screen villainy, by giving us bad guys who are consistently more intriguing, charismatic, and fascinating than the ostensible heroes of those pictures. "Perhaps no movie star has portrayed evil with more charisma, conviction, and gusto than Jack Nicholson," Brian D. Johnson wrote in *Maclean's.* "And after a career of pushing characters to sinister extremes, it is hard to imagine him going any further. But as a villainous colonel . . . he cranks it up one more notch, unleashing previously untapped depths of venom. His appearance, however, is brief. . . . Appearing in just three scenes, Nicholson is the appetizer and dessert. And although his performance is mesmerizing, the rest of the movie is predictable Hollywood fare."

Indeed, it is; though younger viewers may have believed they were seeing groundbreaking drama, anyone with a sense of movie or theater history knows that this is a clever, contemporized knock-off of Herman Wouk's *The Caine Mutiny,* and ought to be treated with about as much respect as one would have for a convincing imitation of a genuine Gucci handbag. Essentially, Nicholson is playing the legendary character of Captain Queeg, only with another name. That may not in any way dim the gloriousness of the performance, though it certainly makes the extremely well crafted entertainment containing it seem a far cry from true, original theatrical or cinematic art. Almost everything in the script is lifted, consciously or otherwise, from some fine previous courtroom drama; the best thing that can be said about Sorkin's writing is that he's extremely adept at picking out what was best in past plays of this genre, aligning them with some basic facts of a more recent actual case, then neatly stitching them together into a work presented as his own.

"A conventional but compelling story," Schickel tagged the film, settling for a balance between an appreciation of the movie's remarkable ability to pay off the viewer and an understanding of how derivative the narrative in fact is. In the *New Yorker,* Michael Sragow was less complimentary when he said essentially the same thing in a more unforgiving tone: "a military-courtroom drama that puts on stale airs of importance." Still, there was no denying that the film was an enormous hit with the public, at least in part because of the immense popularity of Tom Cruise and Demi Moore with youngish moviegoers, but also owing to the continuing dynamo of Jack: "Nicholson is so riveting," critic Brian Johnson went on, "that he makes one bad man seem infinitely more interesting than any number of good ones."

The only possible complaint about his work came from those critics who believed that Nicholson had over the years amassed such a larger-than-life presence that his recent performances could be compared to the later work of John Wayne. One of the few critics to dismiss Nicholson's performance was John Simon; writing in the *National Review,* he argued: "The movie's biggest loss is the absence of Stephen Lang, who made Jessep into an absolutely persuasive, bone-chillingly scary, and ultimately pathetic monster [on the New York stage]. . . . Nicholson, however, who recycles his Joker from *Batman,* comes across frequently laughable, full of jeering malevolence. . . . a sinister mountebank, whose patent anomaly lets the system off the hook."

In a similar vein, Sragow wrote: "The role of a Marine megalomaniac is a natural for Nicholson—the warped flip side of his Navy signalman in *The Last Detail*. At first, the cheap ease of it all works for him. Nicholson de-livers a full assortment of sly intonations and mannerisms. . . . The excess energy he emanates when Jessep is spewing bile or idling carries suggestions of banked resentment and bitterness, and a tinge of self-loathing. . . . But Jessep is the script's fall guy, and after pulling off a couple of tough scenes Nicholson has nowhere to go but down. He turns into a TV movie version of himself—William Devane, perhaps."

Those words may seem way too harsh for all but the most cynically sophisticated *New Yorker* reader; almost everyone loved the movie, especially Nicholson's eye-popping incarnation of evil. Still, there is at least a grain of truth to the criticism. Like past stars ranging from Wayne to Brando, Nicholson has survived at a price, that being the possible transformation into finally seeming a satire on himself.

Nicholson, the young comer of the sixties, had been elevated into one of the key American male stars of the seventies; then, in the eighties, he had proven to be a survivor who could outlast the decade that had defined him, if oftentimes in less than stellar roles. Throughout the first half of the nineties, he has again outlasted most of his contemporaries, once more proving his immense popularity with viewers, though doing so by means of pleasing their expectations for an actor who has become a star, a star who has become a legend.

Rob Reiner (right) offers direction to Jack as they plan a particularly emotional scene.

IRON, GRANITE, AND COJONES:

Hoffa

(1992)
A 20TH CENTURY FOX RELEASE

Jack Nicholson and Danny DeVito, who had costarred in *One Flew Over the Cuckoo's Nest*, were reunited in *Hoffa*, which DeVito also directed.

CAST:

Jack Nicholson (*Jimmy Hoffa*); Danny DeVito (*Bobby Ciaro*); Armand Assante (*Carol D'Allesandro*); J. T. Walsh (*Fitzsimmons*); John C. Reilly (*Pete Connelly*); Frank Whaley (*Young Kid*); Kevin Anderson (*Robert Kennedy*); John P. Ryan (*Red Bennett*); Robert Prosky (*Billy Flynn*); Natalija Nogulich (*Jo Hoffa*); Nicholas Pryor (*Hoffa's Attorney*); Karen Young (*RTA Woman*); Cliff Gorman (*Solly Stein*).

CREDITS:

Director: Danny DeVito; producers, Edward R. Pressman, Caldecot Chubb, Danny DeVito; screenplay, David Mamet; cinematography, Stephen H. Burum; production design, Ida Random; editors, Lynzee Klingman, Ronald Roose; music, David Newman; running time: 140 mins.; rating: R.

The *Hoffa* project began taking shape some five years before it finally reached the screen as a Jack Nicholson vehicle. The concept for the film was to present in a highly positive light the former Teamsters boss—who did hard time for jury tampering until freed via a Nixon presidential pardon, only to disappear mysteriously and, apparently, die violently at the hands of the very mobsters with whom he'd earlier aligned his union. This "revisionist" approach to the tale of a man often thought of more as a member of organized crime than of organized labor came from Frank Ragano, who had been employed as Hoffa's lawyer for years, and Brett O'Brien, whose father, Charles "Chuckie" O'Brien, had served as

a Teamsters official and Hoffa's handpicked successor. With the supposed support and cooperation of Hoffa's estate, Ragano and O'Brien took the idea to Joseph Isgrow, a California record promoter.

Isgrow was excited by the proposal, though it's important to note that he shortly would be indicted by federal authorities for alleged complicity with organized crime. As Princeton history professor Sean Wilentz reported in *The New Republic*, Isgrow had aligned his corner of the record business with crime in much the same manner that Hoffa had earlier broken down the barriers between unionism and organized criminal activity. Apparently Isgrow—who in 1989 was preparing for trial on fifty-one federal counts—felt that in telling Hoffa's story from a positive perspective, he could by implication redeem his own activities: "I really identified with Hoffa's plight . . . I could relate to the kind of government pressure he was subjected to." The deal fell apart, however, and there followed a lawsuit in which Ragano brought charges of breach of contract against Isgrow, who nonetheless proceeded with the project, now insisting that he was going to film the "Chuckie" O'Brien story instead—a story which of course included a great deal of information about O'Brien's old cohort, Jimmy Hoffa.

Isgrow was able to get Robin Moore, author of *The French Connection*, involved as the initial writer; once that was accomplished, it wasn't difficult to sell Edward R. Pressman, a Hollywood producer who seeks out controversial material (*Wall Street, To Sleep With Anger*), on the project, perhaps with Oliver Stone directing. Pressman, in turn, was able to interest then—20th Century Fox executive Joseph Roth, so the *Hoffa* film moved forward, despite the fact that one Hoffa relative publicly described Chuckie O'Brien—now the key source of the material on Hoffa—as "a pathological liar, a mooch, and an opportunist." It's also worth noting that when Hoffa disappeared, O'Brien was a leading suspect in the abduction, his relations with his former friend and boss having grown strained.

Moore (some would say to his credit) found himself unable to bring this material into focus, and so left the project. He was replaced by playwright David Mamet who had a longstanding reputation for admiring tough guys living on the edge, viewing them as sympathetic characters rather than stereotypical villains. Mamet's name was strong enough bait to intrigue Danny DeVito (then riding high as the star and director of hits like *Throw Momma From the Train*), since he would get to direct as well as play the fictionalized Chuckie role; though Al Pacino and Robert De Niro had already been seriously discussed for the lead, DeVito contacted his *Cuckoo's Nest* and *Terms of Endearment* pal Nicholson, always loyal to colleagues from the past, insisting this was the dream project they'd hoped to do together ever since their earlier hits.

"That's major," Nicholson reportedly said to Pressman, which was Jack's informal way of signing on. He was already set to star in *Man Trouble* for Bob Rafelson, so the Hoffa shoot was delayed six months, commencing in February 1992; Nicholson received a salary reputed to have been between $5 and $10 million, bringing the once modest film's total budget to more than $40 million, necessitating that it be released as a mainstream picture rather than a serious art film.

All of which explains why at Christmas 1992, Jack was in the awkward position of competing with none other than himself, playing the title character in *Hoffa* as well as the ostensible villain of *A Few Good Men*. However, audiences ate up the latter while all but ignoring the former. *Hoffa* was not a huge hit with either the critics or the public; though clearly intended as Fox's prestige year-end picture, it did not reap many Oscar nominations when the choices were announced early in 1993. Though a "quality" film in all respects—from the elaborate re-creation of the past, to the serious-minded themes, to the meticulous craftsmanship of set and cos-

tume design, to a script by one of the most highly regarded (some would argue overrated) writers of the New York stage—*Hoffa* nonetheless emerged as a bloated superproduction, boasting many interesting elements but suffering from an overall lack of focus and a dubiousness of intent.

It might have been interesting to see a film that made Hoffa seem sympathetic despite his dark side, as Martin Scorsese's world-class *Raging Bull* did for boxer Jake LaMotta. However, *Hoffa* emerged as less a balanced biography than a brazen, scattershot whitewash. According to this revisionist piece, Jimmy Hoffa was something of a saint, a misinterpreted and maligned man who always had his workers' best interests at heart. At moments the film manages to stir up some of the intended feeling for a character widely dismissed as a common thug; too often, though, *Hoffa* is unable to convince most viewers that its subject was as likable as Mamet's slanted screenplay would have us believe.

In *Time*, critics Richard Schickel and Richard Corliss argued that *Hoffa* was "an utterly externalized view of the corrupt, crusading boss of the Teamsters, James R. Hoffa. The R stood for Riddle, and Mamet's lean script is content to leave him at that. Hoffa does stuff—bullies management, connives with the Mob—but who is he? The movie gives not a clue . . . instead of a hard-edge portrait, we get painting on velvet. It's epic-style vamping around the void of epic character." The story of that epic character is told in flashback, as on July 30, 1975, an aging Jimmy and his longtime pal, the fictional Bobby Ciaro, drive toward what they believe will be yet another assignation, which we sense is fated to be Hoffa's last ride; their years together are summoned up by their conversations.

The two met during the 1930s, when a young Hoffa literally leapt into the truck that Bobby (an Everyworkingman figure) was driving, gradually convincing the noncommitted and frightened Bobby that he really ought to give up his "worry about Number One" attitude and join the union (which at this time had less than 100,000 members), finding strength in solidarity. From then on, Ciaro is Hoffa's constant companion, as the union membership eventually reaches two million and Hoffa rises—by hook and, occasionally, crook—to a position of towering importance and unbridled power.

At the end of their current journey, Hoffa and Ciaro park at a truckstop outside Detroit, where Hoffa has arranged to meet with an ambivalent gangster in hopes of restoring his faded power. Jimmy remains in the limo, while Bobby strolls inside and has a cup of coffee with a kid (Frank Whaley) who listens to Bobby's musings. What seems to be a chance meeting turns out to be anything but: The Kid is actually there to bump off Jimmy Hoffa, which he does at the film's end. This is Mamet's attempt to give the movie an element of Hitchockian suspense; we assume the killers will be dangerous-looking goons, and are waiting for them to drive up until, at the last moment, we realize that the baby-faced kid is the triggerman.

Mamet had previously penned the script for Brian De Palma's *The Untouchables*, about the life of federal agent Eliot Ness, and his writing here suffers from many of the same deficiencies. Though it is sparked by Mamet's love of pungent prose, he introduces Mrs. Hoffa, much as he did Mrs. Ness, as a generic/cipher wife. We could learn so much about the man through the dramatic device of this key relationship, yet Mamet does not tap into any of that. What a pity, because this was one of the truly fascinating elements about Hoffa: Though many of Hoffa's colleagues were notorious womanizers, even his worst critics insist he was scrupulously faithful to his wife and a fine and decent father. As Stanley Kauffmann wrote in *The New Republic*: "He was . . . as puritanical at home as he was profane elsewhere. A pity that this contradiction couldn't have been included."

Nor does Mamet explain the motivations of the man; Jimmy Hoffa's initial entry into the strike scene, colorful as it may be, is not made comprehensible. The film proceeds as a series of fragments, moments from history that never quite meld into an organized portrait. As David Ansen put it in *Newsweek*, "Hoffa is painfully short on historical context, and it never gets far enough inside the man to make a case for him as a misunderstood tragic hero. This is one very odd epic, shot with deliberate artifice by DeVito, complete with fake sunsets and bird's-eye vantage points. The razzmatazz is striking, but . . . as a portrait of unionism's most controversial figure, it offers only flickering illumination."

To be fair, it must be noted that Nicholson himself does make that illumination—however flickering—vivid. This is precisely the kind of role that, in his later years, Nicholson hungered for and demanded, making it all the more disappointing that the middling script and show-offy direction failed to properly service his impressive acting. In *Variety*, Todd McCarthy wrote that "Hoffa presents the controversial labor leader as public icon, a man of iron, granite and cojones who bullies his way across the union and political landscape of the mid-century all for the good of the working man. Unfortunately, this grimly ambitious biopic goes no deeper than that, offering hardly a trace of psychology . . . or inner life. . . . Mainly because of Nicholson's galvanizing performance and Mamet's peppery dialogue,

all this is not exactly dull, but it is very dry and uninvolving."

One of the film's most obvious disappointments is its depiction of the famed Jimmy Hoffa/Robert Kennedy feud, which erupted when the new president's younger brother, now attorney general, went after the mob and those labor leaders who had aligned themselves with organized crime. In the film, a heroic Hoffa has reluctantly dealt with D'Allesandro (Armand Assante, as a composite of several real-life mobsters) only because he had to if his union was to survive. Without forging a deal to bring the mob in on their side, the union would have been crushed by the power and influence of the bosses they were fighting. The bosses had been hiring thugs to beat the union people; the union people had to fight fire with fire.

So in the film, Hoffa is simply a man who did what a man's gotta do. Kennedy (Kevin Anderson) is the upscale slimeball—a supercilious American aristocrat, out of touch with the compromises that blue-collar workingmen must make, who seizes on the mob connection and uses it to destroy, in the service of his own ambitions, a hero of the people. The filmmakers simply ignore ample evidence that Hoffa lined his own pockets through mob connections. In actuality, the Hoffa/Kennedy feud escalated into a duel of epic proportions (brilliantly dramatized on TV in 1983 in *Blood Feud* with Robert Blake and Cotter Smith as Hoffa and Kennedy), though the scope of that conflict is never effectively presented in *Hoffa*. Their confrontation, which is set up carefully, leads only to a brief interchange, then is dropped without explanation; the audience only inadvertently learns both the Kennedys must be dead when we see Hoffa walk past posters advertising movies from the early seventies.

According to popular mythology, Hoffa was jostled late one spring night in 1968, then told by an accomplice that RFK had been killed. Legend has it Hoffa looked at the man as if he were crazy, muttered, "You woke me just to tell me that?" then rolled over and went back to sleep. This would have made a marvelous moment on film, but it isn't included.

Whatever the limitations of the film itself, most critics had kind words for Jack. "Despite an uncharacteristically controlled performance by Jack Nicholson," Brian D. Johnson wrote in *Maclean's*, "Hoffa kneecaps the facts and elevates a corrupt union bureaucrat to absurd heights." Those sentiments were echoed by dozens of other critics: "What one comes away with," *Newsweek*'s Ansen observed, "is Jack Nicholson, superbly made up, scheming and fuming with showy, mesmerizing skill." Todd McCarthy of *Variety*, while noting that the film was "too one-dimensional and chilly to put this in the winner's circle," nonetheless insisted that "Jack Nicholson's powerhouse lead performance will command attention and respect. . . . Decked out in an entirely acceptable hairpiece and built-up nose, Nicholson meets everything here head-on, shrugs and rights himself whenever he takes a hit, and charges ahead as fearlessly as Joe Frazier or Mike Tyson in the ring. In a rare tackling of a real-life character (Eugene O'Neill in *Reds* was another), Nicholson triumphs again."

But even amid the praise, there was a sense that Jack had reached a point where his realistic roles and over-the-top performances—kept scrupulously separate for more than two decades now—were at last melding into one single approach. In *Commonweal*, Richard Alleva wrote: "Nicholson obviously realized that he was hired to do a star turn and picks up his paycheck with honor. The actor has done his homework admirably; the stiff neck, the bantam strut, the slavically slitted eyes, the whine that is both self-pitying and menacing—the Hoffa carapace has been admirably assembled by this dynamic actor and he struts his stuff. I enjoyed this performance without taking any of it seriously for a second. It's a contraption, not a characterization."

There's another aspect to the film, and that's an autobiographical one. Like Hoffa, Jack began in the humblest of origins; like Hoffa, he rose to extreme power and prestige through steadfast ambition coupled with a strong sense of personal destiny. Though Hoffa chose the world of the unions, politics, and (though you'd never know it from this film) organized crime, and Jack went to Hollywood, both men reached the top in their chosen worlds, despite the fact that all odds were against them. As Stanley Kauffmann noted: "Hoffa's color, flash, egotism, bulldog brutality [and] tenacity are all in the film—the guts, the crassness and cleverness, together with a top man's blindness to the turning of the calendar page. Who is the American actor who could best embody all these qualities? Exactly the man who plays Hoffa—Jack Nicholson."

A man of the people: The film romanticized Jimmy Hoffa, depicting him as dedicated to the common workingman, while downplaying his connections to organized crime.

SOMETHING WILD WITHIN:

Wolf

(1994)
A COLUMBIA PICTURES RELEASE

CAST:

Jack Nicholson (*Will Randall*); Michelle Pfeiffer (*Laura Alden*); James Spader (*Stewart Swinton*); Kate Nelligan (*Charlotte Randall*); Richard Jenkins (*Detective Bridger*); Christopher Plummer (*Raymond Alden*); Eileen Atkins (*Mary*); David Hyde Pierce (*Roy*); Om Puri (*Dr. Vijay Alezias*).

CREDITS:

Director, Mike Nichols; producer, Douglas Wick; screenplay, Jim Harrison, Wesley Strick; cinematography, Giuseppe Rotunno; editor, Sam O'Steen; music, Ennio Morricone; production design, Bob Welch; running time: 121 min.; rating: R.

Throughout his career, Jack Nicholson has beautifully balanced two kinds of roles: his finely etched, essentially realistic performances as normal, fundamentally decent men (*Easy Rider, Five Easy Pieces, The Passenger, The Border, Ironweed*) and his larger-than-life portrayals of evil incarnate (*Tommy, The Shining, The Witches of Eastwick, Batman*). It seemed only natural, then, that sooner or later he would bring his two disparate images together in a single film that allowed him to simultaneously showcase the poles of his screen persona. The werewolf film was more or less made to order, considering its traditional theme of a regular guy who goes out of control, a civilized fellow suddenly giving in (via the dramatic device of an animal bite) to the darker side of his natural self.

Only a few years earlier, a horror film might have

The most significant continuing theme in Jack Nicholson films is the notion of men who lead double lives; that idea, so prevalent in films like *The Passenger*, was taken to its logical conclusion with *Wolf*, as mild-mannered Will Randall finds himself transforming into an antisocial creature.

seemed inappropriate for a star of Nicholson's current magnitude. After all, the golden days when great film actors like Lon Chaney Sr. (*Phantom of the Opera*) and Spencer Tracy (*Dr. Jekyll and Mr. Hyde*) relished playing the meaty horror roles in classy productions were but a memory. Throughout the 1940s and 1950s American horror movies had degenerated, first into respectable though unexceptional B-budget studio programmers, then during the 1960s to an even lower level of lurid drive-in junk, including several of Jack's early low-budget items. For the longest time, no respectable actor would touch the genre, at least in America. Beginning in the early 1980s, however, the so-called movie brat directors, who had grown up loving fantastical thrillers and were eager to revive and redeem the genre, began mounting formidable horror films. The trend, begun in 1974 with William Friedkin's *The Exorcist*, continued with Kubrick's *The Shining*, John Landis's *An American*

Werewolf in London, and Joe Dante's *The Howling*. Then, from the esteemed Francis Ford Coppola, came *Bram Stoker's Dracula*, which garnered enough critical praise and box-office receipts to make clear that the horror film was once again respectable.

The *Wolf* premise began taking shape in the early 1980s, when paperback novelist Jim Harrison (*Warlock, Legends of the Fall*), alone in an isolated backwoods Michigan cabin where he'd holed up to write, experienced what he later considered a sudden bout of lycanthropy. Stressed out and half asleep, Harrison noticed what were either car lights rapidly moving in his direction or lightning in the night sky just outside the window. Without warning, the writer—already in something of a depressed state—went wild, surrendering to something primal inside himself, running around in the nearby forest until the mood passed. He did mention the incident in passing to close friend Nicholson and his then-girlfriend Anjelica Huston, who were intrigued by the story, though nothing came of it, at least not for the time being.

Years later, Harrison and film producer Douglas Wick were sharing a plane ride (and a round of bloody marys) when something in the conversation caused Harrison to again relate his wild-man anecdote. Fascinated, Wick insisted it might serve as the proper starting point for a film. Though he did not immediately agree, Harrison was eventually persuaded to write the first draft of a screenplay. When he met while in Paris with longtime friend Nicholson, Harrison vividly recalled the actor's interest in the idea. Jack felt that there was something in the manuscript that spoke to him. He gave his permission for Harrison to contact Wick, informing the producer that the superstar would indeed sign on if one of five directors he greatly admired could be persuaded to helm the project: either Peter Weir (whom Jack had deeply regretted missing the chance to work with on *Witness*, passing on what seemed a thin formula script before learning that Weir would be bringing his unique style to that project) or one of his former well-regarded collaborators: Kubrick, Bertolucci, Polanski, or Nichols.

Since Wick had previously collaborated with Mike Nichols on *Working Girl*, Wick's only previous film as producer and a considerable hit for all involved, Wick called his friend first, and since Nichols was eager to work with old friend Nicholson again, the deal was quickly struck. Considering the high-powered creative team, Columbia Pictures had no hesitation in financing, though at that point the project bogged down. Rather than a smooth ride, what transpired was a 2 1/2-year artistic war for the soul of this film. It would prove to be a war that, sadly enough for the finished product, would never be happily resolved. Perhaps things would have been very different if Wick had first contacted Kubrick or Polanski, both directors with a strong sense of the dark side of life, each possessing a singular style that effectively shows such edgy material onscreen. Nichols, on the other hand, is best known for his witty, urbane social comedies. His most successful films sharply observe the so-called sophisticated levels of society he knows so well, especially in the upper reaches of trendy Manhattan, subtly spearing the pretentions found there. His idea from the start was to play down the werewolf element in the script, reducing it to the point of metaphor, emphasizing the psychological story of an upscale city dweller who is horrified to find himself giving in to unspeakably primitive urges that have previously lain dormant.

That approach might have served the story nicely, had Nichols been allowed to follow it through without interference. Harrison, on the other hand, was highly influenced by Native American thinking, and he saw the story the other way around: For an individual to revert to the level of an animal was a healthy, rather than horrific, way of getting in touch with man's natural origins. Harrison was also intrigued with the pulp-fiction aspects of the werewolf story as they might be realized in the fabulous state-of-the-art special effects that now made the transformations of man to wolf frightfully realistic, as compared to the once scarey, now silly-looking stop-motion photography that had been employed for Lon Chaney Jr. back in the 1941 genre classic *Wolfman*.

Essentially, Harrison's story would reset Robert Bly–new-man thinking in the trappings of a thriller, an approach that Nichols was uncomfortable with. Or, as Nicholson himself would later admit to *Newsweek*, "It's one [kind of] guy who thinks it's very nice to turn into a wolf, and another [kind of] guy who thinks you lose your humanity if you do." Later, Nicholson would attempt to defend the "tension" in his role, stating that "It's the argument between the two that makes the movie not become boring." Perhaps he's right, as *Wolf* is not boring; then again, it is neither fish nor fowl, the finished film revealing elements of what Harrison and Nichols each wanted but failing to develop either approach to its utmost.

Harrison rewrote the script five times, then left the project, realizing he would never satisfy this director; Nichols was ready to walk as well, though Nicholson talked him into toughing it out. Screenwriter Wesley Strick, who had written the *Cape Fear* remake for director Martin Scorsese and his star Robert De Niro, then came on board to create yet another draft that was hoped would bring the project more in line with Nichols's vision. By this point, Columbia executives were growing ever more nervous, knowing that despite the artistic conflicts, the company needed a film with plenty of contemporary sex and graphic violence if it were going to prove a commercial success. Those businesspeople were far from comfortable with Strick's reply to their questions about what was happening with *Wolf*: "We're still trying to figure out what 'it' is!"

No one knew if the movie would be an updated genre piece, a serious drama that told the werewolf story more intelligently than ever before, a tale of a doomed May–December romance between older man Nicholson and younger woman Michelle Pfeiffer, a wicked social comedy, or a broad burlesque on werewolf movies. There were elements of all the above in the script, though no clear "through-line" that allowed anyone a sense of the film's primary, central ambition. And there was more to come: Though Harrison and Strick share screen credit, the final shooting script was actually whipped up by Nichols's onetime partner in writing and stand-up comedy, Elaine May, who came in for a large unspecified sum, wrote a final draft, then turned down an offer to have her name added to those listed in the credits. By all reports, May was the one who added at least a little meat to the role of Laura (making her the malcontent and free-spirited daughter of Nicholson's boss rather than a veterinarian), allowing Pfeiffer to reverse her original decision (she'd turned the film down flat, sensing that the earlier version of Laura was a cipher) and agree to play the female lead. Pfeiffer had enjoyed her brief scenes with Jack in *Witches*, and she relished having him virtually all to herself rather than sharing him with two other actresses, which may explain why she was looking for an excuse to do *Wolf*, since not even Elaine May could do much with the character, who remains the female victim stereotype from old werewolf movies.

Though Nichols had himself made the decision to reset the story in the world of publishing (a far cry from Harrison's concept), May seized on this notion and added endless pithy details and bits of telling dialogue. As Nichols later told critic David Ansen, "She and I share a sense of satire about modern life, and I knew that we could coax that out of the material." It was Jack's job, though, to hold all the elements together: the only reason Columbia hadn't long ago pulled the plug was the reigning superstar's involvement. Nicholson remained insistent that the final film must be acceptable to Harrison, who may have been gone but was not forgotten, at least not by the man who would play the lead: "He has that sort of completely improbable fidelity to his friends," Harrison admiringly explained. Producer Wick, meanwhile, continued to believe that this was not merely one more part that Nicholson would play extremely well, but the role he'd been born for: "The difference between Jack and a wolf is not all that great." Even Nicholson himself was aware this was a unique,

perhaps necessary meeting of actor and role: "They're not selling me [on the idea] that if I wasn't doing it, they wouldn't find somebody else," he stated on the eve of the film's release, pausing to add: "They might be right in this case, though. I realize it's a part I'm good for."

Indeed, that proved to be putting it mildly. The actor once more received raves for his work, even though most reviewers noted that the film failed to ever find itself, too many cooks long since having spoiled the broth. Janet Maslin of the *New York Times* wrote that "Jack Nicholson perfectly embodies the courtly New York executive as an endangered species," nonetheless insisting that "this would have been a far better film" if the actor "had never been made to sprout fangs and grow hair on his hands." The werewolf motif works best in the film's first half, when it is allowed to serve as a metaphor for the mean-spirited competitiveness in today's publishing and business worlds, proving less adequate when it becomes literal and the film degenerates into a formula film, then an outrageous and unpleasant gore fest combined with a special effects extravaganza. In the Sunday *Times*, Caryn James agreed, insisting that "*Wolf* is a film that half works, and its success is all in the first half." In that first half, Nichols dutifully avoids genre and plays the concept of lycanthropy as a mental problem for the main character, Will Randall, who has noticed that his publishing colleagues have degenerated into a virtual pack and that he, mild-mannered fellow that he is, must become a lone wolf and fight back, tooth and fang, if he is to survive.

James also noted that Nicholson managed to effectively nudge the portrayal from specific character or genre cliché into the realm of pop icon, something the star had been doing ever since the early seventies when, without pretension, he found ways to suggest that his vividly specific roles were in some way symbolic, touching on the lives of the audience that flocked to his films. Or, as Jack himself once put it decades earlier, he survived not merely as a fine craftsman but as an ongoing superstar by continuing to ride the crest of the current social waves, however constantly they might change. As James wrote: "the Nicholson wolf is perfectly in tune with today's pop psychology. He is the male version of the heroines in *Women Who Run With the Wolves*, Clarissa Pinkola Estes's popular book [in which the wolf person] represents the essential self, powerful and benign but also informed by the natural predator in humans . . . his introspective werewolf is the man of the moment—a moment when we are all supposed to be looking for our inner wolf cubs. If *Wolf* (had been made) with more assurance, Mr. Nicholson might have been a wolf for the ages. As it is, he makes an amusing wolf for the moment."

The first half is fine, with its smart visual observations

about a world where the fine old wood is all polished and nattily attired men and women still ride up and down to their offices in old-fashioned wrought-iron elevators. But the sophistication is all show: Cold-blooded magnate Raymond Alden (Christopher Plummer) has taken over the publishing house, and senior editor Will Randall's job is about to be assumed by softspoken but cut-throat Stewart Swinton (James Spader), a Yuppie combination of Iago and Uriah Heep who is not only stealing Randall's position but also sleeping with his wife Charlotte (Kate Nelligan). Randall appears absolutely helpless to do anything about the situation until, one winter night, he stops on a Vermont country road (he's been to visit an author) after hitting a wolf, only to be bitten by the beast.

Shortly he finds himself transforming into something of a beast himself. Will's doctor (Om Puri) insists that he's contracted lycanthropy, either a physical, mental, or physiological condition in which the bitten takes on the characteristics of the animal that attacked him. The good doctor insists, though, that "Not all who are bitten change—there must be something wild within." And though there was little to suggest that the Clerk Kent-ish man had a dark side, the film's theme seems to be that there is often an animal in even the least likely of sad souls. Before long, Will—walking through Central Park—spots a ruthless mugger lying in wait for his next victim and mangles the man. More than just another bit of business in a horror film, the scene serves as a kind of release for audience members who have dreamed about

performing just such an act, but are constrained by civilization. Movies have always effectively allowed audiences to vicariously live out their fantasies, and *Wolf* is no exception.

What a shame, then, that the film falls apart as it progresses. The romantic moments between Will and his boss's daughter are embarrassing clichés, a surprise from Mike Nichols, who some twenty years earlier broke all the rules for cinematic sex when he guided Nicholson and female companions through *Carnal Knowledge*. Though Rick Baker's make-up/F/X is certainly state of the art, the uncomfortable feeling sets in midway through that the movie has given up its earlier ambitions and is now just another werewolf movie, no better or worse than Landis's *American Werewolf*, except for the presence of Jack Nicholson. That presence, though, remains one to be reckoned with. As Anthony Lane wrote in *The New Yorker*, "Wolf is a broken-backed, ill-fitting piece of work, which only makes sense—only comes together, really—in the person of its star. This is not a great performance by Nicholson, but it's courageous and astute, because it forces into the open all the tensions that keep him wired and insure his potency as a star. . . . Will Randall is the part that Jack was born to play. . . . He was a wolf man long before this picture was ever conceived. *Wolf* is like a one-movie retrospective of [his] schizoid career." And, as such, not merely another part that he played well, but a watershed role in his always fascinating career.

Everything changes when, by accident, Will is traveling on a remote road at night and hits a wolf, which then bites him.

A MAN OBSESSED:

The Crossing Guard

(1995)
A MIRAMAX RELEASE

Jack Nicholson as Freddy, the embittered alcoholic who wastes his time with "dancers" (Kellita Smith and Priscilla Barnes) instead of nurturing an enduring relationship. Could the superstar have been offering a proposed psychological portrait of the father he never knew?

CAST:

Jack Nicholson (*Freddy Gale*); David Morse (*John Booth*); Anjelica Huston (*Mary*); Robin Wright (*JoJo*); Piper Laurie (*Helen Booth*); Richard Bradford (*Stuart Booth*); Robbie Robertson (*Roger*); John Savage (*Bobby*); Priscilla Barnes (*Verna*); Kari Wuhrer (*Mia*).

CREDITS:

Director, Sean Penn; producers, Sean Penn, David S. Hamburger; executive producers, Bob Weinstein, Harvey Weinstein, Richard Gladstein; screenplay, Sean Penn; cinematography, Vilmos Zsigmond; production design, Michael Haller; editor, Jay Cassidy; music, Jack Nitzsche; costume design, Jill Ohanneson; running time: 114 mins.; rating: R.

Of all the young actors to emerge during the 1980s, none had as much in common with Jack Nicholson as Sean Penn. Like Jack, Sean immediately established his ability to create searing screen portraits of alienated loners (*Bad Boys*), alternating those rebel-hero roles with subtly delineated character parts (*Carlito's Way*) into which he virtually disappeared; like Jack, Penn lived an on-the-edge personal life, including his three-year marriage to Madonna, as well as endless battles with the tabloid press; like Jack, Penn early on expressed a desire to leave behind his role as a cinematic chess piece and assume creative control by directing. His first attempt, *The Indian Runner*, received mixed reviews for its depiction of a difficult sibling relationship, and did almost no box office. Nonetheless, Hollywood honchos were im-

pressed by Penn's potential, as his uneven but oftentimes stirring first effort suggested that in time Penn might emerge as an important filmmaker.

So it was that Penn was given a green light to proceed with a sophomore project. His inspiration derived from two musical influences. First, Penn learned that the four-year-old-child of blues guitarist Eric Clapton had fallen to his death from the window of the musician's fifty-third-floor New York condominium. Penn's pleasure at the birth of his own children with actress Robin Wright—Dylan (named for Bob) and Hopper (after Dennis)—was undercut by the realization that anyone, even an artist-celebrity, was vulnerable, and could have such joy ripped away by a trick of fate. Penn was suffering from terrible dreams in which he proved unable to keep his own children alive. Though no such tragedy personally touched him, he resolved to exorcise his emotional demons by writing about the situation. He happened to hear a Bruce Springsteen song that made reference to a crossing guard; then Penn began work on his story about an ordinary man obsessed with killing the person who accidentally ran over his four-year-old daughter.

To acknowledge his debt to Springsteen, Penn would eventually use the key song (as well as other blue-collar ballads by the self-appointed pop poet of America's white underclass) on the soundtrack. In the meantime, Penn completed the script for his tale of Freddy Gale, a Los Angeles jeweler who cannot cope following the death of his little girl. The incident has led to the destruction of Freddy's marriage; Freddy's wife Mary hoped they might together sum up the strength to go on, but left Freddy after sensing that, instead of gradually adjusting to the terrible reality, he had succumbed to bitterness. While Mary has managed to make a new start with Roger, a supportive man, Freddy has descended into a lifestyle of joyless encounters with prostitutes like Tanya and Verna.

The only thing that keeps him going is the knowledge that someday John Booth—the man who robbed his life of meaning—will leave prison after serving a six-year sentence for drunk driving. On the day of Booth's release, Freddy will stalk and murder him; it is this mission of vengeance to which he has quietly dedicated himself. What Freddy, lost in his obsession, doesn't realize is that, during the intervening years, he has himself become an alcoholic. So while driving to his appointed mission of death, Freddy—pulled over for drunk driving after nearly killing someone else's child—experiences an epiphany. Booth has emerged as what the German philosophers called a *Döppelganger* and novelist Joseph Conrad would have tagged Freddy's "secret sharer." In attempting to kill Booth, Freddy actually hoped to act out his repressed desire and eliminate everything Freddy hates most about himself.

Relentlessly bleak until its somewhat contrived ending (intended as modern tragedy but striking many viewers as soap opera), *The Crossing Guard* was hardly the kind of project that commercially minded producers would rush to finance. However, Bob and Harvey Weinstein of Miramax—longtime champions of the offbeat, original, and eccentric—were attracted to Penns' singular if harsh vision. They offered to help arrange financing and re-

lease the film, especially after Nicholson agreed to star. Jack was just coming off *Wolf*, a film that allowed him to once again go over the top, as he had done gleefully before in *The Shining*, *The Witches of Eastwick*, and *Batman*. Clearly it had been too long a time since he'd approached the kind of delicately crafted, finely etched character part he'd played to perfection in *King of Marvin Gardens*, *The Border*, and *Ironweed*. "I was in a mood to do something like this," Nicholson later told interviewer Bernie Weinraub. "I wanted to do something without any augmentation. So many of my [recent] films have been melodramatic. To be honest, I wanted to do the kind of acting I don't do that often." As for working with Penn, Nicholson added: "I've hung out with Sean. Our esthetic is similar. I like his instincts, his intelligence, his poetry."

Penn had often noted that Nicholson, in addition to being one of his favorite actors, had encouraged Penn greatly with his occasional stabs at direction. The other major influences on the young filmmaker were John Cassavetes and Robert Altman, whose organic, improvisational styles Penn clearly emulated. Yet far from being overwhelmed by a chance to work with the living legend, Penn explained that the world-class Nicholson went out of his way to make the writer-director's work much easier than it would otherwise have been: "If Jack is better at anything than acting, it's at supporting the director. I mean, he will take away any chance of you being intimidated, and not in any overly deferential way, not in a condescending way. He's there to serve you in a way that's emotionally effective." Upon completion, the film's release was delayed for more than a year when it received negative reaction at preview screenings, causing Penn to carry his work back into the editing room. When—like Styrofoam filling a void—it finally reached theater screens in late fall of 1995, during the deadly dull week just before the major holiday releases open, the critical reaction can best be described as guarded respect for a fascinating failure that again suggested—but did not fully deliver—Penn's potential. Owen Gleiberman of *Entertainment Weekly* tagged it "a work of talent and, on occasion, raw passion, but it's also a willed exercise in purgative alienation—imagine *Death Wish* remade by Michelangelo Antonioni."

Most critics agreed on one thing: The film's main appeal was Nicholson's performance, marking his belated but appreciated return to Method realism. Gleiberman took delight in noting that Penn "coaxes a soul-torn grief out of Nicholson that's shocking to behold." The great fear among Nicholson fans had been the possibility that—like the hero of Eugene O'Neill's play *Long Day's Journey Into Night*, based on that author's own actor-father—Jack might have spent so much time working in the crowd-pleasing Grand Guignol style that it would now be virtually impossible to bring down the level of performance to its old naturalistic levels. Indeed, many critics—while lauding the performance—suggested this might be the case. Janet Maslin of the *New York Times* noted "Mr. Nicholson brings presence and sodden gravity to" Freddy and that he "lurches through this role with rekindled intensity, only occasionally summoning his trademark movie-star mannerisms." That final quip suggests Jack had indeed become such a cinematic icon that total believability was not possible; he would always bring something of his canon of work to the part, not a problem early on simply because the *oeuvre* did not then exist.

Variety concurred, noting that "a taste of quietly maniacal vintage Nicholson is supplied in a scene with a tetchy woman returning a ring" to the jewelery store, going on to argue that "Nicholson at times is accompanied by a little too much of his own screen persona to completely serve the character; his dangerously lupine glare threatens occasionally to push Freddy too far off-kilter. But the performance is mostly quite a surprising one. The actor ushers in a softer side than has been customary in his roles of late, and his desolately emotional, tearful recap of a dream [provides] one of the film's most potent moments."

A few critics did feel that Nicholson managed to entirely put his persona aside, including Peter Travers of *Rolling Stone*, who wrote that "Nicholson tones down his star shine to reveal a man ravaged by loss and rage. It's a shattering performance," while Leah Rozen of *People* lauded Jack's "wrenchingly dark performance." For most critics, the highlights of this awkward, unbalanced, fervently sincere, ultimately unsatisfying film were the confrontations between Freddy and Mary, as the people who had shared so many years of their lives attempt to achieve a difficult reconciliation despite the immense amount of anger still resonating between them. The scene worked—or, for some, failed to work—because it clearly played off the real-life situation, the film taking on a remarkable subtext as Nicholson and Anjelica Huston had, like their screen characters, barely spoken since their acrimonious breakup of four years earlier, when the first couple of Hollywood went separate ways after he admitted to an affair—and a child—with another woman.

"Curses are spit out that seem to reach beyond the script," Weinraub noted. When questioned, Huston flatly stated: "I can't speak for Jack, but I brought my experience with me to the table. It's one of those backlogs you can't rid yourself of easily." In a more subdued tone, Nicholson insisted that Penn had cast them not for the added dimension this would inevitably create, but because each was the precisely right actor for the role. Sean

Guilt-ridden Freddy finally confronts his ex-wife (Anjelica Huston); much of the scene's power derives from the subtext these two Oscar-winning performers–longtime lovers though now embarked on separate paths–brought with them to this unique movie moment.

"didn't want it to be precious or anything. I hadn't seen her for quite a while. It was good to see her, and it was always about the work. And the work was good." For *Variety*, this confrontation was the key to the film's appeal despite an occasional clumsiness in the plotting: "The screen reunion supplies the drama with a considerable share of its power. Sparks ignite in a scene [that has the characters looking] back on rosier times, inevitably recalling the former couple's off-camera history." Travers felt that "Nicholson and the stunningly effective Huston achieve a rare poignancy in two scenes that anchor the movie on firm emotional ground." Only Roger Ebert of the *Chicago Sun-Times* complained that the casting diminished the scene, arguing that while it "is played very well, for me it was between Nicholson and Huston, not Freddy and Mary. After it was over, everyone must have been drained by its honesty—but it was honest to them more than to their characters."

Almost every other A-list critic argued the other way, insisting the element of self-revelation added an extraordinary resonance to what otherwise might have been a sympathetic but soon forgotten moment. Maslin noted that "one of the film's more audacious exercises is a tearful, late-night argument between Freddy and Mary that draws an element of exhibitionism from the actors' real-life love affair. Like much of *The Crossing Guard*, this scene reaches for candor and insight that remains elusive, but it still comes remarkably close to getting what it wants." Jack also appeared to have gotten what he wanted from the project. The film allowed him to play a fictional character very much like his own unknown real father must have been, or for that matter the kind of character he might have turned out to be had things not clicked for him in the movie business. As always, Jack Nicholson managed to assume a temporary dramatic mask that, upon closer inspection, revealed something essential about his own inner self.